THE
ALPINE JOURNAL
2008

Adieu Johanna

September is usually a quiet month in the traffic of email between the *AJ* editor and the production editor (February to July can be frenetic). So what was concerning Johanna at this time? It is 4 September 2007 and I open a message that begins as follows:

Dear Steve
> *It seems an appropriate moment, with the 150th edition behind us, to ponder the future of the AJ and I think I ought to warn you that next year's AJ will probably be my last...Best wishes, Johanna*

The floor shakes a little beneath my desk. I've been editing the journal for several years without ever fully understanding the intricacies of how it is put together. And now the only person who does tells me she is going to retire...a cold sweat moment.

Since then I've had almost a year to get a grip and adjust to the idea that Johanna won't be there to ensure the journal is kept on track. How typical that she should serve such a long period of notice, allowing publisher Peter Hodgkiss and I plenty of time to consider an alternative *modus operandi* for 2009? Even so, the departure of Johanna Merz after two decades on the editorial team leaves a big gap.

The purpose of this insert – the only bit of the 2008 *AJ* that Johanna has not seen – is to express my personal thanks, those of Peter Hodgkiss and all associated with the *AJ* past and present, and the Club as a whole for her devoted service to the *Alpine Journal.*

Johanna's name first appeared on the title page of the *AJ* in volume 92 (1987) as one of a small group of assistants to editor Ernst Sondheimer. She took over as editor in 1992, launching with a major examination of threats to the mountain environment. The editorial baton passed to Ed Douglas in 1999 but Johanna stayed on as production editor, remaining in that invaluable backroom role to the present. Both Ed and I, coming from the rude world of journalism, have probably tried Johanna's patience and sense of propriety from time to time, but she has always shown a readiness to innovate and a keen awareness that the *AJ,* like the Club itself, has to move with the mountaineering times and world around it.

Few AC members understand what is involved in the job of production editor. Suffice to say that I use the word 'job' deliberately – it is one of several hours per day for much of the year. Meanwhile, for Johanna, there were grandchildren to entertain, dogs to walk and a large Putney garden to keep in order. And as she put it in that fateful September email: 'I would like to leave myself a little space to do other things before I hit 80!'

Johanna knows I'm normally quite hard on exclamation marks. Perhaps she slipped that one in out of mischief. In the circumstances I'll let it stand, for seldom can that 'little space' have been so richly merited. Thanks again Johanna.

Stephen Goodwin

Photo: Ernst Sondheimer

AC super-athlete Lizzy Hawker ascending Ama Dablam in October 2007. After the climb Lizzy went on to break the record for the run from Everest base camp to Kathmandu, completing the 188 miles of rough trail and tarmac in 3 days 2 hours 36 mins. This cut 4 hours 34 mins from the previous record set by Nepali Kumar Limbu in 2000. Lizzy's run has so far raised £4,400 for Community Action Nepal. A full account of her achievement will appear in the 2009 *AJ*. (*Victor Saunders*)

THE
ALPINE JOURNAL

2008

The Journal of the Alpine Club

A record of mountain adventure
and scientific observation

Edited by Stephen Goodwin

Production Editor: Johanna Merz
Assistant Editor: Paul Knott

Volume 113

No 357

Supported by the
MOUNT EVEREST FOUNDATION

Published jointly by
THE ALPINE CLUB & THE ERNEST PRESS

THE ALPINE JOURNAL 2008
Volume 113 No 357

Address all editorial communications to the Hon Editor :
Stephen Goodwin, 1 Ivy Cottages, Edenhall, Penrith, CA11 8SN
e-mail : sg@stephengoodwin.demon.co.uk
Address all sales and distribution communications to:
Cordée, 3a De Montfort Street, Leicester, LE1 7HD

Back numbers:
Apply to the Alpine Club, 55 Charlotte Road, London, EC2A 3QF
or, for 1969 to date, apply to Cordée, as above.

© 2008 by the Alpine Club

First published in 2008 jointly by the Alpine Club and the Ernest Press
Typeset by Johanna Merz
Printed in China through Colorcraft Ltd., Hong Kong

A CIP catalogue record for this book is
available from the British Library

ISBN 978 0 948153 91 4

Foreword

In a thought-provoking article in this 2008 *Alpine Journal*, Claude Gardien, editor of the magazine *Vertical*, asks whether the limits of alpine-style climbing at the highest altitude have been reached. I suspect the answer of most *AJ* readers would be 'No'. In this, as in other fields where the top performers are pushing at both physical and psychological barriers, the answer must surely be in the negative until all the hard faces of Himalaya reaching above, say, 7000m have been climbed alpine-style by the hardest discernible routes. And that leaves some way to go.

Claude's answer to his own question is a non-committal, 'Only time will tell.' Interestingly, since he wrote those words, the old 'whirligig of time' has not been silent, though his message is mixed. Two new routes in particular bear on this debate, both outstanding, both by Russians and both of about 3000 metres, but in complete contrast to each other: the siege-style ascent of the west face of K2, with 11 climbers reaching the top, and the alpine-style ascent of the west pillar of Jannu by Valery Babanov and Sergey Kofanov.

Babanov's account of the climb is featured here close by Gardien's article in a chapter entitled 'Pure Alpinism'. The Jannu route was just that, two climbers setting off with only what they carried on their backs and arriving back, after nine exhausting, mind-bending days, having established a mark in climbing history but left none on the mountain.

Left of the Babanov/Kofanov route lies Jannu's extremely steep north face; how the pair must have looked across to it and wondered. It has yet to be credited with a first alpine-style ascent, Tomo Cesen's claim to have soloed the face in 1989 having been cast into grave doubt. However, it is not exactly a pristine landscape. The Russians who made the first ascent in 2004 left a lot of fixed rope in place and theirs was at least the ninth expedition on the face.

The technical ability, fitness and sheer grit of the Russians on K2 and Jannu humbles most of us; unfortunately the detritus that siege stylists often leave behind – operating at such an extreme it can be suicidally difficult to remove gear – can queer the pitch for those bold enough to contemplate the line alpine style. Purity of the kind that Babanov and Kofanov found has thus been compromised; part of the element of the unknown has been removed. The ideal for pure alpine style should surely be untrodden ground, or at least uncluttered. It would be a shame if the barrier to what is ultimately possible at high altitude for the boldest alpinists proved not to be within themselves and their equipment but in a lack of clean lines up the hardest faces.

AC members will warm to Gardien's depiction of AF Mummery as a kind of father of alpine style. Mummery's name was on the lips of many at the Club's 150th anniversary gathering in Zermatt as they gazed up at the Matterhorn and recalled his 1879 ascent of the Zmutt ridge. The climb was used to convey two related messages: Mummery's adventurous, unencumbered style is the one the Club still espouses today; and the Zmutt, like other classics, should remain free of the blight of unwarranted ironmongery. Outgoing president Stephen Venables touched on this theme and the contradiction of bolts and adventure in his Valedictory Address, published here along with reports and photographs from what seemed to be one long year of partying. There were also three '150th' expeditions – Kyrgyzstan, Garhwal and the Caucasus – plus a seminar on change in the mountains over the Club's lifetime, notably the effects of global warming. This 113th *AJ* also records the passing of two more 1953 Everesters, the New Zealander who summited to become the most celebrated mountaineer of all time, Edmund Hillary, and the man whose calm efficiency as transport officer played so crucial a part in that success, Charles Wylie.

Each year, production of the journal is a balancing act – trying to ensure that we reflect enough of what is going on at the sharp end of mountaineering (the exploits of the Fowlers, Bullocks and Babanovs) as well as the less sensational but equally enjoyable (maybe more so) adventures of the majority. There is the wider mountain milieu to consider: the hill people whose lives we intrude upon, the environment and sometimes turbulent politics of mountain regions, the art they inspire and the science they inform. And then there is the balance to be struck in recording the affairs of the Alpine Club without making the *AJ* appear too parochial.

The first essential in achieving all this is a lively flow of articles and information from AC members and the wider mountaineering fraternity. Your journal needs you! So many thanks to all those who have contributed to this 2008 *Alpine Journal*, for me the most satisfying of my tenure so far. Vitally important to any editor is the team that brings the various components together. In this I have been fortunate: assistant editor Paul Knott, who brings authority to the Area Notes, production editor Johanna Merz and publisher Peter Hodgkiss at Ernest Press, have once again worked wonders.

But sadly the cast is changing. The *AJ* you hold is the first since 1976 that does not bear the name of Geof Templeman. Starting as 'editorial assistant' to Edward Pyatt, in all Geof saw service with six *AJ* editors, most recently taking care of Reviews and Obituaries. Now a further departure looms. Johanna Merz is to retire as production editor, a job she has done for 10 years. She has been on the *AJ* team since 1987, has typeset every volume since 1993 and was honorary editor for seven volumes (1992-98). It is hard to think of the *Alpine Journal* without Johanna's careful eye on its welfare and appearance. Her absence is going to give me sleepless nights, but seldom was retirement so well earned and Johanna, like Geof, deserves the thanks of all Club members for such loyal service.

Stephen Goodwin

Contents

Front cover photo:
Two climbers from the Kangwon National University Expedition to
Nepal on the south ridge of The Fang (7647m). The peak in the background is Annapurna South. The summit of The Fang is behind the
camera. (*By courtesy of Kangwon National University*)

Back cover photo:
Graeme Schofield leading the crux jamming pitch on the east ridge of
Quesillo (5600m), eastern Huayhuash, Peru. (*Tom Bide*)

Front endpaper:
Prayer flags on the Zetra la, Nepal. Looking over the cloud-filled
Khumbu to Khumbi-yul-lha (*centre*) and distant Cho Oyu.
(*Stephen Goodwin*)

Back endpaper:
Sunset and moonrise over the Hongku Himal, Nepal. Kangchenjunga
shimmers in the distance. (*Stephen Goodwin*)

Illustrations

Pure Alpinism

Rowan Huntley *Castor and Pollux ~ Pink Dawn*
Chroma on canvas, 40cm x 40cm. (*Private collection*)

MICK FOWLER

Matterhorns Lost and Found

In 2005 Chris Watts and I climbed the mountain that the renowned Japanese explorer Tamotsu Nakamura had christened 'The Matterhorn of the Nyenchen Tanglha'. Except that we didn't.

Such an apparently contradictory statement might sound rather odd but one of the joys of exploration is that you sometimes get it wrong. The problem here was that the Nyenchen Tanglha East range in eastern Tibet has a fine selection of outrageously impressive peaks but is not exactly over-photographed. Also the names of the peaks, those that have names, are largely unknown outside the local community. Tom's photograph was certainly the one he meant to caption 'Matterhorn of the Nyenchen Tanglha' but it was not the mountain called Kajaqiao (6447m) as he understood it to be.

So when Chris and I endured two years of challenging bureaucracy to secure the permits necessary to attempt Kajaqiao it was something of a shock to realise that we were actually authorised to climb the wrong mountain. But Kajaqiao was very fine. In fact it was very Matterhorn-like although one could hardly help but notice that the mountain right next door, Manamcho, was arguably even more so. Imagine having two unclimbed Matterhorns side by side. We felt spoilt. I could feel an urge for Manamcho even before we had done Kajaqiao.

And so in April 2007 I was back in Lhasa. Three of the original four-person Kajaqiao team couldn't make it. Chris, a seriously enthusiastic cyclist, was training for a non-stop road race from Paris to Brest and back. Adam Thomas was braving sweaty hostilities working for Medicins Sans Frontiers in the Congo and Phil Amos suffered much internal anguish before finally deciding that he couldn't make it. But finding a team was never going to be difficult.

Ultimately it was agreed that I would climb with Paul Ramsden and our companions were to be Steve Burns and Ian Cartwright. Steve is a computer analyst with Experian and a long-standing climbing partner on the Peak District evening scene while Ian is a member of the Williams Formula One support team based in Oxford. Paul and I have climbed irregularly together for the last 10 years. A health and safety consultant based in Nottingham, his jobs range from delivering dry lectures about health and safety legislation to considering whether or not the James Bond team are safe to drive very expensive cars about on frozen Icelandic lakes. One would think that this expertise would stand him in good stead for judging ice conditions. A collapsing icicle incident in Scotland could have called such skills into question but, with some justification I suppose, he had blamed that on over-enthusiastic encouragement from the second. Anyway, the quickest route to Manamcho crosses a sometimes frozen lake, the testing of which would appear to be within his specialist area.

Access to Lhasa, once the 'Forbidden City', now feels unethically easy. Having left England at 17.00 hrs on a Friday and arrived in Lhasa at 16.00 hrs on the Saturday, the tourist brochures advertising 'true adventure' holidays to Lhasa seemed rather short of the mark. At a superficial glance it is difficult to imagine that anything is forbidden here now. Neon signs flash bold advertisements, plastic palm trees throw shade on the entrance to the Playboy Club and shiny boutiques line the city centre streets. Mountaineers approved by the China Tibet Mountaineering Association (CTMA) are put up at the Himalaya Hotel, an incongruously plush establishment graced by Michael Palin and featuring lift carpets stating the day of week. I suppose this might be useful if the staff remembered to change them at the stroke of midnight.

In line with normal practice the CTMA designated a gentleman named Dawa to accompany us. His bread and butter routine was to accompany Everest trips and socialise with other CTMA representatives. He had never been anywhere near the Nyenchen Tanglha East and clearly wondered what the hell he was going to do with himself whilst we were off climbing.

Two days out from Lhasa our two jeeps pulled off the 250km dirt track, drove under an ornate scaffold entrance arch and rolled onto a concrete dual carriageway. We had arrived in Lhari, the regional centre of this remote area. In pre-Chinese days the nomads hereabouts would drift around and not always reassemble at the same spot. Every time they did assemble though they called the spot 'Lhari'. This history has resulted in a confusing number of minor settlements or once-occupied tracts of land known as 'Old Lhari'. Now, though, permanence has arrived. Modern Lhari is a small town of perhaps 2000 inhabitants that has been fully converted into a Chinese-style settlement. Lock-up shop units with metal roller blinds predominate whilst important looking tinted glass buildings break up the skyline and speak of officialdom.

Our government hotel occupied rooms above a row of shops and was memorable for the fine yak dung stoves in the bedrooms and a complete lack of any toilet facilities. On instructions we kept hidden and nursed continuing altitude headaches whilst Dawa presented our numerous permits for inspection. Outside the wind blew fiercely and the snow horizontally. A yak and a dog faced up to each other over the contents of a bin whilst two old Tibetan ladies swept the concrete gutter with twig brushes. Meanwhile police officers cruised the street in a luxury 4 x 4 vehicle, using a loudspeaker to reprimand people for minor misdemeanours. The whole place had a bleak and extreme feel about it.

'Would you like to live here?' we asked Dawa. He looked at us incredulously.

3. The Manam valley. Fowler and Ramsden believe they were the first westerners to look across Little Silli lake to this array of unclimbed peaks. (*Mick Fowler*)

4. Hiring porters. The 'rich' villagers of Tatse proved hard bargainers. (*Paul Ramsden*)

Lhari is at an altitude of about 4500m. We spent the night clutching our heads and occasionally urinating into a plastic bowl. In common with the piss of other guests, the contents of the bowl were poured out the back windows in the morning.

The villagers of Tatse, some 25km from Lhari, proved hard bargainers over porterage charges. 'They are too rich,' bemoaned Dawa. 'Thousands of yuan in the bank.'

There seemed to be more than a grain of truth in Dawa's words. The population numbered perhaps 40 yet several jeeps and at least 10 motorbikes were visible. The first people we asked to help turned out to be builders brought in from Shigatse, about three days' drive away. The local people, being traditional nomads, had never learned house-building skills, we were told, and so just paid others to do the work for them. The source of this wealth was caterpillar fungus. A traditional Tibetan remedy for just about any illness known to man, caterpillar fungus has been enthusiastically embraced by the Chinese and prices have rocketed to the extent that Tatse men spend about one month a year collecting fungus and 11 months resting in preparation for the next season. Meanwhile life for the women continues in the traditional yak tending, family caring manner with fungus hunting thrown in as an extra.

It took a promise of 200 yuan a day to persuade the Tatse men to carry for us, five times what Dawa felt was the usual wage in the Everest area. None the less, we were immediate beneficiaries of the new-found local wealth in that a bridge had been built across the Yi'ong Tsangpo exactly where we needed one. This saved us running along behind bike-driving porters to another bridge a mile or so away as we had done in 2005.

There was clearly less snow plastering the steep mountains in April than there had been in October 2005. However, the kitchen shelter we had constructed with such care that year was now choked with winter ice. Into its replacement we fitted a flat stone table that pleased chef Ramsden enormously.

There were only seven bags carried up by the porters so, in theory, it should have been an easy job to sort ourselves out at what we rather grandly called base camp.

'Anyone seen the bag of vegetarian food? The pan grip? The lighters?'

It would appear that passing years prompt greater forgetfulness but increased resourcefulness. Improvisation and borrowing solved all but the lack of vegetarian food. Ian looked crestfallen but resigned to losing more weight than expected.

After some serious wallowing in 2005 we had decided to bring snowshoes. This increased the challenge within our 20kg allowances and was a new experience for me. My competence level in using the things seemed about on a par with my skiing ability. Somehow I kept standing on the other snowshoe and tripping over. Paul found this very amusing. I did take them off in disgust but, again to Paul's amusement, had to concede that his accelerating into the distance was at least partially due to his using the things.

It took two days to reach the head of the icefall above our base camp. Later, when acclimatised, it would take 3.5 hours. Acclimatising is odd and the contrast between pre and post acclimatisation activity never ceases to amaze me. It was here that our path diverged from the line we had followed to Kajaqiao in 2005. Then Chris and I had climbed straight up above us to the base of the west face. This time our route lay across a snow plateau to the foot of Manamcho. We knew that in 2005 it had taken Adam and Phil a whole day of serious wading to cross the plateau. This time, acclimatised and with snowshoes, half a day was ample, even with me regularly falling over. Paul celebrated being ready to climb by stretching to do his boots up and inducing a prolapsed disc. Thereafter the Ramsden body moved in a carefully robotic manner, frightening me occasionally with talk about the immobilising effect of previous seizures.

Although it would involve more snow plodding, we decided to continue to the col between Kajaqiao and Manamcho with a view to having a look at the north-east ridge of Manamcho. After a day of more heavy breathing, some dithering over the unhappy state of the Ramsden back, and an appreciation of the obvious difficulties high on the ridge, we ended back where we had started – and a decision to give the north-west ridge a go instead.

After an obligatory short fall into the bergschrund, we managed to get established on the right-hand side of Manamcho's north face. Thereafter lots of panting on 55-degree ice slopes followed by powder-covered Grade IV mixed ground saw us gain the foot of the north-west ridge and the high point reached by Adam and Phil in 2005. This was an exposed spot and being caught here by challenging weather had prompted their retreat. Meanwhile Paul and I could not help but notice that the wind was rising and black clouds were approaching fast. Finding a flat knoll on the ridge after 100m or so we decided to pitch the tent whilst we could and hide from the gusting snow. To begin with all was well. We brewed contentedly, discussed the pros and cons of what food goes down best at altitude and generally lounged about. Having snuggled cosily into our sleeping bags I looked forward to a good night's sleep. It was not to be. By about 2am the wind was such that other concerns than sleep were beginning to surface.

'Perhaps it's worth you climbing on top of me a bit?'

Paul had never made such a suggestion before but the circumstances were indeed unusual. The problem was the wind. Our little knoll was a lovely camping spot but it was very exposed. Also the belays were 5m in front of the tent and there were overhangs beneath us on the lee side. Any slide off over the overhangs would result in a painful pendulum into a jagged rocky groove. Not a pleasant thought. We had taken the risks on board when pitching the tent but had tempted fate by being optimistic and relishing the prospect of a good night's sleep on a flat spot. We were even confident enough to insert a little cross pole that improved ventilation but created a

5. Manamcho (6264m) from the Manam valley. Fowler and Ramsden's ascent line marked in red. (*Mick Fowler*)

small sail for the wind to get under. We regretted that now but it was impossible to remove the pole without getting out of the tent. And as the tent was clearly in danger of lifting, the thought of subtracting the weight of one of us, albeit temporarily, was not appealing. 'Perhaps it will release the pressure if we open the ventilation flaps?' I wondered out loud, noting that the two flaps were very close to each other at the top of the tent.

I unwisely unzipped them. Instead of the wind blowing straight through and reducing the pressure, my efforts simply unleashed a powerful blast of spindrift that covered everything with a film of snow.

'Nice one,' commented Paul.

I gave up that idea and settled down back on top of Paul.

The night was memorable and morning dawned dreary. The wind had dropped but a peek outside suggested that a lot of snow had fallen. Mind you, within reason, conditions mattered little. The basic ethos was to carry on unless there was an exceptionally good reason to turn back. And in fact, with wind-blasted snow overlaying granite, conditions were such as to prompt comments about what good training this sort of climbing is for the Cairngorms. There was no doubt about it; with no pressing reason to turn back we had to carry on.

6. Manamcho from pt 5935m. (*Ian Cartwright*)

Clearings in the cloud revealed an array of spectacular peaks to the west and south. All we knew to be unclimbed but most we were unable to pinpoint on our rudimentary maps. There is indeed a worrying amount of detailed exploring that still needs to be done in this part of the world.

Gaining height gradually, we alternately led up the ridge. Difficulties consisted of short steep rock steps that it was difficult to avoid because of deep powder on slabs to the right and typical north face terrain to the left. One step was noticeably harder than the rest and was my lead.

To the horror of any watching ethical purists I was soon dangling forlornly from a skyhook that I habitually carry on my harness. My finger was bleeding profusely where I had clumsily caught the skin under the skyhook. Paul looked bemused.

'I'll leave my rucksack here,' I grunted.

Soon I was grappling with the overhang above searching desperately for the right nut to slot in a perfect tapering crack.

'***t! Where's all the gear?' I cursed at my empty harness.

A calm voice from below had the answer.

'It's hanging on your rucksack gear loops.'

The step was perhaps 6m high and probably avoidable with a bit of sound route-finding judgement. It is indeed fortunate that greater experience allows one to cope more easily and get less flustered when such minor misjudgements occur.

7. Paul Ramsden on day 3. (*Mick Fowler*)

8.   Mick Fowler at the final bivvi before the summit. 'It was clear the weather had changed ... for the worse.' (*Paul Ramsden*)

By the end of our third day above the bergschrund, our sixth out from base camp, we were approaching the steep summit towers which looked likely to give the technical crux of the route. Our plan had been to join the summit ridge at the apex of the north face and follow it to the summit whilst soaking up a splendid panoramic view of unclimbed and unexplored peaks. This now seemed an unlikely finale. Not only was visibility poor but also the way ahead looked challenging. Ever optimistic, we sat waiting for a clearing before finally giving up and descending half a pitch to try and bypass some difficulties via an exposed ledge line below the crest.

It was whilst descending to the start of this line that Paul made the memorable discovery that some of the new snow hereabouts was overlaying smooth slabs and very prone to part company. A 20m rope-testing slide added interest before we settled down for the night on a reasonable nose-to-tail ledge, me wrapped in the tent fabric and Paul in a bivvi bag. At least we were separate so I didn't have to worry about Paul asking me to climb on top of him in the night.

I had an excess of fabric whilst Paul discovered that his enormous sleeping bag wouldn't fit in his modestly sized bivvi bag without badly crushing the down and giving him a stifling sense of claustrophobia. Conversely I was cosy and comfortable and started snoozing happily. Some time later I awoke wondering what it could be that was pinning me down to the ledge. Surely Paul hadn't thought I was in danger of being blown away? I peered cautiously out to an eye-opening discovery. At least two feet of snow had fallen without waking me. Our ledge was now banked out and the wind was getting up again. Equally noteworthy was the temperature. It had risen to the extent that condensation from our breath was causing problems by dripping onto our down sleeping bags. This change was remarkable considering that, when we left base camp, night-time temperatures, 400m below, had been in the region of minus 10 degrees. We could but wait and see whether this sharp change would herald a further change in the weather. Perhaps we would have a glorious, clear summit day after all?

By daybreak it was clear that the weather had changed ... for the worse. The howling wind had all but cleared our ledge of new snow, the sky was slate grey and visibility was perhaps 10m. And all indications were that conditions were worsening. Paul greeted the day with a customary blunt Yorkshireman's assessment of the situation.

'One of the worst nights I've ever had. My back hurts, weather's crap, view's crap. Let's get up and get the f*** out of here.'

I had to agree. We felt that the top couldn't be much more than 70m higher but the way ahead looked hard and the conditions were truly wild. Ice crystals massaged our faces in a manner which no doubt improved complexions but was not going to be conducive to pleasant climbing. The whole scene seemed reminiscent of a wild winter day on Ben Nevis with a touch of remoteness thrown in for added interest.

I led an unmemorable pitch and then Paul's challenge was to find a way up the summit tower. Being unable to see much he firstly ended up back on the main crest and then reached a cul-de-sac beneath a blank wall. Things looked bleak before he eventually found a tricky mixed groove leading through to an easing of the angle. A wildly windy final 10m then led to a sudden knife-edge on which we dutifully shook hands.

It was as we prepared for the ritual of summit photos that a brief clearing opened up the uncomfortable possibility that a corniced edge about 40m away might be slightly higher.

'***t!'

Perhaps unsurprisingly the view from our new 'summit' was equally non-existent and from here it was debatable whether our first 'summit' was higher. Our summit photos could have been taken on any cold, snowy, misty and windswept place anywhere in the world. And yet somewhere out there in the mist we sensed some of the finest unexplored peaks anywhere in the world. We vowed to do our best to stand on top of more of them.

9. Mick Fowler (*left*) and Paul Ramsden on the summit of Manamcho.
    (*Fowler collection*)

Summary: An account of the first ascent of Manamcho (6264m) in the Nyenchen Tanglha East range, Tibet, by Mick Fowler and Paul Ramsden. The summit was reached on 25 April 2007.

Acknowledgements: Mick Fowler and Paul Ramsden are grateful to the following for their support: W Gore Associates (Shipton-Tilman Grant), Mount Everest Foundation, British Mountaineering Council, Alpine Club, The North Face, Black Diamond, First Ascent and Scarpa.

NICK BULLOCK

Bittersweet Desire

Bursting from a billowing dust cloud, the lorry has a battered, pugilistic face. Its split windscreen forms a pair of dark, evil eyes; the white-painted grill wears a fixed sneer. Thundering by our taxi with inches to spare, the horn screams, 'Get out of my way'. I slide along sweaty plastic to the side farthest away from this menacing spirit of the road. The humidity is stifling, the noise deafening ... cars, bumper-to-bumper, screaming horns, revving engines, the jostle of so many people ... bumper-to-bumper. Returning from the solitude of the mountains, an Indian interior is too much. And my mind has not stopped questioning since we left base camp.

'We should have tried harder.'

We saw, we climbed; we turned and ran. I felt a fraud. The year 2006 had brought new routes in Peru, the Himalaya and the Alps. I had tasted brilliance, and now failure burnt like bile.

I remembered a line from a conversation at a party in the summer.

'In the mountains, if you successfully climb everything you attempt, the lines are obviously too easy.' Well, returning to India for the third time had brought failure for the third time and it hurt.

The plan to climb Kalanka had hardened over the winter as Kenton Cool, Andy Houseman and I shared an apartment in Chamonix ...

'Get on with it.'

Crampon points scraped against a smooth wall. I leant back from the picks of my axes twisted deep into a crack at the back of an overhanging corner. Vain smashing for a placement above the lip of the corner had loosened rocks. A chunk teetered and fell straight into my lap. It was as big as a football. The wind screamed, lifting snow from the Vallée Blanche and throwing it across the Tacul's east face, searing my face. Spindrift and dirt mingled with sweat and fear. I looked at the rock, my feet, my future and the last glow of the setting sun lighting the jagged crests of mountains. Kenton belayed in the gully directly below.

'Watch out!'

Smeared feet skittered and sparked. The rock's weight was pulling. Gravity was pulling. The dark and the wind hissed at me, 'So you think you're good.'

I tilted my groin. The rock rolled ...

10. Kenton Cool seconding the first pitch of *Slave to the Rhythm*, Mont Blanc du Tacul. (*Nick Bullock*)

11. Kenton Cool leading the second pitch of *Slave to the Rhythm*. (*Nick Bullock*)

My eyes followed its bouncing course until it was lost to the dark. Screaming, clinging, waiting ... waiting ... waiting for the tug of the rope as Kenton was hit and fell. But it didn't come. My calves burnt, thighs shook. I returned to smashing into the loose for something solid to pull up on. Eventually hooking a rock that didn't move, I crawled over the lip to finish the climb – *Slave to the Rhythm*, one of four hard routes on the east face of Mont Blanc du Tacul.

Stuck ropes, re-climbing, down-climbing, closed eyes and blinding snow made the descent testing, but the crux of the day was still to come. Two hours later we cowered beneath the Midi Arête, its crest weaving up to the shaft of light from the téléphérique tunnel high above. The wind was now a gale. Kenton shouted in my ear as in the small circle of light from our head-torches we struggled to attach frozen rope to frozen bodies. Tied on, Kenton crawled away into the dark-white-spindrift-cloud whipping over the crest. Picks bit into snow compacted by a thousand skiers' feet. Lumps of ice flew into the night. I began to crawl when the rope ran out. The rope, all 60 metres, billowed in an arc over the sheer north face of the Aiguille du Midi. Chamonix street lights shimmered thousands of feet below. The rope pulled. I crawled. Picks and knuckles smashed into hard ice ... crawling, my knees grew sore. Eyes closed ... *thunk* ... eyes open ... *thunk* ... two more placements ... two feet crawled ... the rope pulled.

At 10pm we entered the glowing snow tunnel leading into the warm-womb peace of the téléphérique station and collapsed. I constantly have to remind myself that the experience is everything. Success is not always reaching a summit.

'Set off in the night, climb through the next day and we'll be on the shoulder. We'll have a big bivvi site, sun, warmth and recovery before climbing the pillar to the summit. Three days up, two down ... We'll take four days' food.'

Kenton and I stood beneath Kalanka's massive north face trying to decide on tactics. Snow-shrouds swept down and across runnels carved by spindrift. Two rock bands cut the face horizontally. Ice glistened. Nobody had attempted the left side of the face. Hardly anyone had attempted the north face at all. And nobody had walked to its foot with just two ropes and their packed sacks and begun to climb ... until now.

Plugging through the night, nervous anticipation was left behind once the bergschrund was crossed. This was my first big climb with Kenton and his brooding beforehand had affected me. I now only climb with a group of very experienced friends who are mainly mountain guides. I nearly always bow to their training, but the climbing partners I most relate to are those who realise I am not a client. Kenton falls into this category. Sometimes in the mountains the only way is to forget the manuals and go with intuition.

Moving together with the occasional ice screw placed between us was the only way this climb would end in success. However as dawn arrived the first steep rock band had to be pitched. Near-vertical snow-ice that would not take protection or secure pick placements gave sickening hot-aches and concern. Once through we carried on moving together. The afternoon brought cloud swirling and hiding the summit. Snowfall began soon after, sloughing and hissing. Earlier than expected, and a long way from the top of the shoulder, we cut a small ledge into hard ice to sit out the night.

'You should be climbing this with someone else.'

I was surprised at Kenton's comment. He had climbed so many hard routes in the past and suffered. The bivvi was uncomfortable and the constant spindrift tiresome but it could have been worse. I wasn't going to allow Kenton's negative attitude to affect me. I knew, deep down, he would not give up. He had climbed Everest five times and endured so much; but on a climb and a face like this, it takes both of you to be driven and supportive; there is nobody else. I prefer to suffer in silence, and for my partners to lie in preference to honesty. Honesty is for the valley.

Shivering on the icy-ledge, the night was long and uncomfortable. I slipped in and out of dreams and memories; rock climbing on the Lleyn Peninsular in North Wales, before travelling to India, passed the hours.

Dan McManus cleared rubble to make a space before sitting like a pixie on the large ledge just above the sea. Cilan Main Cliff loomed dauntingly isolated and bigger than anything at Gogarth. Pale bulbous rock covered in bird shit and shale surged into the sky like stacked tombstones. Rainbow spectrums hung in the mist blown from a waterfall pouring out of a slimy gash in the cliff top. Apart from an occasional sailing boat we were on our own. Dan was twenty, talented and bold; he was extremely driven with that touch of arrogance necessary to succeed. We were on a Dan mission where there would be no room for doubt. The abseil to the shelf where he now sat was totally free-hanging. A rigging-rope joined the marginal pieces of gear that anchored the abseil rope; it twisted across the grassy headland running over rabbit holes and around dry tussocks. The only way out from the base of the cliff was to climb or swim.

Littlejohn and White's *Terrorhawk*, a route with a reputation for adventure, was our chosen climb, but neither of us feared it because Caff, (James McHaffie) had told us, 'It only has one hard move ... just a bit-of-a pull near the top of the final pitch, you boys will cruise it.' And our egos lapped it up.

Pulling up on overhanging weather-worn teeth, height was quickly made. The protection was abysmal but the climbing was relatively easy, as long as the thought of what would happen if a hold ripped was shut away. Sixty overhanging feet later, I balanced on a ledge strewn with rubble. A corroded karabiner hung 30 feet to my right marking the first belay. A corner looked like it may have a gear placement, so I climbed to its top and nonchalantly grabbed a large hold. It ripped. Still gripping the lump of rock, my arm swung like I was throwing a discus. As my body twisted I threw out the other hand. Fingers hit a ledge, clawing deep into mud. My twist slowed for a second ... just a second, before momentum pulled and I dived head first down the cliff.

I filled my lungs and screamed. Tender skin at the back of my throat tore. My lungs emptied. Rock rushed past in a blur. The sea lapped indifferently and I screamed again. Dan's belay ledge hurtled toward me. I threw my arms above my head. Dan looked up before being plucked from the shelf with the tug of the rope. My fall stopped 10 feet above rock. I hung upside down looking into Dan's face and laughed. Dan looked shocked.

Re-climbing the pitch was fine until I drew alongside the wire nut that held my fall. The nut was placed sideways into the lip of a crack and the rock surrounding the nut was splintered like a broken chicken bone. Feeling nauseous, I grovelled through the dirt to the old corroded karabiner and belayed.

The rest of the climb went ... overhanging, technical, run-out, loose and wet. Our eyes grew wider and wilder with every move. The exposure crawled into our minds. Our limbs worked ... just ... pushing us higher as the worm of doubt wriggled deeper.

We pulled onto the grass headland a full seven hours after our abseil. A breeze blew through our sweat-soaked clothes. Exhausted, we collected the gear and staggered across the cliff tops. Big round mushrooms glowed white in the evening gloom. Rabbits bolted into bushes. Life flowed through our veins.

Slipping from the ice-ledge my head snapped back. Cold and covered in snow, the memories of the Lleyn had warmed me and brought a reminder that giving up is more painful than perseverance.

The second day passed in a fight for the ridge.

'We'll be there tonight, sat on a big flat ledge out of the spindrift ... no problem.'

'You're fucking mad if you really think that ... it's miles.'

I knew my optimism was distorted, but optimism on a big face is sometimes all you have.

We moved together all day but the ridge didn't appear to get any closer. Scratching and inching along we grew tired and deflated with the lack of progress. The afternoon snow started and we continued to climb through the spindrift until the hunt for a bivvi began. I climbed a steep corner and looked down onto a rock covered with a triangle of snow.

'If we dig that out, it may be flat enough.'

Slings bound Kenton in tightly while my harness cut me in two. Spindrift poured. We attempted to drape the tent over the two of us but it wasn't big enough. I didn't dream that night.

'This is shit ... I'm not doing another of these trips.'

It was miserable and frustrating, so we decided to forgo the direct line toward the summit spur and head left to the ridge in the sun and what we hoped would be a good bivvi site. But the nagging voice of concern whispered, 'Once on the shoulder you'll never get across to the spur.' We had seen the corniced ridge running along the top of the shoulder from the acclimatisation slopes opposite. It reminded me of un-climbable things I had come across in Peru, but what could we do, we needed a good night didn't we?

Plunging arms up to the shoulder in bottomless powder and mantling on buried axes, the cold stung and our lungs heaved. We had reached the snow arête leading to the left-hand side of the shoulder. Over to our left and beyond a col, Kalanka's neighbour, Saf Minal, appeared to have its own perfect weather pattern and easy access along its summit ridge. We imagined Jon Varco and Sue Knott attempting Kalanka's north buttress (to our right) in 2003 and looking with longing at Saf Minal. It was obvious why Varco had returned the following year in the company of Parnell to successfully climb this striking peak.

We had chosen Kalanka and I didn't regret it. I needed a climb that would challenge me completely. I just didn't know if I was strong enough to face the disappointment of failure. Stopping early, we dug a large cave and for the first time in three days could sit without the fear of falling. Some 10km Ten away the tiny specs of our tents could be seen at base camp. I didn't long to be there. I was content, wrapped in damp down and eating a fraction of the food my body begged. The thought of what tomorrow would bring burned even more calories. Tomorrow would decide the outcome of the climb. We would make it across the shoulder to the summit buttress or we would be abseiling. What else in life is this simple? I realised I had not chosen this mountain, it had chosen me; climbing had chosen me.

I slept fully clothed without a harness and surrounded by flickering stars. Spindrift poured over the roof of our ledge, missing us. The wind rocked our perch, reminding me of sleeping in my van through the summer in North Wales. Tomorrow was Day Four, our imagined summit day. Kenton's altimeter put us at a height of 6300 metres. The 800m to where we now were had actually been 1300m, leaving 700m to the summit. We surmised that if it were possible to reach the bottom of the summit pillar it would then take another two days to climb to the summit and a further two days to abseil the line. We reduced the food intake.

'I don't know how to climb this.'

Standing in knee-deep snow on the crest of the shoulder I was confronted with a snow-covered rock tower. I expected the ground beneath my feet to collapse with each cautious plunge. The ridge was overhanging on the left. Brown rubble like the Lleyn Peninsular was welded together with grey ice and fell straight to the glacier. There was no walkway, no ramp or secret hidden path, I felt cheated. Ahead, I could see Nanda Devi standing proud beyond Kalanka's south ridge; behind were Kenton and Saf Minal. Kenton was sat in a hole with the rope running around his body. Gravity was the belay.

12. Kalanka (*left*) and Changabang north face. The ridge to the heavily corniced shoulder on the left was Bullock and Cool's high point. (*Nick Bullock*)

13. Kenton Cool on steep ground on day one of the Kalanka north face climb. (*Nick Bullock*)

'I don't know how to climb this.'

'How about dropping down on the right?'

The 'right' was nearly vertical snow flutings, unknowable and uninviting, but if we were to get anywhere I would have to give it a go. About an hour later I had passed beneath the rock tower and climbed a deep fluting to hang beneath the crest of the ridge and belay. It had been unprotected roulette, but seeing what was to come I realised it had only been a hors d'oeuvres. *'Kenton's lead.'*

'That was sketchy.'

'If you think that was bad, take a look right.'

Leaning out from the fluting Kenton stared at what was to come.

'I'm not going out there, it'll be suicide.'

I was disappointed and relieved; Kenton had made the decision I was too scared to voice.

The taxi weaved among cyclists and tractors pulling trailers stacked with sugar-cane. Another lorry burst from the cloud of dust that hangs permanently over Indian thoroughfares. I gulped hot, humid air and fought travel sickness. And still my mind raced.

My first thought on seeing the ridge ahead had been that to go on was unjustifiable, and pointless given our dwindling food supply. Kenton's refusal to continue was confirmation, though I had kept my belief to myself, needing his unbiased opinion. Had it come from someone other than Kenton, with his wealth of experience, would I have pushed to continue? Should I have been more forceful? Or would it merely have delayed the same outcome? Was Kenton waiting for my insistence, needing that impetus in order to continue? Questions, too many questions ... but that was the problem ... I felt a fraud.

Summary: An account of an attempt by Nick Bullock and Kenton Cool to climb a new route, alpine style, on the north face of Kalanka in September 2007 (plus digressions to the east face of Mont Blanc du Tacul and the Lleyn Peninsula). The 2000-metre north face of Kalanka (6931m) is a continuation of Changabang's north face in the Uttarakhand Region of India on the border of the Nanda Devi Sanctuary. The face has one established climb, opened in 1977 by a Czechoslovak team using fixed ropes. Several teams have failed to climb the north buttress, a line in the middle of the face. This, with other untried lines on the north face, remains one of the great prizes in the Garhwal.

Acknowledgements: Nick Bullock and Kenton Cool would like to thank Mammut, the Nick Estcourt Award, the MEF, the BMC, DMM, Vasque, Mountain Hardware, Science in Sport and Lyon Equipment for their invaluable support.

CLAUDE GARDIEN & NEIL BRODIE

Alpine-style
Mummery's legacy squandered and reclaimed

In 1895, Albert Frederick Mummery did not waste much time wondering whether he should attempt to climb Nanga Parbat alpine-style or siege-style. He started up the Diamir face with just one other climber, Gurkha Raghobir Thapa, and managed to reach the end of the technical climbing, at an altitude of almost 7000m, without having used any fixed ropes or camps and without the help of a support team. Mummery, along with two Gurkhas, disappeared a few days after his audacious attempt whilst trying to cross a high col on the Rakhiot side of the mountain. His route on the Diamir face had to wait until 1978 to get its first alpine-style ascent, when Reinhold Messner climbed it solo.

The death of Mummery did not, however, mark the end of alpine-style climbing in the Himalaya. In the early 20th century Alexander Kellas, a Scottish doctor, climbed a number of peaks in the Sikkim region of India. Perhaps his most notable achievement was the first ascent of Pauhunri (7125m), which he made in impeccable style with several Sherpas. Kellas used his knowledge of physiology to study the effects of altitude on the human body. He asserted that it was quite feasible to climb the highest peaks on the planet without the use of bottled oxygen, and even managed to calculate the rate of ascent that Messner and Habeler would eventually manage on the first 'free' ascent of Everest in 1978.

Kellas died on a joint Alpine Club/Royal Geographical Society reconnaissance trip to Everest in 1921. Before his death he had remarked on the extraordinary capacity of Sherpas to sustain physical activity at high altitudes. His observations were to have a profound effect on the strategy for subsequent Himalayan expeditions, the Sherpas becoming the power horses of the European-led attempts to climb the 8000m peaks.

After the First World War, the West was impatient to conquer the world's highest summits, even though very little was known at the time about the effects of the high-altitude environment on the human body. There were

14. *Left*
    Pure alpinism: Yannick Graziani, on day three of the first ascent, with Christian Trommsdorff, of Pumari Chhish South (7350m) by the south face, Karakoram, 8-13 June 2007 (2700m, ABO 5.10 M6 A1). Yannick is at the head of a ramp at 6400m, just before the route's first M6 pitch. (*Christian Trommsdorff*).

literally hundreds of six and seven-thousand-metre peaks which could have been used gradually to push the limits further in this rarefied atmosphere, but the European governments were in far too much of a hurry for that. The strong nationalist undercurrent of the day meant that the general public wanted to see their compatriots on top of the highest mountains first. Mountaineering had been hijacked by politics.

Expedition-style attempts, with massive logistical support for the climbers, were considered to give the best chance for success. Indeed this option became the only one feasible when it was decided that bottled oxygen would be indispensable for a summit push. The assumption that supplementary oxygen was necessary became universally accepted despite the fact that climbers using it on Everest in 1924 had not managed to go any higher than those without it.

This dependence on heavy equipment meant that high-altitude porters had to be used, camps installed and ropes fixed, and for 75 years mountaineering in the Himalaya was generally carried out according to this model. Although it had been demonstrated that the human body could function at high altitude, the equipment available to climbers was seen as being much too heavy and cumbersome to allow them to move fast enough to attempt big mountains in small teams. Lightweight ascents, such as that made by Freddy Spencer Chapman and Pasang Dawa Lama on Chomolhari (7314m) in 1937, were very much the exception.

Speed was the key to climbing high summits in good style and in 1907 Longstaff and Brocherel had shown what was possible by covering 1800 vertical metres on their summit day on Trisul (7135m). Almost 70 years later Reinhold Messner would take this concept further, bringing it to the highest altitudes. Messner was fast – in 1974 he had famously climbed the north face of the Eiger with Peter Habeler in just 10 hours – and he had also begun to gain a considerable amount of experience on 8000m peaks, having been on Nanga Parbat in 1970 and Manaslu in 1972. In 1975, whilst participating in a big siege-style attempt on the south face of Lhotse, he began to think about a new way of climbing these mountains. Not long after he returned from Nepal he left for Pakistan, but this time he was accompanied by just one other climber, his Eiger partner Peter Habeler. Just two days after starting up Gasherbrum I (8068m), the pair reached the summit by a new route that had involved sections of technical climbing. The challenge had been laid down for the coming generation.

Over the next 10 years Habeler and Messner's vision was accepted and developed by a new breed of Himalayan climber. These mountaineers had a high technical standard which gave them the necessary margin to be able to move quickly and climb difficult terrain at high altitude. Like their predecessors they were fit, determined and ambitious, but the cumulative experience of high-altitude climbing gained over the previous 50 years also gave them the confidence to head up into the unknown without the need for a lifeline back to the bottom of the face.

15.   Yannick Graziani exiting the first sustained mixed section above the ramp, c6500m. 'During this section Yannick led a 60-metre pitch up an overhanging, icy chimney – no place to fall!' (*Christian Trommsdorff*)

However, perhaps the most significant development during this period was the erosion of the close-knit national team. Organising and financing a small alpine-style attempt was simple compared to a large expedition, and it was no longer necessary to appeal to the general public for funding. Individual climbers met and joined forces to tackle the big Himalayan faces with little concern for nationality. Ideas spread faster through this diversity and the momentum of the alpine-style ideal accelerated. A mere 10 years after Chris Bonington had led an expedition comprising 124 porters, eight climbers and several Sherpas who fixed 4000m of rope on the south face of Annapurna, Réné Ghilini and Alex MacIntyre set off up it with just one ice screw and three pitons between them. MacIntyre had already proved to himself that this strategy could work on the south face of Shishapangma the previous year, but this time the technical difficulty of his chosen line proved too great for their sparse rack. Forced to retreat from beneath a vertical rock wall, he was hit by a falling stone and fell to his death.

16.   'For alpinists who specialise in lightweight, high-altitude climbing, these high peaks are the ultimate on this planet.' Near the exit of the headwall at 6950m, day four, Pumari Chhish South. (*Christian Trommsdorff*)

The challenge of an alpine-style ascent of this huge wall was taken up two years later by the Catalans, Nic Boghias and Enrico Lucas. Even with considerably more equipment, they took a whole day to overcome the 50m-high rock wall that had thwarted Ghilini and MacIntyre's attempt. Reaching the top of the face after six days, Boghias and Lucas whipped their secret weapon out of the bottom of their sack – 80 metres of 7mm cord – and rapped the neighbouring Polish route to the bottom of the face in a single day, using their last piton to equip the final anchor.

MacIntyre had developed his ruthless approach to Himalayan climbing with the Polish climber, Voytek Kurtyka, with whom he had shared several major ascents. Kurtyka was keen to explore the spiritual aspects of high-altitude climbing, searching for what he called a 'State of Nakedness', by which he meant lightweight and vulnerable but confident. However, he freely admitted that this state of self-belief was usually preceded by long periods of doubt and fear.

Kurtyka began his quest with an epic ascent of the 2500m-high east face of Kohe Bandaka (6643m) in the Afghan Hindu Kush in 1977 with MacIntyre and John Porter over six days. The next year they were joined by Krystof Zurek on the south face of Changabang (6864m), a huge 1700m rock wall which they climbed in a single eight-day push. In 1980 he took his vision to the highest altitudes when he climbed the north-east face of Dhaulagiri (8167m) over three days and in appalling weather with MacIntyre, Réné Ghilini and Ludwik Wikzynski.

After the death of MacIntyre in 1982, Kurtyka began a partnership with Jerzy Kukuczka, another Pole. In 1983 they teamed up to establish two new routes on Gasherbrums I and II on the same trip and in the following year traversed all three summits of Broad Peak. Despite these impressive achievements, their partnership was never destined to last a long time. Kukuczka was obsessed with climbing 8000m peaks and shunned technical difficulty, choosing only to pit himself against the challenges of survival in the 'Death Zone'. Kurtyka preferred to dedicate himself to the vision that he had shaped with MacIntyre where 'the summit was the ambition (but) the style became the obsession'. In 1985 he teamed up with Robert Schauer to complete what is undoubtedly one of the greatest ever ascents in the Himalaya – the west face of Gasherbrum IV. This 2500m face culminates at 7925m and the pair took eight days to climb it – eight days during which they had to overcome several pitches of grade 5 climbing on rotten, unprotectable marble, bivouac on tiny ledges up to 20m apart, and sit out a two-day storm high on the face. When they eventually reached the summit ridge they were both exhausted and hallucinating, Schauer imagining himself to be a raven flying across the wall and looking down on his decrepit body. They had run out of food and water and renounced continuing along the almost horizontal ridge to the summit, preferring to maximise their chances of survival by descending immediately.

Since these landmark ascents of the late '70s and '80s, climbers trying to pursue technical, alpine-style ascents on the highest summits have been few and far between. At the same time, it seems that most significant ascents at high altitude are once again made by teams of climbers of the same nationality. In the '90s the energy that invests certain climbing communities at different times moved to Slovenia, perhaps as a result of the incredible new routes that were claimed by Tomo Cesen on Jannu and Lhotse in the late '80s. Marko Prezelj and Andrej Stremfelj climbed the south ridge of Kangchenjunga in 1991 and Tomaz Humar and Janez Jeglic made the first ascent of the east face of Nuptse in 1996, Jeglic unfortunately being blown to his death from the summit. Humar went back to the Himalaya in 1999 to attempt the south face of Dhaulagiri solo. His ascent was certainly impressive but his willing exposure to serious objective dangers, his inflation of the technical difficulties and the presence of a massive media machine covering the whole operation detracted somewhat from the purity of his climb. More recently Steve House and Vince Anderson from the USA made a fast, lightweight ascent of the 4000m-high Rupal Face of Nanga Parbat in impeccable style, just a month after Humar had been plucked from it, at an altitude of 5900m, by helicopter.

However, whilst these ascents are truly impressive, and for the most part were undertaken in the same spirit as Kurtyka's search for his 'State of Nakedness', they have not taken the concept any further than the pioneers of the early '80s, despite a huge increase in technical climbing standards and significant improvements in equipment. Have the limits of alpine-style climbing at the highest altitudes been reached? Are the last great Himalayan faces destined to be sieged into submission by climbers who are too impatient to wait for the next generation? Only time will tell.

Acknowledgement: This article appears with the kind permission of *Vertical* magazine in which it was first published in issue 5, April-May 2007.

Above left:

17. Yannick Graziani, 50m from the summit of Pumari Chhish on day five of his climb with Christian Trommsdorff.

     'The wind suddenly got stronger, and at about a hundred metres from the top we were caught in 80 to 100 kph gusts. Despite being very close to the summit, we began to doubt again.' (*Christian Trommsdorff*)

Below left:

18. Rapelling down in the early evening of day five. The pair had climbed the face with four bivouacs, summiting at noon on 12 June. They down climbed and made approximately 35 rappels along the line of ascent over the next day and a half. (*Christian Trommsdorff collection*).

19. Face of an alpinist: Christian Trommsdorff back at the last bivvi on the descent. (*Christian Trommsdorff collection*)

20. Pumari Chhish South (centre) as seen from Trommsdorff and Graziani's base camp at 4500m. Note that Khunyang Chhish East (7400m) on the left side and the 6800m unnamed peak on the right are both unclimbed. (*Christian Trommsdorff*)

After the climb Christian Trommsdorff's next stop was the Alpine Club's celebration in Zermatt where Trommsdorff was an honoured guest who still had enough reserves of energy to party.

VICTOR SAUNDERS

For Alpine-style read Scottish-style

In the 1980s there was a small club of mountaineers from North London. I guess it was not much of a coincidence that it was called the North London Mountaineering Club. With barely 100 members the club punched way above its weight. (Today it has about 250 members.) I was lucky to live in North London in those years, and this is the story of how the Club dragged me, kicking and screaming, into the terrifying world of grown-up climbing. There was no doubt about it, the things those boys (and girls) got up to in the greater ranges were strictly for consenting adults.

The skills we were to use in the Himalaya were discovered by accident during weekends in Scotland, so the Scottish Weekend really belongs to the Himalayan Alpine Experience. It was our entrée. The Scottish rules were very simple: you had to be at work at 5pm on Friday and 9am on Monday. In between there were two overnight car journeys, as many climbs as possible and the delights of sleeping rough like beer-soaked tramps. The climbs began before dawn and always finished too late for supper. We got used to not eating.

Some weekends were more memorable than others. For example, there was that one journey to the island of Skye. There were four of us. It always had to be four drivers, that way the 12-hour drive could be shared by all. Three hours driving, three hours talking to the driver and six hours laid out in the back of the estate trying to sleep on top of the ice-axes and crampons. It would have been perfect for a fakir: a bed of crampons. This time there was Phil, Mick, Chris and me. Phil sometimes worked in a hospital, Mick in the tax office, Chris in a climbing shop and me, well I passed my idle hours in front of an architect's drawing board thinking about the next weekend. We used Chris's company car for this journey, it was a brand new Astra with go-faster stripes and even faster low-profile wheels. Chris was proud of the little red monster.

We arrived in Skye just before dawn and, travelling fully dressed for ice climbing, began the day energetically. By 5pm Mick and I had just completed our third climb of the day, a wonderful ephemeral line of blue ice with three free-standing icicle pitches and a final blue umbrella which felt like climbing up the inside of a giant frozen jellyfish. We named the route *The Icicle Factory*. It had been perfect weather, rare and beautiful. We stood on the summit, watching the sun sinking inexorably over the snow-tipped Cuillin, across the foam-tipped waves, and on to Canada.

Chris and Phil were also late getting down that night – we missed the pub and slept in a shed; that was normal. By 4pm on Sunday we had finished off another new route and began our long haul back to London. From

Kyle of Lochalsh to Fort William it is 66 miles. Chris covered that in one hour. The road was a single lane, just wider than the car. I cowered in the back seat; that was also fairly normal. This cowering sort of behaviour was normal because the most dangerous part of the Scottish weekend was always the driving. When they built the new roundabout at Ballachulish, Bert drove his hire car right over it. As 'Ballachulish Bert' later said, if you are going to write off a car, make sure it is a hire car. Dr John English dove (yes) his Sirocco into Loch Lomond. He landed on a submerged beach and after finding a tractor to tow him out, dried out the car on the long drive home. Henry Todd flew his brother's car into Rannoch Moor and there were many more similar stories.

I cowered in the back of Chris's beloved car for the next 500 miles. It really was a quick little machine, we were all home in bed by 2am on Monday morning. Chris lived two streets from me in a rough quarter of Islington. The next morning, tired and half asleep, he could not understand why, when he let the clutch out, the car did not move. The surly locals watched him revving up the car again and again, but did not tell him his car was propped up on bricks. The wheels had been stolen during the few hours he slept. Weekends such as these laid the foundations for the North London Club Himalayan outings.

We were used to climbing with just two ropes and whatever we could carry on our backs. Large expeditions with fixed camps and loads of rope? We had no idea how to do that. We were far too incompetent to manage more than small teams of two with the simplest of strategies and equipment. So, climbing Alpine-style in the Himalaya was, for us, not a matter of ethics or choice, but one of necessity. It was a matter of shortage of money, gear and above all, know-how. We did not know how.

Sometime in the 1980s we started knocking around in the Karakoram. Knowing no better, we hired expedition cooks who only cooked fiery lentil curries. To prepare for the 1987 trip to Spantik, Mick went to his nearest curry house and trained by eating the hottest, meanest curry he could find. I think it was called a Bangalore Phal. He also decided that the most dangerous part of any expedition was, like the Scottish thing, the approach. Not just the roads, but also the food and drink. He had read that giardia is carried in the water, so he decided to avoid any further stomach upsets by not drinking any (not even boiled water) before reaching base camp. By day three he had turned a funny colour. As usual, the colour did not affect his ferocious climbing skills.

In our ignorance we had to invent techniques to get us down. On one summit the weather turned nasty. First there was the casual flick of lighting and we hid as deep in the snow as we could until it left. Then the ensuing blizzard covered our tracks that had zigzagged through a crevasse field. We discovered that by crawling down on all fours and probing with the axes, like a mine clearer with his bayonet, we could sense the soft traces of our tracks under the surface.

21. Scottish style – 'the only way we knew'. Victor Saunders gimaces his
     way up Minus One Buttress, Ben Nevis. (*Mick Fowler*)

Four years later, on Kangchungtse, Steve Sustad lost our compass (he says it was me who lost it, but he would say that). We had tried to climb the 1000-metre west face of Kangchungtse (7600m) in a day. So we took no sleeping bags or stoves. The climb was harder than expected and a storm blew up while we were en route, putting down a metre of snow at base camp. We reached the top of the climb at around midnight and in the early hours of the morning were forced to bivouac somewhere on the Makalu La, digging small trenches to get out of the wind. That was where the compass was last seen.

22. Saunders on the second winter ascent of *Pointless*, VII, 6, Ben Nevis. (*Mick Fowler*)

3. Saunders on the first winter ascent of the Upper Girdle Part 2 of the Triple Buttresses, Beinn Eighe, Torridon, VI, 7. Part 1 was done by Fowler and Chris Watts. (*Mick Fowler*)

We needed to leave the plateau to the west if we were to descend into Nepal and not wander over the eastern séracs into Tibet. So, when the wind dropped briefly at 5am and in the grey half-light we glimpsed Makalu, Steve threw down an ice axe in the direction we guessed to be west. Steve went first on a tight rope (it was his fault after all) and followed the direction of the axe, while I tried to steer from behind. It worked, and by that night we were looking for our tent, which had disappeared under the fresh snow.

There is something peculiarly enjoyable, or at least satisfying, about solving problems in the mountains. In a way that is what climbing is really about. It took us a while to dig out the tent and crawl into the sleeping bags, light the stove and make some drinks. Before falling asleep I realized it was now early Monday morning; we had been climbing all Saturday and Sunday and spent the intervening night in some kind of a hazy dream. Our idea of climbing Alpine-style in the Himalaya had returned to its roots. We had finally come home; we were climbing Scottish-style. It was the only way we knew.

Cast note: Phil = Phil Thornhill, Mick = Mick Fowler, Chris = Chris Watts, an AC vice-president.

24. Babanov and Kofanov's new route to the summit of Jannu via the west pillar. (*Babanov collection*)

25. Puja at the establishment of base camp at 4700m in readiness for the west pillar ascent. (*Babanov collection*)

VALERY BABANOV

Nine Days on the Way that has no end

Translated from the Russian by Yuri Lipkov

Jannu west pillar, 16 October, altitude 6400 metres ...
A powerful gust of wind hits me in the spine, and everything that follows
occurs in one instant. I cannot believe my eyes. Transformed from a cozy
shelter into a huge paraglider, our tiny tent is torn from my hands, soars
high into the air and rushes towards the place 200 metres away where the
mountain face is broken by a kilometre-high drop-off that we have just
ascended. Savage horror, mixed with despair that this may be the end of
our climb, releases into my blood a huge dose of adrenalin, which is
immediately turned into a whirlwind of energy.

Without even thinking, sinking up to my knees in deep snow, in a
superhuman surge to halt our disappearing hopes at any price, I throw
myself in the direction of the abyss. Everything happens like in a movie. In
a few seconds I cover a good hundred metres and, thanks to a miracle that
has momentarily halted the flight of our 'house', I dive onto the tent. I am
drained of all strength. Breathing heavily, with my pulse racing, I slowly
come back to my normal self.

26.   Sergey Kofanov on the glacier at 5400m on day one of the climb.
      (*Valery Babanov*)

What *was* this? Was it a warning against some unknown danger, or a blessing from above to continue the upward journey? Time will tell ... Half an hour later the night embraced us, while the gusts of wind twirled the snow in a crazy dance. The weather had turned bad. Thunderclaps could be heard, emanating from God knows where. Nature toyed with us until morning.

Now, after some time has passed, I cannot understand where I got the strength for that surge. Only a second before that my entire body had been weak with fatigue, and my only desire had been to sit down in the snow and lose myself in a desert of do-nothingness. At such high altitude, thoughts become viscous and the world seems to turn still.

Jannu is a beauty 7710 metres high. Bizarre and proud, ridges of rock and ice rise to the sky, forming stately shoulders reminiscent of the wings of a giant bird. Above all this, like a head of this bird, towers the summit pinnacle. In Nepali the mountain's name is Kumbhakarna, but climbers prefer to call her Jannu. French alpinists led by Lionel Terray made the first ascent in spring 1962. Approached siege-style from the south, with intermediate camps and fixed ropes, it was considered at the time to be one of the most technically difficult ascents in the Himalaya. Since then only a very few lucky ones have managed to scale this Himalayan pearl. An ascent of Jannu is a leap into the unknown. Technical difficulties are exacerbated by the hardships associated with very unstable weather, hurricane-force winds, thin air, and very low temperatures. Any route to this summit is a challenge, a test of one's capabilities. It is a conquest of oneself.

17 October, altitude 6700 metres ...
The weather has deteriorated; visibility has fallen to a few dozen metres, sometimes to nothing. I don't know what motivates us to go up; we are definitely crazy. Gradually the slope gets steeper and in places bare ice appears. We are climbing tied together with a thin, five-millimetre static rope. I understand perfectly well that this is silly; the static rope will never withstand a hard pull if either of us falls, but we don't want to change anything. Anyway, it seems easier with the knowledge that you are tied to your partner.

And what about the bad things? Here, it is better not to think about them. This is an intense battle of two exhausted bodies with nature gone mad. I know that we will never win, but something still pushes us forward, does not let us stop. Probably it is stubbornness; or could it be a love of life? Because what we are doing right now – it is real life, a life that reveals its treasures on a razor-edge of struggle.

Sometimes I get an impression that we are climbing inside an enormous, mountain-sized, vertical aerodynamic tunnel. The wind accelerates the snow grains with such a force that they become like pellets of lead shot. I can feel their impact even through the thick layer of my down jacket.

27. The alpinist's view. Looking up to the west pillar from the col at 6350m. Jannu's steeep north face is on the left. (*Babanov collection*)

28.   Babanov astride the west ridge of Jannu at 7000m. (*Sergey Kofanov*)

29.   'Emptiness around us.' Sergey   Kofanov at 7100m.
      (*Valery Babanov*)

30. Day six: Valery Babanov at 7200m with Jannu's summit tower beyond. (*Sergey Kofanov*)

We climb almost blindly through the rising storm, taking the elevation metre by metre away from the mountain. I notice a huge, looming sérac to the right of us. Having quickly weighed pros and cons, I suggest to Sergey that we traverse towards it in order to hide from the raging storm, at least for a while. He agrees. In any other situation it would never have occurred to me to seek shelter beneath this overhanging mass of ice, but now – the tired body begs for respite.

Man is a strange creature. Having sat for two hours in our retreat, we convince ourselves that this place is safe enough, so safe that we can set up the tent here. We don't have much choice. The storm is continuing and soon it will start to get dark. And what will we find above? God only knows.

18 October, altitude 7000 metres ...

Twenty minutes have passed already, but I am still standing in one spot without knowing what to do. Sergey is motionless on belay somewhere far below me. He cannot see me because of a bulge in the cliff. Maybe it is better that way. Right now, I am better off alone, as I struggle to evaluate the situation and overcome the wave of doubt that is rushing through me. The situation is simple: I am in the middle of a steep ice gully and the way up is blocked by a band of near-vertical yellow granite. From here it looks impassable. It would be fine under most circumstances, but now the entire wall is being swept by a torrent of snow. This is not the kind of a snow that falls when everything is enveloped in heavy clouds; right now it is very cold and the sun is shining. But the wind ...

The ridge is being whipped by a raging wind that is picking up tons of snow and throwing it all downwards. Fortunately we do not yet feel all of the wind's power, as we are slightly below the ridge.

Two sides of my personality are struggling inside me. One of them is always in doubt. It is the careful one. It whispers, 'Stop; look around. You have already reached the limit. Impassable cliffs are ahead, and what lies after that? There lies the Unknown, and there are only two of you. You have no backup whatsoever. Isn't it better to descend now and choose something easier? Think about it. Maybe you will never return from here alive.' The second one is the optimist. It cheers me on, gives me energy and guides me through life. It says, 'Don't worry, everything will be fine. You call these difficulties? This is nothing but a game. Play and you will win. But if you descend now you will never come back again. Don't stop at the place you have already reached. The one who believes in something will attain it.'

At some point it appears to me that the snow torrent has weakened a little. It is even possible to lift my head and look around. I peer at the folds of granite high above and notice that in several places they are smeared with thin streaks of surface ice, barely visible from here. This could be the solution. I silence the pessimist inside me and move up. Right away there comes a feeling of relief. The perception that I have passed some critical barrier lifts my mood. I climb higher, the entire length of the rope, and come up to the cliff. Yes indeed, the problem is complicated, but it is possible to get through.

I build a station with two ice screws and pull on the rope three times, a signal for Sergey to ascend. Yelling is of no use; the wind and the distance between us muffle all sound.

Sergey comes up and I climb further on his belay. I am ascending on thin surface ice. In some places bare rock forces me to move over to another ice streak. But that is simply a matter of mastery and technique. In my head a thought flashes about how the experience of so many winter ascents is helping me now.

Metre by metre we are immersed ever deeper in the unknown territory of the Himalayan giant whose name is Jannu. Where we are climbing now no person has ever gone before. Ahead lies the uncharted Earth. The awareness of that fact makes me stronger. I begin to feel a gradual upward tide of energy. Despite all my doubts and inner torments, I am happy here in this upturned world.

Sometimes I ask myself: 'What do I need all this for?' And the answer is, 'I simply like it, and I do not want to stop at what has been achieved. At the end of the day, this is my way of life and I don't want to change it.' I like Reinhold Messner's reply to a journalist who asked about his lifestyle: 'All people are alike, but at the same time entirely different from one another. Everyone has his own way of life. One who finds his own proper way and who has enough courage to follow it cannot be wrong. It is simply that as a rule people are discouraged from remaining who they are.'

It seems to be that I have found my way, although it cannot be called an easy one. Several times, in extremely tough situations, when I was at the limit of my capabilities both physical and psychological, the ascent itself has lost all meaning. But at the same time I knew that if I managed to survive I would hardly stop going to the mountains. Therefore, I never made myself any empty promises to quit. Mountains and mountain climbing have always occupied too large a place in my heart just to take them and throw them away. And the core of the matter is not the adrenalin that, supposedly, is released during risky ascents. The real reason is that mountains live inside me. They are a part of me. I cannot remove and cast away a part of myself. There would be nothing left.

The mountains change us; we become different. And the more time we spend among the peaks, the stronger and more irreversible this process becomes. The success of one ascent leads us to try another, often a more difficult one. We invent our own rules and put up our own barriers to overcome. This is The Way that has no end. It is hard and it is magnificent, and I would never trade it for anything else.

31.   Valery Babanov hard mixed climbing at 7400m. (*Sergey Kofanov*)

19 October, altitude 7300 metres ...
We are moving, alternating the lead, along the knife-sharp ridge. It is almost dark, yet we still haven't found a suitable place for a tent. The icy wind is howling. All of this makes us tense. Associations with a tightrope artist, walking on an endless rope stretched high above the abyss, flash through my head, which is a bit foggy from effort and altitude.

I move slightly to the right in order to avoid stepping on a cornice hanging over the north wall. A huge slab of firn slips out from beneath my feet. Silently, it falls away to the south, dissolving in the darkness of the chasm. The realisation that I managed to jump off the slab only just in time, forces me to wake up and shake off the grogginess of altitude. I gather myself, understanding all too well that this is not the time to relax. Here every upward step is a battle. Any slight mistake or negligence on our part, and that's it, only memories of us shall remain.

At some point I realise that continuing to climb in darkness is becoming too risky. We need to find a tent site now, right where we are standing. But in truth, on a ridge of snow and ice with steep drop-offs to either side, the choices are not many. Sergey and I exchange a couple of phrases lamenting the situation and begin slowly to chop out a tent pad using our ice-axes. Each of us lasts for only a few minutes at this work before having to take a long rest. In order to save effort I chop the ice while on my knees. Time seems to stand still, but at the same time it rushes forward mercilessly.

It seems to me that we have been building this pad for an eternity. It turned dark long ago, the cold has enshrouded our exhausted bodies and the whole world seems to have shrunk to the size of our tiny tent, lost somewhere high in the Himalaya. In such moments I feel myself to be infinitesimally small and helpless in this frozen world of the highest and most beautiful mountains on Earth. This is our sixth night on the mountain and, except once, we have had to chop out a tent pad each time.

20 October, altitude 7500 metres ...
We find ourselves in the middle of that summit pinnacle, the very thing that makes Jannu so attractive and coveted. This morning we decided to leave almost all of our provisions and a part of our equipment, including the sleeping bag, on the ridge at 7300m. With us, we have only the tent and the gas stove with one cartouche; of the food, only several energy bars and tea. We took such extreme measures knowing full well that everything would depend on today. It was literally either today or never. With heavy packs we would not have been able to maintain the necessary tempo for the final push.

As we approached the base of the pinnacle, I grew tenser and tenser at the forbidding sight of it. The cliffs soared steeply and without compromise. Our only hope was to negotiate the steep ice ramps cutting through the pinnacle in several places. But even those did not look easy. Of course, had I been faced with similar sections of climbing somewhere at a lower elevation, for example in the Alps, they would have seemed routine. I would have made quick work of them. But here, at an altitude of nearly 8000m, where the air contains three times less oxygen than on the plain, and with our reserves of strength now practically gone, they appeared insurmountable. We had to surpass ourselves.

I climb on. Sergey belays me. I descend a couple of metres on ice smears and carefully begin traversing to the right, balancing on the front points of my crampons. I am climbing underneath an overhanging rock roof, almost butting my head against it. What appeared at first to be secure ice turns out to be just snow plastered onto the cliffs. I have no choice. As softly and smoothly as possible at this altitude, and while wearing high, double boots, I place my foot where the laws of physics say it should not even hold. I transfer my body weight onto that foot. Hmm ... It holds. I am utterly concentrating on every movement. In order to keep my balance, and for greater confidence, I hook the uneven features of the cliff with my ice-axes, even though I understand perfectly well that, should I lose my foothold, the ice-axes will hardly be of any help. Nevertheless, I am experiencing no fear of falling whatsoever. Maybe all feelings within me have died, stifled by the altitude. Maybe it's better that way.

For intermediate protection I use two stoppers and a Friend, which I put into a crack under the roof as I move along. Underneath my feet, the wall drops away steeply. Far below, we can see a huge snow-covered plateau bearing a pretty name, 'The Throne'. I expect the French named it so during their first ascent. They are masters at giving places beautiful names.

With every metre that we wrest from the mountain, we become ensconced ever deeper in a different reality, one where man ceases to exist as a physical entity, into a state where our actions are based on inner voice and intuition. We are entering a different world.

21 October, altitude 7600 metres ...
It looks as though we have survived this endless night. It was as if the unearthly cold had managed to stop even Time itself. Obviously there was no chance to sleep. Instead, we had to light the gas stove every 10 to 15 minutes for a short time in order to maintain what little warmth remained in our cold and tired bodies. It has just turned light and the watch shows six o'clock. We are ready to start moving. Sergey leads a horizontal traverse to the right, the length of an entire rope. Perhaps the route is located further in that direction, because the ground directly above us looks completely impassable.

I cross to Sergey, take over the lead, and climb on to enter a rock chimney that widens into a steep dihedral. I ascend it for another 10 metres or so. Where I am standing there is virtually no ice left. Even the small patches of centimetre-thin ice that I have been climbing on have petered out. An overhang with a small roof looms above. From here on up it is pure dry-tooling of a very high order. Experience tells me I will likely be unable to

32.   Sergey Kofanov belaying at 7500m. (*Valery Babanov*)

free-climb this section without falling. Yet I begin to climb. At one point I
look down, and my emotionless gaze pauses at an intermediate piece of
protection far below. Altitude and fatigue are at work; I am completely
indifferent as to whether I fall or not.

It probably would have been difficult for me to survive all the events and
ascents of my long years of climbing had it not been for a deep-seated sense
of caution. This sense has pointed the way out of many dangerous situations,
intuitively leading me in the right direction. And so it happens this time.
A barely discernible warning comes from my subconscious and reaches
my altitude-fogged brain. Something tells me that I must search for another
way up, in a different place. As slowly and carefully as possible I begin to
descend. The key, I feel, lies a few dozen metres to the right. My hunch is
confirmed; over there looks a bit easier, and in a mere half an hour I am standing
at the top of the pitch and hammering two pitons into an ice-filled crack.

I yell down that the belay is ready.

Altitude 7650 metres ...
The rock band, which had taken us so much time to get through, is now
below us. Slowly, as our remaining strength allows, we ascend a steep snow
slope. We are climbing simultaneously. High above we can see the coveted
ridge leading to the summit of Jannu. The bulges of the slope we are
ascending obscure the actual summit from view. Even though we have been
under the spell of this huge and powerful mountain for many days, only
here, near the summit, can we fully sense the energy that it radiates. And
that energy gives us the strength to keep moving.

Altitude 7710 metres ...

The summit is right in front of me. The final steps are made through an effort of sheer willpower. A few more metres and the shockingly huge massif of Kangchenjunga comes into view, filling the entire expanse to my left. It seems very near.

Leaning with my ice-axes against the ridge, which is thankfully devoid of a cornice, I throw my leg over it. Momentarily, I am sitting astride the ridge. This is the actual summit of Jannu. It is truly the moment of the realization of my dreams. How many days, maybe years, have I waited for this moment, and now it is reality? From experience I know it will take a long time to fully understand and absorb the enormity of what we have accomplished. Right at this moment we simply do not have the strength or energy to comprehend it.

I take a look around. Snow-clad peaks stretch all the way to the horizon. Everest, Lhotse, and Makalu are in plain sight. The landscape is spellbinding; it expresses eternity itself. I take in the rope and Sergey comes up towards me. I can see that the last steps to the summit are costing him a lot of willpower also. We are both happy but we restrain the outpouring of emotions, knowing that a long and dangerous descent lies ahead.

22 October, altitude 7350 metres ...

Seven o'clock in the morning. The cold is unearthly. I am trying to fold the tent but the crazy wind wants to rip it out of my hands. My entire morning procedure of heating boots and rubbing my feet has been for naught. Five minutes after exiting the tent I have already lost the feeling in my toes. My frozen hands also refuse to obey me. This has nothing to do with boots and mittens; quite simply, the internal energy that has kept us warm all these days is quickly dissipating.

I am fully aware of the seriousness of the developing situation, especially when I take in the altitude and the amount of vertical space beneath our feet. It is almost unbelievable that we still have to cover all that. Sometimes it seems to me we have become the prisoners of this mountain and it no longer wants to release us – at least not alive. We come out onto the ridge. The wind speed is incredible. If yesterday had been as windy as today we would never have reached the summit.

In order to lose altitude as quickly as possible we decide to go unroped on the ridge. This is a risky move but it gives us an edge in speed and right now this is very important. We both understand that in this wind and cold neither of us will last very long. Every additional minute spent at this terrible altitude saps more of our strength. We descend facing the ridge, exercising utmost concentration. If we make one wrong move there will be no way to stop. Two days ago we were ascending here roped together and, in many places, swinging leads.

Finally we reach the place on the ridge where we must begin descending to the west, towards the pillar where we came up. We will be doing double rappels.

33.   'The moment of the realisation of my dreams.' Valery Babanov on the summit of Jannu. Kangchenjunga in the background. (*Sergey Kofanov*)

34.   Japanese ridge from the summit of Jannu. Kangchenjunga in the background. (*Valery Babanov*)

The wall drops away steeply to a cold emptiness. An abyss two and a half kilometres deep is before us. The sun will not arrive there soon. I hammer in two snow stakes, thread the rope through them, and start descending. The feeling of those first steps into the void is not the most pleasant one. Lurking in the back of my mind is the fear that this whole dubious anchor system may fail under the weight of my body, and then ... brrr, it's better not to think about it.

I have lost count of rappels and of holes drilled in the ice. At some point, time simply ceases to exist, and we become as two abandoned dinghies, lost on the waves of eternity.

23 October, 4700 metres ...
One o'clock in the morning ... I have a feeling that I am watching myself from outside and that I see two exhausted and tortured creatures, barely moving their feet; two nocturnal ghosts shuffling along the glacier. They are walking towards the base camp. A distance that had previously taken about an hour now stretches on forever. Sometimes I have a vision that our base camp does not exist at all, that it is merely a figment of our sick, altitude-inflamed imagination.

The stony chaos of the enormous glacier is weakly illuminated by moonlight. I am watching my shadow on the rocks and it seems that this shadow is all that remains of me. There are no feelings, only great fatigue and resignation. I have an impression that the world has fragmented into a multitude of separate, disconnected worlds, and that I am lost somewhere among them, a wanderer in search of something, but unable to find it.

Music has been playing in my head for several hours. I don't even attempt to stop it or analyze it. I know the cause of it, but it just does not matter anymore. There are no thoughts in my brain, only emptiness. I ask Sergey whether he is hearing anything. He answers negatively, but tells me that sometimes he perceives a presence of a 'third person' along with us.

We sense that we are beginning to lose our minds. And that is not surprising. We have been on our feet 19 hours and during the last three days we have eaten only a couple of energy bars each. Altitude kills hunger, and with it our strength, leaving behind only thirst. In order to leave the glacier, gain the lateral moraine, and then the site of our base camp, it is necessary to overcome a huge rise. Even when we were fresh this had taken a massive amount of our strength and energy. Now it seems completely impossible to climb up to the place where we are awaited.

I notice a weak light somewhere high above. It is my wife Olga's headlamp. She has been waiting for us since that very first day when we left base camp to start our ascent. How long ago was that? It feels as if it happened in another life long ago. The perception of time disappears completely. I crawl upwards at a snail's pace. I presume that I am getting closer, only because Olga's headlamp is getting brighter. Just a little bit left.

35. 'Home.' Kofanov (*left*) and Babanov after nine days on the mountain. (*Babanov collection*)

I know that only in a few moments, as soon as I take another step forward, our world, and the internal perception of our surroundings, will change irreversibly. That world which we lived in for nine days, but which contains several years' worth of intense events and experiences, will dissolve deep inside of us to be replaced by another world, temporarily forgotten, but always close to us – the world of warmth, of people, of those we hold dear.

One more step, and I am standing on the grass, in Olga's embrace. We are looking at one another, she is telling me something, and I see how the tears are rolling down her cheeks. A second later, her words make their way through to my tired brain. 'You are both crazy,' she says, then adds her congratulations. In these words, I sense so much love and warmth that in an instant I feel good and calm, peace comes over me. I understand that there is no need to go further. This is it, I am already home.

Summary: An account of the alpine style first ascent of the west pillar of Jannu/Kumbhakarna (7710m) in eastern Nepal by Valery Babanov and Sergey Kofanov, 14-23 October 2007 (3000m/VI, WI+4, 80 degrees, M5). Descent via the route.

Acknowledgements: Babanov and Kofanov thank their sponsors Scarpa, Grivel, Bask, Beal and Julbo.

Climbs

Rowan Huntley *Les Drus ~ Study from Grands Montets*
Watercolour and pencil, 16cm x 23cm

MICHAEL COCKER

Frost, Dust and Tear Gas

Exploratory Mountaineering in the Peruvian Cordillera Carabaya

At the southern end of the Peruvian Andes lies the remote and rarely visited Cordillera Carabaya, a compact and attractive range of mountains with summits between 5000 and 5780 metres and an area where the level of exploration and development approximates to that of the Alps at the end of the Golden Age. In other words, all the major summits have been climbed but there is considerable scope for new routes with a few minor peaks still virgin. In the early summer of 2007 Jonathan Preston, Stephen Reid and I spent 17 days in this area climbing three new routes and one previously unclimbed summit. No detailed maps were available and our primary sources of information were a verbal recommendation from South American specialist John Biggar and a handful of old articles published in mountaineering journals. The principal aim of this paper is to provide a summary of the exploration to date, to clarify some of the confusing and contradictory records and to give an account of our own modest endeavours. It should be noted that these mountains have never been properly surveyed and that altitudes given in this article are only approximations; best estimates based on those recorded by earlier expeditions and ourselves.

For millennia the local Quechua Indians have farmed and grazed livestock in the high valleys below the glaciers. The mountains themselves were (and still are) considered sacred; *Apus* (deities) govern the weather and water, and the mythical place of origin of alpacas and llamas. Traditional names exist for three prominent peaks – Allinccapac, Chichiccapac and Huaynaccapac. The highest, Allinccapac (5780m), takes its name from a legendary pre-Inca king, Allin, who buried his wife Macu at the foot of the mountain (near the town of Macusani). In Quechua, the word *capac* means chief, hence, Chichiccapac means small chief. Huaynaccapac was the name of an important Inca king. The identities of the first two summits, Allinccapac and Chichiccapac, are apparent, as they form distinct massifs. However, Huaynaccapac is in the middle of the range, and, depending on where the mountains were viewed from, may have referred to more than one peak, leading to some confusion for latecomer mountaineers desiring clarity on the matter.

The first survey of the Carabaya was made in 1954 by Dr and Mrs Godfrey Francis and Tim Fisher. This was a geological expedition to study a mass of unusual rock rich in aluminium trioxide. On 9 July they climbed an

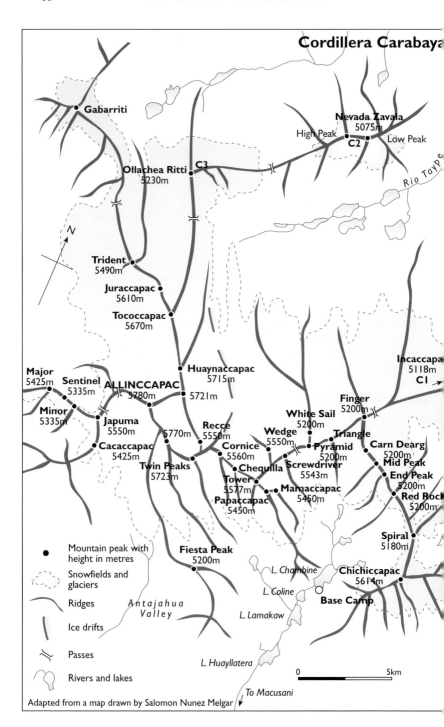

Cordillera Carabaya

Gabarriti

Nevada Zavala
5075m
High Peak
C2
Low Peak

Ollachea Ritti
5230m
C3

Rio Taype

N

Trident
5490m

Juraccapac
5610m

Tococcapac
5670m

Incaccapa
5118m
C1

Major
5425m
Sentinel
5335m
Minor
5335m
ALLINCCAPAC
5780m
Huaynaccapac
5715m
5721m
Finger
5200m
White Sail
5200m
Japuma
5550m
5770m
Recce
5550m
Wedge
5550m
Triangle
5200m
Carn Dearg
5200m
Cacaccapac
5425m
Cornice
5560m
Pyramid
5200m
Mid Peak
Twin Peaks
5723m
Chequilla
Screwdriver
5543m
End Peak
5200m
Tower
5577m
Mamaccapac
5450m
Red Rock
5200m
Papaccapac
5450m

Spiral
5180m

Mountain peak with
height in metres

Snowfields and
glaciers

Ridges

Ice drifts

Passes

Rivers and lakes

Fiesta Peak
5200m

Antajahua
Valley

L. Chambine

L. Coline

L. Lamakaw

Chichiccapac
5614m

Base Camp

L. Huayllatera

0   5km

Adapted from a map drawn by Salomon Nunez Melgar

To Macusani

outlying peak, which they named Japuma (5550m). In 1959 Francis led a second expedition to the area to attempt the three highest peaks–Allinccapac, Huaynaccapac and Chichiccapac. On 30 June, Francis, Simon Clark, Beverley Holt and Julio Cardenas climbed Chichiccapac (5614m) by its west glacier. Having assumed this was the first ascent, they were disconcerted to find footprints and rope marks in the snow near the summit. Cardenas, their chief porter, made enquiries and discovered that the Italian mountaineer Piero Ghiglione and a local porter, Fortunato Mautino, had made the first ascent, via the same route, eight days earlier. At the time Ghiglione was 76 years old. He and Mautino also made the second ascent of Japuma and an attempt on Allinccapac before moving to other areas where they made another 13 first ascents. Francis's party also tried Allinccapac but, hindered by soft snow, were unable to find a suitable line. In 1960, Francis, who wrote the instructional manual *Mountain Climbing* (1958), was killed by stone fall on Pillar Rock.

The first ascent of Allinccapac I, an imposing flat-topped massif encircled by steep cliffs overhung with huge ice séracs and cornices, was made on 25 July 1960 by Robert Kendell and Michael Binnie via a short steep couloir on the west side. The three other members of this Oxford University party – John Cole, Keith Meldrum and Nigel Rogers – made the second ascent two days later by the same route. From a high camp west of Allinccapac, they also climbed the lower of Huaynaccapac's two summits (5715m), which they named Huaynaccapac I, by two separate routes on the same day – the north-west ridge (Cole and Rogers) and south-west face (Binnie, Kendell and Meldrum). The following day Binnie and Kendell forced a track through soft snow up the south-west face, to a col between Juraccapac (5610m) and Tococcapac (5670m) before continuing up the south-east ridge of Juraccapac to make the first ascent. The next day the rest of the party used their tracks to regain the col and made the first ascent of Tococcapac via its north-west ridge. Kendell and Binnie made the first ascent of Allinccapac II (5770m), climbing 300m of steep snow on the north-west face. Recce Peak (5550m) was ascended by Cole, Rogers and Meldrum in order to inspect the four impressive rock and ice towers that they named: Screwdriver, Wedge, Tower and Cornice. They also made a complete north to south traverse of Japuma and included Cacaccapac (5425m), a rock peak to its south. Towards the end of the expedition Cole and Kendell made the first ascent of the second, slightly higher and south-westerly summit of Huaynaccapac (5721m). Finally, during the evacuation from their high camp, 'Pico Carol' (5670m) 'a prominent gendarme on the east ridge of Allinccapac' was climbed. The party had their base camp in the Antahoua valley, directly under the formidable south-west face of Allinccapac, and spent six weeks in the mountains.

In July 1965 a Keele University expedition made the third ascent of Chichiccapac, following the same line as previous parties, before making the first ascents of Tower (5577m) (which they confusingly and erroneously refer to as Huaynaccapac), Screwdriver (5543m) and nine other peaks. It took the best part of a week to find a way up Tower, which Brian Chase, Rodney Gallagher, Geoffrey Bonney and Andrew Tomlinson eventually climbed via 'a huge ice-gully' on the north-east side. During their exploration of Tower they named two subsidiary peaks, east of the main summit, Papaccapac and Mamaccapac, both c5450m. A spell of bad weather and the theft of some equipment detained them for a few days in base camp before a high camp was established in the glaciated cirque below Screwdriver and Pyramid. From here Chase, Tomlinson, Bonney and Gallagher made the first ascent of Pyramid (5200m) by two independent routes. Chase and Tomlinson followed this with the first ascent of White Sail (5200m), another snow peak, possibly Vela Blanca (on the same ridge and slightly north of White Sail) and, on 16 August, Screwdriver via its north ridge – a pure rock climb with two VS pitches. Bonney and Peter Floyd made the first ascent of Red Rock (5200m) and a peak 'just east of Pyramid' (prob-ably Triangle). Chase and Tomlinson devised 'a superb ridge traverse on snow and rock' over the summits of End Peak, Mid Peak, Carn Dearg and Finger Peak, all around 5200m. At the end of August bad weather set in 'and only minor rock peaks nearby were ascended'. The party established base camp at Laguna Lamakaw on 15 July and departed on 9 September.

The first expedition to approach the mountains from the north was a team from the New Zealand Alpine Club which, in 1967, set up a base camp near the head of the Rio Taype. On 14 June, Alex Parton, Dave Massam, Bryan Dudley and Alwyn Chinn made the first ascent of C2 (5075m), an impressive snow peak overlooking their camp, finding it harder than expected, the crux section being a 100m rock buttress which was iced in parts. On 18 June a high camp was established on the glacier north-east of Trident. From the lower reaches of this they 'climbed steep fluted ice and rock to a ridge' leading to the top of C3 (5230m), the first ascent. On 21 June second ascents of Juraccapac and Tococcapac were made via a long snow couloir, presumably on the north-east face, by Parton, Dudley, Massam, Chinn and Roderick McKenzie. The following day the same party made the first ascent of Trident (5490m) their main objective. Steep snow and ice led to a col between the middle and north peaks where 'an interesting rock ridge' led to the summit. After a couple of days back in base camp, second ascents were made of Screwdriver (repeating the line taken previously), Tower and Huaynaccapac II (both allegedly by new routes) and, on 4 July came the first traverse of Allinccapac I and II (third and second ascents respectively of the individual peaks). Massam and Parton made the first ascent of Cornice (5560m), finding it 'longer and more difficult than was anticipated', but left no details of the line taken. Eight other peaks were climbed from base camp, the most spectacular being a subsidiary summit of C2 involving a height gain of more than 600m.

Also in the area at the same time, based on the south side of the range, was a British team led by Roger Whewell. They too had come to attempt

Trident but turned their attentions to Wedge Peak (5550m) after meeting with the New Zealanders. In the event, due to a combination of bad weather and soft snow, they failed to climb Wedge and, instead, made first ascents of three minor peaks on the ridge north of Chichiccapac. Whewell returned with his wife the following year and succeeded on Wedge, the last significant virgin summit.

In August 1971 five British mountaineering instructors – Kate Dilworth, Barbara Spark, Mollie Porter, Carol McNeill and Janet Richards – climbed Japuma from the north and made the first ascents of three peaks on the ridge running west from this: Sentinel (5335m), ascending the south and descending the west side, Minor (5335m) via the south face and west ridge, and Major (5425m) via the east ridge and south face. Spark, Porter and Richards also made the first ascent of Spiral Peak (5180m), one mile north of Chichiccapac, via the south-west ridge, while McNeil and Dilworth made repeat ascents of Triangle and Pyramid.

In October 1973, Steve McAndrews (American), Ian Haverson (Australian), and Michael Andrews (New Zealand) made the fifth ascent of Chichiccapac by the normal route up the west face. On 2 August 1980, from a base in the Antajahua valley, a Chilean team – G Cassana, D Delgado, G Naccicio, and A Neira – made the first recorded ascent of Twin Peaks (5723m) via the south-east ridge. This was the last expedition to visit the Cordillera Carabaya for 25 years as political instability and an aggressive campaign by the *Sendero Luminoso* (Shining Path) guerrillas made Peru a virtual no-go area. By the time climbers did return, in the 1990s, the Carabaya, no longer having the lure of significant virgin summits or peaks over 6000m, slipped into obscurity.

First to rediscover these mountains was John Biggar who led a commercial expedition to the area in 2005. On 14 June, from a base camp at Laguna Chungara, south-east of the Chichiccapac massif, they climbed Chichiccapac via a new route, the east glacier and north-east ridge, a technically straight-forward ascent which they graded alpine Facile. The following day Biggar and two others climbed the minor peak of Chichiccapac South-east (c5285m), which they believed to be a first ascent; an easy glacier on the south side was followed by rock climbing on the north-west ridge up to VS. The party then moved their base camp to Laguna Chambine, west of Chichiccapac, from where, on 19 June, Biggar and three others climbed an unnamed rock tower (c5267m) by two separate routes, the north ridge and west face. No location for this peak is given. They thought the summit may have been reached before but were fairly certain the climbs were new as there was clear evidence that the lines had only recently emerged from the glacier. Ascents were also made of peaks they believed to be White Sail and Red Peak; the latter via a straightforward scramble up the south ridge, possibly a first ascent. Various members of the team climbed Quenamari (c5294m), which lies south of the main range, Iteriluma (c5270m), just south of Chichicca-pac and an unnamed peak (c5057m) near Laguna Chambine. It is not clear if any of these were first ascents.

38. North-west face of Chichiccapac, showing the line up the north ridge (Alpine D
(*Stephen Reid*)

39. Base Camp at Laguna Chambine. (*Michael Cocker*)

Jonathan, Stephen and I arrived in Lima, on 14 June 2007 and the following day took an internal flight to Juliaca and a bus to Puno, on the edge of Lake Titicaca, where we spent four days acclimatizing and acquiring essential supplies. A luggage allowance of 20kg each on the international flight had pared our equipment down to a bare minimum and all the food, fuel and base camp kit had to be purchased locally. A minibus and driver were hired to take us the 300 or so kilometres of dirt roads to the unprepossessing town of Macusani at the foot of the mountains. Here, having little or no choice in the matter, we found a room in a basic hotel, next door to the local brothel.

With no established infrastructure to facilitate onward transportation into the mountains we wandered the streets enquiring in broken and inadequate Spanish if it was possible to hire a vehicle. No one was forthcoming until we were introduced to Alex, a local wheeler-dealer and likeable rogue who had spent time working on construction sites in the USA. Significantly, he had a car, a beaten up old Peugeot with bald tyres. After agreeing a price, he drove with alarming speed and confidence up a rough track leading to a dam at the road head so we could recce the start of the trek to base camp. On the way back we stopped at a farm where two rather toothless middle-aged ladies, wearing the traditional Derby hat and hooped skirt, agreed to act as porters and lend us pack animals. The following morning a friend of Alex's arrived at the hotel with a minibus that looked even more of a wreck than the Peugeot. However we were assured that it was good for the journey and, as if to prove the point, both the driver and Alex brought along various members of their families for the ride. Remarkably, despite living virtually in the shadow of the mountains, they had never been to the lakes at the head of the valley. All went well and a couple of hours later we were met at the dam by the ladies from the farm with two horses and three donkeys. After an hour or so preparing the loads a small caravan, that now included not only the ladies and their pack animals but also the driver, Alex, various family members and a couple of children, set off on the two and a half hour trek to base camp, which we established at the edge of the picturesque Laguna Chambine.

The winter solstice was almost upon us and the locals had told us about the *Allinccapac Raymi* or festival that was due to take place at the head of the adjacent Antajahua valley on 23 June. Thinking the walk would be a good acclimatisation exercise and that we would probably be the first outsiders to participate, we set off that morning to join in the festivities. However, by the time we got to the top of the 5000m pass giving access to the next valley, it became clear we would not be able to get there and back in a day, so instead we decided to traverse the ridge leading north-west towards Allinccapac. A couple of hours' easy scrambling bought us to the foot of a rock tower that projected 50m or so from the ridge. Drum beats, pan-pipes and voices drifted eerily up from the valley below as we soloed

40. Stephen Reid on the crux pitch during the first ascent of the north ridge of
Chichiccapac. (*Michael Cocker*)

up the tower, finding the final short, loose and technically severe wall, just
below the summit, disconcerting in big boots without a rope. There was
no cairn on top and as it had no name and didn't appear to have been
climbed before we called it Fiesta Peak (5200m).

Base camp was a delightful spot. The sun hit our tents at seven in the
morning and for a few hours the air was still and warm. Then around midday
the wind picked up, producing clouds of dust that would deposit their
contents over the camp, invariably just as we were about to have lunch, the
main meal of the day. We were a little concerned about the wisdom of
leaving the tents unattended while we were away climbing, but, in the event,
the only visitor we had during our stay was Marco, a 30-something family
man from Macusani who came three times a week on his bicycle to fish the
lake for trout, which he later sold in the market. Just after 3.30pm the sun
disappeared behind the surrounding peaks and within minutes the
temperature plummeted, driving us into our tents for extra clothing or
clambering up the hillside to stay in the sunlight a little longer. Being midwinter, and just a few degrees south of the equator, days were short and the
darkness lasted a full 12 hours with the temperature dropping to around
– 8°C in the early hours of the morning.

Our original objective was the unclimbed south face of Chichiccapac but a preliminary inspection quickly ruled this out. Although we could see a feasible route up a series of connecting snow gullies the whole face was overhung by massive séracs and cornices. So we turned our attention to the north side of the mountain where we found a fine rock ridge, with three distinct towers, leading directly to the upper snowfields. A chilly bivouac in the corrie below and an early start enabled us to reach 'Preston Col' at the foot of the ridge just after dawn on 29 June. To avoid having to re-arrange the ropes at each stance we had agreed that the leader would climb three pitches before changing the order. Jonathan took the first shift and set off up a chockstone-filled chimney on the east side of the ridge. From an icy belay two thirds of the way up this, a short wall and traverse took us out onto the front of the ridge, where a series of open grooves and corners led to a platform at the foot of the middle tower. We swapped leaders and Stephen donned rock shoes to tackle what was clearly going to be a difficult pitch. Technically it was probably only MVS, but the holds were small, the rock friable and it was only moderately well protected. We were also all acutely aware of the altitude and the sacks felt heavy. It was an impressive lead and when I came to second it, in big boots, I found myself calling for a tight rope on more than one occasion. A couple of pitches of easier climbing took us to the foot of the third tower, which we were able to avoid by a rightward traverse onto the snow. We had noticed a band of ice-cliffs above the ridge the previous evening and had been a little uneasy about the difficulties these might contain, but in the event a straightforward passage was found through them and only a few hundred metres of steep snow and the occasional crevasse separated us from the summit, which we reached at 1.30pm. Far below we could see Macusani, a small stain in the khaki altiplano. To the east, a sea of cloud lay over the Amazonian rainforest while to the north rose the Allinccapac massif and, in the far distance, Ausangate, the highest mountain in southern Peru. After a bite to eat we set off down the west face, the start of which would be difficult to locate in poor visibility. This contained one short steep ice section, but otherwise led easily down to a snow col where we veered away from the normal route and abseiled down the corrie headwall to descend scree and boulder fields back to our bivvi site. It was 5.30pm and almost dark, but rather than endure a second night out we stumbled on down for another hour and a half to reach base camp utterly exhausted. It had been an excellent day's climbing – a new route (which we thought about alpine Difficile), the first complete traverse and seventh overall ascent of Chichiccapac.

Four days later, and after another cold bivouac and predawn start, we scrambled over exhausting, ankle-twisting moraine to access the unnamed glacier below the south face of Screwdriver, our main objective for the day. The snow on the glacier was soft, we moved slowly, and it was already 9.30am before we were near the foot of the face; rather too late, we felt, to embark on a major mixed route of unknown difficulty with no bivouac gear (we had left this below the moraine). Furthermore, we could see no practical line up the face. After a brief discussion we opted for the unclimbed, more amenable and impressive looking Mamaccapac. A steep snow slope led to a col between the twin peaks where we belayed and I set off up the shaded south-west face, the rock rather cold on the fingers. The angle eased after a few moves but the rock became horrendously loose and the climbing akin to tiptoeing up a pile of precariously perched roof tiles. Three nerve-jangling pitches took us to the summit where we built a cairn and wondered how we were going to descend. In the event, delicate down climbing and one abseil landed us safely back at the col where we began the long and wearying return to base camp.

With time left for only one more sortie, we decided to explore the mountains at the head of the valley we had crossed on the way to Fiesta Peak; the elegant looking south ridge of Cornice had in particular caught our attention. On the walk in, and just as we were approaching the bivouac site, I slipped on a loose boulder and landed heavily on my left wrist. I didn't think much of it at the time but next morning, as we walked up the moraine to the foot of the glacier, it was painful every time I put weight on it and I thought it unwise to embark on a long snow and ice climb that was going to require the use of two ice tools for most of the day. Reluctantly, I dropped out, leaving Stephen and Jonathan to complete the route. They reported it as superb, with 13 pitches of climbing at about Scottish grade III/IV that took most of the day and descent down the same line. They didn't get back to the bivouac site till 10pm and, as I had taken our only MSR stove back to base camp, endured a second cold night with only a few mouthfuls of water and some boiled sweets as sustenance. We had all anticipated a return to base camp the same day, so their absence caused me some concern during the night and I was mightily relieved to catch sight of them strolling back up the valley early the following morning. This was only the second ascent of the mountain and the first ascent of the south ridge, which they graded alpine Difficile. The adjacent peak to the north of Cornice, Chequillia, remains unclimbed.

During our time in the mountains the weather remained remarkably stable with only one day of low cloud and drizzle, but on the last evening thunder rumbled in the distance and lightning forked across the eastern sky. We had arranged for our porters and transport to return on 8 July, but being aware that Peruvians have a rather elastic sense of time we were unsure if anyone would materialise. However, our doubts were misplaced and they arrived at base camp early that morning and before we were ready. In the hour or so it took to tidy up the camp and load the pack animals the sky changed from milky high cloud to thick fog and heavy snow that lasted for the rest of the day.

Back in Macusani there was talk of political unrest and a national strike that would bring the whole country to a halt. As we approached Juliaca, the following afternoon, the roads were already strewn with boulders and makeshift barricades. Early next morning troops and tanks surrounded

41. Mamaccapac, showing the line up the south-west ridge (Alpine PD+).
(*Michael Cocker*)

42. Chichiccapac reflected near the bivvi site below Mamaccapac.
(*Stephen Reid*)

43.   Jonathan Preston on the first ascent of the south ridge of Cornice (Alpine D).
       (*Stephen Reid*)

The Allinccapac massif showing the line up the south ridge of Cornice (Alpine D). Chequilla, the smaller peak immediately right of Cornice, is still unclimbed. (*Michael Cocker*)

5. Jonathan Preston near the summit of Cornice (Alpine D). (*Stephen Reid*)

46. Running to dodge the missiles at the outskirts of Arequipa.
(*Michael Cocker*)

the airport, vainly attempting to hold back large crowds of protestors who broke through the cordon and smashed lights on the runway, inflicting enough damage to render it inoperable for several days. Avoiding the demonstrators, we returned to the hotel and were effectively besieged for the next 48 hours whilst sling-shot wielding protestors battled it out with troops and tear gas on the streets outside. At the first opportunity we boarded a bus to Arequipa where we understood the airport was still operational. However, unbeknown to us the protests were still at full pitch in the shanty towns surrounding the city, and the bus driver dropped us 25 kilometres short of our destination, refusing to go any further.

With no alternative, we started walking, carrying the gear as best we could. A short distance down the road we came across a number of abandoned vehicles. On the cliffs above, protestors were hurling rocks and boulders down on anything that moved below. Taking our chances, with debris landing all around us, we moved through this section as fast as we could, only to walk around the next corner to find a pitched battle taking place between protestors and heavily outnumbered riot police. The police ordered us to leave the area, but with nowhere to go and the road ahead completely blocked, our only option was to follow the railway line in full view of the rioters. The uncertainty of the outcome during the next few hours, as we made our way past protestors fuelled with anti-government, anti-capitalist and anti-western sentiments, eclipsed anything we had experienced in the mountains. Nonetheless we survived to tell the tale and that evening wined and dined in style amidst the colonial splendour of Arequipa.

Summary: A historical overview of the exploration to date and account of three first ascents in the Cordillera Carabaya, southern Peru, in June and July 2007 by Michael Cocker, Jonathan Preston and Stephen Reid.

Acknowledgements: Generous financial support was received from the Mount Everest Foundation and the British Mountaineering Council. The map accompanying this article is adapted from one originally drawn by Salomon Nunez Melgar in 1967.

REFERENCES

1. Michael Andrews, 'Chichiccapac and Other Peaks, Cordillera Carabaya' in *AAJ*, p190, 1974.
2. Cesar Morales Arneo, 'Climbs and Expeditions: Cordillera Carabaya' in *AAJ*, vol 12, pp145-146, 1960.
3. Humberto Barrera, 'Ipsi Riti, Southeast Ridge, Cordillera Carabaya' in *AAJ*, pp185-186, 1982.
4. John Biggar, 'Cordillera Carabaya' in *AAJ*, pp252-253, 2006.
5. Michael Binnie, 'Cordillera Carabaya' in *Mountain Craft*, no 57, 1962.
6. Brian Chase, 'The Cordillera Carabaya' in *Cambridge Mountaineering*, pp7-11,1966.
7. DE Cooper, ANH Chinn, BC Dudley, 'The Cordillera Carabaya' in *New Zealand Alpine Club Journal*, pp291-304, 1968.
8. Correspondent (14th July), 'When Ice Turns to Water: Climate Change in the Andes' in *The Economist*, p51, 2007.
9. K Dilworth, 'Cordillera Carabaya Expedition 1971' in *AAJ*, vol 18 , pp211-213, 1972.
10. K Dilworth, 'Japuma and Four Nearby First Ascents' in *AAJ*, vol 18, p173, 1972.
11. Rodney Gallagher, 'Expeditions: Peruvian Andes – Keele University Expedition, 1965', in *AJ*, vol XXII, pp124 -125, 1967.
12. Rodney Gallagher, 'Climbs and Expeditions: Chichiccapac and Other Peaks in the Cordillera Carabaya', in *AAJ*, vol 15, pp181, 1966.
13. Godfrey Francis, 'Invitation to the Andes', in *AJ*, vol LX, pp280-285, 1955.
14. Godfrey Francis, 'Expeditions: The Eastern Cordillera of Southern Peru', in *AJ*, vol LXV, pp85-87, 1960.
15. KI Meldrum, 'Climbs and Expeditions: Allinccapac, Cordillera Carabaya', in *AAJ*, vol 12, pp398-400, 1961.
16. AK Rawlinson, 'Godfrey Herbert Francis 1927-1960' in *AJ*, vol LXV, pp262-264, 1960.
17. Nigel Rogers, 'Cordillera Carabaya: Oxford Andean Expedition 1960' in *Oxford Mountaineering*, pp5-11, 1961.

GRAEME SCHOFIELD

No Place for the Chicken-hearted

I had been warned not to underestimate my feathered foe. 'It has spurs on its heels,' Carl had exclaimed. Armed with a walking pole, I circled it, confident I'd show the damn cockerel why we humans were at the top of the evolutionary pile. Up it jumped as I fended it off with the pole. The bird looked angry and willing to duel to the death. I, on the other hand, was not, and made a dash for the sanctuary of our tarpaulin shelter.

We had arrived the previous day, after a two-day trek, at Huayhuash village, a small settlement in the heart of the Cordillera Huayhuash in the Peruvian Andes. The killer chicken belonged to one of the villagers and, allied with some particularly unfriendly dogs, it was becoming a bit of a handful.

Tomorrow was to be our first day of climbing; we had spotted a long, dramatic line up the unclimbed east ridge of Quesillo (5600m). The idea was to set off at around 2am, summit at midday and be back at the camp in the evening. The alarms sounded implausibly early. I tried my best to appear moderately psyched as I chomped down entirely unappetising cornflakes and powdered milk. Two hours of contouring around scree slopes and laborious plodding up scrub hillsides led us to the beginning of the rock ridge. It started relatively easily and we scrambled along unroped as the sun began to transform the landscape.

We moved fairly quickly to the first gendarme where a short but steep jamming crack threatened to halt progress. Earlier, we had decided that one of us should bring rock boots in case the climbing was difficult and I, in a flash of genius, had volunteered. This meant I got to lead the pitch in rock boots, opting to haul my rucksack up afterwards, whilst everyone else had the desperate job of sketching up the pitch with mountaineering boots and a full pack. I sympathised of course.

From this point the climbing was excellent, albeit a little trickier than we imagined. An abseil down the first gendarme was followed by a rising traverse back to the crest of the ridge, an excellent series of quality rock pitches, and then mixed climbing. It was midday before we were at the foot of the snow section, two hours later than we would have liked. However, as the weather looked good and there was no particularly easy way down we decided to push on for the top.

The snow ridge was initially fairly stable and despite our exaggerated gasping due to lack of oxygen we made reasonable progress. The climbing

47. Tom Bide (*foreground*), Martin Lane and Graeme Schofield climbing unroped near the beginning of the east ridge of Quesillo. (*Carl Reilly*)

was relatively straightforward except for the odd steeper mixed and ice section, but it was deceptively long and we were becoming aware of ominous dark clouds moving towards us, rapidly engulfing Carnicero and Jurau to our north-east. More worrying were the flashes of lightning and rolls of thunder. We were still some way from the summit when it began snowing and things started to get exciting.

Carl was out in front, with about 30m between us, when he turned and shouted.

'Can you stick me on a belay?'

'What!' I screamed back, disbelieving what I had heard.

'The snow is getting sketchy. I can't get it to take my weight.'

We were at 5500m in a snowstorm, with no gear between us, a 600m-drop to certain death if either of us slipped, and now Carl was telling me the snow didn't hold his weight! I pushed in a couple of token snow stakes and created a not very reassuring ice-axe belay. Carl stomped and thrashed up for another 15m before I had to follow. I turned around to Tom as I was about to climb,

'How's it going?' I enquired, trying to appear casual.

'A bit scared really,' Tom replied, without irony or trace of panic.

48. The east ridge of Quesillo (5600m) – the objective. (*Tom Bide*)

49. Graeme Schofield leading the crux jamming pitch on the east ridge of Quesillo. (*Tom Bide*)

With no protection to place we climbed on tenterhooks. Finally, after an hour of thinking we were pretty much at the top, I saw that Carl had found somewhere to sit and was giving me a body belay. I climbed up to his position. Carl was sat straddling the ridge, legs worryingly close together, providing no belay to speak of. He gestured to the top about 50 metres above us: 'The top looks pretty nasty.'

'Yeah, I think there is an ice cave just down to our right. I think we can probably get down the north face,' I replied, thoughts of going over the top and down the west ridge now fading into the distance. 'Give me a belay, I'll climb down into the ice cave and stick an ice screw in, we can re-group from there.'

Tom and Martin soon joined us as lightning flashed over Huaraca, only a mile away.

'F****** hell, let's go.' Panic seeped into my voice.

I climbed down quickly, desperate to get away from that ridge, and was into the ice cave in no time. I shouted that I was safe and grabbed an ice screw from my harness. I pushed the spikes against the ice and turned the screw rapidly to make my belay, turning and turning until suddenly my arm was jolted violently away from the screw. At the same time there were shouts and screams from the ridge.

Tom: The flash and electric shock was immediately followed by Martin collapsing, thankfully into my arms. He was out cold for around 30 seconds, which in our position on a knife-edge ridge felt like an eternity. He woke up disorientated, confused and in a state of shock.

I knew we had been struck by lightning as soon as it had happened. Thankfully, other than some slightly twitchy fingers, I felt fine; then I heard a voice of desperation sound down from Tom above.

'Graeme, are you alright?'

'Yeah.'

'We've all been electrocuted,' Tom shouted.

'Join the club.'

'Martin is pretty bad,' yelled Tom.

What did 'bad' mean? Dead? Incapacitated? Moderately perturbed? I had no idea. It was no small relief when I saw Martin climbing slowly down towards the ice cave. I steered him in, trying to sound reassuring as in a trembling voice he asked where he was and what had happened. Carl and Tom soon followed, and after stripping all the metal off our harnesses we were able to appreciate our surroundings. The cave was around 6m high and stretched at least 30m across the north-east face. At the part of the cave nearest the ridge there was a hole leading through to the south side of the mountain.

Tom was taking care of Martin while Carl and I began to discuss what to do next. Thunder rolled on over the mountain and the storm continued

50. Trying to keep warm in the snow hole. (*Carl Reilly*)

undiminished. We looked over at Martin who was still very much in the land of the fairies. There was no real decision to make: with only a couple of hours before nightfall we would have to dig in and stay where we were for the night. There was no way we could have expected Martin to down climb a serious face in the state he was in. A struggle began to create a snow hole large enough for us all to sleep in. Unfortunately the snow had no cohesive properties and as soon as a hole was enlarged sideways the roof would collapse. Two hours of effort produced a rather pathetic snow hole. At an incredible squeeze, it could fit us all, but only if we all lay in the 'spoons' position.

A very cold night ensued. At minus 15C without sleeping bags or bivvi bags, and only two basic layers of clothing under a down jacket, none of us felt cosy. I would not say that any of us are particularly 'huggy' people, but nobody was trying to be the alpha-male that night. For my own part, I have never been so glad to be sandwiched between two strapping young men. We had one stove and forced ourselves up a couple of times to have a hot drink and make sure everyone was alright. At first I did everything in my power to stop myself from sleeping, desperately aware of the possibility of not waking up, but as the hours past I realised that, although cold, I wasn't about to die of hypothermia and I allowed myself the odd little nap.

After 12 hours of utter misery the sun began to creep over the horizon, breathing life into the landscape and our limbs. Martin seemed the liveliest of us all; clearly being struck by lightning had charged him up somewhat. We made one, 60m abseil off an abalakov thread which took us from the cave into the expanse of the heavily fluted north-east face. There were no ice or rock belays to abseil from so there followed a series of precarious down climbs passing over extraordinarily high, sugary flutings. Protection was, quite frankly, pathetic and a slip wasn't really an option. It was a great relief to reach a rock band from where we could make a couple of abseils to reach the glacier. The descent of the glacier was not made any easier by having to take my contact lenses out part way down, and finding that my spares were just empty packaging.

We walked at our own pace once we reached the valley floor and I was some distance behind everyone else. It should have been a great relief to be off the mountain, but alas not. I could hear barking, snarling dogs and spent the whole of the walk in a state of heightened anxiety. From a distance I mistook two Peruvian children for dogs and picked up some stones to throw at them. It was only the cry of 'caramelos' (sweets) as I cocked my arm that made me realise my mistake.

Finally, I descended back into the Huayhuash bowl and towards our tents. Across the river, past the houses avoiding the dogs, past the tents of trekkers and into our camp. And there he stood, waiting for me. The cockerel was primed for another round.

Summary: An account of the first ascent (almost) of the east ridge of Quesillo (5600m), Eastern Huayhuash, Peru, 2-3 August 2007 by Tom Bide, Martin Lane, Carl Reilly and Graeme Schofield.

Acknowledgements: Thanks to the Alpine Club Climbing Fund, British Mountaineering Council, Mount Everest Foundation, Mammut and DMM for the financial support that helped make this expedition possible.

PAUL KNOTT

Rock Vultures in Arabia

Desert climbing, for me, is a great antidote to the big mountains. I gained a taste for it when I lived in Morocco in the late 1990s, and more recently on two trips to Oman with Geoff Hornby. As exploratory climbing destinations go, the mountains of Oman are pure luxury. A modest drive on brand new roads leads to peaceful camping next to the car and to readily accessible climbing. The Oman of Wilfred Thesiger's *Arabian Sands* has long gone. Fortunately, the warmth and hospitality of the people has not changed. The convenient access leaves time and energy to explore the huge expanses of wonderful rock. The exotic limestone on Jabal Kawr and Jabal Misht has a sharply pitted surface with exceptional friction for climbing. There are usually plenty of features for nuts and cams, and the routes can be 1000 metres long. Despite these temptations, only a select group of climbers have really discovered the area. Many of these have been Alpine Club members, including Mike Searle, Pat Littlejohn, Tony Howard, and especially Geoff Hornby. The area has also seen notable interest from certain Austrian, Italian and French climbers, who are surely in a position to know about good quality limestone.

In December 2007, I enjoyed a delightful third visit to Oman with Richard Simpson. One of my main aspirations for this trip was to complete a new route on the huge south face of Jabal Misht (2090m). The face has a steep upper section that presents few lines of weakness. One opportunity that caught my eye was an apparent ramp line circling up around the second tower, well to the left of the next route, *Madam Butterfly*. If we could reach this, so I thought, we had the key to a new line on a neglected part of the face. A thorough reconnoitre was in order, so we spent a day driving around the available viewpoints in different lights. We eventually worked out a likely line that zigzagged up to a big chimney and moved across it and up to reach the ramp.

Mindful of the flash flood hazard, we waited a day for storm clouds to clear. We made an alpine start from the village of Ghayl Subayh, walking up wadi beds and scrambling into an atmospheric hanging valley for the start of the route. As always on Misht, the rock was a delight. After three varied pitches we passed the crucial passage through a line of overhangs and onto the easier ground that led us into the huge chimney splitting the face. The pitch above the chimney, we hoped, would take us onto the ramp, and with any luck out of trouble.

Richard tried the likely-looking ways up and right to where the ramp should start. Neither of them worked, so instead he moved to a steep crack in search of a higher traverse. I followed to his exposed belay and set about

Rock Vulture
Vulture
TD- VI 505m

Madam
Butterfly
TD VI 700m

51. *Rock Vulture* route line on Jabal Misht (2090m). (*Paul Knott*)

climbing the crack. After a couple of athletic moves, I saw that the ground continued steeply, with no way across to the ramp. Lacking other options, I sized up the offwidth above and shifted the big cam as high as possible. I shoved my arm deep into the crack, ignoring the ravages of the hoar-like crystals inside, and moved up. Reaching a small tussock, I found that far from representing easing ground this signalled looser rock. I was now some distance above the last runner, and unable to retreat. There was no more gear, as the crack flared unevenly and was full of friable crystals. I kept climbing, sending debris down to the belay and pulling on small stuck-on flakes. Eventually, the difficulties eased and I scrambled eagerly into the haven of a deep horizontal cave.

Our outlook improved dramatically on the next pitch, when Richard stepped around the corner to find a putative ledge below. A short abseil to the ledge left us looking to the top for escape. As we climbed up and around the tower we were relieved to find the ledge steadily widen. Two easy pitches and some scrambling took us to the broad col. We relaxed, taking in our surroundings with satisfaction. Later we named the route *Rock Vulture* (TDinf VI (HVS) 505m), recalling the soaring birds that had watched our progress. Below us on the north side of the mountain was a thousand metres of notoriously unrelenting descent. After traversing ledges across the next tower, we followed a long slabby rib to our camp and much-needed sustenance.

52. *Above*
Richard Simpson
completing pitch 10 (VI)
(HVS 5a) on
Rock Vulture. (*Paul Knott*)

53. *Right*
Pitch 12 of *Rock Vulture*,
above the crux at the
start of the circling
ledge. (*Paul Knott*)

54. Jabel M'Seeb north face route lines. (*Paul Knott*)

The next day my fingers were zinging. As luck would have it, the Eid holiday provided a great excuse for a day of rest. On rest days, when not driving around scoping routes, we often passed the time by visiting local tourist sights. For me, this ticking of sights seemed shallow. Guidebook-designated sights always seem to be full of fellow tourists and hawkers, and devoid of insight into the real country. More enriching, I found, were the places and people we came across in the course of our climbing. The day we drove around Jabal Misht, for instance, a young Omani student, keen to practise his English, treated us to lunch at his house. He extolled the virtues of his devout upbringing, from the social cohesion of frequent prayers to the variety and nutritious value of Omani dates. He gently discouraged us from misguided activities like dancing, shaving, and eating with cutlery. Perhaps it was fortunate that he had no particular views about climbing.

We climbed two other routes in the vicinity of Jabal Misht. On Jabal M'Saw, a south-western outlier of Jabal Misfah, we climbed *White Knight* (Dsup V+ 545m) on the buttress left of the existing *White Magic*. On Jabal Assala's furthest east tower, referred to by the friendly villagers below as

'Lorbib', we climbed the delightful *Orange Roughy* (D V+ 383m) on the main north pillar. The villagers here remember the names of the climbers who have visited and the lines they took on the mountains. Climbers are still a novelty here; we met no others during our stay. This situation is beginning to change. What I hope does not change is the established clean climbing ethic, using only leader-placed protection.

After our success on Misht we moved to the south-west side of Jabal Kawr, camping near the hamlet of M'Seeb. This remote settlement has no permanent buildings, but instead wire mesh enclosures with palm-frond covered shelters and canvas tents. The villagers here were virtuoso goatherders, with an impressive range of rhythmic calls that produced outstanding obedience from the goats. They were also very welcoming, plying us with exquisite spicy coffee and, after their Eid celebration, with succulent fresh goat's meat. Though we shared no common language, we thought they respected our enthusiasm for their stunning surroundings. For several nights to come we watched the progression of colours on the rock towers overlooking the hamlet, and shortly afterwards the full moon rising above the ridge. As it did so, the ever-present dust in the air produced a succession of dramatic moonbeams. The effect was enchanting.

The technical highlight of our climbing from here was the two routes we climbed on the shady north face of Jabal M'Seeb. This face is something of an enigma. Although hidden, overshadowed and dark, it offers up to 500 metres of engaging climbing that links together walls, ramps, corners and slabs. Geoff Hornby and I first investigated it almost as an afterthought in early 2005 and found a fantastic juggy route up its central watercourse that we called *Juggernaut*. This time, we looked for a line that would take us to the overhanging head at the left side of the face. The route worked beautifully, producing technical interest where we did not expect it and lines of weakness when we anticipated potential trouble. At the top, a ramp line sneaked right up through the big overhangs. We named the route *Bloody Sunday* (TDinf VI- 395m) for the havoc a dislodged flake caused to the back of my hand. Later we returned to try a line up the huge square-cut blocks near the right-hand end of the face. The blocks provided several steep, energetic pitches before the ground eased, making the shorter but still excellent *Moonshadow* (Dsup VI- 276m). Once again, we returned to camp satisfied, but thanks to M'Seeb's shaded climbing and easy access, not depleted.

We could not ignore the sunny face of Jabal Kawr itself. After a reconnoitre of some pillars that we decided were too complicated, we looked over from our M'Seeb camp in the warming afternoon light and noticed a shallow buttress that appeared to provide a straightforward route to the plateau. We walked up to it early next morning. The hiss of a snake startled us on the entry pitches, but after this, the climb was pure pleasure as we moved fast up wonderful brown rock. The route we made, *Sunset Serpent* (Dinf IV 503m), probably takes the easiest line on this part of the mountain.

55. Jabal Misht south face from Ghayl Subayh (sunset). (*Paul Knott*)

56. Campsite at M'Seeb, Kawr Tower and Jabal M'Seeb behind. (*Paul Knott*)

At its top, we were surprised to discover a carefully wedged, faded cap sporting the coat of arms of the UAE. This, I suspect, marks the celebrated *National Day Climb* (also Dinf 500m), an early Oman route climbed in 1984 by Bill Wheeler and friends. If so, this route must have taken the old watercourse just to the right of *Sunset Serpent*, some way from the line suggested by existing information. Once on the plateau, we traversed to the end in search of an expedient descent. Finding only a lengthy and complex scramble, we wondered if it would be easier to descend our route.

We made our final ascent on Christmas Day, weaving our way up exposed slabs and stepped ramps to the summit of the Nadan Pillar. This is a striking feature rising 800 metres from the gorge leading to the hidden cirque of Nadan. It sports an alluring but somewhat inaccessible black and orange south face, from which our route would make an expedient descent at ADsup (IV). There appears to be no easier way to the summit. Below us in the gorge, work continued on the improbable and somewhat destructive project to build a road through the ancient boulder choke to Nadan itself. From the summit we saw that this hidden spring-fed village had most of its terraces abandoned and few buildings in good repair, though we did hear the voices of children playing.

Our trip was over but for an important social engagement. The day we arrived, I had spotted a former student of mine in Starbucks. Omani hospitality evidently extends to the city as well as the mountains, and we happily took up her invitation to dine gratis in Muscat's best restaurant. It was a memorable evening, not only for the food and venue, but also for the insight into the lives of our fellow diners. Their liberal attitudes provided an illuminating contrast with the people we met in the mountains. I left feeling enriched and intrigued.

Summary: Rock climbing in Oman, Paul Knott and Richard Simpson, December 2007, including new routes *Rock Vulture* (TDinf VI (HVS) 505m) on the south face of Jabal Misht (2090m), *Bloody Sunday* (TDinf VI- 395m) and *Moonshadow* (Dsup VI- 276m) on the north face of Jabal M'Seeb, and *Sunset Serpent* (Dinf IV 503m) on Jabal Kawr.

JOHN TOWN

The Sliding Snow of Tachab Kangri

You have to have a good reason for visiting the far north-west of Tibet – it's a long way, the roads are appalling and you never know what you are going to find when you get there. On the other hand, perhaps these are reasons enough.

Seven thousand metre peaks are rare on the Tibetan plateau, compared with the Himalaya to its south. There are none in the eastern Nyenchen Tanglha and only two in the western part of the range – Nyenchen Tanglha (7162m) and Jomo Kangri (7048m). A third, Loinbo Kangri (7095m), lies further west in the Gangdise Shan. Other candidates have come and gone as maps have changed over the years. Intriguing then, that in 2004 another seventhousander appeared.

Between the northern and southern highways that traverse west Tibet is a vast tract of country patterned by a seemingly endless array of inland lakes. There are high mountain ranges here, though many seem almost lost, both on the map and on the ground, in the vastness of the landscape. A number of these ranges run north-south, though there is little overall pattern. The most westerly is the Lungkar Shan, the first section of which runs south from the Gertse area to the Rinchen Shubtso lake. While the Lungkar Shan proper then bends south-east in a series of lesser peaks, the line of high mountains is continued south of the lake towards the Southern Highway in the form of the Surla range, a total of 180 km. The highest peak on most maps, given as 6860m and lying towards the southern end of the northern part of the range, is named in the literature as Kuhanbokang and on Russian maps as Jang. Kading Kangri (6730m) lies towards the northern end of the Surla range. No climbers appeared to have attempted any of these mountains or taken any pictures.

This was how things looked until two new maps of Tibet appeared in 2004. They showed an unnamed peak of 7216m at the northern end of the northern half of the chain, near the village of Marme. Older maps showed a peak of 6704m at this point. I was naturally keen to find out if this new 7000m peak existed and to get there before anyone else. Satellite photos and Google Earth revealed a relatively gentle massif with apparently straightforward glaciers on its various flanks. I showed these photos to Kevin Clarke, a fellow university administrator working as Secretary at Stirling University, and he in turn tempted Richard Sant and Mike Dawber, from Strathpeffer and Aberdeen respectively. Richard and Mike were 20 years younger and had climbed considerably harder than Kevin or I, so I pinned our hopes of avoiding humiliation on the levelling effects of altitude. The early start of Scottish universities meant that we would have to go in

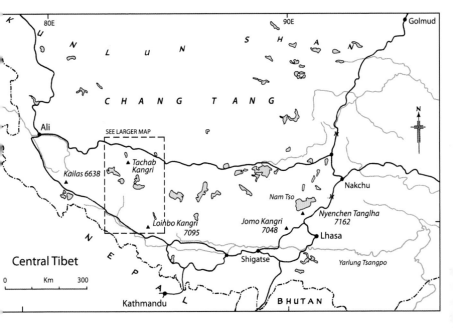

Map showing the position of Tachab Kangri (6704m). The larger map on page 87 provides more detail. (*John Town*)

August but I hoped that the area was so far north and west of the Himalaya that the monsoon would have little effect.

We left the UK on 28 July 2007, meeting up in Nepal with Richard, who had gone out earlier to deal with the lengthy and expensive business of extracting our freight from the Kathmandu customs shed. Mig Ma, our Tibetan agent, had arranged numerous trips for me in the past. He met us in Kathmandu and accompanied us on the drive to Kodari on the Tibetan border, across which our two Land Cruisers and lorry were waiting, together with Pasang and Kusang, our liaison officer and cook.

In normal times, a night at Zhangmu would have followed, but, in a fervour of pre-Olympic investment, the initial section of the Friendship Highway was being upgraded by an army of Chinese and Tibetans. Uphill travel was only permitted after 8pm, so it would pay to head for Nyalam that night rather than wasting a day. Never ones to miss a trick, our companions had discovered that it was possible, for a consideration, to get an early start, so by 5am we were part of a select echelon forging the wrong way up 30km of one-way street. Our luck held and we were in Nyalam in time for dinner.

Entering Tibet by the Friendship Highway is an acclimatisation nightmare, it being possible to gain 2800m in less than five hours, reaching 5153m at the Thong La. We duly spent two nights acclimatising in Nyalam (3762m), most of which I spent in the toilet block with a stomach bug while the others drank beer. On 2 August we set off over the Thong La and Lalung La before turning off the main highway and heading west across the high plains south of the Shishapangma range. These provided spectacular views of Shishapangma and the lesser-known peaks that run north-west from it. After passing south of the aquamarine expanse of the Pelkhu Tso, we turned north towards the valley of the Yarlung Tsangpo and the garrison town of Saga, with its military checkpoint. There were spectacular views of Jomo Uchong (6236m) that lies to its north. I had been told that this peak was attempted in 2004 by a bi-national team including Tibetan climbers but I have not been able to find any record of an ascent. In the north-west could be seen a fingernail outline of Kangchung Kangri (6003m) and in the north-east the snowy pyramid of Gainbu Ri (5997m).

Saga has restaurants and hotels to cater to the military, Indian Kailash pilgrims and the small number of western tourists for whom this is a key waypoint, but its attractions are easily exhausted on a first visit. In any case, these were not on offer and we were consigned to the Post Office Guest House, which boasts a collection of disused satellite dishes and an elevated communal toilet whose horrors are beyond description.

The next day we drove east for 60km before branching north onto the S206 which links Tibet's Northern and Southern Highways, running north-south for 400km via the county town of Tsochen, also known as Mendong. We made good time but I was becoming increasingly frustrated by our driver, a third Pasang, whose youth, inexperience and macho driving style worried me. You cannot win travelling by Land Cruiser in West Tibet – if you have the windows open even a few inches, you and your gear are covered in dust. If you keep them closed it is hot and abominably stuffy. Normally it is possible to attain some form of compromise, but on this occasion young Pasang, who had a master switch for the windows and was inordinately proud of his upholstery, won the battle hands down. Just outside Tsochen, we finally got out of the car at a police checkpoint. Mike, who is 6ft 4in and had been squashed into one corner of the vehicle for hours, took a hesitant step, turned and collapsed in a dead faint. He recovered quickly but we spent an extra day in Tsochen as a precaution.

Tsochen is the most heavily policed town I have seen in Tibet and they sent a message saying we were not allowed to visit the local monastery. This kind of thing is unusual in Tibet these days, though the number of monks at a given monastery still remains under state control. I thought of making a fuss, pointing out that this was exactly what gave the regime and the local authorities a bad name, but didn't want to delay the expedition. Shame on me; shame on them.

The next day was a long one. The road rises gradually to a low pass leading over to the basin of the Dawa Tso, then climbs again over the southern part of the Shakangsham range to Yak Skull Pass (Nor Chung La) and on along the eastern side of these impressive mountains. Some way north of the range the road joins the Northern Highway by the large salt-pans of the Dong Tso and we turned west. By late afternoon we had arrived at Gertse, the biggest town on the Northern Highway, with its

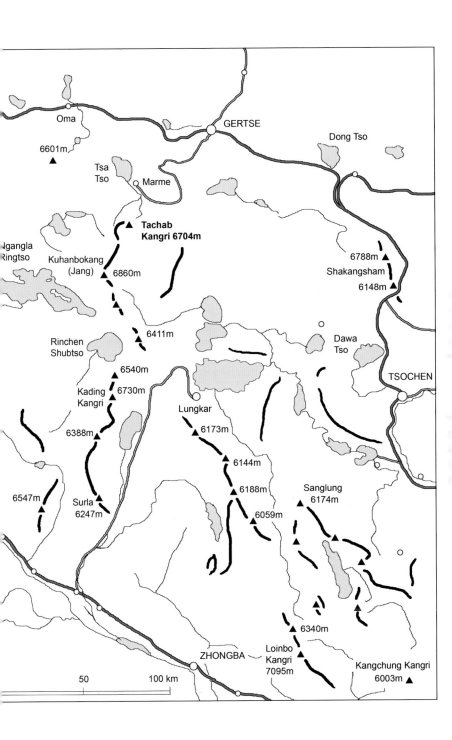

The Lungkar Range and Tachab Kangri. (*John Town*)

restaurants and guesthouses. After a great meal of roast lamb and noodles at one of the Muslim eating-houses, the decision was made to continue, though this was easier said than done. We wanted to get to Marme, which is reached by a minor road that finds its way along and through the hills to the south of the Gertse plain. None of our Tibetans had been that way before and few of the locals seemed to be able to identify the right way out of town. After a time-consuming false start we got on our way, but distances and surroundings did not fit with the map. The road was being rebuilt and re-routed, said the locals we met at the first pass, but they confirmed that it did get to Marme eventually. We were in unknown territory for the first time and somewhere on this road should provide our first view of the mountain. We continued for hour after hour, with little idea of exactly where we were, until we crested a high pass. In the half-light the mountains were laid out before us, looking much as we had been led to believe by maps and Google Earth. I don't know how the others felt, but I was a little disappointed that there was no savage spire to put fear into our hearts, just rounded curves of glacier and shattered rock leading to a serene dome of snow. Tibetans often name their mountains after deities and, if so, it was surely a benevolent god that looked down upon us.

The road ran swiftly down an enclosed valley leading eventually through a short gorge and on to the wide plain leading to Marme and the Tsa Tso. We made a hasty camp in the valley and talked with Dawa at the picnic table late into the evening. Above and below us great squalls of hail traversed the valley, while thunder and lightning crashed on the surrounding ridges.

Next day there was much poring over GPS and satellite photos to get us to the right spot for base camp. This was high above the Marme plain, at about 5000m, at the start of a deep narrow valley leading directly towards the glacier basin below the main peak. We never did get to see Marme village, though we can confirm it has a doctor, a lama and a mobile phone mast (Vodafone only). A side road took us away to the south and provided a bridge over the major river. Shortly after that we set off cross-country over boulder-strewn plains and shallow gulches, with the lorry leading the way. As we gradually climbed towards our objective, distant white dots resolved themselves into tents and more came into sight down beside the river. As we ground to a halt and said our hellos, family after family bestirred themselves – a new and welcome diversion from the routine of camp life was in prospect. They probably thought the same about us.

Communications are always a little hesitant to start with, since the nomads here speak a version of Tibetan as strange to our Lhasan companions as medieval English is to us. The mountain was called Tachab Kangri, the river the Tachab Kang Chu and our route of approach the Tachab valley. No prizes for guessing what we called the glacier.

We explored the lower part of the Tachab valley the first day, then made a more significant reconnaissance by climbing the ridge system to the north of the valley direct from base camp. Black clouds and thunder rolled over

59.   North-east face of Tachab Kangri, approaching camp 1. (*Mike Dawber*)

60.   Tachab Kangri from advanced base camp. (*Mike Dawber*)

the higher peaks throughout the day and we were poorly acclimatised, but we struggled 5km to reach a fine viewpoint at about 5700m where the glacier and the whole of Tachab Kangri's north-east face was laid out before us. The mountain did not look to rise as high as 7000m, but fitted with the original figure of 6704m. We would have to decide which of the two cols either side of the main peak gave the best access. Both were approached by straightforward snow slopes. Mike favoured the south-east col and I favoured the north-west, which, though steeper and longer, gave more scope for avoiding avalanches.

Well satisfied with our day, we made plans for moving to advanced base camp, about 8km up the valley below the glacier snout at 5670m. Next day was spent packing and there was a further day's delay as a storm pinned everybody in the tents. The thundery weather was a surprise and the lightning displays at night had monsoon written all over them, even though we were 250km north of the Himalaya. On our return we found that India had suffered particularly severe monsoon weather at this time. It was clear that a significant amount of snow had fallen on the mountain over the last few days, although below 5700m it melted away as quickly as it had fallen.

On 11 August the storms abated and yaks carried our equipment to advanced base. The next day the weather closed in again and we had to stay in the tents, but the day after that we were able to establish Camp 1 up on the glacier at just over 6000m. On the 14th we occupied the camp and, feeling the results of our efforts in the calf-deep snow, took the next day off in preparation for the final push. There was no great build-up of snow on the glacier and I felt happier about heading for the south-east col, where we intended putting a last camp. Strong winds battered the tents at night but it dawned clear on the 16th and we got away at about 9am. We had been going about 20 minutes, descending slightly at first and then traversing towards the foot of the slopes leading to the col, when there was a loud crack. A huge section of the steeper slopes above us and to the left, perhaps 100m high by 150m wide, detached as a body from the ice beneath it and slid steadily towards us. I was the only one to run, if that's the right word, but I didn't get far. The slide came gracefully to a halt about 100m away, momentum lost in the tumbled mass of its own bow-wave. There was a long silence as we stood and looked, before starting to discuss alternatives to our present route.

Right

61.   Lungkar Shan (*right*) looking south from space. Tsa Tso at lower right. (*By courtesy of Image Science & Analysis Laboratory, NASA Johnson Space Center*)

62.   Route on Tachab Kangri. (*By courtesy of Image Science & Analysis Laboratory, NASA Johnson Space Center*)

The alternative involved the rocky flanks of the ridge bounding the far side of the north-west col and it took about an hour to climb up and across the basin towards it. I led this section and in places there was an air gap between the frozen surface layer and the ice beneath, leading to sharp cracks as sections collapsed under my feet. Kevin, who was second on the rope, had been making appreciative noises, but on level ground it was harmless enough. After one particularly loud crack he produced another gasp and I turned to ask him to keep the noise down. The look on his face caused me to turn again, in time to see the whole of the 300m slope above us beginning its inexorable slide in our direction. This time we had kept a respectable distance from the slope and were separated from it by a dip in the glacier. The scale, though, was awesome: the entire slope leading to the col had gone, perhaps 300m across and an estimated 20,000 tons of snow. The break line at the upper margin scythed across the slope in an overhang of up to 2m. Once again the slide had been self-limiting, the lower margin a jumbled chaos of massive blocks.

For me, that was enough, but the sheer scale of the thing was hard to take in. We talked of possible ways through or round and Richard and Mike cached some gear for a possible return the next day. We slogged back down to the camp from our 6300m high point and, as things sunk in, further plans were quietly abandoned. The yaks arrived at ABC on the 19th, as agreed, leading their owners up hill and down dale on the descent and trashing rucksacks and barrels indiscriminately as they cavorted. Finally freed of their broken burdens, they sat and watched us. We could match their exhaustion, if not their look of smug satisfaction. At least we had lived to fight another day.

Summary: An attempt on Tachab Kangri (6704m) at the northern end of the Lungkar Shan in central Tibet by Kevin Clarke, Mike Dawber, Richard Sant and John Town, 28 July to 26 August 2007.

DAVID PICKFORD

From Russia With Love

War Games in Kyrgyzstan's Wild West

At five past four in the morning, the ancient Aeroflot Tupolov smashes into the runway at Manas airport. There is an audible intake of breath from the passengers as overhead lockers spring open, spewing their contents across the cabin floor. The plane is filled with a cacophony of creaking hinges, interspersed with other, less identifiable noises, culminating in a tremendous growl from the bowels of the fuselage. The aircrew look on, unflinching. Clearly this is a perfectly normal landing. A great cheer rises from the back and curls like a gust of wind through the plane. The trio of Poles in the row behind me are in high spirits. They've been drinking vodka with kamikaze determination throughout the flight and now propose a new round of toasts:

'To zee great naztion of Poland! To zeez exzellent Russian Kapitan! To ze great naztion of Russia! To ze Republik of Kyrgyzstan! Stolsch!

Their words slur into cheers and I smile at the post-Soviet solidarities. Mikhail Gorbachev would have been proud of our welcome to Kyrgyzstan.

As pre-dawn arrivals go, this is unconventional. We shamble out into the hush of the arrivals hall chattering loudly, like the after-party crowd leaving a nightclub at closing time, and whisk through immigration with the vodka fumes from the Poles building behind us. The revelry continues. Sam (Whittaker) and Zippy (Mark Pretty) head for an empty bar with die-hard determination. Having woken the bartender, who had been snoring on his chair with an empty vodka bottle in one hand, they return with several beers. Too tired to stomach Russian export lager, I crash out under the table to the sound of their chinking glasses. The hum of a distant vacuum cleaner in the terminal building lulls me into sleep.

A chill wind engulfs the mountains about us. The massive slab kicks back as I fight the creep of my rock shoes on its tiny crystals. Gear swings about my harness, useless. There is no protection. I must decide to move. I move. The sky overhead turns dark. The sound of rushing cloud fills my ears. Am I falling?

ZZZZZSSSSSCCCCHHHHH... I awake to the sound of a gigantic Hoover scooping across the floor beside my table. Peering up, I am momentarily unsure whether my dream has ended, as I see that the man controlling the Hoover massively dwarfs the enormous contraption itself. Or perhaps it is I who have disappeared, once again, into that traveller's looking-glass, where everyone is Alice and the world is Wonderland.

Five hours later we shamble out into the heat of the day. High summer on the steppes of Central Asia is defined by a fervid haze that begins around 10.30am and lasts well into the evening. The heavy air of Bishkek, capital of the Republic of Kyrgyzstan, hangs a few centimetres above the asphalt and shakes. Finding the Twin Otter at last in the far corner of the runway, I seek shade under the left wing and notice a well translated bit of Cyrillic plastered on the fuselage: CHOP HERE WITH CRASH AXE. Reaching into my pack for a camera, I become aware that a military policeman with the physique of a medium-sized adult gorilla is walking in my direction. As the camera appears, Rambo raises his Kalashnikov towards me. Momentarily forgetting the Russian for 'terribly sorry old chap', I quickly stash the SLR out of sight. Rambo howls with laughter, revealing a well-polished set of gold teeth. Gold teeth are a hallmark of wealth and status in Kyrgyzstan, a sort of Central Asian equivalent of a BMW X5 with tinted windows.

We are bound for Osh, the main town on the Kyrgyz side of the Fergana Corridor, a long strip of fertile land that stretches west towards Samarkand and on to the deserts of Uzbekistan and Turkmenistan. Looking out of the window of the little plane as it begins its descent, the Pamir Alai rise sharply to the south. An immense wall of jagged spires and glinting white summits lifts out of the plains, defining the point where the steppe of Central Asia gives way to the westernmost end of the Greater Himalaya. Two days later Ian (Parnell) arrives in Osh, having flown in via London on his way back from Everest. The team is thus complete: Sam, Zippy, Grimer (Niall Grimes), Donie (O'Sullivan), Ian and myself – the 'Kyrgyz Six' as we would come to call ourselves. We are to leave for Ozgouruch next morning.

I wake at dawn to the drift of the call to prayer from the mosque across the street. We breakfast on black Kyrgyz tea and eggs; the tea is always strong in this country and the men seem to drink it constantly. One local proverb translates roughly as, 'If he does not drink tea, a Kyrgyz man will die'. In the eerie half-light we hear the approach of the Beast. Several minutes elapse between the first sound of the contraption and its tremendous arrival. With a demonic puff of foul black smoke – an exotic mixture of diesel and other, more obscure petrochemicals – into Ury's yard scowls the Beast. It is a fearsome sight. Best described as a mechanical rhinoceros with extra sound effects, the remarkable Uuaz is one of the engineering hallmarks of the former USSR. With a flash of gold teeth in the dawn light, our driver appears behind the Beast's enormous wheel. He speaks almost no English but has a gentle, determined manner that instils confidence. Quickly he becomes known as 'Shortcut'. His Kyrgyz name sounds almost identical to the English word, and, more to the point, it sounds good. If anyone can get us across 400 miles of potholed desert roads in this unlikely contraption, Shortcut is our man.

The Beast's starter-motor erupts with the noise of a squadron of MiG-28s on take-off and we hit the road west towards Ozgouruch (also known as Voruch), the tiny village at the road head to Karavshin.

Less than an hour out of Osh, The Beast grinds to a belching halt.
'Problem, Shortcut?' I enquire.
'No problem. I fix. Ten minute.'
Shortcut looks unperturbed. After 10 minutes of fiddling with the engine,
he establishes the fault – a broken distributor rotor – and attempts to fix it
with part of a baked bean can fashioned with a penknife. Firing up the
engine again, The Beast revolts at his repair and spits out the entire assembly
in an explosion of bolts and fragments of tin. Our prospects of reaching
Ozgouruch today are not looking good. Shortcut merely shrugs, wanders
across the dusty highway and hitches a ride with a truck back to Osh. A
sand-coloured sun rises over the desert to the east as the dust-cloud of the
truck disappears. We play football in the road as the chill of dawn fades
with the creeping heat of the morning. After a while, another dust-cloud
appears in the distance and a battered Lada rolls to a halt. Shortcut! Our
unflappable driver swings out of the Lada wielding a new distributor cap
and bolts it on, cigarette dangling precariously out of his mouth over the
oil-caked engine. He turns the enormous crank and The Beast belches into
life with renewed vigour.

In the burning midday heat we lurch down an endless road through a
desert full of gigantic potholes. At an unmarked crossroads two Kyrgyz
soldiers emerge from a hut bristling with weaponry and ask for our passports
with languid curiosity. Clearly mystified by our presence, they wave us on,
making a vague gesture of their AK47s towards the mountains to the south.
It is almost dark as we reach Isfara. Children are playing in the dusty street,
wide eyes flashing with the light from roadside fires. At the edge of the
small town we turn south again, then west towards the castellated dusk
sky. From here, the road curls tortuously up a steep valley towards
Ozgouruch. Just before midnight, as we cross a bridge of recycled wooden
railway sleepers, I hear the Kara Su river roaring through the darkness below.
A blast of icy air hits me as I open the Beast's rear window, craning my
head. Far above, the ridgeline is in strong silhouette against a night sky
dense with stars. Further to the south, the snowy peaks of the Kara Su
valley dim the star-sheen slightly. The journey from Osh has taken 19 hours.
Nothing you might have heard about Karavshin, a remote village deep in
the mountains of south-western Kyrgyzstan, will prepare you for the
spectacle of arrival. With tired legs after two days of hard walking we emerge
from the arid lower canyon onto high pasture. A short way ahead of our
horsemen, we stop beyond some mud-brick houses at a small clearing among
stunted pines where the glacial Ak Su river levels on to a gravel flood plain.
It is almost dusk and a cold wind is blowing off the high mountains to the
south, from Tajikistan. Through the trees, three immense shapes begin to
define the western rim of the valley while to the east loom another two
monolithic summits. We set up base camp as night gathers among the
boulders under Central Pyramid, its monumental outline cut sharp against
the night sky of the Pamir Alai.

63.   The line of *From Russia With Love* between the Central Pyramid and the Russian Tower (*right*) above the Ak Su valley, Kyrgyzstan. (*David Pickford*)

64.   On the map, just. The 'village' of Karavshin, tucked in the mountains of south west Kyrgyzstan. (*David Pickford*)

After a few days of unstable weather the sky clears one evening after a thunderstorm, promising a change. Sam and I have set our hopes on a slender, unclimbed pillar rising out of the back of the massive couloir between Central Pyramid and the Russian Tower. We fall into a restless sleep with fingers crossed, daunted and intrigued by the forthcoming challenge.

A chill wind engulfs the mountains about us. The massive slab kicks back at me as I fight the interminable creep of my rock-shoes on its tiny crystals. Climbing gear swings about my harness, useless. There is no protection. I must decide to move. I move. The sky overhead turns dark. The sound of rushing cloud fills my ears. Am I falling?

I wake in the icy chill before dawn, peering out of the tent to see the early light catching the three summits to the west. The air is cold and still, the morning sky an inky, polarised blue.

'Sam, are you awake?'

A furtive reply comes from the depths of his sleeping bag.

'Looks like it's settled.'

A local hunter who stayed with us last night has rekindled the fire and is squatting in front of it, warming his hands, breaking sticks for kindling. We gulp down tea with a few pieces of indigestible Kyrgyz flatbread before beginning the steep ascent across the scree-cones under the enormous bulk of Central Pyramid.

65. Woman making flatbread in Karavshin. (*David Pickford*)

66. and 67.
Left and below:
Sam Whittaker enjoying the open groove early on *From Russia With Love*.
'... immaculate climbing on equally perfect granite.'
(*David Pickford*)

An hour later, we're gearing up at the head of the couloir. Sam sets off up a slabby rake from which the great pillar rises. He climbs quickly across initial slabs of lichenous granite. As he arranges a belay I get a chance to take in where I am.

The sun is still hidden behind the icy bulk of the Russian Tower's north wall. The silence of the couloir is shattered intermittently as huge chunks of ice and rock peel away from the wall and plunge more than a thousand feet to the scree. From the safe distance of our position on the pillar I watch the tumbling debris with an alarmed fascination. Occasional chill gusts eddy around the couloir; a pair of lammergeiers circle on an early thermal coming off the moraine under Wolf Peak.

'Ok Dave, when you're ready.' Sam's voice brings me back to the rock and the challenge in wait above. I follow the pitch slowly, kicking my toes against the granite crystals, trying to get the blood back in my feet. By the time I arrive at the belay the sun has just swung over the Russian Tower and we shed thermals, enjoying the warmth. Above our marginal stance soars a perfect open groove, disappearing just before the arête that bounds the right-hand edge of the pillar. We swing leads and I climb on into the groove. All too soon, after 60m of immaculate climbing on equally perfect granite, Sam warns that I've run out of rope. Above, the groove vanishes after about 10m and is capped by a series of daunting overlaps. Sam leads on through, eager to get on with the climbing. Moving out right from the top of the groove, his progress slows, eventually coming to a halt at a final overlap.

'How does it look?' I enquire.

'There's just a sea of granite up here Dave, I don't think it'll go this way.'

There is an audible silence. I think we are both weighing up exactly how disappointing a retreat would be from this point.

'How about reversing back to the groove and breaking out left around the arête?' I suggest from the security of the belay.

Sam arrives back at the top of the groove, the slack already looping out on his right rope, the way ahead uncertain. After a while, he chalks up, cleans his boots and makes a delicate, precise move out left on to the arête. I can hear him breathing with those brief, deep exhalations that say far more than any words can about the gravity of a climb. After another short pause, he says with a quiet assurance:

'Ok Dave, watch me here, I'm going for it.' He disappears around the arête and out of my field of vision. The ropes inch out. Vagrant gusts come and go, blowing chill air from the shadows of the icy couloir to the right. When the air is still I can feel the warmth of a thermal rising from the open slabs way beneath us. Occasionally there is a hollow boom from the depths of the couloir as another massive chunk of ice and granite explodes into the scree. Then suddenly there is a different sound from high to my left - a brief shout of adrenaline release, and relief.

'Nice one Sam,' I reply, hoping he's cracked the invisible puzzle around the arête.

'It's not over yet, keep watching me.'

I detect the urgency of his movements as the ropes pull out quickly, pause for a second, inch back, pull out again, inch back, stop. After an indeterminate moment, they haul out firmly for another metre. As I hear Sam's holler of success I feel my own nerves settle. Instinctively knowing the meaning of his exclamation, I shout an enthusiastic reply into the wind.

And all too soon I'm above the groove, back-stepping through those wretched overlaps. I remove the final, small cam Sam has placed high on the right rope with trepidation, watching it loop, slack and useless across the wall to the left. I guess it must be at least 20m to the side runner above Sam's belay. Switching off, I reverse the intricate moves back to the groove, soon peering around the arête with some relief.

A faint line of chalk weaves across a featureless slab to Sam's belay in a tiny niche 15m to the left. He beams across at me:

'That was the hardest bit of onsight climbing I've ever done.'

I congratulate him on his astonishing lead. Simultaneously, with rather less enthusiasm, I'm calculating the length of a potential pendulum. I'm precariously balanced on minute footholds and although not as unquantifiably dangerous as on the lead, a fall from here would take me on an extensive and accelerating sideways tour of the abyss. Never a fan of bridge swinging, I try to zone out from my position on the arête.

Eventually, I get the better of the weight of my camera and the monster pendulum yawning back at me, and make a series of intricate and balancy moves left to a rest on a tiny edge. Part of it crumbles away and I stab my foot back at it, holding on friction. Sam laughs. I look up left, smiling back with incredulity at the seriousness of the pitch.

'Shit, a fall from here on lead would have been a monster.'

'Er, yeah!

Safer now, having closed the angle to the last gear considerably, I enjoy a brilliant final sequence to join Sam on the belay. With a sudden flashback to last night's conversation in base camp about James Bond, I compliment him, tongue-in-cheek:

'Nice lead, 007.' As our laughter subsides, I realise we've found a perfect name for the route. It has to be *From Russia With Love*, even though the nearest Daniella Bianchi look-alike would surely be drinking vodka with Russian mafiosos in downtown Bishkek.

After a while, I set off up the daunting crack-line in the impending wall above us. I'm reminded of those classic extreme climbs on Gogarth's Main Cliff as I move strenuously through wild terrain, studiously avoiding a giant, booming flake apparently welded to the wall by lichen alone. Pulling through the last of a series of small but awkward overhangs, I find a secure belay, content in the knowledge that we have finally unlocked the puzzle of this climb, one of the most perfect, elegant lines either of us have ever seen.

68. Whittaker high on *From Russia With Love*. (*David Pickford*)

Sam soon appears around the roof, his grin even wider now, and races on up the easier-angled continuation of the crack. After another massive pitch, I belay on the apex of the pillar. We revel in our new perspective on the surrounding world of towering granite walls and snow-capped peaks, sharp in the late afternoon sunlight at 4500m. Eventually, we find the top of a reasonable-looking abseil line down an enormous corner system we'd spotted from below. Halfway down, the evening shadows race up from the couloir to overtake us.

Only a few hundred feet from the scree and we look back up at the line. The last sunlight falls across the pillar, just discernible among the deep shadows of the couloir, a slender orange brush-stroke against the vast, darkening wall. Pulling the ropes on the final abseil, we watch and remain silent. That last moment of light captures everything we might have said then, about why we had chosen to make the long journey to Ak Su, or why we ever go climbing.

At dawn, from somewhere down the valley, comes the crack of a Kalashnikov, probably fired by those half-trained, half-mad Kyrgyz soldiers from Batken. The soldiers arrive and we find we are leaving Ak Su under a very Russian kind of 'unofficial arrest'. We have no permit, they tell us. Where is our permit? Yes, we reply. We tried many times to get one, but you cannot get one in Batken.

Thirty-six hours later I'm in a small cell in the army barracks in Batken with two Kyrgyz officials cross-examining me in a mixture of Russian and Kyrygz . The fat man on the right calls himself 'The General'. The skinny one – who looks and smells like he's had a few vodkas already – calls himself 'Mister Zulu'. One or two English phrases are thrown in for good measure.

'You zwatch footzbal?'

'Arzenal?'

'Manchzesta United!'

'You have many western girl?'

"Western girl strong at night. Ha Ha Ha!"

'You have girlfriend? I get you very nize Kyrgyz girl. Ha Ha Ha.'

'You have vodka?' (I reply with a vague negative.)

'Zen maybe ve call ze Miniztry in Bishek. Ha Ha Ha.'

It is like being a contestant in a Russian *I'm A Celebrity Get Me Out Of Here*, with a strong staging reference to Tarantino's *Reservoir Dogs*. The General and Mister Zulu are playing good-cop-bad-cop, but cannot decide which of them is which. Like a couple of teenage boys desperate to impress, they carry on until the absurdity of the situation slowly dawns on them. Mister Zulu slinks off for his vodka and the General opens the door, suddenly assuming an air of military seriousness:

'You may tell zur frientz zat maybe you stay in zis platz for some days.'

I break the news to the others, my throat parched from the dry air and the General's cigarette smoke. In need of refreshment, I go over the road to where a small boy has arrived on an enormous bicycle laden with watermelons. Biting into a slice, I walk back to pass the melon round to the others. They are convulsed with laughter.

'What is it Sam?' I ask. Turning back towards the barracks, I see Mister Zulu greedily knocking back another shot by the main gateway.

'Now they… they want a couple of hundred som for more vodka…!'

Hours later, we are rattling back across the featureless desert on the Uzbek border when Shortcut pronounces he is lost.

'How can we possibly be lost?' Grimer enquires, to a murmur of agreement. It is nearly midnight and we are all knackered. Shortcut has stopped his interminable chain smoking, so even he must be in need of a break. We shamble out of The Beast and crash out instantly on the sand.

A chill wind engulfs the mountains about us. The massive slab kicks back at me as I fight the creep of my rock shoes on its tiny crystals. Gear swings about my harness, useless. There is no protection. I must decide to move. I move. The sky overhead turns dark. The sound of rushing cloud fills my ears.

Twenty-six hours after leaving Batken, we arrive back in Osh at mid-afternoon and bid goodbye to Shortcut, tipping him handsomely for getting us to and from Ozgouruch in such style. He departs with his signature flash of gold teeth. That evening, I read the news on the Internet. A couple of weeks have passed since the 7 July bombings in London. In no mood for sleep after everyone else has retired, I stay up reading. After a while, I hear a woman's voice beyond the curtain separating the courtyard from the house. It is Ury's wife, beginning her late reading of the Koran in its original ancient Arabic. It is unusual to hear women reading the language. Her voice is clear and sharp, lifting and falling through the air like windblown snow. It sounds like the voice of a woman far younger. Fig leaves rustle in the empty courtyard and the vine rattles from time to time overhead. The night air smells of dust and wood-smoke. Suddenly, the woman's voice rises in crescendo, and with a final 'Al-Laa-U-Akhba' falls silent.

Another gust of wind blows through the fig tree, colder now, stiffening the quiet courtyard with the reality of our time in history; a nightmare time when the Bush-Blair projects in Afghanistan and Iraq seem almost identical, in their pseudo-religious extremism, to the terrorism of Al Qaeda. Both camps share a blind lust for a single world order, as intellectually arcane as it is morally destitute. To me, this Kyrgyz woman's hauntingly beautiful reading of the Koran, now seems an elegy – for the Americans who died on 11 September 2001, the British and American servicemen killed in Iraq and Afghanistan, for the countless Iraqi civilians who have died since 2003, and an elegy for the Londoners blown up just two weeks ago.

Two days later, we're back in Bishkek. After the wildness of the Pamir and the wild-west characters of Karavshin there is a certain refreshing austerity to the glum Soviet blocks and monolithic heaps of concrete masquerading as public art that line the streets of the capital. Two gorgeous Kyrgyz girls in fluffy boots and matching hot-pants sashay across the boulevard from where we're drinking coffee, snatching cheeky glances at every opportunity. Even the beer is cold. Urbanity is an odd place after several weeks in the high mountains of Asia.

It is 4.15am and the hatchet-faced Russian clerk at the Aeroflot check-in desk wants money. She is trying to weigh our baggage and all manœuvres to try and divert her prove ineffective. Even the two bottles of vodka I produce as a goodwill gesture fail to register. Ian is convulsed with hysterical laughter as we wait to board our plane to Moscow, completely stripped of our last reserves of cash but happy to have made our great escape from Kyrgyzstan, the Batken Barracks, the vodka fumes of Mister Zulu, and the ire of the General.

Just before we taxi away to take off, at the back of the plane the door swings open and in strides a uniformed official.

'Are zere six Engliz Alpinistz on zeez airkraft?' he asks repeatedly as he strides down the cabin.

'Shit.' Zippy breathes through clenched teeth.

Sam's eyes roll with anxiety and sleep deprivation. Donie and Grimer left on an earlier flight, so at least there aren't six of us. Zippy, Ian and Sam have their hand baggage checked for climbing gear, which, fortunately, they are not carrying.

'Alpinists?' Zippy asks with a confused expression.

'No, no, we're just tourists,' Ian chips in immediately.

'We have been on a wonderful holiday in your excellent country,' adds Sam.

Lacking the linguistic ability to contest our explanation, the official nods slowly. After a while, he turns around with the painfully disappointed expression of a man who has just lost a game of poker, and walks back towards the door of the plane. The grins widen and as the door finally closes we burst into paroxysmal laughter.

'The Kyrgyz Six,' Zippy proclaims triumphantly.

'Long live the Kyrgyz Six!'

The voices of my friends fade as the engines roar into life, and I'm pulled back into my seat as the decrepit Tupolov lifts into the summer night. I watch the lights of Bishkek fade below until they vanish altogether. Leaning back against the window, I am overcome by waves of sleep.

A chill wind engulfs the mountains about us. The sky overhead turns dark. The sound of rushing cloud fills my ears.

69.   Sunset over the emptiness of Uzbekistan. (*David Pickford*)

Summary: An account of the first ascent of *From Russia With Love* by Sam Whittaker and David Pickford (500 metres, E7 6b / 5.12 X / ABO), Ak Su Valley, Kyrgyzstan, in July 2005. On the same expedition, Niall Grimes and Donie O'Sullivan established a long and sustained route called *Amazing Grace* (1000 metres, E4 5c / 5.10d / ED3) further up the valley, where Ian Parnell and Mark (Zippy) Pretty also made the first ascent of *Long Live the Beast* (500 metres, E4 6a / 5.11a / ED3).

Journeys

Rowan Huntley *Grands Charmoz and Grépon in swirling cloud*
Chroma on board, 28cm x 45cm. (*Private collection*)

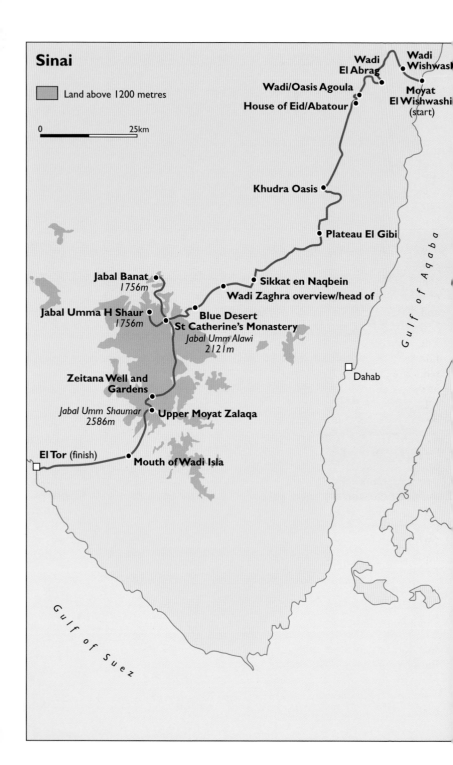

Sinai

Land above 1200 metres

0   25km

Wadi
El Abrag

Wadi
Wishwashi

Wadi/Oasis Agoula

Moyat
El Wishwashi
(start)

House of Eid/Abatour

Khudra Oasis

Plateau El Gibi

Jabal Banat
1756m

Sikkat en Naqbein

Wadi Zaghra overview/head of

Jabal Umma H Shaur
1756m

Blue Desert
St Catherine's Monastery
Jabal Umm Alawi
2121m

Gulf of Aqaba

Dahab

Zeitana Well and
Gardens

Jabal Umm Shaumar
2586m

Upper Moyat Zalaqa

El Tor (finish)

Mouth of Wadi Isla

Gulf of Suez

GEOFF HORNBY

Sinai: the long way down

Exploration in Arabia has been sanitised. The days of extended camel crossings of the Empty Quarter have been replaced by jeep-supported trips. The incentive to look deep into the heart of an inaccessible mountain range has been replaced by the fast-fix trip of Airbus and Land Cruiser, leading to minimal discomfort and maximum footage climbed. Hard core today is travelling without beers in an icebox.

Whilst this trend is unavoidable for most, I think it has an unfortunate side effect. Deep exploration of the mountains is only going to occur where vehicle access is achievable. Use of a jeep dramatically reduces the issues of water management. As the insidious use of power drills extends further and further into the mountains, so does dependency on the Land Cruiser both to carry equipment and support the electrical needs.

In 2003 I crossed Oman's deserts and mountains in as light a manner as I dared, but ultimately the jeep was never far behind. I knew that I had to reduce dependency on transport and, as a pay-off, increase the penetration into the mountains that only walking could achieve.

David Lucas is the 'Gaffer' regarding climbing on the mountains of the Sinai Peninsula. We had climbed together around St Catherine's monastery and I suspected that his domain would provide the perfect venue for my plan: to cross an entire mountain range on foot from one coast to another; to take a route that is inaccessible to jeeps and camels; to climb as many new rock walls along the way as possible; to leave nothing but footprints; to share time with the local Bedouin.

I drew a line across Sinai, from the Heights of Taba at the Gulf of Aqaba to the town of El Tor on the Gulf of Suez. My crude ruler made it look like 250 kilometres. I knew little more. Whilst Gaffer filled in the plan in Sinai, I quickly recruited Susie Sammut and David Barlow. Susie had shared the Oman traverse with me three years earlier and David had a long record of climbing in Musandam, Oman, the Emirates and Jordan.

Gaffer's planning was exquisite. He recruited a Tarabin Bedouin, M'Sallem, to be our guide for the first 10 days, and two of his relatives, Eid and Farrag, as our camel men. The plan was that the four of us, with Am, would walk the entire route, exploring hidden wadis and canyons, whilst Eid and Farrag would fill up with water at wells and meet us nightly at pre-arranged points in the mountains.

We left the shore at the entrance to the Moyat El Wishwashi and made a camp by midday to allow us time to climb in the canyon. The two Daves added a new butch E2 5c whilst the B team retreated ignominiously off the line of a waterfall to one side.

72. Dave Lucas and Susie Sammut new routing on the House of Eid.
(*Geoff Hornby*)

73. Bedouin delivery systems at a meeting point in Wadi Isla.
(*Geoff Hornby*)

The next day set the tone for the trip. We left the camels at dawn and we climbed and traversed ridges and wadis, passing through the Ghoula Oasis, over the col at El Corhelai, down through the Closed Canyon and out onto the plain of Wadi El Abrag. Sure enough at sunset the camels arrived, having taken a route through the main wadi systems.

Foregoing the jeep was the first step to liberation; now we were to experience the Bedouin style – no stove and no packaged food, fresh baked bread from the coals of the fire, pulses and rice, salad and veg and of course the endless sweet tea. Our plan for the next day involved a traverse of the mountain ridges to the west, followed by the Rainbow canyon and a descent south to surreptitiously cross the black top road that runs through the middle of the Peninsula. Inshallah, this would be achieved without the authorities spotting us and a rendezvous made with the camels that night at the Agoula Oasis, 10 kilometres south of the road.

As we assembled the next night in camp I could sense the release of tension in our Bedouin team. Avoiding the police and army in Sinai is essential for a happy trip. 'Rules' governing hiking and climbing in Sinai are dependent on whoever in authority you ask and who you meet. Taken together with Egypt's draconian restrictions on the movement of Bedouin within Sinai, it is advisable to keep as low a profile as possible.

The Wadi Agoula is a wide sandy wadi that twists and turns to the south. On one of the great bends we found ourselves below a beautiful-looking wall that immediately commanded the setting up of camp and the pulling out of ropes. 36 hours later we had made six new routes from Severe to E1 and 50m to 150 metres in length. We decided to name the wall in Eid's honour and all the routes are named after his family members.

Heading south, we climbed slowly up a long sandy wadi to find ourselves in the open desert of El Helal. The climbing possibilities were limited, as the sandstone is particularly soft, so we set off west and then south past Jabal Rum and on to the oasis at Khudra. An inspection of the surrounding sandstone walls provided little incentive to climb so we continued through the White Canyon and headed south past Jabals Abu Ghuzaiyat, Matamir and Muzayrah until a camp could be made on the Plateau El Gibi below Jabal Barqah.

Turning to the west we re-entered granite country and noted many possibilities for future rock-climbing trips. However, I suffered the ignominy of filling my water bottles with salty water from the well at Bir Sa'al without checking the quality first. The Bedouin team thought this was the height of incompetence. As we neared the end of the perfect wadi system of Sikkat en Naqbein, we knew we were fast approaching a major police facility in Wadi Zaghra. The Wadi Zaghra drains the high mountains of Sinai through a wadi system flowing south-east to the coast near Dahab. It did not suit our agenda to drop in from above on the police, so we kept our camp whilst Gaffer and M'Sallem rode our baggage camels to a nearby Bedouin village to get the beta on the safe route westwards.

74. Geoff Hornby on the 1st ascent of *Bilhana wilshiffa* ('health and power')
– west face of Jabal Umm H Shaur. (*Susie Sammut*)

Stick to the high ground was the advice and so we did, for two days
across granite ridges and passes until we could drop into the Blue Desert.
At this point it was time to let our Tarabin camels leave us as we were now
entering the tribal area of the Jebalya. We left our equipment dumped in
the desert whilst we continued on foot across the desert and up over the
pass to the north of Jabal Umm Alawi to then circle around St Catherine's
monastery and so into St Catherine's village.

With the change in tribal areas we recruited Nasser and Mohammed
from the Jebalya. Am stayed with us as a friend rather than a guide and
having walked for 12 days he was looking forward to finishing the trip
through country that was new to him. First though we had some serious
climbing objectives to fulfil. Heading north from the monastery for 10
kilometres we then camped below the east face of Jabal Banat.

On the big north face the Daves set about a thin crack system which they
felt would provide possibly the hardest big route in Sinai. Unfortunately
encroaching darkness and a fiercely cold north wind forced them down
from three-quarters height.

Whilst they were away, Susie and I added a new route immediately left
of *Call of the Wild* on Banat's north-east face. The route, *Palestine*, was just
short of 400 metres in length and HVS 5b. We returned the next day to
finally straighten out an old project of ours to the right of *Call of the Wild* via

bold slab climbing. This 400-metre route was named *Jerusalem* and has possibly the best E2 5b slab pitch outside of Froggat.

Turning west out of St Catherine's, the posse then set about the west, south and east faces of Jabal H Umm Shaur. Camp was established in a cave under a boulder, which made our friend Mohammed very emotional as he had been brought up from the age of two to 12 living in this cave with his mother. Having lived in a welfare state which produced a generation of 'dole climbers', I can only say that I felt ashamed at this man's childhood hardship.

The Shaur provides top quality granite and the Daves hoovered up crack line after crack line. I particularly enjoyed their affair with the Nun, a pillar feature on the south-east face, resulting in the crack line on the left side *Kicking the Habit* and the crack line on the right side *Dark Side of the Nun*. However, their choice addition was the 200-metre crack line on the east face that weighed in at E3 5b.

Susie and I climbed a great line up the west face of Shaur at 250 metres and HVS 5a. We named the route *Bilhana wilshiffa*, which is a standard Arabic toast meaning 'health and power'. We also added a 250-metre route to Shaur's south face at HVS 5a called *Sharouk Il Shams* translated as 'Sunrise' in Arabic.

Heading south out of St Catherine's was the usual exercise in deception. We set off looking like four day-trippers, only we never came back. Long after dark, 25 kilometres to the south, our camels arrived with all the baggage. We were now a truly Sinai posse with Bedouin from the Tarabin, Jebalya, Ulad Sayid and Mizena tribes all travelling with us.

A long day took us across many ridgelines to climb eventually to the summit of Jabal Umm Shaumar, the second highest summit in the range and the outlier in the south-west. This stunning granite mountain provides superb views of the Egyptian mountains in Africa round to the Saudi mountains of Jabal Mazhafa.

Some 2600m below us and across a sand desert lay our final goal, the town of El Tor. The camels were circling around the Wadi Isla route whilst we dropped down Wadi Umwayjet, a rock gorge with endless scrambling and ridge traverses, to bring us out two days later at the edge of the final desert. We were now exposed again and the Bedouin wanted to get back into the mountains as soon as possible.

Dumping our gear we bid an emotional farewell to our support team and they returned the way they had come. We were only left with a walk of 27 kilometres to the coast. Perhaps we should have avoided the 12km-long artillery range, but it wasn't marked as such on the maps. Whatever, now I know what anti-tank missiles, mortar bombs and even Stinger missiles look like. We marched in a spread-out single file, all following David Barlow's footprints, to minimise land mine potential, and finally staggered onto the coast road trying desperately to look like tourists out shopping – a tense end to a long journey.

75. The Posse: (*clockwise from left*) Eid, Susie Sammut, Dave Lucas, Geoff Hornby, Farrag, David Barlow, M'Sallem. (*Geoff Hornby collection*)

Summary: An account of a 250-kilometre continuous foot traverse of the mountains of South Sinai from the Gulf of Aqaba to the Gulf of Suez between 21 November and 17 December 2007. The expedition made first ascents of 20 rock routes along the way and recorded further potential for new routes. Without vehicle support or the use of pitons or bolts, the journey was carried out by David Lucas, Geoff Hornby, Susie Sammut, David Barlow and M'Sallem Farrag Eid.

JOHN SHIPTON

Mount Burney: a centenary visit

In March-April 2007 Jim Wickwire led an expedition with Japanese climbers Otani Eiho and Yamanushi Fumihiko and myself to make an attempt on Mount Burney in southern Chile. In his article on the first ascent of this mountain in 1973 (*AJ* 1974, pp1-4) my father, Eric Shipton, started with an apology that he should be mentioning the ascent of a paltry 5000ft peak. However, anyone who has travelled in the Chilean Magellanes knows this to be preposterous modesty. The weather is the worst in the world and the country requires special stamina.

Mount Burney is the southernmost volcano on the South American continent, the most southerly, therefore, of the great chain of Andean volcanoes, though very much detached from the others. Although it is an ice-capped massif with glaciers and icefalls on all sides, it provides no great technical challenges. The key to the mountain is the weather. Perched on the end of the uninhabited Munoz Gamero peninsula, a country of bog, lakes and dense primeval temperate rain forest, the mountain is almost always shrouded in cloud and seldom seen by the occasional boats navigating the complex channels and fjords of southern Chile. Even its true altitude, variously given as around 1500m and 1700m, is uncertain. Persistent cloud cover has meant that it remains a blank spot on Chilean surveys. But very occasionally a patch of settled weather allows Burney's ice spires to appear as they did for Robert Cunningham when he was surveying the area in the 1800s, and then miraculously for Eric in 1973.

Probably even greater apologies are due for mentioning a trip to the same mountain, of a mere 5000ft, and not managing to make the ascent. However, 2007 was my father's centenary year and Mount Burney was his last great climb. The mysterious mountain held a special fascination for him. He made two audacious journeys in 1961 and 1962 using a single inflatable on the then totally unexplored fjords and lakes of Munoz Gamero peninsula, one trip brilliantly recorded on film by John Earle.

The 1973 ascent with Perry and Radcliffe was Eric's last great climb and one of his finest adventures. As Radcliffe says, the climb was made more by luck than good judgement. However, Eric's calm confidence in the face of enormous challenges was the hallmark of his greatness as an explorer and, I think, created the luck. Some years ago the mountain began to fascinate me too. In 2001 I travelled to Burney with Paddy Freaney, Rochelle Rafferty, Brede Arkless and others, repeating some of Eric's earlier approaches with inflatable dinghies. It was a terrific journey through stunningly beautiful, untouched country, but the mountain remained as stubbornly shrouded as on Eric's first two journeys.

77.　View east from the slopes of Burney. (*John Shipton*)

It wasn't my intention to go back to the rain and bogs of Munoz Gamero too quickly but Jim Wickwire, having picked up the piece I had written on that Burney trip, asked me to accompany him and Japanese climber Otani Eiho. I could hardly refuse an invitation from such an accomplished veteran to make a more direct effort to climb Burney, especially as I could meet Otani who had led the 1989 ascent of Monte Shipton/Darwin, in Tierra del Fuego. Jim and Otani were both deeply inspired by Eric and were keen to have a look at his last climb. Later, Otani recruited his fellow Japanese mountaineer and film-maker Yamanushi Fumihiko.

Unfortunately, from our point of view, a second ascent of Burney had been made in 2003. After a prolonged siege, an American NOLS (National Outdoor Leadership School) team based in Puerto Natales was gifted that magic lull in the weather and followed Eric's 1973 route from the west. Jim was not put off by this, but felt there were further climbing aspects to the mountain, a new route up the north-east glacier, for example, and the higher of the two summit pinnacles. He opted to approach from the north, landing at Ancon sin Salida. This would bring us closer to possible new routes and a far cheaper boat ride than all the way round to the west of the mountain.

76.　*Left:* Map of Burney reproduced by courtesy of John Earle.

History suggested April might offer a better than average chance of one of those magic settled spells, so on 22 March we found ourselves standing in drenching rain on the beach of Ancon sin Salida. Captain Conrado and his 40ft motor-sailer Foam had conveyed us on an eight-day voyage from Puerto Natales through the spectacular inland seas and channels. A problem with the bay is that it faces north-west, from where the prevailing winds hurtle onshore. Fortunately two tiny, forested islands protect the beach where we landed and, astonishingly in this deserted place, a little fishing boat was anchored in their lee. Bundling everything into the nearest trees we established a shore camp and immediately started our battle with the wet.

It was wonderful to see again all the plants that I had become familiar with on previous trips. The evergreen *Nothofagus betuloides* dominates, an indication, if any further were needed, of the soaking conditions. Also at our woodland camp were *Drimys winteri* and Calafate *Berberis ilicifolia* whose prickly leaves are relieved by the juicy berries so well known in Patagonia, and on the floor a carpet of *Gunnera magellanica*, another Patagonian speciality.

To the south the lower slopes of Burney were occasionally visible and when the cloud lifted above its customary 800m level we could see a part of the great north-east glacier which gleamed ice blue even without sunshine. Between the beach and the bottom of the mountain lay miles of pampas bog. Our immediate concern, as is usual when landing anywhere in the Magallanes, was to find a way through the dense coastal forest to open pampas bog beyond. Captain Conrado had left us with an old inflatable to negotiate the glacier river next to our camp. On the first day we crossed the river and walked along the beach of Ancon sin Salida; a Spanish explorer's 'Bay with no Exit', so named on his fruitless mission to find a new route across to the Atlantic.

The beach is of rounded pebbles of Burney volcanic rock, the many-coloured porphyritic andesite which makes up the ramparts of the caldera. We soon came to a river and in an attempt to find a good crossing found ourselves struggling through extremely dense bush. A second river confronted us and with rain pelting down we decided to postpone the necessary disrobing for a crossing. Next day, having waded up to our waists to cross the first river, we found the second too swift and deep. We decided to somehow bring the inflatable down the beach and use a tiny inflatable I had brought to do the ferrying on the glacier river. In prospect lay several days work just to get off the beach.

On the way back, as we considered the logistics with inflatables, we came across fishermen collecting firewood. It was an extraordinary piece of good fortune. One of them, Arnoldo, said we didn't need to cross the rivers to get to the pampas. I couldn't see how this was possible as the coast appeared to be completely guarded by dense bush. However, he insisted and eventually decided to show us the way. Without Arnoldo there is no chance we would have found the little track that cut its way through bog and bush for a

78. Primeval *Nothofagus betuloides*. (*John Shipton*)

kilometre to the open bog beyond. Arnoldo said he used it to go fishing fresh water fish and hunting. Later, by way of acknowledgment of our debt to Arnoldo, we rowed across to the island where the fishermen were anchored. The island, called Islota Caro, was covered in *Desfontainia spinosa*, in flower with its scarlet and yellow blooms being fed upon by humming birds, as was the great pink bell-flowered scrambler *Philesia magellanica*. Arnoldo was out with his rowing boat bringing in nets but later he brought four huge fish. Next day Arnoldo and his boat were gone.

In the morning we started the business of carrying two loads towards the mountain to establish a base camp. Once through our marked trail through the coastal forest, we were on the pampas heading due south. With visibility fluctuating, a compass was needed much of the time. Yama's GPS was a useful backup for finding our return route, but we soon got used to navigating on the trackless bog. Carrying 30kg loads across the turba of Patagonia is something of an art form, the trick being to get into a rhythm despite the varying terrain. This ranges from swampy grassland reaching our waists, to a spongy bog often dominated by *Astelia pumila* with stretches of impossible *Nothofagus* copse. On four occasions our way was blocked by canyons full of thick luxurious forest dominated by *N.betuloides* which,

Otani agreed, look somehow very Japanese with their layered branches, along with more *Desfontana spinosa* and *Berberis ilicifolia* and great clumps of the fern *Blechnum magellanicum*. We struggled through, and on 26 March were established at our base camp in a sheltered spot, the mountain above us blanked out by cloud. Rain came in vigorous pulses and always seemed to be heavier as we took down or put up tents. Interestingly, Otani and Yama had forgotten their flysheet, a slight oversight in the wettest place on the planet, but they rigged a canopy and made their tent so comfortable that it became our gathering place for meals.

From our base we explored a route around to the base of the north-east glacier. This involved a plunge through dense forest dominated by ancient, moss-covered *Nothofagus pumilio*. We emerged into a large open valley beneath the great mass of blue ice we had seen from the shore. An easy route looked possible to get onto the ice above a large icefall, and beyond a ramp which seemed to lead up into the cloud towards the invisible top half of the mountain. Jim had initially envisaged doing a circumnavigation at the same time in the manner of Eric's 1962 epic journey. However, travel in this region is an arduous affair. Endless rain means that moving camp leads to getting almost everything soaked. Double loads need to be carried from place to place for much of the time. It was an exercise to which I was not averse, but it soon became apparent that it would preclude the objective of climbing the mountain. By 29 March we had established our 'glacier camp' and decided to await the weather.

It was a glorious place to be and, as in 2001, I felt sure that we were the first people to be on this spot since Eric passed by, probably several metres above us on ice that has since disappeared. An easy stroll around the valley brought us onto the glacier from where we walked up a ridge to the base of the ramp, overlooking a vista of wild country. Ancon sin Salida and Seno Union lay to the north and the uninhabited lands of Munoz Gamero to the east with its myriad rivers, lakes and mountains. To the south was the spur off Burney that Eric and John Earle had called Tryfan as it shares the craggy appearance of the Snowdonian favourite. Between Tryfan and Burney itself was the ridge that Brede Arkless and I had peered over in 2001 on a trip up from our camp on the south side of the mountain. Above us were great walls of volcanic conglomerate made up of welded blocks of the same several-coloured andesite we had found on the beach.

As in 2001 the cloud base hardly ever lifted above 800m, just the point where our ramp tantalizingly turned a corner into the caldera of the volcano, and this time it was often much lower as sheets of driving rain swept around the mountain. Over the next few days we caught just the occasional glimpse of the pinnacles on top of the mountain. When the weather was a little less wet we made exploratory forays, but for much of the time we were forced to shelter and wile away the time amusing ourselves with tales of America, Wales and Japan and games of cribbage that I introduced to the assembled company. On 4 April, Yama and I walked along the ridge above the glacier and climbed what I called Mt Yamanushi, which I now think must be what Eric and John called Tryfan II. From here, in a tempestuous wind, we could see a little more of the crevasse conditions on our ramp. That evening the wind eased and the sky started to clear. We saw the Southern Cross, and indeed stars, for the first time, and felt that the moment had arrived.

Preparing for the climb and a pre-dawn start we were full of anticipation. Conditions looked good until 2am but soon afterwards the cloud rolled back along with rain heavier than ever before. Enough was enough. The weather was not going to give us a break. Using Jim's satellite phone we called Puerto Natales to get Captain Conrado to pick us up from Ancon sin Salida on 11 April rather than the 15th.

If we had any concerns that cutting our attempt short would lose us the chance of climbing Mount Burney we need not have worried. If anything the weather worsened with temperatures starting to fall, signalling the approach of the southern winter. The rain that accompanied our journeys back to the shore turned to snow on quite low ground. Back at the shore camp the day before our pick-up there was a strange calm and a whole assortment of birds, along with porpoises and sea lions, gathered round the little islands, but the cloud never left the mountain. The wind soon picked up the next day and was bitterly cold, forcing us into the shelter of the trees as we waited for the welcome appearance of Foam.

Although we signally failed to make our ascent of Mount Burney, we all felt it was worth the effort. Travelling in this wild and extremely beautiful part of the world, still unexplored in parts, is always fascinating. For me it was a privilege to walk with Jim Wickwire and two great Japanese climbers who were tremendous company in harsh conditions. It was in any case justifiable as a small tribute to my father in his centenary year. Mount Burney now may well see few other climbers in years to come, holding its secrets secure behind a shroud of mist and snow.

Summary: An attempt to climb Mount Burney, the southernmost volcano on the South American continent, by Jim Wickwire, Otani Eiho, Yamanushi Fumihiko and John Shipton, March-April 2007.

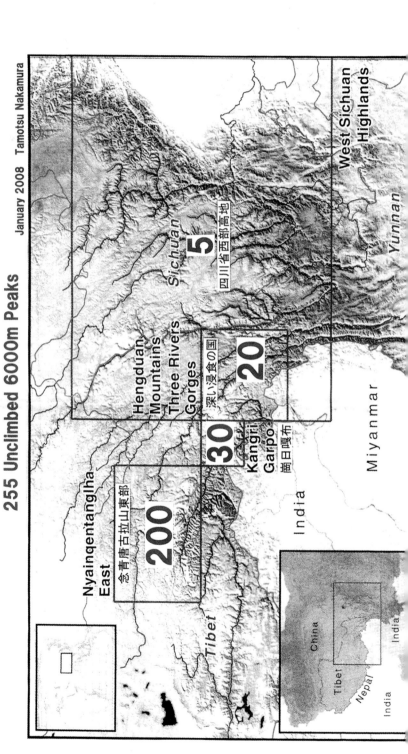

ヒマラヤの東―チベットのアルプス

未踏の6000m峰 255座

EAST OF THE HIMALAYA–ALPS OF TIBET

255 Unclimbed 6000m Peaks

January 2008   Tamotsu Nakamura

West Sichuan
Highlands

Yunnan

Sichuan

四川省西部高地

5

Hengduan
Mountains

Three Rivers
Gorges

深い浸食の国

20

30

Kangri
Garpo

崗日嘎布

Nyainqentanglha
East

念青唐古拉山東部

200

Tibet

Miyanmar

India

China

Tibet

Nepal

India

India

TAMOTSU NAKAMURA

Return to Gorge Country 2007

In spite of a chilly wind, I sat for some time gazing at this colossal chaos of mountains flashing in the sunlight, the deep valley of the Wi-chu at our feet, and then range beyond range to the Salween, and beyond that again more mountains. Why yes! I must be looking at the very sources of the Irrawaddy itself, and there in the south-west, one, two, three, I know not how many ranges away must be the gorge of the Taron, and beyond that Burma. Wonderful!

The Mystery Rivers of Tibet
Frank Kingdon Ward, 1913

My voyage of discovery to 'East of the Himalaya – the Alps of Tibet' was triggered by the enchanting narratives of Frank Kingdon Ward on his travels to the remote Tibetan marches of north-west Yunnan and south-east Tibet. This paradise for plant-hunters has an equal allure for mountaineers, with 255 unclimbed 6000m peaks mapped in the whole area of 'East of the Himalaya'. They are distributed as follows:

> Nyenchen Tanglha East – 200 peaks
> Kangri Garpo range – 30 peaks
> Deep Gorge Country of the Hengduan mountains – 20 peaks
> Sichuan West Highland of Hengduan mountains – 5 peaks

In autumn 2007 I led an expedition of six members to Deep Gorge Country to revisit an isolated borderland that has been of particular interest to me. It is a land of natural wonder where great rivers have eroded the Tibetan plateau into deep valleys with gloomy shadows and forbidding gorges. This was the hunting ground of Kingdon Ward whose footsteps I have been tracing since 1990.

A wave of changes, however, is sweeping China, reaching every corner of its frontier in the west. The Deep Gorge County, which the Chinese call 'Three Rivers Parallel Streams' (Salween, Mekong and Yangtze), was registered as a world natural heritage site by UNESCO in 2002. Playing on the Shangri-La of James Hilton's *Lost Horizon*, the Chinese government has highlighted the Meili Snow Mountains on the Yunnan-Tibet border and Mekong River valley for the development of tourism. Nevertheless, there still remain many unfrequented and lesser-known mountains and valleys to attract an old explorer. I have been fortunate, though I must admit our 2007 expedition was rather hard and uncomfortable.

Deep Gorge Country

Baxoila Ling-Salween/Yu Qu Divide-Nu Shan in Three Rivers Gorges

Tamotsu Nakamura

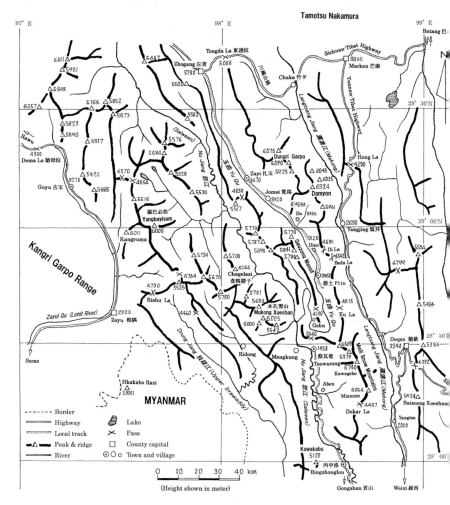

(Height shown in meter)

Our original plan was to go up the Salween River (Nu Jiang) north-westwards from Tsawarong by horse caravan, but the muleteers refused, saying the trail was too narrow and dangerous for pack animals to pass carrying loads. We were forced to choose an alternative route along Yu Qu (Wi-chu), a tributary of the Salween, which I had already traced twice. Extraordinarily heavy snowfall in mid-November closed the high passes, including two, at 4900m and 5300m, that we had intended to cross, forcing a further change of plan. In addition, all six of us caught serious colds in the smoky Tibetan houses where we stayed.

Nevertheless, our journey achieved a satisfactory outcome, shedding light on two 6000m mountain massifs and one 5700-5800m massif, as follows:

Baxoila Ling. The northern part of this large mountain range is on the Lohit-Parlung Tsangpo-Salween divide; the southern part is on the Irrawaddy-Salween divide in the Tibetan Autonomous Region and changes its name to Gaoligong Shan in Yunnan Province. There are three outstanding mountain massifs: Yangbayisum (6005m), Chagelazi (6146m) and Mukong Xueshan (6005m) ('Xueshan' means snowy mountains).

Range on the Salween-Yu Qu divide. Comprises three massifs: Geuzong massif opposite Jino to Do villages, 5700-5800m, many outstanding rock peaks in its northern part; central massif opposite Bake to Jomei villages, 5300-5700m, many peaks; northern massif opposite Zayi, 5400-5600m, few attractive peaks.

Nu Shan / Taniantawen Shan: This is also a large mountain range on the Salween-Mekong divide. Nu Shan in the southern part has a famous holy peak of Meili Snow Mountain (6740m) with well-developed glaciers, while Taniantawen Shan stretching north of Nu Shan has the rocky massifs of Damyon (6324m) and Dungri Garpo (6090m) with no eminent glaciers.

Itinerary: 6 to 30 November 2007

We flew from Kunming (1950m) to the ancient city Dali (1900m) on 6 November and returned to Kunming from Shangri-La/Zhongdian (3280m) by air on 30 November. (Air temperatures shown below were taken at 8am.)

By Land Cruiser through Salween canyon
6 Nov: Cloudy, 11°C, From Dali (1900m) – across Mekong – Liuku (850m) Salween bank.
7:      Rain/cloudy, 17°C, Liuku – Gongshan (1560m) [Yunnan].
8:      Cloudy/fine, 10°C, Gongshan – Longpu (1860) – Tsawarong (1950m) [Tibet].

16 horses caravan along Yu Qu valley

9: Rain/cloudy, 11°C, organising caravan at Tsawarong.

10: Cloudy/fine, 10°C, Tsawarong – Tongdu La (3340m) – Zaji (2360m).

11: Cloudy/fine, 7°C, Zaji – across Yu Qu – Gebu (2460m) – Wobo (2730m).

12: Fine 5°C Wobo – Razun/Radoun (2880m). Perfect view of east face of Mukong Xueshan.

13: Fine, –1°C, Razun – Tong La (3270m) – across Yu Qu – Pitu (3060m).

14: Fine/cloudy, –2°C, Pitu – (this section by a car) – Dino (3130m).

15-16: Snowing –0°C. Stay at Dino owing to heavy snowfall.

12 horses caravan from Yu Qu to Do Qu - Reconnaissance of Damyon

17: Rain/cloudy, 1°C, Dino – (entering Do Qu) – Do (3350m).

18: Fine, 0°C, stay at Do. Perfect view of west face of Damyon.

19: Cloudy/fine, 0°C, Do – (Do Qu) – camp site at 3560m.

20: Fine, –5.5°C, camp site – (Do Qu) – pasture for yaks at 4140m – camp site.

21: Fine, 2°C, camp site – Do. Viewed Geuzong massif on Salween-Yu Qu divide.

13 horses caravan northwards along Yu Qu

22: Fine/cloudy,–6°C, Do – Bake (3270m).

23: Fine, –7°C, Bake – Ge La (3960m) – Meila (3750m). Central massif of Salween-Yu Qu divide viewed from Ge La.

24: Fine, –10°C, Meila – Jomei (3320m).

Return from Yu Qu via Sichuan-Tibet Highway

26: Fine, –9°C, Jomei – Zayi (3470m) – Zhogang (3780m) – Sichuan-Tibet Highway – Tongda La (5008m) – Chaka (across Mekong) – Markam (3860m) – (across Upper Yangtze) – Batang (2530m) [Sichuan].

28 to Fine, –2.5°C, Batang – (along Upper Yangtze) – Derong

29: (2410m) – Shangri-La [Yunnan]

Highlights

The **grand canyon of the Salween** runs northwards from Liuku, capital city of Nu Jiang Lisu Minority Autonomous Prefecture, where we arrived by three Land Cruisers on 6 November. The canyon scenery is rich and varied with magnificent gorges, great bends, rope bridges, rapids, pools and beautiful forests. The people are friendly with colourful costumes, raised houses and Catholic churches.

A paved road runs from Liuku to Bingzhonglou, 40km north of Gongshan, and in 2005 a new vehicle track was opened, 56km as the crow flies, from Bingzhonglou to **Tsawarong** on the left bank of the Salween.

& 82, North-east face of Mukong Xueshan – North peak (6005m, main peak) seen from Wobo village. North peak and South peak (6000m) (*left*) seen from Razun village. (*Tamotsu Nakamura*)

This new road forms part of the ambitious West Development Plan and is connected to the Sichuan-Tibet Highway from the south. Thanks to this road, we were able to reach the administrative centre of Tsawarong in six hours from Bingzhonglou, whereas the old path required three to four days on foot.

Kingdon Ward loved the people and culture of Tsawarong, visiting in 1911, 1913 and 1922. It is said that the pine-forested valley of the Yu Qu, to the north, is the most beautiful in eastern Tibet. It is also, as Kingdon Ward noted, a valley of pretty females. The people are hospitable and we were welcomed in Tibetan houses, lodging at Dino, Do, Bake and Meila villages on the route of our caravan.

The grandeur of the first bend of the **Yu Qu gorge** is breathtaking. The traveller has a bird's-eye view while descending the trade path (pilgrimage trail) from Tongdu La (3340m) to Zaji village. This was the first highlight for us along the Yu Qu, and the second was to come near Tong La (3270m). The well-maintained trade path crosses the Yu Qu at Gebu village and ascends about 300m before levelling and continuing northwards. Down to our left was the meandering turquoise stream of the Yu Qu while to the west we could see prayer flags at a pass on the ridge separating the Yu Qu and Salween. The mysterious view of the Yu Qu [Wi-chu] from the pass would be similar to the one we enjoyed at the Tong La, near Razun village (2880m) and enthusiastically described by Kingdon Ward.

> Now we see the Wi-chu at our feet, flowing southwards ... plunge into thicker forest, and climbing steadily soon reach a low pass, Tong-la. Wonderful! We have just this minute turned our backs on the Wi-chu and certainly it was flowing due south; yet here it is at our feet again, this time flowing north! Surely I must be dreaming!

An examination of the highly tilted rocks led Kingdon Ward to a conclusion that this extraordinary loop of the river was made up of fragments of two or three older rivers, which had been gradually forced into each other's embrace as the result of earth movement, or cutting back by head erosion.

I woke at dawn on 13 November and went out from Razun village so that I could at last take a full picture of **Mukong Xueshan**, the snow mountains. Kingdon Ward had also seen the peaks near the same place, though I regret that no pictures of 'Orbor', as he referred to Mukong Xueshan, are found in his book *Mystery Rivers of Tibet*. He wrote:

> The sun was setting behind the twin crystal peaks of Orbor, and black cliffs crowded up one behind the other from Wi-chu to the Salween, their feet in the curdled mist, their heads amongst the brilliant stars. Darker and darker grew the shadows, the crimson faded from the sky, and indigo dusk curtained a scene of savage grandeur.

South face of mountain goddess Damyon (6324m) seen from Do village.
(*Tamotsu Nakamura*)

4. South face of c 5800m rock peak south-east of Damyon seen from Do Qu.
(*Tamotsu Nakamura*)

Deep Gorge Country – Mountain Ranges

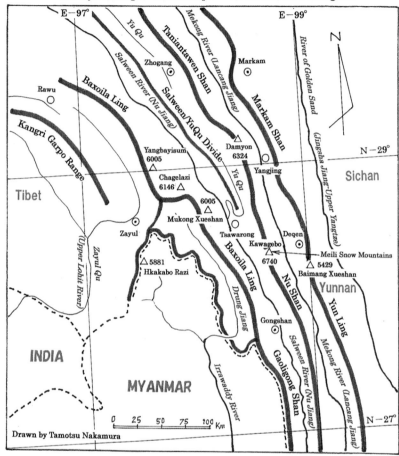

Drawn by Tamotsu Nakamura

Mukong Xueshan is a large mountain massif with sizeable glaciers. It has twin peaks, the north of 6006m and the south of 6000m. The northeast face looks magnificent, comprising precipitous walls of snow and ice.

It might not be exaggerating to say Mukong Xueshan had become one of my mountain obsessions. I had tried to view it several times before. There were two chances in autumn 1996 from the pilgrimage trail round Meili Snow Mountains, when I crossed a ridge of Yu Qu loop and later as I crossed the Xu La (4815m) on the Yu Qu-Mekong divide. In autumn 2003 as I traversed the Gorge Country from Zayu to Mekong, one late afternoon I hurried on our caravan to reach the Tsema La (4710m) on the Irrawaddy-Salween divide, but thick clouds already hid the peaks. Two days later I expected to get a view from another high pass, the No La (4269m), and stayed there for more than two hours, but I could see only part of the south face of the main peak, which had a large glacier. Another chance came at Razun, but I only caught a glimpse of the summit for a second. Ninety per cent remained in the cloud.

In November 2007 the gods finally blessed me. I saw the main peak from Wobo village and a whole panorama of the north-east face appeared before me at Razun. The AC's email *Newsletter* of January 2008 included a paragraph on my visit to Gorge Country illustrated by photographs of Mukong Xueshan and Damyon.

Though the Meili Snow Mountains are now famous among tourists, few are aware of **Damyon** (6324m), which has long been worshipped by the local Tibetan and Nashi minorities as a sacred mountain. Damyon and Dungri Garpo (6090m) are located at the southern end of the Taniantawen range which is 50km long from south to north and has five unclimbed 6000m peaks. Kingdon Ward first saw Damyon from the east in 1911 and again in 1922 when he approached from Yangjing (2680m), a place of salt wells on the bank of the Mekong. He wrote of an 'abrupt climb from the Mekong gorge to the crest of the ridge, over 3,000 feet above the river' (*From China to Khamti Long*, Journey 1922). He went up a trail to the north-west and when this soon disappeared ascended screes and moraines to about 5500m, where he found dead glaciers that had supposedly retreated hundreds of years earlier. For my part, in 1998 I had a perfect view of the east face of the two massifs from Hong La (4200m) on the Mekong-Yangtze divide, but the south and west sides of Damyon remained quite unknown till 2007.

After two days of heavy snowfalls our 12-horse caravan departed from Do village (3350m) on 13 November to reconnoitre Damyon from the west. We ascended through primeval conifer forest along the Do Chu, a tributary of the Yu Qu, and camped at 3560m. The following day we reached a pasture at 4140m where yaks are grazed in summer. Above were lofty rock peaks of c5800m ranging south from the main peak of Damyon. In summer we would have found a fairy meadow.

According to an old villager, the west face of the main peak lies to the north of a small ridge running east-west. To reach this face one must cross a high pass (4850m) called Zeh La near the headwaters of the Do Qu beneath the south face. There is a lake called Uke Tso just north of the Zeh La and a muddy lake called Nacha Tso directly beneath the west face. Camping is possible at a pasture just north of Uke Tso. A trail passes northwards from Uke Tso to a pass of 4000m near Chaka where the Sichuan-Tibet Highway crosses the Mekong.

The old man also explained that each of the rock peaks ranging south from Damyon has its own name. From north to south, the names are Lamyon, Gonmyon, Nachamyon, Suzemyon and Kashonmyon. *Myon* means goddess and each has her own legend. More peaks named after the goddess sisters of Damyon extend to its north. We were fortunate to be able to photograph the whole of the south and west faces of Damyon, soaring to a blue sky, from Do village – the first time the challenging Damyon had been photographed from this southern aspect.

86. East face of 5770m peak in Geuzong massif on Salween–Yu Qu divide. (*Tamotsu Nakamura*)

87. East face of 5841m peak in Geuzong massif on Salween–Yu Qu divide . (*Tamotsu Nakamura*)

Caravan crossing a suspension bridge over the Yu Qu at Gebu village. (*Tamotsu Nakamura*)

A farewell party with muleteers at Jomei; in the centre is Tom Nakamura. (*Tamotsu Nakamura*)

After his reconnaissance of Damyon, Kingdon Ward entered Pitu crossing the Beda La (4542m) on the Yu Qu-Mekong divide. He described the scene thus:

> If you travel north-westwards from Yakalo (Yangjing), you meet with snow peaks at every turn, growing ever more lofty. There is a perfect botanist's paradise in that mountainous and little-known country beyond the sources of the Irrawaddy.
>
> (*From China to Khamti Long*)

In mid-November 1998, I crossed the Di La (4581m) adjacent to the Beda La to the north-west and saw the same panorama of the mountains as Kingdon Ward. One of the objectives of our 2007 journey was to gain information on the little-known mountains, notably the **Geuzong massif**, that lie between the Salween and Yu Qu. Less attention has been paid to this range as there are no peaks exceeding 6000m and only very small glaciers. A Russian 1:200 000 map denotes many 5300-5800m peaks ranging from north-west to south-east.

I tried to profile as many peaks as I could while marching up the Yu Qu. However the valley path was too close to the mountains to have good views. I could just manage to take pictures of Geuzong from near Do village on the way back after reconnoitring Damyon and the central massif from the Ge La 3960m between Bake and Meila villages. Photos of the northern massif were taken in 1998 on the way to a pass at 4000m west of Zayi.

Our quest finished in Jomei, where the muleteers from Jino and Do village held a farewell party for us – the first time this has happened for me during 17 years of travel 'East of the Himalaya'. We were deeply moved by the kindness and generosity of the people of the Tsawarong area.

Expedition members: Leader Tamotsu Nakamura (72), Tsuyoshi Nagai (75), Eiichirou Kasai (67), Tadao Shintani (64) and Ms Sonoe Sato (48). Interpreter Lu Weidong (58, Han), guide Shaohong Cheng (35, Tibetan).*

---

*   Shaohong Cheng, whose Tibetan name is Gerong, is a guide from Deqen who has travelled with me several times to Gorge Country since a circumnavigation of the Meili Snow Mountains in 1996. Cheng arranged everything for our journey and I proudly recommend him as the best and most reliable guide for trekking in the Hengduan Mountains.

ANDY PARKIN

Peaks and Pastels

Nepal, December 2007 ... Heading into the Khumbu,
solo, painting and prospecting, a notion of a peak to
climb – but which one? – and hopefully a new route ...

Kathmandu to Lukla

Flying in was all sunny, after the clinging morning fog of the
capital; the plane steadying its approach, though in a crazy
landscape of tilted mountains. Kathmandu to Lukla in 35
minutes! As drastic as the change was, the familiar chatter of
employment-seeking porters brought me back to earth. Hastily
repacked loads and a bit of bargaining and we were off, the two
porters as keen as myself to begin the walk-in. To where? Well I
would work out that as we went along.

Namche Bazar

I liked Namche, the hub of it all for the Sherpas. Indeed the
valleys radiate away from it like the spokes of a wheel and
choosing the northernmost one, we left after resting a day. Once
into the valley that led onwards to the village of Gokyo, I felt at
peace. Having made a decision as to my destination and
having a vague idea that somewhere up there I should find a
mountain to climb, I relaxed, taking in the scenery, painting
as I went, feeling as if I were really on holiday for once.

Porters

It was wilder in this upper valley but still there were people
everywhere. Of course the locals were constantly on the move
between villages; small and impressively solid men carried as
much as a hundred kilo loads on their backs. Everything from
building materials, cases of beer, sacks of rice, eggs to cigarettes
by the thousands. I also met the odd trekker, although to be fair
some of them turned out to be good characters.

Glacier

Cold, dry and icy. Such are the Himalayan glaciers in winter.
Terrible winds can scour them, making life out of doors a harsh
experience. People occasionally venture on to them, laden with
supplies and/or ambition. As with all glaciers, it's better to
avoid them where possible. I was lucky throughout the trip;
I never went on one. Villages cling to their edges, huddled for
shelter in ablation valleys, alternatively warmed by the sun or
cast into the shadow of towering mountains.

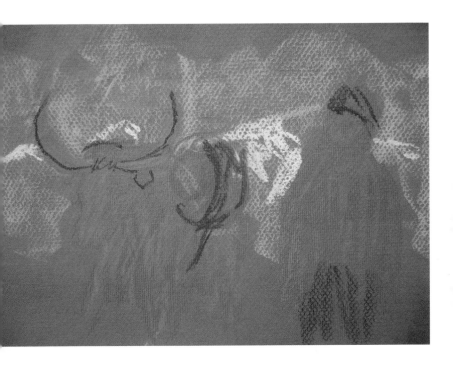

Yak and Sherpa

Generally speaking, if it isn't carried by a person then it's strapped to the back of a yak. Amazing creatures and prized by the villagers, these semi-wild beasts provide transport, wool, milk and eventually meat. Sure-footed, hardy, they somehow find grazing at high altitudes, indifferent to storms and cold. They seem to symbolize this country as horses do the arid steppes of Patagonia.

Sacred lake, Gokyo
Perched on a moraine ridge, above the village of Gokyo, three days' walk from Namche, I painted and attempted to design a route up the walls of Phari Lapcha that dominated the lake. My eyes wandered between the turquoise water and the dark and foreboding face. For once, the weather was good, the temperature not too low, the light just right and my fingers, holding the stubs of pastel colours, not too numb.

Looking from the window of the lodge

It certainly beats the usual style of base camp, the living inside
a house! Instead of being constantly cold it can even be warm.
Add to that good food, and the result is easy winter
mountaineering. Still, across the lake and up there in the sky I
had a climb to do. Using binoculars I studied my chosen line.
Would it go, how hard would it be and how cold?

Phari Lapcha, the north-east face
This is the mountain I had heard of but never seen; that I had come all this way to in order to find a line I could climb. I would follow the snow ramp, on its north-east face and then climb runnels of ice, snow and rock to the summit. The descent would be via whatever route seemed the best. I didn't know the mountain, so would have to make it up as I went along. I had come here looking for an adventure and had a feeling that I was about to get one.

View from the summit, Cholatse and Taweche
Whilst climbing I didn't have the time or inclination to do much sightseeing. Once on the top (6017m), with the sun warming my back I gazed out towards Makalu and its foreground peaks of Cholatse and Taweche. Whilst preparing for the climb I had never tired of painting these two giants. As the friendly sun sank, their western aspects glowed in the rich, clear light of the Himalayan twilight.

AC 150

Rowan Huntley *Breithorn and Breithorngletscher ~ Clouds on the Wind*
Chroma on canvas, 50cm x 40cm. (*Private collection*)

The 150th Anniversary Year

3 February 2007   Shap Wells Dinner, Cumbria
Guest Speaker: Peter Habeler

8 - 11 March   'The Artists of the Alpine Club' Exhibition
John Mitchell Gallery, Old Bond St, London
Launched by Lord (Chris) Smith

April   Ak-Shirak ski expedition, Kyrgyzstan

12 - 13 May   Celebrations at the Pen-y-Gwryd, North Wales

May/June   Garhwal Expedition, with Himalayan Club

22 - 24 June   The Zermatt Gathering:
Reception, Grand Hotel Zermatterhof –
Dinner Hotel Riffelberg
Principal guests:
Walter Bonatti, Kurt Diemberger,
John Harlin III and representatives of the
Swiss Alpine Club

August/September   Caucasus Expedition

21 - 26 September   'Treasures of the Alpine Club' Exhibition
Christie's Galleries, St James's, London

29 September   Scottish Dinner, Atholl Palace Hotel, Pitlochry

4 December   Summits of Learning seminar, London:
'150 Years of Mountaineering,
Mountains and Science',
held at the Swiss Embassy, followed by
Ambassador's Reception

10 December   Formal Dinner, Old Hall,
Lincoln's Inn, London

STEPHEN VENABLES

Valedictory Address

Read before the Alpine Club on 11 December 2007

Brevity might be the soul of wit, but it is anathema to climbers. We thrive on reminiscence and most of us would probably agree that a large part of the pleasure of our perverse pastime lies in ruminative retrospection. We are compulsive regurgitators. So, almost inevitably, this address will look back over the 35 years I have spent as a climber and at the changes I have witnessed. But it will also attempt to look to the future. And I will try to make it mercifully brief. I should stress that any views expressed will be purely personal and in no way a reflection of official Club policy.

I'll start with a late afternoon in 1974. David Lund and I were on the Aiguille du Midi, slogging, far too late, with pitiful slowness, up the so-called snow arête of the Frendo Spur. What had looked so beguilingly white from the valley was actually brittle grey ice and the stubby ice hammers we used in those days were making little impact. The setting sun was obscured by thickening cloud and snow was beginning to fall. The Midi cable car, out to our right, packed with warm bustling humanity, might as well have been a rocket in outer space for the all the help it could offer us. I felt cold, lonely and tired and I was dreading the now inevitable unplanned bivouac.

By the last glimmer of light we just managed to reach the foot of the final rognon, where we installed ourselves on a cramped rock knob, and crouched uncomfortably beneath the Zdarsky sack. Snowflakes pattered on the nylon shell over our heads; condensation dampened the inside. The dehydrated 'Scrambled Egg and Cheese' we heated up on our stove was so disgusting that we ended up tipping it down the north face of the Midi. Life was less than perfect.

And yet, there was a companionable fug inside our bivouac sack – a sense of coping with adversity. I think we even slept a little. And when the time came, in the morning, to re-tighten bootlaces, strap on crampons and shake out stiff limbs, apprehension gave way to a quickening of the spirit. The sun had come out and the rocky rognon was transformed under its glittering new coat of snow. Numb fingers quickly warmed to the task, grappling with granite, snow, ice – even, I seem to remember, a peg or two for aid – delighting in the craftsmanship of it all. Again there was that delight in coping with – even enjoying – the job in hand. We had got ourselves out of a fix, and life, actually, was quite good.

The following year I entered the Frendo Spur – along with the Matterhorn and a few other peaks including the glorious Cassin Route on the Badile – on my application form to become an aspirant member of the Alpine Club (I hadn't yet quite clocked up the requisite 20 routes for full membership).

The ostensible reason for joining was to get reduced rates at alpine huts. In fact, we nearly always bivouacked *outside* the huts; even at half price, they were expensive; and you got a much better night's sleep under the stars.

No, the real reason, which became apparent when I turned up to my first meeting at South Audley Street, was less to do with tangible benefits than a sense of tradition. The room was packed with people, mainly but not exclusively men, nearly all of them wearing suits or tweed jackets, with incongruously garish green and yellow ties. Most of the people had white hair. But then you began to realize who they were. That must be Noel Odell. And that rather jolly-looking old lady must be Dorothy Pilley of Dent Blanche fame, chatting with the legendary *New Statesman* literary editor, Janet Adam Smith. And that's John Hunt. And the rather severe looking man in the chair is Jack Longland, author of *Javelin Blade*, one of the world's very first extreme rock climbs, not to mention that gallant performance on Everest in 1933.

The speakers that night were also a distinguished lot. Their style was a little different – long hair, wide lapels, hipster jeans and no ties – but the story they had come to tell – the first ascent of the south-west face of Everest – clearly entranced the Club elders. I felt rather privileged to be there, in that quite intimate gathering, hearing Bonington, Boardman and Scott deliver their lecture, hot off the press, before they embarked on their big public tour. And the Everest evening was soon followed by other equally riveting talks: Alan Rouse on the big South American extravaganza with Hall, Whittle, Carrington and the Burgess twins. Alex MacIntyre on big new alpine routes. Terry King, actor, climber and raconteur, on everything from Sron Ulladale to the Hindu Kush with Andrei Zawada. Another Pole, Janusz Onyszkiewicz, on the then still unrepeated peak of K2. Joe Tasker on his and Peter Boardman's redefining of Himalayan climbing with the west wall of Changabang. Doug Scott returning to talk about how he *really* liked to climb, without oxygen and fixed ropes and porters, on Kangchenjunga, and Nuptse, and Makalu.

The Seventies were an exciting time to start mountaineering. Even on the very highest peaks, the whole concept of what was possible was being redefined. At slightly lower altitudes, peaks that Shipton and his contemporaries had only dreamed about – spires like Changabang, Trango and The Ogre – were actually being *climbed*. In the Alps, better ice gear was enabling Alex MacIntyre, Patrick Gabarrou and others to start work on a whole new world of north-facing adventure. Now it seems incredible to think that when Lindsay Griffin and I attempted – unsuccessfully – to make the second ascent of Gabarrou's Super Couloir on Mont Blanc du Tacul, it was regarded as perhaps the hardest ice climb in the Alps.

But going back three years to the summer of 1974, the biggest news in Snell's Field at Chamonix actually came from home: Pete Livesey had just climbed the *Right Wall* at Dinas Cromlech. British rock climbing was undergoing its own renaissance. Livesey and his young acolyte, Ron Fawcett –

alongside Leeds-based stars such as John Syrett – were forcing up the standards of free climbing. More exciting, to my mind, were the seaside explorations of Pat Littlejohn, who was – and remains, as Jim Perrin once put it, the greatest British rock-climbing pioneer since Joe Brown (and one of our least-recognized all-round star mountaineers). Later we got to hear about the equally creative activities of Mick Fowler. (The first time I saw his grinning face in a magazine, it was to announce the free ascent of a gritstone route called *Linden*. 'Some parochial Sheffield rock-jock', I assumed, until, a few months later, I read Fowler's article about a new route on the Grand Pilier d'Angle. Ah – apparently this man climbed real mountains too).

On the South-west sea cliffs, Littlejohn and Fowler were following in the tradition of Pete Biven and our own Frank Cannings – a man who, I am delighted to say, still eschews that horrible American import of the late Seventies – *Chalk*. As Joe Brown put it to me recently, at our 2006 dinner, chalk changed British rock climbing irrevocably: not only is it an aesthetic assault on our predominantly dark native geology; by marking up the holds, it also destroys subtlety and takes away the sense of the unknown – the thrill of discovering the route's secrets for yourself.

Ken Wilson, that tireless prophet of our times, flagged up the chalk issue in his *Mountain* magazine. It was he also, a few years earlier, who published Reinhold Messner's 'Murder of the Impossible'. I remember reading Messner's essay as an 18-year-old and thinking, 'this man knows what it's all about'. Reared on the books of Shipton and Tilman, it had never occurred to me that people actually drilled holes in rock; but apparently they did – whole ladders of steel bolts forced inanely up otherwise unclimbable walls. Messner was fulminating against mindless *aid* climbing – the *Diretissima* that bears no relation to the natural features of the rock. In fact, that particular aid-climbing cult proved short-lived and the Tyrolean polemicist probably never imagined that 30 years later, the bolt – placed into what are now electrically-drilled holes – would be used, not for artificial climbing, but to open up whole new kingdoms of previously unimaginable *free* climbing.

But I think the principle *does* remain the same – the notion that if nothing is impossible, then we are all diminished. Of course I admire, for instance, the stunningly beautiful new free rock climbs on the Wendenstock above Meiringen, which could probably not be protected without bolts. Drilled protection has enabled the best climbers to create routes that I will never, ever, be good enough to get up. So do I have any right to complain?

Well, yes, I think I do. Because mountaineering is about aspiration. We need heroes to admire. And we need those heroes to be bold and brave and respectful of the mountain aesthetic. But what is *really* important is that bolts are not just enablers for the extraordinary technical achievements of the *elite*. No, they are being used to mollycoddle the rest of us, to make climbing everywhere – even on the easiest routes – more convenient and more accessible. This so-called '*plaisir*' climbing has less to do with the deep, lasting satisfaction of genuine personal discovery – the *real* pleasure of mountaineering – than a kind of bland instant gratification, peddled by a society ever more in thrall to a pernicious, erosive culture of 'health and safety'.

This is beginning to sound like the rant of an old guard elitist in a green and yellow tie. But just because something is new, is it necessarily good? And, anyway, what on earth is wrong with elitism? I think that our friends in the Swiss Alpine Club, notwithstanding the wonderful generosity they have shown us in our anniversary year, are profoundly misguided when they insist that their job is to re-equip comprehensively the glorious climbs of their country, to make them safer and more accessible. I think that Michel Piola displayed staggering arrogance, recently, when he bolted his way up a 'new route' in southern Turkey, without bothering to find out that an earlier team had already climbed the same line, protecting it with the plethora of excellent modern removable gear available in any climbing shop, using and delighting in the natural features which God – or a few million years of erosion – gave them, and leaving those features unharmed for future generations to enjoy.

Mountaineering is fundamentally about overcoming our own personal fears and weaknesses. It is about surprise, and discovery, and the unknown – or at least the illusion of the unknown. And, whatever Ruskin said about greasy poles, it is about aesthetic sensibility being *heightened* – not diminished – by physical exertion. And if that entails a bit of hardship and even danger, well, so be it. If you don't like it, go to Disneyland. Or play golf.

Mountaineering is also about friendship. Some of the most companionable times of my life have been spent with members of this Club. Tibet with Henry Day. The north face of the Eiger with Luke Hughes. Kohe Sahkt with Lindsay Griffin and Roger Everett. Kishtwar with Dick Renshaw. *Orion Face Direct* with Alison Hargreaves. Snow Lake with Duncan Tunstall and Phil Bartlett. The unexplored wilds of the eastern Karakoram with Victor Saunders, Jim Fotheringham, Dave Wilkinson, Henry Osmaston and Harish Kapadia – that particular expedition made possible by the generous help of our then president, Roger Chorley.

I have also been lucky enough to climb with some of the modern legends of international climbing – John Roskelley, Jim Wickwire, Ed Webster, Tim Macartney-Snape, Reinhold Messner ... I even once went bouldering with Catherine Destivelle. And while we're on the subject of name-dropping, I never imagined, listening to that Everest lecture at South Audley Street in 1975, that Chris Bonington would one day help to save my life on a peak in Garhwal; nor that Doug Scott would, during an Alpine Club symposium, sneak off from the lecture room to lead me up *Cenotaph Corner*, followed by that incomparably macho creation of his old friend Don Whillans – *Grond*.

The really nice thing to report about all those climbing partners is that apart from Alison Hargreaves – and Henry Osmaston whom died of respectable old age – they are all still alive. It would be naïve to pretend

100. *Right*
Stephen Venables – on the
Breithorn media event at the start
of the AC gathering in Zermatt,
June 2007. (*Ed Douglas*)

that our survival has not had at least something to do with luck; we've all had our near misses. I have certainly been lucky to survive. I've also had the good fortune and honour to be president of this Club during the year of its 150th anniversary. Unlike John Hunt, in the centenary, dressing up in evening tails to welcome Her Majesty the Queen, I have been allowed to celebrate more informally. But I think we have still marked the year with an impressive variety of dinners, meetings and expeditions, with special guests including Peter Habeler and Walter Bonatti. Recent lectures by members – or about-to-be members – such as John and Anne Arran, Ed Tressider and Kenton Cool, have demonstrated the vitality of modern alpinism and the talent of its stars to entertain. The Club is thriving, particularly in its ability to see the big picture, beyond the minutiae of pure climbing achievement, with a huge range of thoughtful articles in its *Journal*, ever more ambitious exhibitions and an excellent conference looking at the increasingly urgent need for scientific understanding of the mountains.

I was lucky enough to be born in one of the richest countries in the world, in a generation which hasn't had to fight wars and which has enjoyed unprecedented freedom to travel. The whole world has been our playground. Our possibilities for exploratory mountaineering have been – and at the moment still are, despite the efforts of the Piolas to tame the cliffs – almost unlimited. But I wonder how much longer we will enjoy this fool's paradise of ever cheaper air travel, before the whole fragile edifice of our oil-driven modern economy, built on the mantra of yearly growth, comes tumbling down. Perhaps that sounds unduly pessimistic. But who knows? Perhaps, quite soon, travel will again become difficult. If that does happen we might be more restricted to our own island mountains – the mountains where this gloriously irrational pursuit of climbing was first invented. Just supposing that does happen, these native hills and cliffs will seem even more precious. So, at the risk of sounding jingoistic, I would suggest that we, in the Alpine Club, should remain zealous custodians of those British hills and of that British tradition of enjoying the hills in a spirit of free, adventurous discovery.

RONALD FAUX

Zermatt Gathering

22-24 June 2007

A helicopter clatters low over the slate rooftops of Zermatt trailing a steel cable. It hovers over an assembly of mainly grey heads in the town centre and the cable is ceremoniously attached to a white cloth. At a signal, the helicopter lifts, whisking away the cloth and unveiling the bronze statue of an alpinist from the Victorian era, alpenstock in one hand and hat doffed towards the Matterhorn in the other. A brass band of immaculately uniformed mountain guides strikes up. It is all deeply and theatrically symbolic; the helicopter and its cable signifying a mechanistic age, the bronze figure marking the time 150 years ago when a small group of enthusiasts formalised their passion for alpine peak-bagging and founded the Alpine Club. An inscription states simply that the statue, a striking figure commissioned from Stefan Mesmer, marks 150 years of friendship between Zermatt and the pioneers of alpinism, a friendship that has palpably remained strong ever since.

It was a grand occasion, growing grander by the minute in the run-up with more members and guests wanting to take part than there was space to accommodate and feed them. As the receptions and banquets were re-scheduled to ever-larger venues, a logistical nightmare for the organisers was handled at an unflustered alpine stride by the Swiss hoteliers. Great names of alpinism were gathered together; representatives came from most of the world's leading mountaineering associations and the press and television cameras were there in force to record an undeniably historic event. Even the Matterhorn, icon among mountains, joined in the theatre, initially refusing to appear from behind a solid shroud of cloud; then, Salome-like, giving glimpses of a thinly veiled Furggen, followed by a rump of Zmutt and the dark edge of the Hörnli soaring to an invisible summit. Heavy fresh snow followed by mild temperatures had made this a dangerous place and we were told of six climbers who, days earlier, had been lifted to safety by helicopter.

This first day of celebration had begun with a mass Alpine Club trespass onto the Breithorn, the 4164m snow summit above Zermatt on the border with Italy. How the early pioneers would have reacted to this leap-frogging up mountains by cable car can only be imagined, but time constraints necessitated being swept to the summit of the Kleine Matterhorn from where the Breithorn was but a two-hour plod.

101. Retreat from Moscow? Doug Scott guides his rope of four out of the cloud on the descent from the Breithorn summit media event. Following, in order, are Stephen Goodwin, John Harlin III and Stephen Venables. (*Ed Douglas*)

Conditions were reminiscent of Scotland on a bad day with driving snow and scant visibility. The Zermatt guides, who had charge of the journalists hoping to cover the event from its literal high point, were initially reluctant to leave the shelter of the cable car station. The swift ascent by cable left a couple of journalists ill from the altitude. One mountaineering wordsmith intent on retreat was shamed by a slip-of-a-girl from US *Men's Vogue* who tripped along gaily through the driving hail in jeans and a designer sweater carrying two Pentax large-format cameras. George Band, aged 78, was in the summit party with a sprinkling of other Everesters; at the centenary celebration 50 years ago he reached the same point via the Younggrat. Doug Scott, in fly-fishing hat and Barbour jacket, and AC president Stephen Venables were interviewed for television as the howling wind and driving snow added an authentic touch of alpine atmosphere. Then everyone made a safe descent for the unveiling ceremony which took place in a spell of bright sunshine.

Speeches of welcome drifted on the wind and there were presentations to honoured guests, principally to Walter Bonatti, stocky, white-haired and craggy-faced, whose record as an alpinist is universally admired, to the redoubtable Kurt Diemberger and to Paula Biner, sister of the late Bernard Biner, the Zermatt guide who had such a strong association with British mountaineers. It was a time for memories and I doubt there was anyone of a certain age present who failed to slip back in remembrance to earlier exploits and time out in the challenging landscape surrounding Zermatt. Since I'm writing this I can rewind my own memory banks to the time a girlfriend, a fellow journalist, gave me the boot because she didn't like my style, and I arrived in Zermatt intending to repair my feelings beneath a tree writing a poem. In the cellar of the Bahnhof, the hotel presided over by Bernard Biner, were Dave Mellor, then a teenage rock jock, Brian Nally and Tom Carruthers, who days later made the first British ascent of the Matterhorn north face, and John Emery, survivor of the Haramosh disaster that left his hands and feet mutilated by frostbite. We climbed a crop of summits in the Valais and, without knowing it at the time, established friendships that have proved to be life-long, and which years later led me to three expeditions to Everest and a great wealth of adventurous experience. It was once whilst camping in Zermatt that I had a telegram, via the Bahnhof, offering me a job on *The Times*, which I accepted and stayed for 30 years. I never did write the poem.

I mention this because there were surely others on this 150th anniversary celebration cherishing their own memories of Zermatt that perhaps made a significant impact on the rest of their lives. This was certainly the impression when the celebration decamped to the largest reception room in the nearby Grand Hotel Zermatterhof which creaked at the seams as the drink started to flow and old friendships were noisily revived. It was all delightfully informal and casually dressed, a cut apart from the early days of the Alpine Club when it would have been unthinkable for an Englishman not to dress for such an occasion at any of the leading winter sports centres. But as skier-journalist Arnie Wilson has recalled, it was the Alpine Club members who led the revolt against such formality in the Alps by dressing for dinner in brown serge suits.

The weather cleared the next day as members dispersed into the hills, with a large contingent aiming for sun-warmed rocks on the south face of the Riffelhorn. President Venables and John Harlin III, editor of the *American Alpine Journal*, celebrated the day by establishing a new route, quite an achievement on a cliff that over the years had been so thoroughly worked over. The new line they named *Swiss Hospitality*. Venables counted it an excellent turn-out and a good day with no bolts to cloud the ethical horizon and the Riffelhorn fairly swarming with AC parties. He was also in a group that later climbed the Leiterspitz above Täsch, afterwards walking back to Zermatt. 'Leslie Stephen would have been proud of us,' he declared.

That evening, with hardly time to change into their brown serge, more than 300 members, wives and partners rode the rack and pinion Gornergrat railway up to the Hotel Riffelberg. This lofty establishment with its superb views across the Valais bathed in bright evening light had also burst at the seams, requiring one group of anniversary diners to decamp to an annex restaurant. So speeches were held first, al fresco, with the Matterhorn forming the backdrop to another genial exchange of compliments and gifts.

102. Where it all began: Frank Urs Müller, president of the Swiss Alpine Club, presents AC president Stephen Venables with a painting of the Finsteraarhorn, the mountain on whose slopes, in 1857, William Mathews and Edward Shirley Kennedy decided to found the Alpine Club. 23 June 2007, Hotel Riffelberg, Zermatt. (*Bernard Newman*)

The Swiss Alpine Club President, Frank Urs Müller, presented the Club with a watercolour of the Finsteraarhorn – a well-judged reminder of where Mathews and Kennedy decided to form the Alpine Club – and Walter Bonatti was awarded honorary membership of the Alpine Club. Other honoured guests included John Harlin III, Professor Bruno Messerli, Peter Mäder, general secretary of the SAC, Christian Trommsdorff, and Tom Nakamura of the Japanese Alpine Club. Together we dined on antipasti Riffelberg and ragoût of beef with crème brulée to follow, accompanied by a wine order that might have tested the lifting power of the Gornergrat railway. Walter Bonatti gracefully accepted honorary membership of the club, pointing out that it was highly significant that Zermatt should have been chosen to celebrate the Club's third 50th anniversary. The town and its Matterhorn were two icons inextricably linked to the history of mountaineering. Edward Whymper's scaling of the magnificent and challenging peak in July 1865 highlighted a fascinating epoch, Bonatti said, recalling other famous British climbers who pioneered many difficult mountains in the Alps, among them John Ball, the AC's first president, and his great contemporary Leslie Stephen. Then came great English climbers such as AF Mummery who climbed the Matterhorn aged 15, a strong alpinist with a profound ethical sense.

103. *Left*
Zermatt all stars:
(*left to right*) George Band,
Walter Bonatti, Doug Scott,
Stephen Venables – and the
Matterhorn. Terrace of the
Hotel Riffelberg.
(*Bernard Newman*)

104. *Below*
'Over here … '
Nick Clinch (*left*), former
president of the American
Alpine Club, and John
Harlin III, editor of the
American Alpine Journal.
Zermatt, June 2007.
(*Bernard Newman*)

Bonatti related that in 1965, one hundred years after the first ascent, he had wanted once more to climb the Matterhorn, but in winter, via the north face and alone. That was, he said, his testament to the greatness of Whymper and to the beauty of the mountain. Now, 50 years on, here they were once again – alpinists gathered in friendship at the foot of this 'imposing and mythical Mecca' – to celebrate a history and a spirit of the hills as timeless as the hills themselves.

The festivities concluded with a Sunday morning service at St Peter's, the English Church in Zermatt, which the Alpine Club affectionately regards as its own parish church and where so many distinguished British mountaineers are buried or remembered. Conducted by the Rev Brian Underwood, seasonal chaplain for the Intercontinental Church Society, the special service was organised on behalf of the AC by committee member Rick Eastwood. Sadly, Rick was killed six weeks later in an abseiling accident on the Grand Capucin.

About 150 people, mostly AC members, attended the service, and all are indebted to Rev Underwood, the ICS and the local congregation for their warm welcome and the work they put in. The Bible lesson was read by Club member Sally Westmacott and another member, Ian Thompson, was the organist (Ian had also sung grace in Latin for the Riffelberg dinner). Prayers were read by local Churchwarden Hazel Perrin and by Trevor Letchford and Dave Healey of the ICS. Stephen Venables gave a short introduction for the benefit of visitors who were unfamiliar with the Club. The church was specially decorated with alpine flowers and along the front of the altar was a row of historic ice axes kindly lent for the occasion by the Matterhorn Museum.

Many AC members lingered on into the following week, though the Matterhorn remained well out of sorts. The Riffelhorn saw a good deal more activity, as did (let it be whispered among those who despise ironwork in the hills) the new and remarkably airy *via ferrata* on the cliffs of the Turmwang above the village. A group of nine stalwarts traversed from Zermatt to Zinal, staying at three huts – Topali, Turtmann and Cabane de Tracuit – and ascending the Brunegghorn (3590m) and Bishorn (4135m) en route. Bishorn summiters were Mike Esten, Robin Richards, Hywel and Ingram Lloyd, Peter Payne and Hugh Nettleton. Rob Collister, Lizzy Hawker and Phil Wickens went up the Unter Gabelhorn (3392m), Andy Parkin and Simon Yates climbed the Pointe de Zinal (3789m) from the Schönbiel hut and Stephen Goodwin worked off the stress of organising the whole jolly gathering with a rapid stomp up from the village and over the Platthorn (3345m) and Mettelhorn (3406m). Doubtless there was more.

105. Post-party capers: Ed Douglas (*top*) and Simon Yates in Thermometer
      Couloir, Riffelhorn, 24 June 2007, Zermatt. (*Stephen Goodwin*)

Lincoln's Inn Finale

The last official event of the anniversary year was a black tie dinner, ably organised by Chris Russell and Sally Holland and held in the packed splendour of the Old Hall, Lincoln's Inn, London, on 10 December. A message from the Duke of Edinburgh was printed at the front of the menu cards. Among the guests were the Swiss Ambassador, Alexis Lautenberg and Dr Lodovico Sella of the Sella Foundation. The toast, 'To the Mountain Clubs of the World' was proposed by George Band and responded to by AC honorary member Nick Clinch of the USA. Their speeches are reproduced here:

George Band

TO THE MOUNTAIN CLUBS OF THE WORLD

The AC's Golden Jubilee Dinner took place on 17 December 1907 also at Lincoln's Inn, but in the Great Hall, where Douglas Freshfield remarked: 'Will the company which dines here 50 years hence include the conqueror of Mount Everest?' Indeed it did! At the Dorchester Hotel on 6 November 1957, the President was John Hunt. Among the 410 present were 55 official guests including Tenzing, while among absent friends, Ed Hillary and George Lowe were moving steadily towards each other across the Antarctic. Michael Westmacott and I were present, as were several others here this evening: Alan Blackshaw, Simon Clark, Chris Simpson and Tony Streather. Emlyn Jones, at 92, was on the list but sadly has just fallen and broken his hip. We wish him a rapid recovery. In 1957, the toast to 'The Mountain Clubs of the World' was proposed by Sir Arnold Lunn. Referring to the bond that unites all mountaineers, he suggested it was closer than in any other sport. He said how much this bond meant to him in a period of acute wartime anxiety when at the end of 1940 he spent two weeks in North America. His only comparatively happy hours were those spent in the company of mountaineers.

I had a similar experience when, newly married to Susan, I was posted in 1959 by Shell to the desert oil town of Midland in the wilds of West Texas, not knowing anybody. Out of the blue, I was telephoned by Nick Clinch who I had never met. He invited us to join him and his parents at their home in Dallas on New Year's Eve. We ate the traditional Texas supper of barbeque beef with sweet potatoes and blackeye peas. Next day he had tickets for American Football at the Cotton Bowl: Texas University versus Syracuse. Spurred on by the cheerleaders, with great fervour I sang 'The Eyes of Texas are upon you...' with my hand firmly clasped over my heart. I am really delighted that Nick is here tonight to respond to my toast.

BUCKINGHAM PALACE.

One of the strongest instincts of small children is to explore their environment. In some people this instinct tends to fade with time, but with others it seems to become stronger and more demanding as they mature. For those who see no great value in getting to the top of mountains, the courage and dedication of the addicted climber is a mystery.

Climbers are single-minded, and it should come as no surprise to find that the pioneers of serious mountain climbing very soon formed themselves into a club. The Alpine Club has every reason to celebrate its 150th anniversary, and I am delighted to have this opportunity to send my congratulations and best wishes to everyone attending this anniversary dinner. It will be a great occasion to recognise the achievements of its members over the years, and also to be grateful to all those who have kept the Club going through good times and bad.

Message from
HRH The Duke of Edinburgh KG, KJ
Honorary Member of the Alpine Club

How can I possibly pay tribute to the Mountain Clubs of the World? There are over 300 Clubs in the UK alone, and over 80 affiliated to the International Mountaineering and Climbing Federation, known as the UIAA. The 'Arc Alpine' countries of France, Switzerland, Germany, Austria and Italy, with their huge numbers, provide the core financing and membership of the various commissions on which the UK is well represented. I can only speak from my experience as a delegate to UIAA meetings held by rotation in member countries. When it was the turn of Slovenia, they generously offered a pre-meeting guided tour of the Julian Alps. I applied and was duly met at the airport by an attractive girl in her early twenties, 'Ah, Mr Band, welcome to Slovenia. I am your guide and you are my only client!' So for three days we tripped hand in hand, or should I say from hut to hut, over Triglav and several other fine limestone peaks, before joining some 50 delegates from 20 countries. Mountaineering is important in Slovenia. I learnt that one third of all their parliamentarians were members of the Slovenian AC. When, as UIAA president, Ian McNaught-Davis had an audience with the President of Slovenia, the latter lamented that he had only managed 150 days' climbing so far that year.

Mac has just been to Japan as the AC delegate to the UIAA. I immediately think of Tom Nakamura, editor of the *Japanese Alpine News*, who has been so generous in sharing the results of his 28 expeditions over 17 years to the 'Alps of Tibet' in the eastern Himalaya, with all mountaineers, so that our current stars like Mick Fowler, Paul Ramsden and Chris Watts can enjoy first ascents of these spectacular virgin 6000m peaks.

Harish Kapadia of the Himalayan Club is another generous explorer, and his Club was wonderfully hospitable to us in 2005, celebrating the 50th anniversary of Kangchenjunga in Mumbai and Kolkata, and with our dear friends the Sherpas in Darjeeling. Later in May, at an event organised by the Nepal Mountaineering Association, it was an unforgettable experience for Norman Hardie, Tony Streather and me to be garlanded and then driven in a horse-drawn open carriage through the crowded streets of Old Kathmandu.

Finally, one must reserve a very special place for the Swiss. Their hospitality has been superb, from the early days of 'The Club Room of Zermatt 1864' at the Hotel Monte Rosa; and the first great alpine guides, up until the unveiling last June of the statue 'Marking 150 Years of Friendship between Zermatt and the Pioneers of Alpinism'.

I end on a cautionary note prompted by reading Doug Scott's article 'Resisting the Appeasers' in the current *Alpine Journal*. Inexorably, drilling and bolting is spreading to the high mountains, including the great Alpine classic rock climbs. Mummery's route up the Zmutt ridge of the Matterhorn only just escaped being fixed with iron stanchions on the difficult passages. It is up to us as AC members to set an example in climbing ethics by reminding our friends in other Clubs that the finest memorial to the Pioneers of the Golden Age would be to leave the great routes just as the Victorians found them.

107. Final dinner of the AC's 150th anniversary year in the splendour of the
Old Hall, Lincoln's Inn, December 2007. (*Reproduced by courtesy of
SKM Photographic Studio*)

Nick Clinch

TO THE ALPINE CLUB

First I would like to report that there is a recent achievement of the Alpine
Club of which you may be unaware. Composed as it is of mountaineers,
it is almost impossible to get the board of the American Alpine Club to
agree on anything, but recently a minor miracle occurred, and they voted
unanimously to extend their congratulations to the Alpine Club on its 150th
anniversary. So on behalf of one of your younger and paler imitations,
I am pleased to present this certificate of our affection and high regard.

Once an American primary school teacher asked her class whether, if
Abraham Lincoln were alive today, he would be considered to be a great
man. A boy in the first row raised his hand, then jumped up and said 'Yes!'
Pleased, the teacher asked 'Why Johnnie?' The boy replied, 'Because he
would be 150 years old.' Today the Alpine Club is considered a great
institution and not just because it is 150 years old.

Earlier this year, mountaineers from all over the world gathered in Zermatt to celebrate the 150th anniversary of this, the first alpine club, an institution that inspired the establishment of similar clubs including the Japanese Alpine Club, the Alpine Club of Canada, the American Alpine Club and many others. But they did not come just to pay worthy homage to an organisation which is first among equals. They came to celebrate what it began and for the important qualities that it still represents. For centuries there had been scattered ascents of mountains that has enabled many of us to claim for our countries an early start in the sport. But it was the Victorians who formed the Alpine Club that gave us mountaineering. The Club enabled them to exchange their feelings about challenge and risk, together with the beauty of the mountains and how climbing made them more aware of their natural surroundings. John Ruskin was wrong. AC members did not look upon the Alps as 'greased poles in a bear garden'. They understood that difficulty enlarged their appreciation of mountains, not diminished it. They bonded with others who climbed, first with their fellow members and then with everyone who went into the high hills, as John Muir said, 'to get their glad tidings'. These were the pioneers who set our standards and our expectations and gave mountaineers throughout the world, and not just Britain, our heritage.

This 'brotherhood of the rope' is not a cliché as some cynics might think. Yes, even before Whymper and Carrell on the Matterhorn there had been less than cordial behaviour in the hills. But it is minor compared to the strong spirit of comradeship that comes from being a mountaineer. I know. Almost 50 years ago we climbed Hidden Peak; two Americans reached the summit but the success belonged to climbers from around the world who eagerly went far out of their way to help. Americans, Pakistanis, Baltis, English, French, Swiss, Italian and Japanese mountaineers worked together toward a common end. That is just one example. You all have your own. As a result of this brotherhood, I have the finest friends in the world, as I am sure you have as well. It is for this gift that mountaineers throughout the world celebrate the founding of the Alpine Club.

It is inevitable that the tremendous growth in numbers of people climbing mountains will tend to dilute these feelings; therefore, it is even more important that the Alpine Club remains a vigorous source of renewal of this legacy. So as we celebrate tonight among ourselves this gift of the challenge, beauty and friendship of the hills that the founders of 150 years ago have given us, please join me and the members of mountain clubs throughout the world in a toast to the symbol of our past, our present, and our future – 'to the Alpine Club'.

108. Doug Scott, Dennis Gray, Peter Habeler and Mike Mortimer celebrate at the opening anniversary dinner at Shap Wells, Cumbria, February 2007. (*Dick Turnbull*)

109. AC members and guests celebrating the 150th anniversary at the Pen y Gwryd Hotel, below Snowdon, 12-13 May 2007. Jane Pullee looked after everyone magnificently as some 40 lucky diners – including seven past and present Presidents – emulated the alpine pioneers, drinking sparkling Bouvet and feasting on Rack of Welsh Lamb.

DAVE WYNNE-JONES

Ski Tracks in the Kyrgyz Tien Shan

Alpine Club ski-mountaineering

The scent of lilac drifts about the overgrown parks and leafy streets of Bishkek. Above the marble facades and golden cupolas shimmer the jagged snow peaks of the Kyrgyz range. A day's travel later, apple blossom is opening in irrigated orchards punctuated by an occasional pink froth of flowering peach or nectarine. Above the shores of Lake Issy-kul, mountains appear piled all the way to the Chinese border. It is spring in the valleys, winter in the Tien Shan.

We drive up the Barskoon gorge through herds of sheep and goats, cattle and horses, herded towards higher pastures by nomad children who ride as if born in the saddle. But this is early April and as we approach Kumtor goldmine I realise that not only is the road clear but also most of the slopes below 3800m, hugely different from my experience in 2003 when 6WD vehicles had been abandoned in deep snow after straying off the road.

Fortunately Lake Petrov is still frozen solid, so 40 minutes and 2km after setting foot on the ice we set up camp 1 on a sandy beach beneath the snout of the Petrov glacier. It makes a mockery of the hours of Herculean effort forcing a route through the moraine foreshore alongside the melting ice when we last tried this route in May 2006. Nevertheless there are penalties; the camp is at 3730m and having jumped 2000m in the five-hour drive, headaches are obligatory.

That evening we are surprised to see another pair of skiers crossing the lake towards us. They turn out to be Joris and Wytze from the Netherlands who had read my MEF report on the 2006 expedition. Next morning they head south with their single shared pulk, a bright blue plastic baby bath bought in Karakol. Cheap maybe, but it's nothing like as well-behaved as our sledges.

Meanwhile we struggle up the convoluted glacier to leave a cache. Returning, Stuart is caught by a small avalanche on a short but steep slope amongst the broken facets of the glacier. It's enough to take him off his feet and our concerns about snow conditions are strengthened. Overnight snowfall lingers into a dull dawn; also our headaches are worse, so we take a rest day. During the afternoon, Gordon, Gethin and I find a safer alternative route onto the glacier.

Next morning we break camp and skin across the lake in the lee of the glacier's crumbling cliffs, skirting pressure ridges where the weight of glacial ice bears down upon the frozen lake; it could be a scene in the Arctic. By afternoon, however, we can't tell the difference between blasting at the distant mine and the rumble of snow as it settles in huge plates beneath our skis. At one time or another we all break through the softening surface into disconcertingly unconsolidated snow.

Camp 2, at just under 4300m, has more stable snow conditions, and we're encouraged enough to attempt our first peak next day, though Gordon's headache keeps him in camp. We skirt debris from a collapsing cornice and climb steeply and obliquely to reach the saddle just above it, then ski down onto the glacier beyond. With skins back on, it's a steady pull up to the col on the west ridge of our peak. We manage a little further on skis, then have to scratch across an ice band in crampons until we can kick steps up the broad ridge to the summit at 4836m. We decide to name the peak in true (former) Soviet style – Pik 150th Anniversary of the British Alpine Club – and grade it PD. There are great views of a snow-clad Tersky Ala Too and I linger taking photos and logging the GPS data. In doing so I miss Stuart putting a leg into a hidden slot on the way back to the skis, splitting his knee open. Adele steri-strips the wound. Back on skis, Stuart takes off at speed, hoping to make camp before his knee stiffens irretrievably – and he does. We all get a skiing 'high' on the fine run all the way to the foot of the pass.

Our next peak is to the east and as we climb up under its south-west face we are surprised to find fresh tracks of snow leopard. Ice lurks beneath the snow so we abandon plans to skin up the face and leave skis at a glittering ice boss on the west ridge. Trying to sneak past the boss we find wind-polished, armour plating and rope up for a short pitch. Then deep snow forces us onto the rocks of the ridge, but it's good to swing up from handhold to handhold, kicking steps or balancing delicately on frozen-in rock flakes until we break out onto the upper snowfield and traverse to the summit ridge. The icy conditions lead us to alternate ice screw protected pitches with sections of soloing until we eventually make the corniced summit at 4887m. It has to be Pik Ak Illbirs (snow leopard in Kyrgyz.) There are fine views west towards Pik 150th and we grade the route AD. Afternoon sunshine softens the ice sufficiently to ease our descent and a long schuss down the glacier brings us back to camp where Stuart had been resting his injured leg.

Over the next couple of days we head east again to climb two more peaks from the pass at the head of the glacier. One is a steep whaleback of sheet ice rising to a narrow fin of snow and rock at the 4750m summit (PD+); the other is a corniced ridge that reaches 4815m before dropping off steeply into a fierce little cirque to the north (PD). Later we decide to name them Pik Plavnik, Fin in Russian, and Pik Solidarnost, Solidarity, because it was the only peak that we all climbed. From the latter summit it is clear that our proposed route linking several glacier systems will take us far too low for safety in the prevailing conditions. We decide to break camp and head for the north-facing glacier bays to the south of us.

110. *Above*
Taking a rest on the ascent of
Pik Ak Illbirs. Pik 150th is in
the centre background.
(*Dave Wynne-Jones*)

111. *Right*
Tough hauling on steep slopes
during the ski-out at the close
of the AC Ak-Shirak expe-
dition, Kyrgyzstan.
(*Dave Wynne-Jones*)

Unfortunately as we lose height the snow conditions become increasingly difficult. We make heavy going of the descent and are lucky to find a good campsite on a medial moraine. Next day, whilst making an early crossing of the glacier to the south in an attempt on the peak opposite, the snow repeatedly gives way beneath us with a resounding whump. The collapse of a sérac from the flank of the mountain and plenty of evidence of avalanche from adjacent slopes convince us to back off, climbing nervously up the northern edge of the main glacier to scout the major pass to the east. It's passable but would involve further descent with the attendant deterioration in snow conditions. It's a thoughtful ski back to camp for all of us.

That night we talk it through and decide we've pushed our luck far enough. Gethin wants to have a go at the largely rocky peak to the east of us but Stuart doesn't fancy it and the rest of us are non-committal, saying we'll wait for him in camp. So it's strange that four of us head out next morning for the short skin up the side of the moraine before launching on to the rocky slopes above. Adele and I take too long trying a *direttissima*, scrambling over balanced boulders in ski boots; nothing much tumbles but it all feels like it might. Gethin and Gordon are luckier. Taking an oblique line they strike upon a shallow snow gully that takes them through the rocks to the summit snowfield. There, Gordon doesn't trust his alloy crampons enough on a hard ice band so it's only Gethin who makes the first ascent of our final summit, 4727m at PD. He names it after his Mam, Pik Mari.

And that's it. There's nothing much more we can do. After what had clearly been an exceptionally warm winter, we would have to be satisfied with our five first ascents. I call in our transport on the satphone and we head back down the glacier and across the lake. But there's a sting in the tail. A margin of melt-water circles Lake Petrov. We opt to make difficult double carries over two ice and moraine ridges to gain the beach where we had camped before. By morning however the melt-water has been bridged by two inches of new ice and the old ice beyond is sound so we load up the pulks and skin easily back to the road-head.

The mountains, of course, go on looking spectacularly beautiful. It is clear there is a lot more ski-mountaineering and climbing to do in the Ak-Shirak, but not this time. We have been privileged to know something of what the early pioneers must have experienced in the Alps when virtually nothing had been climbed and they could look out for a likely peak and climb it with some assurance that theirs would be its first ascent. How fitting that we should share this taste of pioneering while celebrating the 150th anniversary of our Club.

Summary: An account of a ski-mountaineering expedition to the Ak-Shirak range of Kyrgyzstan organised to celebrate the 150th anniversary of the Alpine Club. The team explored an extensive glacier system and made first ascents of 5 peaks.

DAVE WYNNE-JONES

Climbing in the Kagbhusandi Valley

Alpine Club 150th Anniversary Expedition

'How quickly can I get home from here?' The thought popped into my head as the sub-surface gave way beneath my feet and I sank from knee to thigh deep in wet snow. I was at 3900m in the Garhwal and the first flurries of the next snowfall were gathering up-valley where clouds swagged around obscured summits. Climbing prospects looked bleak.

Stumping back to camp I thought back over our efforts to reach this point: the night train from Delhi to Haridwar-Rishikesh, the daring, horn-blasting drive to Joshimath, the days discovering elaborate shrines and a family of wild boar in the woods above Auli while Parvan, our fixer, explored the labyrinth of bureaucracy surrounding our permits, the further drive along the Badrinath road to Govindghat, starting point for the Valley of Flowers, where the walk-in began, the 'monsoon' rainfall en route and the regular doses of stomach medication.

It had not all been negative: on the first day's trek we had a timely reminder of the Alpine and Himalayan clubs' links with tradition by a chance meeting with Nanda Sinh Chauhan. Ninety-four years old, he was a runner for Frank Smythe in 1931 and 1937 when Smythe explored the Valley of Flowers. This was, after all, a joint AC/Himalayan Club expedition that Harish Kapadia had organised to celebrate the AC's 150th anniversary: I told myself I should be made of sterner stuff.

Harish had first entered the Kagbhusandi (Tal) valley in early May 2006. Hathi Parvat and Otika Danda had been climbed from the north but the other peaks around the valley had not been touched. With so much left to do, Harish's interest in the climbing potential of the area was soon shared by Atul Rawal and AC members Chris Astill, Mick Cottam, Mark Higton and myself. By returning in late May 2007 we had hoped to avoid the unexpectedly deep snow that had thwarted Harish's attempt to cross the Kankul Khal pass in 2006. Leaving the Valley of Flowers trail at Bhuidhar, we had trekked up the Kagbhusandi valley in three days to a base camp at Chhaiyan Kharak (3815m) with Hathi Parvat (6727m) towering to the north. It was just above base camp that I had recognized that this year's weather was no better and was tempted to cut and run.

Doubts persisted as an attempt to get higher on the glacier foundered amongst the snowed-up rocks of a moraine ridge after taking hours to reach 4127m. Then a fine morning prompted an exploration of the approaches to the Kankul Khal. Mick heroically broke trail all the way to the pass at 4665m despite the difficult snow conditions and deteriorating weather while

I reeled along in his wake nursing a stomach upset and wondering why I hadn't brought skis. We descended the last slopes in a thunderstorm but by evening the weather had cleared and the moon came up like a lamp from behind a ridge of Otika Danda, setting the whole cirque glimmering.

With improving weather, the team then made several forays up the steep flanks of the valley in the hope of spotting likely lines. Plenty of ridges and couloirs attracted attention, but looked to be tough propositions in the prevailing conditions. Ridges were plastered with snow and the couloirs avalanching. Mick pointed out a possible line on the peak immediately west of the Kankul Khal and early on a clear morning we headed up the ablation valley on the left bank of the glacier, going on to kick steps in our old tracks back towards the pass. We camped on a broad snow terrace at 4350m enjoying spectacular views northwards to Gori and Hathi Parvat.

At 6am we were away up the crisp snow to scramble up a wide jumble of boulders that fanned down from the first snowfield. Mick and Chris crossed to a weakness in the rock band ahead near a large avalanche cone while I headed right up a snow slope towards a saddle that looked to access the upper snowfield more easily. It didn't. I emerged at a brèche on a very narrow and technical ridge that did indeed lead to the upper snowfield but not anything like safely enough for me. There was nothing for it but to go back and traverse over to the other line with Mark, by then about half an hour behind the others.

The line of weakness was as scrappy as I'd imagined, a mixture of unstable snow, loose rock and wet earth, but we emerged on the upper snowfield looking forward to using the steps kicked by the earlier pair. Unfortunately that half hour had made a significant difference. Although only 8am, the temperature had risen to a point where the steps regularly collapsed and as the snowfield rose into a broad ridge that then narrowed into a steeper continuation spur, Mark and I found it hard going in the increasing heat. At the spur, Mick and Chris took the couloir flanking it on the left but Mark and I were concerned about avalanche danger and climbed the spur direct in four pitches of about Scottish III.

At the top of the spur our routes converged as a narrow ridge swung west to merge into the east face. We climbed four more pitches of mixed ground to gain a massive granite block that we had originally thought to be the summit. The true summit, complete with blade-like rock pinnacle, was another 60m along a narrow snow ridge and gave a GPS reading of 5030m. Consensus later graded the route at AD. The weather deteriorated and Mark and I descended to camp in a snowstorm to see Mick returning to base camp. We remained at the 4350m camp with Chris, gaining a little more acclimatisation and later having to rescue the tent porch that was ripped off by a ferocious wind during the night.

Next morning I dawdled down alone. A weasel popped out on the snow, took a look at me then popped back under his boulder. Lower still, birds

2. Anniversary mountaineering. On the joint AC/HC Garhwal expedition.
   Peak AC 150 is the nearest of the three peaks left of centre. (*Dave Wynne-Jones*)

3. The west ridge of Dhanesh Parvat at dawn. (*Dave Wynne-Jones*)

were singing and a carpet of tiny purple flowers had sprung up in the waterlogged meadows exposed by the melting snow. Back at base camp, the team was unanimous in its recommendation of a name for the mountain – Peak AC 150.

Much debate ensued about our next route. With Chris unwell, Mick, Mark and I geared up for a night out on the upper Barmal glacier whilst Harish's team made an attempt to traverse the Kankul Khal. In the end they had to settle for a 'picnic in the snow' as conditions were far too dangerous for porters to carry loads over the pass. However, the reconnaissance of the glacier yielded good views of the peaks at its head and the Barmal Khal, a newly discovered pass at over 5000m. Unfortunately the north face of Barmal proved to be uniformly threatened by sérac collapse, but the southern glacier approach to unclimbed 5490m Dhanesh Parvat looked objectively safe. Next day we decided to head north, cache camping gear at the foot of that glacier, and descend the ablation valley on the right bank of the Barmal glacier. This descent proved less than straightforward with a long tricky traverse of a crumbling moraine ridge before we could gain that ablation valley and boot-ski down the soft snow. Around base camp yellow azaleas were opening their delicate pale flowers amongst the blowsier purple blooms of dwarf rhododendrons.

Chris recovered, was unhappy about the glacier route and Mark was suffering badly from sunburn so it was just Mick and I who set out next day, with a couple of porters, to bring down Chris's tent. It was a light load and they went off back to base camp, sliding on their bums, whooping and generally enjoying themselves while we went on to make camp.

Next morning we climbed on up the right side of the tributary glacier where avalanche debris from the couloirs of Otika Danda had filled in the crevasses and well away from the séracs piled on the left. At about 5000m we found a reasonably flat site for camp 2, a safe distance from the nearest couloirs, and settled in for a day of dozing. The couloirs had other ideas and from 2pm until 4pm unloaded an impressive tonnage of ice blocks, snow and rocks. Just as we had convinced ourselves that the campsite was safe, the nearest couloir would unleash a particularly loud roar that had us ducking our heads out of the tent door to check through the clouds of ice crystals that we really were sufficiently far from it. By 4pm the cloud build up was enough to take temperatures down and switch off the avalanche machines. Relieved, we had dinner and snoozed on through the evening.

The moon was casting shadow profiles of the ridges of Otika Danda onto the snow as we left at 1am, but it still didn't seem to be cold enough and we found ourselves post-holing at 5200m. The glacier headwall was little better, however a narrow snow ridge running north to a broader saddle led us to firmer snow below the west ridge of Dhanesh Parvat. We took a rest, snacking and gazing over the pre-dawn mountains. North slumbered Tibet while in the east the glow of the coming day built steadily, silhouetting peaks a deep black against the orange sky.

114. Mick Cottam leading the first pitch on the east face of the summit block of Dhanesh Parvat. (*Dave Wynne-Jones*)

The ridge climbed steeply to a narrow crest of snow and rock running into the sheer face of the granite summit block. It looked hard. Several lines might be possible: a steep crack to the left, a wider chimney crack with a couple of wedged chockstones, a zigzag chimney closed at the top with overhanging blocks, a traverse onto the south-west face to gain a snowy gully filled with precariously balanced blocks. All proved too difficult, loose, cold or unstable to commit to, though we spent two hours establishing this.

Conceding defeat we retreated down the ridge; then from below Mick spotted a narrow snow ramp rising under the overhanging north face of the summit monolith. High above the glacier, the doubtful snow seemed on the verge of sliding off into the void. However, we were able to fix runners in the wall above the ramp and two pitches led to the east face of the summit block. Sun-warmed rock just the right side of vertical rose in cracks and spaced narrow ledges above us. Mick led the first pitch, finding it harder and looser than expected. Above I found it harder still. A good nut unlocked a difficult sequence that Mick reckoned was at least British 4c. I don't normally lead 4c in plastic boots but the moves just seemed to be coming together so I went with it. No one conquers a mountain; the mountain whispers the way, but you have to be listening. A poor runner protected a precarious traverse along a narrowing boot ledge before a series of cracks and broken ledges led to easier ground. And suddenly I was there, pulling over the top block to see the glittering ridges of Hathi Parvat beyond and shouting a great 'Yes!' of delight.

Photos, a bite to eat, and we were abseiling down the icy cracks of the west face before carefully reversing the west ridge. By daylight it was possible to avoid the unconsolidated snow of the avalanche cones on the glacier and we made better time back to camp 2. Time enough, at 10.30, to break camp and get back to base camp, though I was wasted by the time I got there! We graded the route D.

Chris and Mark were away, making the first ascent of the peak lying to the east of the Kankul Khal. From a camp below the pass they first ascended a couloir falling west from the north ridge of the main summit. Wet snow on the ridge obliged them to traverse into another rock couloir on the east face that led to the summit. The peak was given 5080m on the map though the GPS reading was lower than AC 150 and the route was graded at about AD. Kankul Peak was recommended for its name.

Having run out of time for another route, the team retraced its steps to Bhuidhar rather faster than expected, leaving time enough for an excursion to Hemkund Sahib, the highest *gurudwara* (Sikh temple) in the world. Each day 5000 Sikhs were passing Bhuidhar on pilgrimage. Whilst the numbers were something of a culture shock after our relatively remote valley there was no denying the determination of whole families, motivated simply by faith, to leave Birmingham or the plains of the Punjab and climb to more than 4000m. I was glad that I hadn't failed my own test of faith all those days ago, knee-deep in wet snow above base camp.

Back at Bhuidhar we held a memorable birthday party, complete with cake, marking 150 years of the Alpine Club. The expedition had been a superb way of celebrating the roots of both the AC and the Himalayan Club in exploratory mountaineering.

Summary: An account of the joint Himalayan Club and Alpine Club expedition to the Kagbhusandi valley, Garhwal Himalaya, to celebrate the 150th anniversary of the AC. The exploration of the valley included first ascents of three 5000m peaks.

Acknowledgements: Particular thanks are due to Harish Kapadia for proposing the expedition and organising arrangements in India, to Mark Higton for co-ordinating the UK end, and to the Alpine Club Climbing Fund for financial support.

115. Party time at the end of the joint AC/HC Garhwal expedition. (*Dave Wynne-Jones*)

HENRY DAY

Climbing and Kalashnikovs, Part II [1]

Look in any *Alpine Journal* up until the 1960s and even an alpine climb is listed as an expedition. Contrast that with more recent accounts about flying to China, completing an amazing route within a fortnight's holiday, and just calling it a climb. Getting to the mountains is the nub of the difference. Overcoming political, bureaucratic and security obstructions can be as much of a challenge as physical obstacles on the mountains. Add to that a particular yen to drive, say, a beloved Land Rover, to distant countries and what you have is definitely an expedition. Any climb in the Caucasus nowadays is certainly an expedition as there are no huts and what little infrastructure there was disappeared with the Soviet Union.

Georgia was just the place to drive to. The Caucasus were long overdue a visit and consulting the Foreign Office website was no more off-putting than usual. Word of my plan got out and I was asked to make it another event to celebrate the 150th anniversary of the Alpine Club. An open invitation was issued to members to come along and an expedition was born.

The climbing area we wanted to visit, the remote valley of Svaneti, was still pretty lawless. In 1998 an AC group had been robbed there at gunpoint – twice. Interestingly, Douglas Freshfield, on a visit in 1887 to climb Tetnuld, had also been robbed, right under the noses of the party's Cossack escort. Since the demise of the Soviet Union, Georgia had experienced the Rose Revolution and other upheavals and kidnappings had been reported. The *Lonely Planet* guidebook advised taking out hostage insurance – but not telling the baddies! Relations with the Russians had taken a turn for the worse with accusations of missiles being fired, spies being deported – and a lot of this near the Abkhazian border where we would have to venture.

To try to mitigate the risks, we took advice from John Town and Derek Buckle and on their recommendation decided to place ourselves under the protection of the Khergiani family who had been so helpful to them in 1998. My namesake Henry (Mushtakiani, married to Maia Khergiani) was in charge of border security and it was arranged for him to come to Tbilisi and escort us from there. We looked like being a team of 12 at one stage, including Alan Scowcroft, the owner of a second Land Rover Defender. Mine – the 'Maschina' – was of 1998 vintage that had been to the Kun Lun in China and back [2] as well as from Alaska to Tierra del Fuego.

1. 'Climbing and Kalashnikovs. The 1998 Alpine Club meet to the Georgian Caucasus' in *AJ* 1999, pp136-146.
2. 'Travels with donkeys in the Kun Lun. British Kun Lun Shan 2001 Expedition' in *HJ* 2002, p126

116. Strategic road to Ushguli in the remote Svaneti valley. (*Henry Day*)

117. Storm clearing over Tetnuld (4852m). (*Henry Day*)

My wife Sara together with the Scowcrofts were to drive out to Georgia. Starting in Italy and continuing in north-east Turkey and Georgia, we were to visit early Christian churches and view their frescoes. This bit of culture was to add purpose to the journey and make it most interesting. We found a neat way of travelling directly from the heel of Italy to Turkey by vehicle ferry that took 33 hours. We were nearly at Bari when we heard the sad news that Alan and his wife were not able to come because of illness in the family. The climbing team now consisted of Mal Bonner and me in my Land Rover to be joined in Tbilisi by Kate Ross and Margaret Graham.

To our delight, the ferry to Cesme, near Izmir, sailed through the Corinth Canal, in places only a couple of metres wider than the ship. Another delight was to find a troupe of Georgian performers on board who gave us a full-dress performance of national songs and dances. We drove on to Georgia via ancient sites in Turkey, to be met at the border by Eliza Khizanishvili who had been engaged as interpreter at the recommendation of another AC member. She accompanied us to Tbilisi. Once there we were in the capable hands of the Khergiani clan.

On 30 August we camped by the Black Sea for the last time, ready for an early border crossing at Sarpi next day. One lesson learnt from several traverses of the former Soviet Union in recent years was to have a friend at border crossings. We had had too many anxious encounters with venal officials and much preferred to pay an agent an agreed fee rather than hand out US$20 bills at every obstruction. We need not have worried. The Turks were efficient and the Georgians most welcoming. The inevitable delay was caused by the sociability of the officials who seemed to have forgotten what they were there to do.

Our Georgian interpreter was not, in the event, able to penetrate the customs area so we got through on our own. However from the border at Sarpi to Tbilisi we were swept along effortlessly. On learning that we needed a shipping agent to get us across the Black Sea at the end of the month, Eliza determinedly tracked one down near the docks at Batumi before announcing that it was perfectly feasible to drive to the capital that afternoon. The route was a major highway used by transcontinental TIR trucks heading for Azerbaijan and land-locked Armenia as well as by herdsmen grazing cattle on the grass verges. Limos with blacked out windows tore past, forcing a third and sometimes even a fourth lane on the single carriageway road. We saw several smashes but somehow made it intact to Tbilisi and our home-stay, just as it got dark. The 265 miles had taken six hours.

Now we could enjoy the hospitality of the clan. Katya Khergiani, sister of Maia with whom we were to stay when we got to Svaneti, was a Moscow graduate but her degree had been gained in Soviet times and her qualifications were no longer needed in Tbilisi. She introduced us to Henry, her brother-in-law, who we took to immediately; an utterly reliable person whose only drawback was that he spoke no English whatever. This was to prove a major problem throughout the trip. The Georgian language and script are unique and even road signs were unfathomable to us. Russian is being displaced by English as the second language but the younger generation that we encountered had yet to progress much with it. More than once we had to use the mobile phone to ask Eliza to interpret. Later on, calls were even made to another sister in New York for the same purpose. Henry recruited an out-of-work geologist friend to drive us to the airport in the dark to meet the Scottish contingent, Kate and Margaret. We learnt that only a few days earlier a group of Latvian tourists in the area to which we were heading had been invited, at gunpoint, to turn out their pockets. Next morning a *marshrutka* minibus joined the Maschina for what was expected to be a 14-hour drive into the Caucasus and the remote valley of the Svans, home of brigands. Our route saw us retracing the main road almost to the Black Sea before turning north to Zugdidi and following the border with Abkhazia all the way to Mestia, regional capital of the Svan, an ancient people. Although part of Georgia, the Abkhaz feel much closer to the Russians; there had been recent shooting incidents with the Georgians and bad feeling existed. It was intriguing that Russian troops at a check-post on the way to the mountains wore blue helmets though not under UN command. We met many Georgian military vehicles heading our way but that may have had nothing to do with the heightened tension reported in the papers over tit-for-tat incidents involving a missile from a Russian plane and the subsequent arrest and expulsion of some Russians on spying charges.

The main hazard to us remained other drivers and the deteriorating roads, now with steep drops into the Inguri river. The saving grace was being in convoy with the *marshrutka* carrying Henry and the Scottish contingent. Its driver was the safest we came across and never exceeded 45mph on even the best stretches, though this did lead to a 16-hour day. Sara and I had shared the driving all the way from Cambridge but I tried to be behind the wheel for the bad bits so I got the final six-hour stretch to Mestia, home of Henry and Maia. The Khergianis even possessed two of the stone defensive towers for which Svaneti is renowned.

Maia's late uncle, Misha Khergiani, had been a famous mountaineer but he was killed in a climbing accident in the Italian Dolomites in 1966. When John Hunt visited the Caucasus in 1958 with a team that included George Band and other AC members, they climbed with Misha and are still fondly remembered. There is now a museum set up in Misha's memory by the Khergiani family and we were shown around by one of the modern generation who did speak English. George had kindly sent us a copy of a photograph he had taken of Misha in 1958 and it is now on display in the museum. Unfortunately we could not find any mountaineers to come with us who spoke English well.

From Mestia three forays were mounted to the Ushba glacier, Tetnuld and Shkara. Whether due to the lateness of the season (September) or global warming, the mountains were unrecognisable from the descriptions supplied by the 1998 AC group.

118. *Above*
Mt Shkara seen from
above 5000m.
(*Henry Day*)

119. *Left*
Mt Shkara and Ushguli,
Georgian Caucasus.
(*Henry Day*)

The Ushba Plateau proved unattainable, denying us several suitable acclimatisation objectives accessible from there. Henry donned his uniform to come with us to Mazeri and from there to the Ushba glacier as it was close to the Abkhaz border and infiltrations were reported. We hired a local 4x4 as it was not safe to leave the Maschina unattended. Lack of accurate information saw us having to unload our horses at a patrol post and backpack the rest of the way through steep and slippery forest. The icefall at the head of the glacier had largely fallen away so the route to the plateau, reached with ease by the previous party only eight years earlier, was impassable. We found the grizzly remains of a former Soviet climber strewn across ice melted by the fierce summer sun. Our Georgian friends planned to give him a decent burial. Rejoining our escort back in the valley we had the opportunity to fire an AK 47 (Kalashnikov) with some success.

The second trip was to Tetnuld (4852m). Once again horses were arranged to carry up equipment for a base camp. Climbing in the Caucasus remains like the Alps before mountain huts, so help is required. We were accompanied by Georgi, a young guide whose mother Nazo Khergiani hosted the AC climbers in 1998. Georgi's father Nugzar Niguriani, a retired guide, proffered advice on the approach to Tetnuld that was at variance with the limited information we had. Instead of leaving a road-head at Adishi, as Freshfield had done, we took a much better ascending traverse from the Ugyr Pass, only 12km from Mestia.

We had great difficulty communicating with Georgi who, whilst clearly doubting our aged competence, expected limitless energy. When he was seen contemplating riding on one of the packhorses (which already carried his pack) leaving our ladies laden with their packs he got a well-earned Scottish wigging. A stage above our camp, the Abalakov bivouac turned out to be a few levelled tent platforms at about 4000 metres. We planned to copy the previous AC party and make a further bivouac below the long summit ridge. Very heavy snow overnight elicited one of Georgi's few English phrases 'good tent'. 'Crevasse bad' was another and next morning with the threat of another storm to come (it didn't) he hurried us off the mountain and we left feeling rather short-changed.

The final foray was to hills beneath Shkara in the remotest part of Svaneti, to the world heritage site of Ushguli with its 20 stone towers. We took the Maschina up an appallingly maintained road that the Soviets had furnished with huge concrete bridges. We stopped by a Lada that had crashed into the river a couple of days before. All three young men in it had perished. We met oxen dragging sledges loaded with fodder cut from the hillside to keep cattle alive throughout the five months of winter. We even saw bent timbers, cut from the woods, that were to be fashioned into new runners for sledges. There were ancient Christian icons and crosses in the newly opened museum, and also in the old church opened for us by a smiling villager. Perhaps it was having Henry with us again, but we were greeted with smiles wherever we went.

At 5210m, Shkara is the highest peak wholly within Georgia. We got the Defender right up the valley beneath the mountain, level with the snout of the glacier, where we found a great campsite in a wide, vegetated valley. Next morning Shkara sparkled above us. Over the centuries, in times of trouble, this valley has been a place of retreat where people could graze their animals way up the hillsides. We split next day to either side of the valley and traversed all the hilltops we could reach in a day, just above the snowline. Some were in addition to those made by the 1998 AC meet. It was a memorable end to the trip in fascinating terrain.

We declined an invitation from Henry Mushtakiani to join a meeting with Russian border officials on our way back past Mazeri, which was just as well as a fire-fight broke out and two Russian officers were shot dead.

We retraced our route to Mestia and on to Tbilisi where Alex, a Russian student from Cambridge, joined Mal and me as an interpreter. The journey back across the Black Sea, Ukraine and Poland was all new to us; not new, however, were the venal officials who seem to be a common legacy of Soviet times. The Maschina re-enacted the charge of the Light Brigade at Balaclava in the Crimea, where Alex left us to return to university for his final term. Mal and I drove back via Lvov and Krakov fairly smartly, covering the last 500 miles to Cambridge in one go. We had been away for eight weeks and driven almost 7000 miles.

Lessons learnt? The support of the Khergianis was wholehearted and quite delightful and made the trip possible. Another time I would seek English speaking Georgian climbers to join the party as well, possibly through the Georgian climbing fraternity. The Georgian Caucasus are well worth rediscovering by members of the Alpine Club who are up for a proper expedition!

Summary: An expedition to the Georgian Causasus, organised by Henry Day as part of the AC's 150th anniversary. Other members: Mal Bonner, Kate Ross and Margaret Graham. On the overland journey out, Sara Day was co-driver and 'cultural adviser'. In Georgia, Eliza Khizanishvili acted as interpreter and Henry Mushtakiani took care of security. On the return journey, Alex Putau acted as Russian interpreter.

ROB COLLISTER

Cambridge in the Late Sixties

Whether the Cambridge University Mountaineering Club in the late sixties was more or less active than at other times I do not know. There was no one as well known as Nick Estcourt, who was just before my time, or Alan Rouse, who was just after. On the other hand, Ken Wilson's anthology *Games Climbers Play* (Diadem, 1978) contains no less than four articles culled from *Cambridge Mountaineering* of that era. Talks in the Downing Site lecture theatre could attract audiences of up to a hundred and we had the chance to listen to the wise, or more often irreverent, words of speakers like Eric Shipton, Tom Patey and a clean-cut young P.E. teacher called Doug Scott. The Freshers' meet in Derbyshire easily filled a coach, but the six o'clock start on a Sunday morning and a three-hour drive each way ensured that a minibus was normally sufficient for outings to gritstone. The active membership in climbing terms was about twenty, though when I organised a weekend in Wales specifically to walk the Fourteen Threes, a totally different set of people emerged. For the demographically-minded, the majority of the club's keenest members were on the Science side rather than the Arts, most came from the North, and women were conspicuous by their absence.

Twenty-five years later, Olly Overstall organised a reunion in North Wales. It was surprisingly well attended. For some, it transpired, climbing at Cambridge had been a hugely enjoyable but brief interlude before embarking on a career. But for many, mountaineering in one form or another continues to fill their leisure time and for Bob Barton and me, Cambridge proved to be an apprenticeship leading to the *Metier du Guide*. For all of us, however, it was an inherently dangerous period in which we learned many lessons the hard way and accidents did occur. The atmosphere was sombre at the first Tuesday tea-time gathering one Lent term. Roger Wilson had been killed during the holiday period, when his gear ripped on the first pitch of *Haste Not* on White Ghyll. I remember all too clearly reading in a Swiss newspaper of the *chute mortelle* of Rollo Davidson and Michael Latham on the Biancograt. There but for the grace of God ... We were ambitious, competitive and, climbing 'not wisely but too well', we had more than our fair share of near-misses.

Of my immediate contemporaries, the leading personality was undoubtedly Mick Guilliard, a good-natured extrovert from Leek, hard by the Roches, with an infectious laugh and an astonishing appetite for beer. We were in the same college and shared digs for a year so I knew him well and

120. *Left*
John Cardy on *Llithrig*,
Clogwyn du'r Arddu.
(*Rob Collister*)

121. *Below*
Cardy – 'shock of red hair and
the enormous forehead of a
boffin' – tip-toeing up the
Bloody Slab, West Buttress,
Clogwyn du'r Arddu, June 1970.
(*Rob Collister*)

put him to bed more than once. As a climber, I was never in the same league but I remember leading through, with trepidation, on an early ascent of *Dream of White Horses* when a fierce wind was blowing spume from the waves and the ropes billowed out in an arc on the final pitch; and again, on *White Slab* on a grey day with no one else around and wreaths of mist drifting in and out behind the Far Far East buttress, adding to the menace of the Black Cliff. And then there was our disastrous first Alpine season along with John Hamilton and Pete Hughes, when two of our three routes involved a forced bivouac and I nearly died when an abseil anchor failed. Although the most accomplished and enthusiastic of us all, once he had qualified as a vet, Mick took up skiing and fell-running and hung his rock-shoes up for good.

John Cardy, with his shock of red hair and the enormous forehead of a boffin, was another distinctive figure. Neither of us was particularly strong in the arms and when we climbed together we usually chose our routes accordingly. We were in our element on the never-ending girdle of the *West* on Cloggy and tip-toed up *Bloody Slab* in good style; but when it came to *Cemetery Gates*, my hands were actually on the belay ledge when my fingers opened and I fell off. I was not to own a harness for another 10 years, but I came to no harm and still have the garage-nut that held me. Adrenalin propelled me back up onto the stance but I was less than pleased when Cardy announced on arrival that he was too pumped to lead the top pitch. With John, too, I spent several dank, autumnal days dangling nervously beneath ludicrous overhangs on limestone aid routes like *Castellan*, *Twilight*, *Hubris* and *The Prow*, all long since freed. John was something of an aficionado. I did not care for aid one bit but felt it was a necessary part of my education.

Rob Ferguson was a geographer whose keen interest in mountains was not just recreational. Unusual in his dislike of technical rock, Rob was a very confident snow and ice climber and became my mentor on early visits to Scotland and the Alps. When a large party was marooned on Tower Ridge at dusk, it was Rob who was dispatched into the infamous gap while the rest of us sang mournful dirges and yelled obscenities into the night to keep the cold at bay. It was Rob who led me up my first ice-climb, *Three Gully Buttress*, cutting steps expertly with a straight-picked axe (though it was Bob Jones and Gordon McNair who saved my life, calmly fielding me when I tripped over my crampons on the descent to the Carn Mor Dearg arête). And it was Rob who had the audacity to suggest attempting first the Fletschhorn and then the Grosshorn north faces at a time when, the Triolet excepted, Brits just did not climb alpine ice. Rob was always very organized. He was the only one of us properly shod when we bivvied on the crest of the Cuillin ridge, one March, prior to a traverse of the main ridge. I was wearing Hush Puppies because of an Achilles tendon problem. Denis Mollison was wearing baseball boots because they were all he had, and during the night it snowed …

Geoff Cohen was another more experienced mountaineer who initially took me under his wing. Geoff was, and is, a delightful person, famous for his inability to make decisions except, fortunately, when climbing. During my first long vac we visited the northern highlands, cheekily knocking on Tom Patey's door in Ullapool and spending a few nights in the bothy at the bottom of his garden. The doctor took us in person to the obscure Alladale Slabs and pointed us at the second ascent of *The Fiddler* on Ben Mor Coigach. One night we joined him in the pub at Inveroykel where closing time was unheard of. Patey was singing and playing his squeeze-box into the wee small hours and beyond, and while we crashed out in a barn nearby he was driving back across Scotland for morning surgery. The following winter Geoff and I teamed up again on Ben Nevis. The week in the CIC hut had started badly when Gordon McNair, the President, was avalanched by a collapsing cornice while soloing an easy gully. As we struggled to splint his leg and put him on a stretcher brought up from the hut, we were all hit by another avalanche and swept further down Coire na Ciste in a tangled mess of bodies and equipment. In retrospect, we were extraordinarily ignorant to have been launching ourselves up snow gullies in semi-tropical conditions. By the end of the week, it was at least colder, but otherwise the weather was atrocious and everyone else was heading downwards as we set off for the North East Buttress. This was regarded as a long, serious climb rather than a hard one, but it felt quite hard enough for me, chipping steps in earnest for the first time. The sense of commitment at the foot of the *Mantrap* in thick mist and a howling gale, the exhilaration of fighting our way over the summit, and the state of contented exhaustion in which we squelched our way down the boggy path in the dark to Fort William, were all new but were to become quite addictive for a few years. It may have been the same occasion when the police moved us on from a comfortable bivouac in a bus shelter. The night being dreadful and the cells full, they found a railway carriage for us instead, first class at that, with the stipulation that we vanish by seven in the morning.

While my friends were pushing their grades in Wales and the Lakes, the whole of my second long vac was taken up by an expedition to the Hindu Kush. I was recruited by a group of ex-CUMC members – Alan Cormack, Dick Metcalfe and John Peck. Peck was a colourful figure with shoulder-length blond hair and an enormous beard, who lived in a garret in Spittalfields, producing what he called 'semi-pornographic' etchings. The overland journey to Pakistan in an old army truck was a six-week epic in which personal relations broke down almost as frequently as the vehicle. The mountains, when we finally reached them, felt like a rest cure by comparison. Before we could climb anything, however, we first had to rendezvous with Henry Day, who we had last seen in the Officers' Mess of the Royal Engineers in Osnabruck. We had arranged to meet at our proposed base camp beside a lake near Sor Laspur in Chitral, but plans changed when we learned that a party of Austrians were at the same site. Having no

22. The bohemian John Peck at high camp on the North Kohistan expedition. (*Rob Collister*)

23. John Peck and Rob Collister with teachers from Bagral Primary School, North Kohistan, 1968. (*Rob Collister*)

124. Mount Ararat, Turkey, passed en route to the North Kohistan, Swat, in 1968 – a six-week epic drive on which 'personal relationships broke down almost as frequently as the vehicle'. (*Rob Collister*)

permit, it seemed tactful to go elsewhere and we ended up on the other side of the watershed in Swat. Unfortunately, there was no way of letting Henry know. In the event, Alan and I missed him by a day, after a week's journey over untrodden glaciers involving rock-fall, an almost fatal crevasse incident and some scary river crossings. I was learning all the time and discovering that mountain travel could be just as rewarding, and as hazardous, as actual climbing. However, my most vivid memory is of meeting, near the lake, a dignified but courteous Chitrali horseman, a falcon on his wrist, a spaniel running to heel and a retainer walking behind carrying a musket and a bag of provisions. Subsequently we climbed a number of peaks just under 6000 metres and I acquired a taste for that sort of exploratory mountaineering which has never left me.

When Dick Isherwood asked me to join a small team going to Chitral the next year, I jumped at the chance. At the time, Dick was one of the best rock climbers in the country as well as a formidable powerhouse in big mountains. In his company, an awestruck youth, I found myself rubbing shoulders in Wales and the Peak with god-like figures such as Crew, Boysen and the wonderfully voluble Holliwell brothers. On that trip I learned a great deal about alpinism from Dick, and from Colin Taylor too, but above all I learned that in the mountains you must seize your chances with both hands. We oh-so-nearly climbed Thui II, a beautiful peak at the head of the

125. Dick Isherwood at the bivouac on Thui II, Chitral, August 1969. 'We oh-so-nearly climbed it.' (*Rob Collister*)

Yarkhun valley, but we bivouacked early and the weather broke during the night. We were prevented from making a second attempt by our liaison officer, an extremely unpleasant man who later had us turned back at the Khyber Pass because of 'currency irregularities' and did his best to have me thrown in jail.

Skiing was not a sport that appealed to climbers in those days, but I had been on a couple of school ski trips and I was inspired by a picture in Alan Blackshaw's *Mountaineering* (Penguin Books, 1965) of a mountain tent guyed down with skis in a blizzard. Chris Barry was equipped with my Mum's edgeless skis from the thirties, given a day's tuition in Coire Cas and then dragged off over the Cairngorm plateau to Ben Macdui. I was hooked even

126. CUMC Sixties style: David Gundry at Chair Ladder, Cornwall, January 1968.
(*Rob Collister*)

if Chris was not, and the next winter a Land Rover-full of us, including Tim Nulty, an American economist who had been enormously helpful in Pakistan the previous summer, the bohemian Peck and David Gundry, companion on many an escapade before and after, set off on a three-day marathon drive to the Bernese Oberland. Christof Lehrner, a guide in the Lötschental, lent us a straw-filled barn to stay in, warmed from below by cattle and sheep, and a day tour in his company taught us a lot about skins and kick-turns, though not, alas, how to ski difficult snow. Even snapping my brand-new skis, four days stormbound in the unguarded Hollandia hut and a sightless descent in total whiteout did not diminish my enthusiasm for ski-mountaineering.

Times change but topography does not and Cambridge has never been the ideal location for a climber. Purpose-built climbing walls were still in the future, but the notion of training for performance must have been gaining ground, for no sooner had the old lime-kiln at Cherry Hinton, with its carefully chipped if rather slippery holds, been blown up on safety grounds, than the energetic development of disused railway bridges began. The arrival of Harold Gillespie and Mick Geddes from Edinburgh with tales of the Currie Walls must have had something to do with it.

Of course, generations of Cambridge climbers had found adventure aplenty on their doorstep, at night. Geoffrey Winthrop Young with his pre-First World War *Roof Climbers Guide to Trinity* was only perpetuating a tradition which found its finest expression in the thirties with Whipple-snaith's *Night Climbers of Cambridge*. The sixties' contribution to the genre by Hederatus did not match the whimsy and humour of that classic, but it reflects the secretive nature of the activity that I never knew who wrote it. For myself, I loved the heightened awareness created by the dark and the illicit, the sense of being privy to a totally different night-time world when the only other signs of life in the silent town were perhaps a solitary light high up in a tower window or the hooting of an owl. Most of the keenest climbers of my time, though, did not much care for night climbing, with its need for stealth and silence. The metallic clink of a karabiner or the briefest flash of a headtorch could be enough to betray one to a prowling bulldog and the authorities suffered from a sense of humour failure when it came to night climbing, especially on Kings.

Kings is the most famous route in Cambridge and it certainly has some unique situations, but John's is the better climb. It offers laybacking, bridging, a delicate slab, and a final strenuous overhang in a superb position; there is even an easy descent if you have played your cards right. Dick Isherwood described it as 'the finest Severe in England' and he was probably right. One ambition I never achieved was the Senate House Leap. Chris Barry had a room ideally situated high up in Caius. One night we used a plank to measure the distance and practised standing jumps in the corridor. Neither of us could ever quite make the chalk mark on the floor and discretion proved the better part of valour; though on another occasion, after a dinner, Chris used the same plank to walk across.

Night climbing skills could be deployed in other contexts, too. During the Europe-wide student unrest of 1968 there was a sit-in at the Old Schools which I was able to drop in and out of as I chose. It was good fun though I cannot for the life of me remember what we were protesting about. During my final year my wife-to-be, Netti, was at Newnham. Visitors had to be out of the college by 10pm which seemed unduly restrictive so we kept a rope under her bed. Abseiling out of the window into the garden was given an added frisson by a don occupying the room below.

I suppose I had a rather cavalier attitude towards my degree. Hours spent gazing out of the UL at clouds and trees along with subversive texts by Thoreau, Richard Jeffries and Henry Williamson, convinced me that whatever I did in the future was going to be out of doors. In my fourth, final year, the university careers department, mystified by this attitude, arranged only one interview for me, with a firm of rubber traders in Malaysia. Fortunately help was at hand in the form of Noel Odell. Odell was in his eighties then, but still very fit and spry. He had a weakness for crumpets and used to call round at tea-time, usually on a Monday, to compare notes about the weekend. On one occasion, staying at the Pen y Gwryd hotel for a C.C. dinner, he had walked over the Glyders on Saturday and up Snowdon on the Sunday and was full of it when we met. Mick Guilliard, who had also been up to Wales, had already told me at breakfast that the weather had been so vile that they had spent the entire weekend in Wendy's café and the Padarn ... It was Odell who introduced me to the Alpine Club, driving me up to London in his Mini a number of times and later proposing me for membership. Like many of his generation, it seemed, he was a great raconteur, and I loved listening to his stories of Everest and Nanda Devi.

From Odell I learned that the British Antarctic Survey employed mountaineers for its fieldwork and that Sir Vivien Fuchs was giving a public lecture the following week. One thing led to another and a year 'on the ice' with a dog-team made it even less likely that I could settle into an office job or endure the rigours of the chalk-face. Eventually, I drifted into instructing and guiding almost by default, but I have never regretted it, the boundary between work and play often blurring. Looking back, I can see that my years at Cambridge (Selwyn 1966-70) were not just enormous fun, but they gave me a profession, a spouse and some life-long friends. What more could one ask of a university education?

The year 2006 was the centenary of the Cambridge University Mountaineering Club. The Club committee organised a special dinner, which was well attended, and solicited past members for contributions to a commemorative book. This piece was one of those contributions, although the book itself has so far – August 2008 – not materialised.

Mountains:
people, environment & science

Rowan Huntley *Mont Blanc ~ Sunset Glow, April*
Chroma on canvas, 50cm x 75cm

128. Remnants of penitentes, the wind-sculpted ice figures that once guarded the approaches to Aconcagua; these on the Relinchos glacier at c4800m. As the world has warmed, the fields of penitentes have withered. (*Stephen Goodwin*)

Summits of Learning

The AC Seminar on 150 Years of Mountaineering, Mountains and Science

As part of the AC's 150th anniversary celebrations, our member Martin Price, professor of mountain studies at the University of the Highlands and Islands, organised a seminar in London to highlight the radical, and accelerating processes of change that have been underway in mountain environments over the Club's lifetime. Entitled *Summits of Learning: 150 Years of Mountaineering, Mountains and Science*, the day-long event was held at the Swiss Embassy on 4 December and followed by a reception hosted by the Ambassador of Switzerland, Alexis Lautenberg.

While the reception proved a most enjoyable and comfortable soirée, the seminar might best be described as 'stimulating but disturbing'. As one professor after another detailed the consequences of global warming and people pressure on glaciers, plants and downstream populations, the summary that sprang most readily to mind came not from an academic but from Corporal Frazer of *Dad's Army*: 'Doom, doom …We're all doomed.'

For AC members among the 60 people who attended, the facts of glacier retreat and forest degradation were not exactly a blinding revelation – we've been observing it first hand for years. None the less, when glaciologist Wilfried Haeberli of the University of Zurich warned that even on a modest scenario for global warming most glacier ice will be gone from the Alps by 2050, mountaineers winced. The idea of only slivers of glacier left clinging to Mont Blanc and Monte Rosa is quite shocking.

That, of course, is only the selfish climber's reading of the consequences; far more serious, as Haeberli and hydrologist Rolf Weingartner of the University of Berne made clear, is the impact on agriculture and cities on the plains as changed water flow patterns result in drought and floods. Weingartner called for a 'revolution' in water management, the probable alternative, it seemed, in parts of the world such as the Nile region, being war.

Mountains, their environments, communities and vital importance as 'water towers' for the plains, gained a foothold on the international political agenda in 1992, with recognition in Agenda 21 at the UN Earth Summit in Rio de Janeiro. AC honorary member Bruno Messerli, also of the University of Berne and centrally involved in developing the mountain chapter in Agenda 21, said mountains had become a new priority for the scientific and political communities. 'The mountains have a new significance since it has become clear that climate change will first influence these very vulnerable and sensitive ecosystems.' he said.

Research thus becomes increasingly important, not least to make the case for difficult political steps. What then? Even in the event of global warming being stemmed, the mountain world is going to take some time to return to the state in which the AC pioneers found it 150 years ago. In the words of Professor Haeberli: 'Earth will probably need 70,000 years to forget the experiment man is doing now.'

The seminar report that follows opens with a scene-setter by Ed Douglas on the relationship between science, mountaineering, exploration and the Alpine Club followed by abstracts from key speakers. Professor Messerli's article updates his seminar contribution with the very welcome agreement by the UN of a resolution on sustainable mountain development. The report concludes with an article by US geographer Alton Byers on landscape change, particularly in the Everest area, and the remedial work of the Alpine Conservation Partnership. Byers expands on his contribution at the seminar and points to at least one way in which climbers might make amends for their own guilty part, as adventure tourists, airline users and global consumers, in these crises of the mountains.

Stephen Goodwin

SCIENCE AND MOUNTAINEERING
Ed Douglas

Had you been leaving church in the country surrounding London on a winter Sunday morning in the 1880s you might have encountered a group of a dozen or so middle-aged men, some of them powerfully bearded, rushing past the lych gate. This group had not been in church on their knees, like the rest of the population. In fact, their walks were a deliberate escape from worship because these men were not muscular Christians. They were muscular agnostics.

Leading the way, metaphorically if not literally, was Leslie Stephen, former president of the Alpine Club and recently at work on his new *Dictionary of National Biography*. Quite a few of his walking companions on what were dubbed Sunday Tramps would be among the entries of the first edition. If they were talking at all, it was to argue about the great intellectual debates of the day. And in that fashion the procession of jurists and philosophers, journalists and engineers and poets, all of them connected in some way to the angular form of Stephen, marched along country lanes in rude intellectual health.

One of their number was Francis Edgeworth, the influential economist then teaching at King's College, London. He pursued a kind of proto game theory, an early explorer of ideas that seem very contemporary. Born in County Longford, Edgeworth had an unquenchable passion for life, as a friend explained after his death:

'He was an insatiable reader, but his love of walking, mountaineering, golf, and boating, with his strict and regular habits, maintained to the last his wonderful vitality. Every summer, even at the age of 80, he used to bathe before breakfast, and he would often be seen riding his bicycle in the country round Oxford or playing on the course at Cowley. But as a walker he was perhaps most indefatigable; and he was the life and soul of those Sunday tramps. To a courtly grace, derived perhaps from his Spanish mother, he added the Irish characteristics of humour, imagination and generosity. He was the merriest of men, and seemed to possess the secret of perpetual youth, both of mind and of body.'

Like Stephen, Edgeworth was also a founding editor of the *Economic Journal*, a position he held until his death. His successor was John Maynard Keynes, a friend of George Mallory, another link between Stephen's mountaineering world and the Bloomsbury group.

Edgeworth, whose long life spanned the most extraordinary period in British history, was born eight years after Victoria came to the throne and died eight years after the shock of the Great War. I don't know if he was a member of the Alpine Club, but he illustrates how physically vigorous the Victorian intelligentsia often was. Much of society now forgets how physical most of human history has been.

These men, and alas they were almost always men, did not stay in their ivory towers. They roamed across the Earth. The same restless, assured ambition that brought Empire and industrialisation was also present in science. Charles Darwin endured seasickness and fever to sail round the world on the *Beagle*. In 1846, Darwin's bulldog, Thomas Huxley, sailed on the *Rattlesnake* to explore New Guinea and Australia. In 1849 Darwin's friend and correspondent Joseph Hooker was detained in the wilds of Sikkim for illegally crossing the border into Tibet.

So much of nature still waited for a scientific explanation to overtake the version offered by the Book of Genesis that physical exploration and scientific discovery became for a short while intertwined. And, for a while at least, the Alpine Club was caught up in that too.

Historians often portray the Alpine Club as a conglomerate of predictable lawyers and clergymen, and mountaineering as just another bourgeois summer pastime for the middle classes with time on their hands. Sporting clubs were appearing all over Britain at this time. But those lawyers were often radical Liberals, like the great James Bryce, and many of the clergymen leaned towards Anglicanism of the socialist Franklin Maurice. Then there were agnostics like Stephen. There was something surprisingly subversive about the early Alpine Club, which is partly what the Establishment reacted against in 1865 following the Matterhorn tragedy.

Part of that whiff of challenge was also reflected in the Alpine Club's early connections to science. Because while there have always been a surprisingly large number of great scientists with a passion for the mountains and mountaineering, in the mid nineteenth century, mountains were the focus for great scientific discoveries. They were the zeitgeist, in the way that quantum mechanics or artificial intelligence was in the 20th century.

There is a seamless progression from Alexander von Humboldt to the zoologist, geologist and glaciologist Louis Agassiz, whose book *Études sur les Glaciers* transfixed Victorian England, to J D Forbes, who met Agassiz at a British Association meeting in Edinburgh, later working with him in the Alps. After which, in the way of these things, they fell out, starting a cascade of squabbles and spats that punctuated scientific exploration and the history of the Alpine Club equally.

Agassiz and other glaciologists were promoting the idea of an Ice Age to a general public infused with Romantic ideas of the sublime. Suddenly, here was science, a physical understanding of the world, which matched the scale and scope of philosophy. Coleridge asked who could not believe in God after seeing a glacier. Shelley, who pointedly signed himself into his hotel in Chamonix as *atheos*, or atheist, found in glaciers evidence of a random and remorseless natural world. After visiting the Glacier des Bossons, he wrote of glaciers as agents of cataclysmic upheaval and personal annihilation. The possibility of a new Ice Age was for Shelley 'sublime but gloomy'. How ironic, then, that it is the retreat of glaciers that is alerting humanity to a possible apocalypse.

So for a while, leading up to the formation of the Alpine Club, Western society's understanding of nature was undergoing an extraordinary change, both scientifically and culturally, with each feeding off the other. And some of the protagonists in that change met at the Alpine Club. John Ruskin is an obvious example, as is Stephen, and there are others, like Thomas Bonney, but one man stands out in particular as both a leading mountaineer and a leading scientist, John Tyndall.

Tyndall was born in 1820 at Leighlin Bridge in County Carlow. He left school at 17, with no chance of going to university but with a solid grounding in maths. He worked as a surveyor, first in Ireland and later in England, but was sacked by the Ordnance Survey after complaining about how the Survey was managed and its treatment of Irish employees. He worked variously as a private surveyor on the railways and as a maths teacher at Queenwood College in Hampshire. He befriended the science teacher there, Edward Frankland, and together they travelled to Marburg for a scientific education.

Tyndall was by now 28. He had his doctorate within two years, despite being required to study in German, and stayed on in Germany to do further research on magnetism and diamagnetic polarity. It was while a student that he discovered the Alps, walking all the way from Marburg 'trusting to my legs and my stick, repudiating guides, eating bread and milk, and sleeping in country villages where nobody could detect my accent'.

He was an indomitable man, truly self-made. His work on magnetism in Germany brought him to the attention of the British scientific establishment and he became friends with men like Michael Faraday and in particular Thomas Huxley, who shared his passion for the mountains. His first lecture to the Royal Institution was so successful that they invited him to do another, and then a series of lectures, and then offered him a job. Seven years after walking to the Alps as an impecunious student he was back with Huxley, climbing Mont Blanc for three years in a row and doing experiments while he was about it.

He was a truly great mountaineer. In 1858, four years after the so-called Golden Age of Alpinism began with the ascent of the Wetterhorn, Tyndall made a daring and controversial ascent of Monte Rosa, revealing his qualities as an alpinist, just as his lectures at the Royal Institution revealed his qualities as a scientist. 'It is an entirely new experience to be alone amid these scenes of majesty and desolation. The peaks wear a more solemn aspect, the sun shines with a purer light into the soul, the blue of heaven is more awful . . . the feeling of self-reliance is very sweet, and you contract a closer friendship with the universe than when you trust to the eye and arm of your guide.'

His greatest climb was the first ascent of the Weisshorn by its east ridge in 1861. Remoter than the Matterhorn, perhaps less dramatic and as a consequence less prized by the public, it is for climbers, discerning ones anyway, just as appealing a prize. Leslie Stephen called it 'an almost faultless mountain'. It took Tyndall and his guides 19 hours to reach the summit, which when you consider he spent much of his life in poor health is extraordinary. He also came close to the first ascent of the Matterhorn in 1862, missing out to Edward Whymper who rather wrote down Tyndall's contribution in his classic account *Scrambles in the Alps*. Tyndall's own memoir appeared in the same year but was called *Hours of Exercise in the Alps*. Titles are everything.

At the same time as his mountaineering career was reaching its crescendo, he did the scientific work for which he is perhaps now best remembered, the absorption of infrared light or 'radiant heat' as it was then known, by different gases. In 1859, the year he first explored the Matterhorn, he designed an elegant piece of apparatus to test this and within six months had concrete results. Oxygen and nitrogen, which make up 99 percent of the atmosphere, were almost transparent to it. Trace gases like carbon dioxide, water vapour and ozone were almost opaque. Tyndall found that water vapour was the most potent greenhouse gas by far and concluded that water vapour must 'form one of the chief foundation-stones of the science of meteorology.'

These were powerful insights but the marriage of science and mountaineering couldn't last. It was, however, the mountaineers who instigated the divorce. In 1862 Leslie Stephen read a paper to the Alpine Club that mocked the utilitarian value of climbing a mountain during an imaginary ascent of the Ober Gabelhorn:

"'And what philosophical observations did you make?" will be the inquiry of one of those fanatics who, by a reasoning process to me utterly inscrutable, have somehow irrevocably associated alpine travelling with science. To them

I answer that the temperature was approximately (I had no thermometer) 212 degrees (Fahrenheit) below freezing point. As for ozone, if any existed in the atmosphere, it was a greater fool than I take it for. As we had, unluckily, no barometer, I am unable to give the usual information as to the extent of our deviation from the correct altitude, but the federal map fixes the height at 13,855 feet.'

A smart-arse, was Leslie Stephen, and his more serious point was lost on Tyndall, who was deeply offended and resigned his membership of the Alpine Club, despite having just been made a vice-president. The climbing didn't finish though, and in 1868 he made the first traverse of the Matterhorn aged 48. Cleverly, he waited until his mid 50s before he married, very happily, although his death some years later was caused by his wife's tragic misreading of the label on a bottle of medicine. Both husband and wife, almost immediately aware of her error, knew he was doomed.

Tyndall's legacy has comfortably outlasted Stephen's, through the money he bestowed on universities from his lectures, for example, and through his work which is continued by institutions like the Tyndall Centre for Climate Change. But the physical restlessness that also characterised Tyndall is echoed in the career of scientists who have followed in his footsteps, like the glaciologist Lonnie Thompson whose work on tropical ice cores has been so influential in the climate change debate. The antipathy has continued too. One of Thompson's colleagues, the British glaciologist John Mercer, famous for doing his field work in the nude, fell out spectacularly with another president of the Alpine Club, Eric Shipton, on the Patagonian Ice Cap a century after Stephen and Tyndall squabbled.

That antagonism is fascinating to me, a microcosm of the two cultures immortalised by C P Snow. It's the tension between two questions, why we live, and how we live. Scientists are useful for the first, artists for the second, that's the way we tend to look at it. But I think evolutionary psychologists, in particular, would find a proper look at climbing mountains a useful exercise. You can measure air pressure on a mountain, so why not the mind? What is so precious up there that it's worth risking your life for? So far, that question has largely remained the domain of artists.

Samuel Coleridge, for example, captured the state of mind of a risk-taker as well as anyone before or since. 'There is one sort of Gambling, to which I am much addicted;' he wrote to his lover Sara Hutchinson after his experience on Broad Stand in 1802. 'When I find it convenient to descend from a mountain, I am too confident and too indolent to look round about and wind about 'till I find a track or other symptom of safety; but I wander on, and where it is first *possible* to descend, there I go – relying upon fortune for how far down this possibility will continue.'

Not good mountaineering practice, but I love the phrase 'symptom of safety', treating security as though it were a disease. He is caught up in the immediacy of feeling, half thrilled half terrified, as he contemplates climbing and jumping between each terrace and ledge. Finally, the prospect of the

129. *Right*
John Tyndall:
a passion for science
and daring alpinism.
(*Alpine Club Photo Library*)

130. *Left*
Leslie Stephen:
precipitated 'divorce'
between mountaineering
and science.
(*Alpine Club Photo Library*)

next hard move is too much and he is forced to lie down to recover his equilibrium. 'O God, I exclaimed aloud – how calm, how blessed am I now – I know not how to proceed, how to return, but I am calm and fearless and confident.'

The question is, why? It's one of the great paradoxes of human beings that we want security but are bored by it. I once interviewed the psychologist Steven Pinker and was discussing with him the alleged crisis among men in modern Western society. He described to me the circumstances of our social groupings, in which we evolved. 'Small groups of men,' he said, 'working together in a risky environment to solve problems. That's what makes us happy.' That does sound remarkably familiar.

Of course we have an innate desire to seek security, both in terms of the resources we can draw on to survive and bring up children, and in security from threat. But we also have the tools to face an environment that is more dangerous than the one we have created for ourselves. Solving problems, facing risk and working as a team make us happy as individuals. They are their own reward. It is under these circumstances that our brains are doing what they are designed for. Take away risk and adventure – in their broadest meanings – and the kind of boredom that leads to drug abuse and joyriding can prosper. But no one *wants* to live in a dangerous environment, at least not for long. Both Reinhold Messner and Doug Scott have written that the sweetest moment in an expedition is the moment just before you reach base camp, when the climb is almost over.

Mountaineering's image is of an exciting but dangerous enterprise that adds lustre to an individual's reputation as a risk-taker, someone who is determined to live life to the full. Francis Edgeworth would have understood that gamble. For me, it is a satisfying way to live, a way to calm a restless spirit. But climbing is a little world, and ultimately a small but satisfying glimpse of heaven. I think George Mallory understood that even as he set out for Everest for one more try. Knowing John Maynard Keynes and the Bloomsbury set left him with the sense that the world he had chosen was too small to realise his ambition. He guessed, I suppose, that the greatest explorers were never those seeking new shores or hacking through jungles. Those fellows were just the pretty assistants. The real magicians are those with minds agile enough to discover what is both true and unknown, about the world we live in and the way we are.

Right

131. Grenz glacier between Monte Rosa (*left*) and Liskamm. By 2050 this could be among the few slivers of glacier left in the Alps.
      (*Stephen Goodwin*)

THE ALPS WITHOUT ICE?
Wilfried Haeberli

Snow and ice have very different characteristics and functions in high-mountain landscapes. Snow primarily depends on short-term weather conditions and constitutes a *'nervous interface'* with respect to processes and interactions between the atmosphere, the earth surface and living conditions for plants, animals, and humans. Glaciers, on the other hand, are *'safe indicators'* of integrated climatic changes. The global trend of shrinking glaciers is a key indication of worldwide and rapid changes in the complex climate system. Such changes also induce strong effects and long-term disequilibria within deep layers of perennially frozen slopes (permafrost), mainly found above the Alpine timberline. Due to the slow diffusion of heat in the ground, the response of permafrost – the *'invisible deep disturbance'* – to climate change involves a large inertia, but will continue for a very long time (centuries to millennia).

Changes in the snow and ice of high-mountain areas are primarily driven by climate and have taken place in recent decades on a worldwide scale and at high, if not increasing, rates. In the Alps, glaciers lost about half their total volume (roughly 0.5% per year) between 1850 and around 1975, another 25% (or 1% per year) of the remaining amount between 1975 and 2000, and additional 10 to 15% (or 2 to 3% per year) in the first 5 years of this century.

During the 20th century, the warming of permafrost on mountain summits, due to atmospheric temperature rise, reached depths of more than 50 metres. Realistic climate-change scenarios for the Alps indicate that glaciers could largely disappear in coming decades, and that increasing thermal anomalies are likely to affect permafrost down to 100 metres or more, causing deep thaw, penetration of water in ice-filled crack systems and, hence, reduced slope stability and increasing probability of large rock falls above timberline. Seasonal snow may become restricted to high altitudes and a few winter months.

Such developments mean that we are moving ever further from documented past conditions and empirical knowledge. More and more pronounced disequilibria are likely to develop in the water cycle, mass wasting processes, river sediment fluxes, and growing conditions of vegetation. Far beyond the Alps, the combination of earlier snow melt, reduced summer precipitation and vanishing melt water from glaciers may cause serious long-lasting droughts towards the end of hot-dry summers, which could become much more frequent. On the other hand, the decreasing proportion of solid winter precipitation may reduce the dampening effect of mountains with regard to floods during the cold season, which could become wetter than now. As a consequence, too little as well as too much water could constitute an essential large-scale threat from the Alps without ice.

Professor Wilfried Haeberli, Geography Department, University of Zurich, has contributed to all of the reports of the Intergovernmental Panel on Climate Change (IPCC). In 1986 he was appointed director of the World Glacier Monitoring Service.

150 YEARS OF MOUNTAIN MEDICINE
Jim Milledge

When the AC was formed in 1857, our understanding of medicine and physiology was primitive compared to today. For instance, the germ theory of disease was not established and it was another 40 years before the role of oxygen lack and carbon dioxide in breathing was demonstrated. As a result of ascents to high altitude in balloons and on mountains, descriptions of acute mountain sickness, as we would now call it, *did* exist; however, they were mixed with the effects of cold and exhaustion and some seem bizarre to us now.

JS Haldane led an important early Anglo-American expedition to Pikes Peak in 1911 to study the same subject. His work on the mechanisms of altitude acclimatization has withstood the test of time, though the claim that the lungs secrete oxygen was disproved by Joseph Barcroft, who led another Anglo-American expedition to Peru in 1920. A further international expedition to Chile in 1935 undertook studies up to 6140m. The seven Everest expeditions between the wars yielded very little medical scientific data, though they did stimulate interest in the subject.

In 1952, on a pilot expedition to Cho Oyu (8140m), Griffith Pugh studied climbing at high altitude with supplementary oxygen, providing data for the design of an oxygen climbing set. Together with Pugh's insistence on the importance of adequate fluid for climbers at altitude, these were the crucial factors enabling the British to succeed on Everest in 1953 where the Swiss had failed in 1952.

Following these two expeditions, Pugh and Edmund Hillary organised a major scientific expedition, the 'Silver Hut' in 1960-61, on which scientists spent the winter at 5800m before accompanying climbers on an attempt to climb Makalu (8481m). The objective was to study the mechanisms of really long-term acclimatisation at great altitude. In 1981, John West led an American Medical Research Expedition to Everest with similar objectives – but with more modern equipment more could be done. Barometric pressure and temperature were measured on the summit for the first time, and alveolar gas samples were taken there together with blood samples from subjects on the South Col. In direct descent was the mammoth 2007 Caudwell Xtreme Everest Expedition involving 10 summit climbers, 30 or so scientists, and 200 trekkers who acted as subjects. All were studied in London, Kathmandu, Namche, Pheriche, and Base Camp, with further

Left

132. The Silver Hut on site on the upper Mingbo glacier just east of Ama Dablam in the Everest region of Nepal, winter 1960-61. The altitude is 5800m where the barometric pressure is just half that at sea level. This was our home and laboratory for the winter. (*Jim Milledge*)

133. Inside the Silver Hut, John West acting as subject for a control of breathing study. He is breathing from one of the big bags via one-way respiratory valves. The gas mixtures were made up to have varying percentages of oxyygen and carbon dioxide. We measured his ventilation with the gas meter (green box) and collected samples of his alveolar gas (from deep in the lungs) via the device to the left of his face. The results gave us a measure of the change in his sensitivity to carbon dioxide and oxygen lack (hypoxia) with acclimatisation. (*Jim Milledge*)

studies on the core group in the Western Cwm and South Col. Arterial samples for blood gas were taken up to 8400m. In all, some 30 projects were undertaken.

All these expeditions concentrated mainly on the physiology of acclimatization, but the diseases of altitude were being studied at the same time by others. We now recognise three: acute mountain sickness (AMS), high-altitude cerebral edema (HACE), and high-altitude pulmonary edema (HAPE). AMS, a self-limiting condition characterised by headache, nausea, vomiting, and misery, gradually became recognised by the mountaineering world, especially as more people travelled faster to higher altitudes. HAPE and HACE can be fatal in a few hours or days. In the last 40 years, studies have shown that various drugs can help, though the most important action is to get the patient down.

Dr Jim Milledge has been involved in high-altitude medicine and physiology since 1960 when he was a member of the 'Silver Hut' scientific and mountaineering expedition. A general and respiratory physician, he retired from the NHS in 1995.

MOUNTAIN WATERS:
THEIR SIGNIFICANCE IN A CHANGING WORLD
Rolf Weingartner

More and more people are obliged to share the world's water resources and this has far-reaching consequences with regard to food supplies. From the agricultural point of view, a distinction is made between *blue* and *green* water. Blue water flows into rivers and can be used for irrigation. Today, around 20 per cent of food production comes from irrigated land. Green water, which supplies all non-irrigated vegetation, and is present in the root zone, is far more important, contributing 80 per cent of food production.

In view of this pressure on water supplies, mountain water resources are becoming increasingly important. The particular hydrological characteristics of mountain areas can be summarised as follows: (1) considerable runoff as a result of higher orographic precipitation; (2) seasonal delay of runoff owing to the accumulation of winter precipitation in the form of snow and ice; (3) highly reliable runoff resulting from the regularity of the snow and ice melt.

Mountains cover approximately 20 per cent of the Earth's land surface (excluding Antarctica and Greenland) but account for some 30 per cent of total mean runoff (blue water). If only non-tropical regions are considered, the corresponding figures are 24 per cent of surface area and 46 per cent of runoff. For example, the runoff from the Swiss Alps represents 44 per cent of the total volume of the Rhine, although the Alpine part of the catchment is only 15 per cent of the river's total catchment area. In arid and semi-arid regions, this function of mountains as water towers is even more marked: in such areas, over 90 per cent of runoff originates in the uplands, as in the case of the Niger, Nile and Colorado rivers. In the drier lowland areas that rely on this runoff, disputes concerning the use of the water have sometimes led to violence. In the case of the Nile, the former Egyptian foreign minister and UN secretary-general Boutros Boutros-Ghali has expressed the fear that, 'The next war in our region will be over the waters of the Nile, not over politics.'

The latest report of the Intergovernmental Panel on Climate Change (IPCC) states categorically that global warming is a fact and that it is influencing hydrological processes. Mountain areas are especially affected; here the seasonal distribution of runoff is governed by the melting of snow and glaciers – ie those processes that are particularly affected by climate change. For this reason, the seasonal runoff pattern in the Swiss Alps, for example, is bound to change; at the same time, total annual runoff will decrease. This will have consequences for populations downstream; such consequences will be far more serious in Third World countries where the pressure on (mountain) water resources will rise sharply if there is both a marked decrease in precipitation and a rapid growth in population.

International cooperation and solidarity are required if we are to find solutions to these problems, for example by improving water management or cross-border river basin planning, as well as improvements in agriculture. At the same time, the needs of mountain populations must not be ignored, although they represent a minority with only 12 per cent of the world's population.

Professor Rolf Weingartner, Geographical Institute of the University of Berne, has focused on the development of the Hydrological Atlas for Switzerland. He was a scientific expert in a World Bank project to save the Aral Sea and has made many visits to Nepal, Pakistan and China within the 'People and Resource Dynamics in Watersheds of the Hindu Kush – Himalaya' project.

UPWARDLY MOBILE PLANTS
Harald Pauli

The alpine life zone comprises the high mountain area above the treeline. It can be sub-divided into an alpine belt with closed dwarf vegetation and a rock-, scree- and snow-dominated nival belt, where plants only sparsely occur. A common characteristic of all high mountain ranges, in the tropics as well as in temperate or polar latitudes, is that their plant life is controlled by low-temperature conditions. Accelerating climate warming may therefore threaten a unique and outstandingly rich biodiversity treasure when lowland species invade into the alpine belt.

Already in the 19th century, botanists were searching for the upper limits of mountain plants in the European Alps and they have left invaluable data. The oldest reliable information dates back to 1835: Swiss clergyman and naturalist Oswald Herr made the first ascent of Piz Linard, the highest peak of Silvretta in the central Alps, and found a single patch of *Alpine androsace* in the summit area. Seven subsequent visits between 1864 and 2003 showed a successive increase in species numbers on this summit, where 12 different nival plant species now live. The changes on Piz Linard were not an exception. More than 30 other historic summit sites have been re-surveyed since the late 1980s, providing evidence of obvious increases in species richness. Apparently, plants were migrating upward in the course of climate warming during the 20th century.

These findings gave rise to the establishment of high-resolution permanent plots in the high central Alps and to model predictions which suggested a drastic decrease of cold-adapted species as climate warming continues. A temperature increase of + 5°C, which is within the range forecast for the end of this century, would result in an upward shift of bio-climatic zones by more than 700m. At least in the mid- to longer term, this could lead to the disappearance of many alpine regions.

Ecologists have so far been in a difficult situation when asked for the rate of the expected losses. Consequently, at the turn of the millennium, an international network of standardised permanent observation sites was created. This *Global Observation Research Initiative in Alpine Environments* (GLORIA: www.gloria.ac.at) attempts to operate as an early warning system for an increasingly threatened high mountain biodiversity. It began in 18 European mountain regions and is now active in 53 mountain regions on five continents. A low-cost monitoring approach aligned to summit zones, and a worldwide community of concerned ecologists have made it possible to include remote regions in the Andes and in the eastern Himalaya. Resurveys at intervals of 5 to 10 years should allow the comparison of actual changes across mountain regions.

In summer 2008, the first major re-investigation took place across the mountains of Europe, from the Mediterranean to the sub-arctic. Some recent changes can already be visualised: (1) advances of alpine treelines, as seen in the Urals; (2) an expansion of alpine plants and a concurrent decline of nival species in the high Alps within a single decade. Both are very likely to result from ongoing climate warming.

Dr Harald Pauli is a member of the high mountain research group at the Department of Conservation Biology, Vegetation and Landscape Ecology, University of Vienna. He is scientific co-ordinator of the Global Observation Research Initiative in Alpine Environments (GLORIA).

DEVELOPMENT OF A GLOBAL MOUNTAIN POLICY
Bruno Messerli

The last 20 years have seen a new priority given by both the scientific and political communities towards the mountains. In a great surprise, on 12 December 2007 the United Nations General Assembly accepted a detailed resolution recognising the 'crucial' importance of sustainable mountain development and calling on governments to act. Coming just eight days after the AC's 'Summits of Learning' seminar, perhaps we can think of this as the last great gift in the Alpine Club's 150th anniversary year.

Key among the 42 paragraphs was the Assembly's recognition of, 'the global importance of mountains as the source of most of the Earth's fresh water, as repositories of rich biological diversity and other natural resources, including timber and minerals, as popular destinations for recreation and tourism and as areas of important cultural diversity, knowledge and heritage ...' The Assembly also noted '*with concern* that populations in mountain regions are frequently among the poorest of a given country and that there remain key challenges to achieving sustainable mountain development, eradicating poverty in mountain regions and protecting mountain ecosystems.'

The strong orientation of the Earth Summit in Rio de Janeiro in 1992 towards the environment and development provided the setting for an intervention in the preparatory commission of 1991 in Geneva and that of early 1992 in New York to ensure the inclusion of a mountain chapter in Agenda 21. This was enthusiastically supported by delegates from the Himalaya, the Andes and East Africa, who had already experienced international co-operation through the International Centre for Integrated Mountain Development (ICIMOD), founded in 1983 in Kathmandu for the eight Hindu Kush–Himalayan countries, and also by the African Mountain Association (founded in 1986 in Addis Ababa), and the Andean Mountain Association (founded in 1991 in Santiago).

Although the new chapter was unanimously accepted at Rio, its importance was not properly understood by many political delegations. Rather, it was assumed that natural hazards, land use problems, agriculture and forestry, and all aspects of development and conservation were part of national policies and national competences that could hardly be classified as having international or even global importance.

This perception changed for the better five years later in New York at the special session of the United Nations General Assembly for the evaluation of Agenda 21. The UN Food and Agriculture Organization (FAO) was officially designated task manager for implementation of the mountain chapter. Fundamental, too, in providing greater awareness of the mountains of the world, was the work of UNESCO and the United Nations University (UNU) with their mountain research and development programmes, the foundation of the Mountain Forum in 1995, and many local to regional non-governmental activities.

Most important between 1992 and 1997 was the rethinking of the global significance of mountains. As a result, the book *Mountains of the World: A Global Priority* (Messerli and Ives 1997) and an attractive brochure titled *Mountains of the World – Challenges for the 21st Century* (Mountain Agenda 1997) were presented at the special 1997 Assembly. It was at this point that the political delegates began to understand the global case for the mountains. The expression 'water towers' was used as a catchword for the first time, and attention was focused on mountains as areas of biological and cultural diversity, as vital recreation areas for a more urbanized world population, as sacred places for different cultures and religions, privileged regions for protection and, especially, for water resources. These aspects not only have a local or national importance but, more important, an international regional-to-global significance.

One year later, in 1998, water problems were the main topic on the agenda of the UN Commission for Sustainable Development (UNCSD) in New York. For this commission meeting another brochure was created, entitled *Mountains of the World – Water Towers for the 21st Century*, and presented to the national representatives. The headwaters of most major rivers of the world form in the mountains, and probably more than half of humanity relies directly or indirectly on the fresh water that accumulates in the mountains. This message was well understood in the global political arena: the mountains of the world were no longer merely local and national problems, they gained global significance, especially for the 21st century.

Based on this new understanding, it was decided shortly afterwards to designate 2002 an 'International Year of Mountains.' Then in 2000, the General Assembly declared 2003 as the 'International Year of Freshwater'. These two international years on mountains and on freshwater offered possibilities for co-operation and improved information for the political community, and encouragement for the scientific community to take new initiatives and new responsibilities for basic and applied research projects on mountain watersheds and mountain water resources.

Mountain rivers cross borders and create problems and conflicts between neighbours and between countries in the highlands and lowlands about quantity and quality of water resources. Legally binding agreements among all the different countries of a mountain system exist only for the Alps, the Carpathians, and the Rocky Mountains, but not yet for all the other much more critical mountain regions, especially those in the developing countries. Therefore, we need not only political goodwill and good scientific data, but also a better cooperation between policy and science.

We must discuss not only the development of a global mountain water policy as a support for the urgently needed regional agreements, but also the development of hydrological mountain knowledge as a basis for just and peaceful solutions. On this and other cross-border issues, mountains could become bridge-builders for peaceful co-operation between neighbouring states.

Professor Bruno Messerli, Geographical Institute of the University of Berne, was centrally involved in developing and implementing the mountain chapter in Agenda 21 for the Earth Summit in 1992 and the International Year of Mountains in 2002. From 1979 to 1996 he led research in Nepal about natural hazards and soil erosion, and the significance of the Himalayan rivers for floods in Bangladesh.

ALTON BYERS

The Alpine Conservation Partnership

Protecting and Restoring Alpine Ecosystems,
Strengthening People's Resilience to Climate Change

Alpine ecosystems are among the world's most beautiful but endangered landscapes. At the Alpine Club's *Summits of Learning* seminar in London in December 2007, I outlined the research I have carried out in Nepal on the dramatic environmental changes wrought in the Khumbu and Hinku valleys – notably through the burning of juniper at trekker lodges – and global warming, and the ameliorative work of the Alpine Conservation Partnership. ACP works through local communities, strengthening their ability to adapt to change, not just in the Himalaya but also in other mountain regions.

Climbers and trekkers are both agents and observers of change to alpine ecosystems and in this paper I intend to lay out the background to the problem, the work of the ACP, The Mountain Institute (TMI), the American Alpine Club and others, and how mountaineers can become involved – that is, evolve from being part of the problem to become ambassadors of the solution.

Canaries in the coal mine

Alpine ecosystems are characterized by low growing shrubs, cushion plants, and grasslands adapted to the harsh, high-altitude climate between the upper treeline and permanent snowline. Among the most bio-diverse ecosystems in the world, they are also critically important for wildlife habitat, and to millions of people in the lowlands as sources of fresh water for drinking, agriculture, and hydropower. The medicinal and aromatic plants harvested from alpine meadows generate millions of pounds annually in the global market.

Alpine vegetation and landscapes are particularly sensitive to changes in climate, analogous to 'canaries in the coal mine' in terms of their ability to rapidly demonstrate global warming impacts such as glacier recession, upward plant migration, and biodiversity destruction from changing land use patterns. Yet, compared to rainforests, oceans, and coastal regions, alpine environments have been neglected by the international development and conservation communities alike, possibly because of their remoteness, high altitudes, harsh climates, and extremely difficult travel and working conditions.

In the course of 12 research expeditions to the Everest region between 1984 and 2001, including a year spent living in Khumjung village, I was able to show that soil loss processes in the alpine zone (> 4000 m) were 40 times greater than those in the sub-alpine forests and shrub/grasslands (ie 40 tons/ha/year); that more than 50 percent of the protective shrub juniper – the 'geomorphic glue' of the fragile alpine soils – had been removed from the hillsides during the past 20 years; and that more than 80 percent of the alpine zone (4200m-5200m) had been seriously impacted in recent times. Tourist lodges, trekkers, mountaineers, and their porters were using tons of juniper shrubs and alpine cushion plants annually as fuel, in spite of regulations designed to encourage the use of imported kerosene. The removal of these soil-binding shrubs from the fragile and thin alpine soils had contributed not only to dramatic increases in soil erosion, but also to accelerated landscape denudation that local people referred to as 'growing glacial moraines'.

I began collecting substantial evidence of similar degradational processes at work elsewhere in the Himalayan alpine zone, including the Mera Peak/ Hinku Khola region, around Makalu base camp, in the protected areas around Kangchenjunga on both sides of the Nepal/India border, and in the Rongbuk valley of Tibet. In fact the impact has been much the same anywhere in the mountain world frequented by adventure tourism over the last 20 years, notably, Kilimanjaro (Tanzania), Virunga Volcanoes (Rwanda), Mt Kenya, Acongagua (Argentina) and cordilleras Blanca and Huayhuash (Peru). International awareness of the problem was initially extremely limited and remedial action was simplistic, focusing primarily on cosmetic and fashionable garbage trail issues and clean-up expeditions that neglected the critical linkages between people and environment in alpine regions, highland/lowland interactions, and sustainable local economies. Although of vital ecological, economic, and spiritual importance to millions of people, it was clear that alpine ecosystems were among the most poorly understood and neglected landscapes in the world, and in critical need of protection and restoration.

Conservation action in the Khumbu

Interviews with local people in the Everest region during our 2001 research expedition funded by the National Geographic Society showed a clear awareness of the problem of growing alpine degradation, and a strong desire to reverse the trend, but a total lack of financial and technical resources to realistically confront the key threats and issues. Interviewees indicated a desire to launch an alpine conservation and restoration project based on community and participatory approaches, partnerships with local NGOs, project management training opportunities, and the development of educational materials targeted on lodge owners, trekking agencies, national park visitors, and local schools.

On 28 May 2003, during celebrations marking the 50th anniversary of the first ascent of Everest, the American Alpine Club (AAC) announced its contribution of US$21,000 for a 'community-based alpine conservation and restoration project' in the Khumbu. Additional funds were generated by grants from the National Geographic Society's Conservation Trust, United Nations Development Program/Small Grants Program, private donations, and the US Agency for International Development.

Finally, after years of self-financed research, awareness building, and fundraising efforts, 'Community-based Conservation and Restoration of the Everest Alpine Zone' became a reality. We included the word 'restoration' in the project's title since conservation alone is no longer sufficient in many of the world's alpine ecosystems – active restoration through protection, re-planting of seedlings, and new land-use management policies is also needed.

A year later, in May 2004, the Khumbu Alpine Conservation Committee (KACC) was formed by local people – the first body of its kind in Nepal. Under the field supervision of Ang Rita Sherpa, The Mountain Institute's (TMI) Senior Program Manager, the KACC consists of a chairman, secretary, treasurer, and 19 community members. Since its formation it has spearheaded far-reaching changes in the management and protection of the upper Imja Khola alpine zone that include the following:

1. **Banning the harvesting of all shrub juniper** and alpine plants (eg *Arenaria* sp.) for fuelwood, agricultural purposes and incense throughout the Imja Khola valley (the equivalent of 2000 *doko* (baskets), or 80,000kg of wood saved for 2007 alone).

2. **Protecting in perpetuity the fragile alpine ecosystems** (4200-5200m) of the upper Imja Khola watershed through new KACC and National Park cooperation.

3. **Establishing a kerosene and stove depot** (10,000 litres and 100 stoves) in Dingboche that provides alternative energy for local people, lodge owners, and trekking groups as well as a potential source of operational support for the KACC.

4. **Renovating an existing porter shelter** in Lobuche to provide shelter, warmth (blankets and 50 bunks), and cooking facilities to porters. Left to fend for themselves at the end of the day, many porters were previously forced to burn fragile alpine shrubs for warmth and cooking, while sleeping in nearby caves.

5. **Constructing the first alpine cattle-proof exclosure** (50m x 50m) in the Sagarmatha (Mt Everest) National Park above the village of Dingboche as a demonstration of hill-slope and ecosystem restoration.

6. Establishing the **first nursery in Nepal devoted exclusively to alpine eco-system restoration** with a 5,000 juniper seedling and medicinal plant capacity.

7. **Training and capacity building courses given to KACC members** in basic financial accounting, project management methods, problem solving, and monitoring and evaluation.

8. **Establishing educational conservation signboards** along the Everest and Island Peak routes.
9. Publishing informational brochures **to increase visitor awareness of the project** and ways that they can help support project activities.

134. Porter shelter at Lobuche (4900m) on the Everest trail. It provides porters with a warm place to sleep, plus food that is much cheaper than the overpriced lodge *dal bhat*. When Byers visited in autumn 2007 and spring 2008 it was always full to capacity. (*Alton Byers*)

The Alpine Conservation Partnership

In January 2007, the Alpine Conservation Partnership (ACP) was officially launched with a US$150,000 grant from the Argosy Foundation that has since enabled the project to expand the conservation success of the Everest region to heavily impacted ecosystems worldwide. The unique partnership between the American Alpine Club and the Mountain Institute has resulted in field projects characterised by exceptional high impact and cost effectiveness, thanks in part to TMI's existing on-the-ground presence and staff in the field and the AAC's network of international organisations.

Accomplishments in 2007-2008 include the following:

Kilimanjaro National Park, Tanzania: More than 50,000 tourists per year attempt to climb Kilimanjaro. The total number translates to 200,000 individuals per year when support staff are added, creating enormous impacts on the fragile high mountain ecosystems. The park provides important services as an enclave of biodiversity; a source of potential income for community tourism and home stay activities; and as a high income generator whose fees support a number of other, less visited national parks throughout Tanzania.

In January-February 2007, a reconnaissance of the mountain was conducted in the course of developing a major new conservation proposal with Africare and the African Wildlife Foundation. Although the trails and hut systems along the popular Marangu ('Coca Cola') trail were found to be in good shape, expressed priorities included (a) new rescue gear, especially new, lightweight folding stretchers that can be carried to the higher altitudes above Kibo huts (the existing one-wheeled stretchers are too heavy for this), (b) advanced rescue and first responder training for rescue staff, (c) a medical unit hut at Mandara and Kibo with oxygen, Gamow bag, first aid supplies, (d) assistance with managing human waste at high altitudes, and (e) improving working conditions for porters.

Efforts are underway by the ACP to find support for these activities, either as a separate project or built into the larger Kilimanjaro conservation proposal developed in 2007.

The Mera Peak region, Makalu Barun National Park and Buffer Zone, Nepal: The Mera Peak region is located four days walk east of Lukla airport within the Makalu Barun National Park and Buffer Zone. A traditional alpine pasture for Sherpas, Rais, Chhetris, and Gurungs from the Bung and Cheskam regions, the region has become popular among foreign visitors in the past decade as an alternative to the Everest base-camp trek and because of its access to Mera Peak, the highest 'trekking peak' in Nepal at 6476m.

Between 12-21 May 2007, the ACP, TMI staff, and representatives from the Department of National Parks and Wildlife Conservation (DNPWC) conducted a detailed field reconnaissance in order to obtain the best understanding of current conditions in the upper Hinku Khola watershed region. Forest destruction in the sub-alpine regions near Kothe, and the destruction of the alpine ecosystems between Dragon *gompa* and Khare, was found to be occurring at a rapid and unsustainable rate that in turn is threatening the biodiversity and geomorphic integrity of the entire upper Hinku Khola valley.

5. *Right*
Juniper seedlings at a nursery devoted to alpine eco-system restoration, Shomare, Khumbu. (*Alton Byers*)

6. Damber Thapa measuring a stack of juniper in Tangnag (4400m) in the Hinku valley, Makalu-Barun National Park, April 2007. The priority here is to build a kerosene depot to provide an alternative to juniper, which takes a couple of hundred years to get to the size shown. Long-term solutions will be either fuelwood from plantations at lower altitudes, and/or hydro-power. (*Alton Byers*)

137.   Denuded hillside due to juniper harvesting. (*Alton Byers*)

Severe devastation to the shrub juniper and dwarf rhododenron in the Tangnag/Khare region has occurred, with Tangnag and Khare lodges burning 106,312 kg/yr and 77,962 kg/yr respectively, an additional 67,200kg burned by yak herders and an unknown quantity burned by the Rai sheep herders per year. More than 50m^3 of juniper cut for fuelwood was found stacked outside five lodges in Tangnag, with each limb taking more than 100 years to reach its average diameter of 3-4cm. Transect results suggested that as much as 50 per cent of the region's shrub juniper cover has been lost during the past decade.

On 17 May, a meeting with 15 lodge owners from Kothe, Tangnag, and Khare was held to discuss and build consensus on addressing the issues of illegal lodge building, forest destruction, shrub juniper and dwarf rhododendron harvesting, and the need for better land stewardship. TMI then facilitated a second meeting in Lukla in September 2007 where the Mera Alpine Conservation Group (MACG) was officially formed. With financial and technical support from the ACP and Makalu-Barun National Park and Buffer Zone, MACG is in the processing of banning (a) the harvesting of shrub juniper and timber, (b) the construction of all new lodges, (c) importation of all bottles (beer, soda, etc), and (d) the hunting of wildlife, while developing workplans to improve all sanitation facilities at lodges and campgrounds. The project is being supported by the Argosy Foundation as well as by a grant from the National Geographic Society's Conservation Trust received in September 2007.

Huascarán National Park, Peru: On 6 August 2007, following several meetings at the Instituto de Montaña in Huaraz, ACP personnel visited Johnny Ortiz, the new Director General of the Huascarán National Park. Ortiz welcomed the ACP in the park and said that the proposed activities were greatly needed. The group agreed that first year activities would focus on the 'protection and restoration of the popular Ishinca watershed and its high-altitude ecosystems (alpine, pasture, forest) through community-based partnerships, capacity building, and increased awareness'. During the next year, these activities will focus on developing models that (a) improve sanitary conditions, (b) remove grazing pressure on the alpine areas by improving lower elevation pastures, (c) increase tourist, park, and *campesino* awareness of the fragility of the alpine ecosystem, and (d) build the capacities of all stakeholders to practice better alpine ecosystem stewardship. Meanwhile, a detailed plan for the conservation and restoration of major base camp ecosystems within the HNP, beginning with the Ishinca valley, will be developed in 2008.

Khumbu Alpine Conservation Council (KACC), Sagarmatha National Park, Nepal: KACC's success has been substantial since its formation in 2004 and it continues to be a model for all other ACP projects. New KACC activities in 2007 included the following:

(1) With funds from the United Nations Development Small Grant Programme, the KACC built a beautiful new Visitors Centre/ Kerosene Depot in Dingboche in November 2007.
(2) Sea buckthorn (*Hippophae rhamnoides*) juice is now being produced by lodge owners and sold to trekkers on a regular basis. Training was funded by the UNDP under the theme 'conservation by use'.

(3) A new roof was installed on the Lobuche porters' rest house following loss of the original to high winds. When I visited the shelter in November 2007, it was filled to capacity, warm, and *dal-bhat* (rice and lentil peas) could be purchased for NR100 instead of NR180 at the nearby lodges.

(4) The monsoon of 2007 was one of the wettest on record, and the upper Imja Khola region experienced three separate floods that destroyed most bridges, including the bridge co-financed by the ACP in 2003.

(5) Plans are underway to conduct a feasibility study for a mini-hydro plant in Dingboche.

Climate change

Climate change is of manifest importance to mountain people's lives and livelihoods, and to conservation practices. In autumn 2007, I spent 30 days (12 October–9 November) in the Sagarmatha National Park conducting an analysis of contemporary climate change impacts on the region's glaciers and alpine landscapes. Sponsors of the project included the AAC, TMI and the International Centre for Integrated Mountain Development (ICIMOD). Methods included retracing the footsteps of the early mountaineering scientists, replicating their c1950 panoramas of glaciers, then comparing the two to detect visible changes in terms of glacier retreat, volume, or new lake formation.

This was the first time that so many of these historic panoramas had been replicated and, supplemented with informal interviews with local people, resulted in significant new insights regarding recent glacial fluctuation and climate change impacts in the world's highest mountain range. The resultant findings and photographs were unveiled at the Alpine Club's *Summits of Learning* seminar and again at the AAC's *Climbatology* fundraiser for the ACP held in Golden, Colorado on 22 February 2008. In Colorado, Conrad Anker acted as MC, and Dawa Steven Sherpa lectured on his forthcoming 'EcoEverest' expedition designed to increase awareness of climate change. A portable exhibit was display on 18 April 2008 at Everest base camp in conjunction with Dawa's climb and additional presentations were held during the summer and autumn of 2008 in Europe and the United States.

How can climbers become involved?

How can climbers make meaningful contributions to the conservation and restoration of the high-altitude landscapes that we love, but sometimes inadvertently abuse?

An increase in awareness of the problems is a start. I have found that most climbers and trekkers who are made aware of the problems of alpine degradation, and informed of either appropriate behavioral changes or the existence of projects such as the ACP, are more than happy to raise the issue of burning alpine shrubs for fuelwood with lodge owners.

Similarly informed, trekkers and climbers will also insist that their out-fitters provide warm shelter, clothing, and food for porters for both humanitarian and environmental reasons (saving on the burning of shrub juniper if porters are no longer forced to seek shelter in caves). And some-times awareness produces a donation on the spot. One Swiss gentleman wrote a cheque for US$10,000 to Ang Rita Sherpa in 2005 after he and Ang had discussed ACP's work over a cup of tea in Pangboche.

We need to continue thinking of creative ways to raise the profile of the ACP so that its successes, lessons learned, recommended codes of conduct, and future needs reach a much wider international climbing audience. This is an area in which all international alpine clubs could become involved and mechanisms are needed to bring this about.

In summary, support for, and direct involvement in, the ACP is probably one of the best, most direct ways in which the climbing community can have a real and measurable impact on alpine and high mountain conserva-tion, improved livelihoods, and climate change impacts.

MIKE GROCOTT

Caudwell Xtreme Everest

The Caudwell Xtreme Everest expedition during the spring of 2007 was not principally a climbing expedition. The aims were scientific, not adventurous, and the members were physicians who were experienced amateur climbers, not professional high-altitude mountaineers or clients chasing a personal life-goal. For us, Everest offered a unique opportunity to study how humans adapt to hypoxia (low oxygen levels). More than 200 volunteers trekked to Everest Base Camp to be subjects of 60 investigators in an experiment designed to investigate why there is such variation in people's ability to adapt to hypoxia (acclimatise) and perform effectively at altitude. We hope that the results will help to improve our understanding of how our patients with critical illness adapt to hypoxia, and perhaps, to develop new treatments for the critically ill. At the same time, higher on the mountain, climbing doctors (and medical students) made novel measurements at the edge of the human physiological envelope, trying to define the limits of tolerance of hypoxia.

Overall, the expedition was a success: we completed more than 90 per cent of the planned experiments, facilitated several major rescues, and everyone involved returned safely. As it turned out the climbing was also safe and successful. Fifteen Sherpas, two cameramen and eight doctors reached the summit of Everest, but the principal high-altitude goal, a blood sample on the world's highest point, was not (quite) achieved. This article tells the story of the expedition.

Why were we there

We set out to understand why there are such dramatic differences between individuals in their ability to adapt to hypoxia (acclimatise). Much previous altitude research has been conducted on small groups of subjects, making it difficult to explore differences between individuals. We set out to study a large group (222 subjects in total) in order to be able to observe a spectrum of normal variability and relate the observed differences to the different genetic profiles of our subjects. In this way, we hope to be able to identify genes associated with beneficial adaptation and thereby better understand the mechanisms responsible for effective adaptation. We believe that the same mechanisms may explain variations in response in critically ill patients and help us to understand why some survive when others do not.

We are particularly keen to explore whether changes in the efficiency with which cells utilise oxygen are responsible for the dramatic differences in performance between individuals at altitude. Until now, the majority of literature relating to acclimatisation has focused on how oxygen gets to the cells, rather than how effectively the cells use it. Studying hypoxia in patients in hospital is rarely fruitful because of the large number of additional factors (type of injury, previous illnesses etc) which make it difficult to separate out the effects of a single variable such as hypoxia.

Our subjects were studied at sea level and in purpose-built laboratories in Kathmandu, Namche Bazar, Pheriche and at Base Camp. All the subjects trekked from Lukla to Everest Base Camp following the same ascent profile. Consequently, we know that any differences we observe between them will be due to their individual physiology rather than to different ascent rates. The logistics needed to achieve this volume of science were substantial. More than 26 tonnes of equipment were flown to Nepal and then flown and trekked into the relevant laboratory. Each one of more than 500,000 items was catalogued on a vast spreadsheet. It is a testament to the abilities of Mac MacKenney and his logistics team that every item was delivered to the correct laboratory at the right time.

The expedition was the culmination of more than three years' preparation, including two previous successful expeditions over 8000 metres (Cho Oyu) and months of testing in cold and low-pressure chambers. The huge volume of results will keep us busy for at least the next five years.

Everest in 2007
Our climb on Everest in 2007 bears little comparison with the pioneering summit successes of the 1950s, '60s and '70s. Fixed rope is now almost continuous from base camp to summit; only on the flatter areas of the Western Cwm and on the South Col do you move around free from an ascender. The 'icefall doctors', a team of five Sherpas paid by a national park levy, prepare and maintain the route through the Khumbu icefall. Each day throughout the season, they make and mend the fixed ropes and ladders whilst the incessant downward flow of ice continuously erodes their work. Higher on the mountain, we were able to have effective radio and telephone communication from the South Col, along with battery banks to power our experiments. We returned with renewed admiration for the pioneers on Everest who succeeded without all these supports and were truly heading into the unknown.

Safety-Science-Summit
Any expedition with the aim of improving medical knowledge must be very careful not to cause harm. Consequently, our priorities had to be very clear: safety first, then science, with the summit a distant third, and only in the pursuit of our scientific goals. We stuck to this mantra throughout the expedition and it served us well.

Formal risk management (required for ethical approval) in the mountains was new to most of us. At the outset, we identified the icefall and the summit ridge as the principal hazards. The icefall concerned us because of the

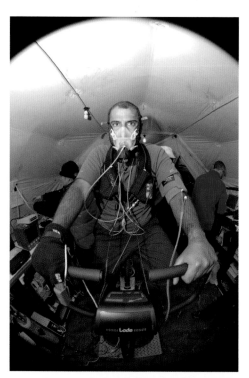

Left 138.
Sundeep Dhillon undergoing a test to measure oxygen consumption during exercise at Everest Base Camp.
(*By courtesy of Caudwell Xtreme Everest*)

139. Paul Gunning passing a gastric tonometer into his stomach in order to measure gut blood flow during exercise.
(*By courtesy of Caudwell Xtreme Everest*)

ever-present objective danger of structural collapse, whereas the summit ridge presented the well-documented risks of overcrowding, queuing and attendant delays in a potentially hostile environment. We planned to traverse the icefall only three times, once for acclimatisation, once for the Western Cwm science and once for a summit attempt, and we were able to achieve this. To minimise the risk of being caught on a congested summit ridge we deliberately waited until most teams had cleared the ridge, risking the possibility that the weather window would close and the summit would become unreachable. When the first teams from other expeditions started heading up to the summit in early May, we descended to Dingboche for food and rest. We returned a week later to find much of the activity past.

Consequently on our first summit day (23 May) we were the only team on the south-east ridge and the second summit team (24 May) shared the ridge with only a handful of other climbers. 24 May was the last day of the 2007 spring season that Everest was climbed from the south. Our strategy worked well, but it was close.

A well-defined leadership structure with clear accountability and frequent effective communication was essential for such a large project. Climbing decisions were discussed by a group of three (MG, SD and CI, *see below*) and all major moves were preceded by team briefings with clear definition of roles and exploration of contingencies. This was unfamiliar ground for most of us, who had grown up on small, less structured, private climbing trips. Nevertheless, all expedition members signed up to the leadership structure before we left the UK and it worked well. One of the criteria for being selected for the summit team was a previous illness-free ascent over 8000 metres, and all of the medical summit climbers had previously climbed Cho Oyu. We stuck to a 'buddy system' above base camp; anyone moving anywhere did so with at least one buddy and always with a radio. Radio schedules were clearly defined and a continuous listening watch was kept from the base camp logistics tent. Our communication plan on summit night was ambitious and the geography of the ridge meant that we were frequently out of direct contact with base camp. The presence of relay facilities at camp 1 on Pumori, courtesy of the BBC team, and at camp 2 in the Western Cwm, minimised the resultant anxiety for those at base camp. We had a predetermined midday turn-around time on summit day. As it turned out conditions were good, we moved briskly and we had everyone back on the South Col before the midday threshold arrived.

On Everest in 2007 we were very fortunate to work with the same core Sherpa team that many of us had climbed with on Cho Oyu in 2006. The bond of affection and trust between the Sherpas, climbing and base camp science and logistics teams was never more evident than at the party to celebrate the descent of the last Sherpas off the mountain. It was probably a good job that most of the other teams had vacated base camp by this time. Without the Sherpas we would not have been able to conduct any of the science above base camp. Our high-altitude Sherpas completed more than 100 carries to the South Col in a round trip from base camp taking only a day and a half. An early start would see them on the Col by late morning with a return to camp 2 by early afternoon, overnight rest, and return to base camp early the next morning. In contrast, the climbers took four days to reach the South Col with substantially lighter loads. We also had the benefit of their climbing experience. Between the Sherpa (81), filming (6) and climbing research (13) teams we had more than one hundred previous ascents over 8000 metres.

Our goal on the summit had been to measure the level of oxygen in the arterial blood of some of our team, in order to make a measurement very close to the limit of human tolerance of hypoxia. We know that the level of hypoxia at the summit of Everest is close to this limit for several reasons. The first 63 successful summiters all used supplementary oxygen; it was nearly 25 years after Hillary and Tenzing's first ascent that Messner and Habeler succeeded in reaching the summit without supplemental oxygen. To this day only about 5 per cent of those who reach the summit of Everest do so without using supplemental oxygen. Even the subtle reduction in barometric pressure that occurs during winter may be enough to make the summit unattainable breathing ambient air except by a very few individuals. Only one individual (a Sherpa) has so far reached the summit under these conditions without supplemental oxygen. Sadly, on the days that we climbed, the conditions on the summit were too cold and windy to make this measurement. However, we did manage to obtain four samples at 8400 metres (27,559ft) and these are the highest arterial samples ever obtained, by a margin of more than 2000 metres. The levels of oxygen in these samples are lower than has previously been measured in humans, and are similar to the lowest levels ever measured in any mammal. Interestingly, the two other comparable values that we have been able to identify have been in diving seals returning to the surface after a long dive and in the human foetus in the uterus. More than 80 years ago the British physiologist Joseph Barcroft first proposed the idea that physiology in an Everest climber would be similar to that occurring in a foetus.

Conclusion

As the handful of commercial operators that go back year-on-year already know, it is possible to manage risk effectively on Everest with a modicum of luck on your side. We owe a huge debt of thanks to the CXE team, our Sherpas, the volunteer trekkers, our sponsors (please see www.xtreme-everest.co.uk) and Jagged Globe who provided our logistical support. We also owe thanks to many of our fellow teams on the mountain. In particular, we found the big commercial operators who run expeditions on the mountain every year to be incredibly helpful and supportive and highly professional in all their conduct. This shouldn't be surprising, but it is in marked contrast to the way these individuals and companies are often portrayed in the media.

2007 was also a year when the AC was well represented on Everest. In addition to the six authors of this article, Simon Lowe, Jim Milledge, Victor Saunders, Henry Todd and Kenton Cool were all on the mountain. At the end of April, in the run-up to the summit attempts, we wondered whether there might be enough AC members at base camp to have a full meeting and change the constitution to pursue more civilised (warmer) goals. Several weeks living in the shadow of the Khumbu icefall can do that to you!

Caudwell Xtreme Everest was a huge team effort that succeeded only because of the combined efforts of all those involved. We returned enormously relieved that the trip was completed without significant harm to those involved. We worked, with other teams, to rescue several sick and injured climbers high on the mountain and collected the data that was the goal of our expedition and which will keep us busy at sea-level for years to come.

As we strolled down the Khumbu valley in early June there was a quiet satisfaction for a job well done, mixed with a relief that it was all over. A year on, the same individuals who said 'never again' are busy putting together plans for the next expedition, with new novel experiments addressing the questions arising from our results; as always in science, new questions arise as old ones are answered.

Team leader Mike Grocott (MG) was assisted in the preparation of this report by climbing leader Sundeep Dhillon (SD), deputy climbing leader Chris Imray (CI), Jeremy Windsor, George Rodway and Graham Hoyland. It is hoped to feature more of the scientific results of the expedition in a future AJ.

140. Circus maximus. Everest Base Camp, spring 2007.
(By courtesy of Caudwell Xtreme Everest)

141. In the interests of science – Mike Grocott, Dan Martin and Sundeep Dhillon on the summit of Everest, May 2007. (*By courtesy of Caudwell Xtreme Everest*)

Acknowledgements

Caudwell Xtreme Everest (CXE) is a research project coordinated by the Centre for Altitude, Space and Extreme Environment Medicine, University College, London. The aim of CXE is to conduct research into hypoxia and human performance at high altitude in order to improve understanding of hypoxia in critical illness. Membership, roles and responsibilities of the CXE Research Group can be found at www.caudwell-xtreme-everest.co.uk/team. The research was funded from a variety of sources, none of which are public. The entrepreneur John Caudwell, whose name the expedition carries, donated £500,000 specifically to support the research. BOC Medical, now part of Linde Gas Therapeutics, generously supported the research early on and continues to do so. Lilly Critical Care, The London Clinic (a private hospital), Smiths Medical, Deltex Medical and The Rolex Foundation have also donated money to support the research and logistics. All monies were given as unrestricted grants. Specific research grants were awarded by the UK Intensive Care Foundation, the Association of Anaesthetists of Great Britain and Ireland and the Sir Halley Stewart Trust. The CXE volunteers who trekked to Everest Base Camp also kindly donated to support the research.

The expedition was filmed by BBC Horizon and a two-part documentary was released in autumn 2007 and has since been shown worldwide. Two BBC Radio 4 documentaries were also produced. An IMAX film of which the expedition forms a part is scheduled for release during 2009.

NICK MASON

Mera Peak Pains

Addressing porter and trekker welfare

The afternoon shadows were beginning to lengthen on the faces of Cho Oyu, Everest, Lhotse and Makalu and the countless peaks in between. My hands were growing cold as I collapsed my tripod and put away my camera gear to return to Mera high camp and capture the light as it faded over Makalu, Chamlang, and distant Kangchenjunga which seemed to float, suspended in the air, away to the east. As I walked the last few hundred metres a solitary porter passed me, his basket empty, trudging heavy-footed and late, back down the trail that earlier in the day had been heaving with porters and trekkers ascending to high camp at around 5800m. His gait seemed a little unsteady and he did not return my breathless 'Namaste' as I willingly stepped aside to allow him to pass.

On arriving back at camp a British trekker from another party asked me if I had passed the lone porter and how he had seemed. He had apparently been taken ill on arrival at camp earlier in the day and complained of a severe headache before vomiting. The trekker was concerned because the porter had been sent down unaccompanied. I asked where I could find the group's *sirdar*. He eventually appeared and I introduced myself: 'I am a doctor who works with the International Porter Protection Group. You never send a sick porter down unaccompanied. He must always have somebody with him.' The *sirdar* smiled, shrugged his shoulders and feigned incomprehension. I could feel anger beginning to grow within me. Fortunately at that moment Dawa, the *sirdar* from my own group, appeared, grinned mischievously, and five minutes after animatedly translating my words into rapid-fire Nepali, a Sherpa was scuttling off down the slope in the fading light to accompany the porter to the safety of lower altitude. The western leader of the group looked sheepish. 'I was concerned,' he said, 'but you know what they're like. They never listen. It needs people with authority like you to make them pay attention.'

This brief episode sums up so many of the problems faced by mountain porters on Mera and in Nepal in general. Misunderstood by the majority of westerners, mountain porters are itinerant workers, often of Rai, Tamang or Chetri origin, from the middle hills of Nepal who have left their low altitude villages to seek better paid work portering to support their families. Frequently and wrongly labelled as Sherpas, and attributed with a Sherpa's genetic adaptation to altitude, they are in fact lowlanders and as susceptible

142. *Right*
Porter ascending from
the lower Hinku valley.
(*Stephen Goodwin*)

143. *Left*
Girl porter from the lower hills
takes a break at 4000m in the Hinku.
(*Stephen Goodwin*)

144. Trail routines: porters prepare tsampa in a mid-morning break en route
up the Hinku valley. (*Stephen Goodwin*)

145. Porter on the Mera La (5400m) heading for the high camp.
(*Stephen Goodwin*)

to altitude-related illness as any westerner, perhaps more so as a result of the heavy loads that they are forced by necessity to carry. Problems with altitude illness are compounded by an understandable unwillingness among porters to admit to illness for fear it will result in being paid off, sent back down the mountain and losing the opportunity for future work. Porter unemployment is now a significant problem in Nepal, as anybody who has flown into Lukla recently and been met by hundreds of porters jostling for work will realize. With the majority lacking any form of health insurance, too many hide their symptoms until it is too late.

The descending porter I had met was fortunate. At least his condition had been recognised and appropriate action taken in sending him down. Others are less fortunate. That morning at breakfast just below the Mera La we had been shocked to hear of the deaths of two porters in the remote Hongu Valley a week previously. Details were sketchy, but it appeared that while returning from carrying loads to Baruntse base camp they had been caught out in a storm, and inadequately clad and without shelter had perished. We shall never know who the porters were who died so that westerners could enjoy a mountaineering holiday on a peak that has already had in excess of 200 ascents, and we shall never know how many children their widows must now struggle to raise unaided or how, if ever, they learnt of their husbands' deaths. Flimsy clothing and footwear are the norm for the majority of porters and a source of amazement for unthinking westerners. They marvel at the seemingly superhuman strength of their porters, toiling under the weight of several trekkers' bags wearing only thin clothing and only plimsolls or flip-flops on their feet.

Rarely do people make the connection that the porters are only there and working so poorly equipped in such an extreme environment because they, as tourists, have chosen and paid to go there. Even more rarely do people grasp that they can influence and improve their porters' welfare for the better.

I was visiting the Hinku valley, and the village of Khare in particular, as a member of the International Porter Protection Group (IPPG) to investigate problems rumoured to exist there for both porters working for the trekking industry and the trekkers themselves, and to look into the feasibility of expanding a small, tented aid post sponsored by a major trekking and climbing company into a formal, medically staffed rescue post and porter shelter. Each season reports have filtered back to organizations such as IPPG and Community Action Nepal (CAN) of injury, altitude illness and even deaths on and around Mera. It was four and a half years since I had last visited the Hinku valley and I was surprised to see the development that had taken place during that time. On my last visit the valley had been under Maoist control with trekking groups receiving visits in camp from heavily armed guerillas asking for generous contributions to the cause. The Maoist presence remained but now, since a ceasefire and political changes, it was no longer covert and hidden. Posters extolling the Maoist leader Prachandra's vision for a new communist Nepal were proudly displayed in every village next to the fading Maoist graffiti from an episode everybody but the Nepalese government had recognized as a civil war.

A number of possible approach routes lead to the Hinku valley but all converge on the village of Khote, also known as Tashing Ongma, at 3600m. This village had doubled in size since my last visit with the building of substantial new lodges. In 2003 we had been one of the few groups in the valley, but now many parties were ascending or descending, on their way to or from the climb of Mera Peak. From Khote the path gains 800m along a wide, boulder-strewn riverbed and over moorland to the village of Tangnag (4400m). The riverbed was gouged out when a glacial lake above Tangnag burst in 1997 sending a giant wave of water tearing down the riverbed. Some of the boulders were the size of houses. It seems extraordinary that nobody was reported killed by this unimaginably powerful event. Tangnag sits opposite the imposing north face of Mera. Here I met a group who had had to evacuate a member of their party with high-altitude pulmonary oedema and the following morning had to organise a helicopter rescue for a woman with life-threatening high-altitude cerebral oedema. She and her husband had descended overnight from Khare after realising that the woman's condition, which had developed at Mera high camp, was not resolving despite the 1000m loss of altitude.

The path from Tangnag to Khare, some 400m above, crosses moraines and winds up a narrow river valley before opening onto summer yak pastures criss-crossed by streams and ringed by spectacular snow peaks. On my first attempt to ascend to Khare I came across a porter sitting shivering, breathless

46. Tangnag (4400m), staging post on the Mera Peak trail. Boulder debris fills the valley bottom from a glacier lake burst in 1997. (*Stephen Goodwin*)

47. Graffiti of civil war. A fading reminder of who called the shots – and still does – in the Hinku during Nepal's years of turmoil. (*Stephen Goodwin*)

and coughing at the side of the trail. He was screwing up his eyes against the bright morning light. A number of groups had already passed him despite the fact that he was obviously sick. It transpired that he too had taken ill in the Hongu valley while portering for an expedition on Baruntse and had been sent back on his own down the Hongu and over the Mera La. He had had to cross this glaciated pass at 5400m wearing a thin jacket, tracksuit bottoms, a scarf wrapped around his head and plimsolls on his feet. Sunglasses were conspicuous by their absence. An initial assessment suggested that he was suffering from hypothermia, pneumonia and probably high-altitude pulmonary oedema, and a degree of snow blindness. We evacuated him, initially on foot, and then on the back of a porter, to Tangnag where, with the loss of altitude and appropriate treatment, including a number of hours in a portable hyperbaric bag, he made a good recovery. The following morning we were able to leave Tangnag in opposite directions, he to descend with another porter and me to attempt to reach Khare again.

My first impression of Khare was that it had changed little from my previous visit. It remains a collection of poorly constructed yak herders' huts, surrounded by trekking parties' tents and toilets, clinging to the hillside below a landslide. Yet while in character it may have changed little, it had increased considerably in size. According to figures from the Nepal Mountaineering Association, just under 800 climbers attempted Mera each year between 2003 and 2006, although this has fallen from more than 1000 a year in the late 1990s. A brief survey on my first night revealed 10 groups of varying sizes with a total of around 80 trekkers, 50 trekking staff and nearly 150 porters. Predictably, with so many people in the village, many porters were forced to sleep outside at an altitude of nearly 5000m and with night temperatures dropping to well below freezing. Inadequate shelter remains one of the major problems faced by porters who, having spent the day carrying trekkers' tents, sleeping bags and down jackets, are left to fend for themselves and sleep in caves or rough shelters. While the problem is being addressed in more developed areas such as the Khumbu with the construction of dedicated porter shelters such as the CAN-built IPPG shelter at Machermo in the Gokyo valley, the shelter built by the monks of the Tengboche monastery and the planned CAN shelter at Gorak Shep, in more remote but increasingly frequented areas such as the Hinku, porters continue to suffer while their clients sleep in comfort. Further afield, in areas such as the Langtang, the problem is even worse.

During the week that I spent in and around Khare my time was divided between talking to the locals and treating sick trekkers and their porters. News of a doctor in the village led to frequent visits to my tent door. The majority came with the usual assortment of high-altitude coughs, sore throats and mild symptoms of acute mountain sickness (AMS), but worryingly I saw five cases of frostbite to the foot, all of which required helicopter evacuation, and two cases of frostbitten fingers. I also heard of a further case of high-altitude pulmonary oedema that had also been flown out by helicopter. My experience was rapidly confirming the problems rumoured to exist in the Hinku and the cause of much of the altitude-related illness was easy to see.

Although there are several routes into the Hinku valley, increasing numbers choose to fly into Lukla at 2800m and cross into the Hinku via the Zetra La. It is possible to acclimatise perfectly well before crossing this 4600m pass but few groups appear to be doing so. Instead many are spending only one night at Chutanga on the west (Lukla) side of the Zetra La before crossing to Tuli Kharka, the first huts on the east side at 4200m. The result, predictably, is significant altitude illness. On the night that I spent in Tuli Kharka the 'village' seemed to be full of people with bad hangovers, shuffling around gaunt-faced, holding their pounding heads in their hands, or pushing their food disinterestedly away – all classic signs of a completely avoidable epidemic of AMS. People think they can get away with this reckless approach to acclimatisation because the following day they descend to Khote at 3600m and their symptoms will resolve. Unfortunately once in the Hinku there is only one village, Tangnag at 4400m, between Khote and Khare at almost 5000m. One of the many things known about acclimatisation is that everyone acclimatises at their own rate and this will vary widely across a group often randomly thrown together for a trek or a climb. Ideally, for good acclimatisation, it should take four to five days to get from an altitude of 3600m to 5000m but few groups in the Hinku seem to choose to follow this well accepted wisdom. The result is that many trekkers who are paying considerable sums of money to be guided up Mera in safety and in a condition to maximise their chance of reaching the summit, arrive at Khare inadequately acclimatised for the ascent. The same, of course, applies to their porters who have no choice but to be there.[1]

The number of cases of frostbite that I saw was unexpected but not difficult to understand. Despite the technical ease of the normal route up Mera – providing nothing goes wrong, it requires no more than the ability to put one crampon in front of the other – reaching any summit at almost 6500m places considerable physiological stress on the climber. For many, Mera seemed to be a first experience of a glaciated snow peak and a first experience of such altitudes. Alpine experience appeared to be the exception rather than the norm and many were learning to use crampons for the first time. All of those who had frostbitten feet had been wearing leather boots. The arguments for and against the opening up of the Himalaya by commercial operators have been rehearsed countless times; there are companies who

---

1   In autumn 2007 the editor entered the Hinku with a Himalayan Kingdoms group via the Pangkongma La, well to the south of the Zetra La and almost 2000m lower. Though this adds two more days to the trek from Lukla to Khote, most of it is spent around the 3000m contour and is a boon to good acclimatisation.

insist on appropriate experience from their clients, ensure that clients are properly equipped, who follow sensible ascent profiles that optimise the chance of acclimatisation and place the welfare of their native staff on an equal footing with those of their clients; sadly there are other companies who do not do these things and the look of almost shock on the wearied faces of those walking back into camp, and their incredulity at the cold and wind speeds that they had experienced on the summit, was eloquent testimony to this fact.

My discussions with Karmi Sherpa and other members of the Mera Alpine Group Committee, effectively the Hinku valley council, were both encouraging and daunting. The committee was aware of all of the problems I had come to investigate, yet each one we talked about seemed to throw up several others that I had not envisaged. In addition to porter welfare and the high incidence of altitude illness, they had identified other serious issues. A clean and safe water supply is needed for Khare. The absence of a safe water supply and the proliferation of toilet tents mean that it can only be a matter of time before there is a major outbreak of gastrointestinal illness. Almost every group arriving digs at least one fresh toilet rather than using the dilapidated and admittedly quite offensive village toilets. Rubbish disposal is also a major problem along with deforestation lower down the valley. The scree slope above Khare is also unstable. Karmi and Dendi Sherpa showed me two potential sites with good water supplies where a porter shelter could be constructed. They were keen that the tented porter aid post be incorporated as a permanent rescue post and ideally staffed by a doctor during the trekking seasons along the lines of the Rescue Post and Porter Shelter run by IPPG at Machermo. From what I had seen, a rescue post would be immensely useful, not only for medical services but also for the provision of education on altitude illness. At Machermo, as at the Himalayan Rescue Association (HRA) posts at Pheriche and Manang, there are daily, well-attended talks for trekkers on both altitude illness and porter welfare. Research from the HRA at Pheriche has demonstrated a fall in the incidence of AMS amongst westerners from more than 50 per cent in the mid-1970s to 30 per cent in 1996; the most probable cause for this reduction is increased awareness and understanding of the condition. Interestingly, the incidence of AMS amongst porters passing through Pheriche during the same period in the 1990s was found, at almost 40 per cent, to be considerably greater than among westerners.

While there is an undoubted need for a porter shelter and rescue post in Khare, the crux of our discussions centred around how to fund and safely run what would become the most substantial building in a village that is not inhabited all year round. One possible solution would be to set up a tented, seasonal, rescue post along similar lines to that operated by Dr Luanne Freer and the HRA at Everest base camp. A permanent building such as the Machermo post would cost around US$100,000 to build and equip.

148. Pitching Mera high camp. At 5800m this can be a place of headaches
      and worse for trekkers and porters alike. Beyond are Makalu and
      Chamlang (*right*). (*Stephen Goodwin*)

Despite the numbers of people now passing through the Hinku, there is certainly not that kind of money available within Khare. Nor could money be found locally for the other improvements sought by the Mera Alpine Group. The reasons for this, and why the development which has taken place in the Hinku is of such poor quality compared to the Khumbu just a couple of valleys away, are complex and beyond the scope of this article.

The Mera Alpine Group expressed their frustration that they receive none of the money from the permits to climb Mera that they rigorously police for the Nepal Mountaineering Association. While there clearly is injustice in this situation, is it really beyond the means of the mountaineering community to fund these greatly needed projects for the benefit of all? Is it too radical to suggest that instead of an equipment or clothing company sponsoring yet another climber they sponsor the construction of porter shelters where they are so desperately needed in Nepal?

On descending from Tuli Kharka I came across a porter perched, bird-like, in the branches of a bush. We both watched as another porter struggled past carrying the kit bags of three trekkers. I commented that to be expected to carry such a load was inhuman and should not be allowed. The porter in the bush looked at me and shrugged. '*Kay garnay, sahib*? What to do? Our politicians are too busy fighting among themselves. What interest do they have in the lives of us poor porters?' The politicians of Nepal may care very little about the lives of mountain porters, but this does not mean that we should follow their example.

Immediate action

Important though the matters discussed here undoubtedly are, the welfare of mountain porters could be improved overnight if those of us who visit Nepal took ownership of the problem and insisted on our porters being treated to the same standards as ourselves. The International Porter Protection Group has published guidelines that may be summarised as follows:

1. The provision of adequate clothing and footwear for all porters for their protection in bad weather and at altitude.
2. The provision of adequate shelter, food and drink.
3. Access to the same medical care and insurance as western clients.
4. Accompanied descent with appropriate care if porters fall ill.
5. No porter should be asked to carry a load that is too heavy for their physical ability or safety.

Anybody using a commercial company to trek or climb in Nepal should ask whether these guidelines are followed and if they are not, explain to the company why they are going elsewhere.

Arts

Rowan Huntley *Argentière Glacier ~ Turquoise Ice*
Chroma on canvas, 40cm x 50cm. (*Private collection*)

150.   Rowan Huntley painting at Montenvers, June 2007

ROWAN HUNTLEY

Beginnings

The first time I peered into the ultramarine abyss of a glacial crevasse, I saw my future life's work fall into place. With my face to the wind, crampon claws dug deep in the ice and my axe to hand, I stood fixated. The colours, textures and even sounds which surrounded me there on Norway's Nigard glacier seemed to touch my very soul. I had entered an icy paradise where, amongst the rock debris, all around me lay small snow crystals, glistening crunchy surface granules, larger clumps of melded, rounded ice marbles, water-worn runnels, turquoise surface pools and the polished and compressed, glass-like walls of deep blue crevasses. The sheer enormity, power and beauty of a glacier were finally real to me.

My quest to experience a 'living' glacier had begun two years before while painting in Snowdonia, more of which later. However, my love for snow and ice has been part of my life for as long as I can remember. I grew up in the Scottish Borders where I was always first out and last home in a blizzard. I'd spend hours playing in snow, running around and best of all, just staring upwards as it fell. I was captivated by its mesmerising qualities and the way in which it completely transformed everything it touched, even if - as was often the case – it was just for the briefest of moments.

I spent my childhood roaming the countryside near our home with my late father, Eric Huntley and, more importantly, I also watched him paint it. The landscape within just a few square miles comprised the river valleys of the Tweed and the Whiteadder, the north-east coast, and the Cheviot and Eildon Hills. These subjects, together with a wide open sky and our tiny, rural village provided endless inspiration for dad's paintings over a period of nearly 40 years. This proved a doubly valuable lesson for me; that there is great importance in really getting to know and understand your subject and that a subject can be painted many, many times before you run out of things to say about it.

Dad was a very accomplished painter, inspired initially by the 'Euston Road' approach. He trained under Sir Lawrence Gowing, Sir Roger de Grey and Sir Robin Darwin at Durham University (graduating in 1950 with First Class Honours) and later was elected RSW (Royal Society of Watercolourists). My own path to becoming a painter is somewhat more tenuous. There was never any question that I would become an artist of some kind but, in an attempt to ensure that I'd have several career options to choose from, I chose to train as an Illustrator. This, though, was like trying to walk with your mountain boots on the wrong feet. After graduating as a 'Wildlife Illustrator', it soon became obvious that I was anything but. Employment (both voluntary and paid) in graphics departments within the Museums service followed for a brief period, but in my heart, I wanted to paint.

So I got married (!) and my painting career was launched shortly after, with my first picture winning a Trophy at the Derby City Open Exhibition. This gave me the confidence to believe that maybe I could achieve at least part of my dream with some success. Needless to say, I haven't looked back since.

Establishing one's self as an artist is no slight task; there are many routes to take and all have hurdles to contend with. But early on, what became apparent to me was the importance of having faith in, and being true to, myself.

Sadly, my father died at this point and I found myself for a time, artistically at least, very alone. But I persevered and determined even more to 'carry on where I [Dad] left off', as he warmly encouraged me to do not long before he passed away.

We moved to south-east Wales and I busied myself with painting the beautiful Glamorgan coastline and the austere moorland of the Brecon Beacons but there soon came a point where I was no longer happy to paint the area's 'scenes which sell' just for the sake of it, as the local galleries demanded. I wanted to be challenged, stretched, inspired, interested in what I was doing and learning things along the way. Not just in terms of painting but also in building a thorough knowledge and comprehension of a subject that fascinated me. So I headed for higher ground and it was here that I knew I had found where I wanted – perhaps even *needed* – to be.

Repeatedly visiting the wonderfully mysterious Cwm Idwal in Snowdonia, I became acutely aware of the natural ice-carved beauty around me as I painted. This led to an intense desire to discover more about the actuality of how such a jagged and mountainous landscape had been created – to look beneath the surface of the scenery I could see. This would enable me to really begin to understand the natural processes such as upheaval, erosion and, primarily, glaciation, which had been instrumental in its shaping.

So I took myself off to Norway, to the Jotunheim National Park and the Jostedal ice cap, a breathtaking world of mountains and ice. Here I was able to immerse myself in painting the alluring mystery and bleak splendour of a frozen mountain world which yields, for me, the endless inspiration and artistic challenges I seek. My intimate adventure on Nigardsbreen was my first encounter with a 'living' glacier and as such, it remains intensely special to this day. That experience alone opened up a whole new world to me in terms of where I wanted my painting to take me and, in turn, where I wanted to take it. From then on, my aim has been to really 'get under the skin' of rock, ice and snow in order to portray them as truthfully as possible in the representational manner in which I paint.

To do this, (and therefore) to interpret the rawness of the mountain environment with probity, I need to feel it, be part of it. I need to witness ephemeral skies and the dramatic light that emanates from them affecting everything below. I need to experience the enormity and power of nature in a place that renders us so small. I need to get in amongst the snow and the rock to touch and embrace them, to build awareness of their substance and textures with my fingertips. Only then can I begin to understand the relevance of each individual element and how they work together to create such scenes of mystery, awe, turbulence and serenity.

Mountains have intrigued and attracted artists throughout history and will absolutely continue to do so. There are many such painters whose work I admire tremendously and who have, undoubtedly, had some influence on my own approach. The Norwegian painters; J C Dahl (1788–1857) of the Romantic era, Even Ulving (1863–1952) and the Finn Eero Järnefelt (1863–1937) are of particular note, my specific interest in the latter being more about the rendering of snow than about mountains. Other favourites are Gabriel Loppé (1825–1913) and E T Compton (1849–1921) who were painting at an incredibly exciting time during the formative years of Alpinism and T H Somervell (1890–1975), first and foremost a medical missionary and mountaineer of great merit but an accomplished and revered painter nonetheless. All lived at different times and all had their own unique style of working but what they had in common was a shared fervour for exploring and painting the Alpine world. What is of enormous interest and significance to me is that each sought to do so in a representational way, paying great attention to direct observation.

In my own paintings, I inherently seek to identify and emphasise the natural rhythms and patterns in a landscape, something which is probably due largely to my illustrative background. Thankfully, my subject matter is extremely giving in this respect in that there is much to work with even in the simplest of compositions. Skies play a central role in many of my pictures as they are directly responsible for the light that, together with the weather, creates atmosphere. What goes on above is directly responsible for what we see below in the landscape – just think of the shadows cast long by a low winter sun or from scudding clouds as they speed by on the wind. There are endless types of cloud and many ground-based features to play with: snow layers, flutes, meringues and cornices, rock slabs, strata, facets and fissures to name just a few. All these provide infinite appeal and possibility, colour and design and are indeed enhanced to great effect by the transient light of continuously changing weather and, of course, the seasons.

My recent work in the Alps has served only to fuel still further my passion for painting snow, rock and ice – the more I discover the more I want to find out. Barely having scratched the surface of this captivating subject matter, I look forward greatly to the many stimulating challenges – painting and otherwise – I will encounter as I continue to explore and be enthralled by it, hopefully for some considerable time to come.

WILLIAM MITCHELL

Rhythms of the Alps

A review of the exhibition of Rowan Huntley's work at the
Alpine Club, 9 October – 9 November 2007

*Over the slopes of the Col du Géant was spread a coverlet of shining snow, at
some places apparently as smooth as polished marble, at others broken so as
to form precipices, on the pale blue faces of which the horizontal lines of bedding
were beautifully drawn.*

John Tyndall, 17 July 1857

Just as Tyndall applied his exacting and scientific mind to the study of
glaciers and mountains, Rowan Huntley's work is a result of extensive
craftsmanship and observation.

This exhibition of a large selection of paintings and drawings again
confirmed Rowan's status as an eminent *peintre alpiniste*. On the one hand
she is the geologist picking up her brush and, on the other, the meteorologist
capable of mastering the reduced palette so often elusive in landscapes at
altitude. Geology and atmosphere are the *Rhythms* vying for attention in
her craft as an artist. Rowan's professed fascination with rocks and geological
formations owes much to a 1996 study trip to Norway and she paints them
in chromacolour, highly concentrated artist's pigments that give strong,
opaque colours. Rowan's background in illustration gives her the confidence
to tackle the snowfields in complicated tonal values opposed to muted
colouring, rendering *'a coverlet of shining snow'* perfectly.

The mass of spires and needles in the foreground of *Dent du Géant* throws
the onlooker's gaze off to the left into an abyss of thermals and backing-up
clouds. Part skilful composition and part deft handling of flat light on the
glaciers of the Dent itself, Rowan combines finely drawn crevasses and
rivulets with strong shadow.

Cosmiques 2 mixes vertigo with dazzling light in perhaps the most daring
composition of the exhibition. The opacity of Rowan's medium lends itself
to such contrasting colours in the rocks and snow. These more familiar
rooftops of Europe become studies of masonry and geology offset by vast
spaces built up in tones. Rowan's first-hand knowledge of alpine meteorological conditions is a clear advantage in her painting and distinguishes
her as a true *peintre alpiniste*.

151. *Dent du Géant and Aiguille de la République – Early Light*
Chroma on canvas, 50cm x 70cm. Private collection

152. Left:
Cosmique 2 – Rock and ice
Chroma on canvas
70cm x 50cm
Private collection

153. *Les Grandes Jorasses – Morning Sun, June*
Chroma on canvas, 50cm x 75cm. Private collection

Les Grandes Jorasses is majestic in its panorama and complexity and relies heavily on Rowan's 'lights and darks' in the many glaciers and snowfields. The central ridge epitomises Rowan's work – a mass of baroque lines encasing bold brushwork and a myriad of hues. Looking at her drawings, it is clear that detailed draughtsmanship is essential although *Rhythms of the Alps* was far from an exhibition of studies.

The pair of pure glacier pictures are marvellous exercises in asymmetry. The turquoise in the ice looks freezing and impenetrable – another aspect of the unglazed medium. A patient hand has delineated every buckle and crack of the moving ice and the undisguised 'love of rocks' and geological formations permeates the exhibition. Some of the smaller canvases retain great impact through the treatment of rock and ice as visual sculpture. Built up, bit by bit, the paintings and drawings are absorbing beyond their two dimensions. At close inspection the tumbling ice fields and skewed angles of ridges and needles owe their forms to an inquisitive but firm line meandering throughout. *Rhythms of the Alps* is a craftsman's skilled response to vast tracts of snow, rock and sky.

JULIAN COOPER

Kailas: A Painting *Khora*

154.   Kailas north face, afternoon. 2007, oil on linen.
71 x 99ins/180 x 251cms (*Julian Cooper*)

Kailas and its neighbouring Lake Manasarowar have dominated the Indian imagination for millennia. It is both a real mountain, 6714m high, and a conceptual mountain, central to a world of myth and literature, architecture and sculpture, music and dance.

Called by the Tibetans Gang Rimpoche or Ti-se, it is the source of four major rivers, Indus, Sutlej, Ganga and Brahmaputra. In geological terms Kailas is the world's highest deposit of tertiary conglomerate, laid down in the period immediately preceding the arrival of early man. And of course it is both a fascinating and a strikingly beautiful mountain to behold.

A sacred geography of Hindu, Buddhist, Jain and Bon cosmology centres around Kailas (as Mt Meru, *axis mundi*). Different interpretations are given to the physical features of the mountain, the cardinal directions and the river systems which emerge from the mountain. For the Hindus it is the seat of Shiva and Parvati, for the Buddhists it is a gigantic mandala, for the Jains it is the locale of the celestial world *loka*. Its four clearly defined walls match the points of the compass. It is forbidden to climb the mountain; only to circumnavigate it.

Parallel and concurrent to the literature of the mountain is the myth recreated and replicated in stone and brick temples and monuments, innumerable reliefs, stone sculptures, bronze images and countless miniature paintings from the 5th to the 18th centuries. These are found all over India.

My ambition in making this series of paintings of Kailas was to extend the range of meanings that a mountain subject had offered me in previous painting projects. The Kangchenjunga series of paintings 2000-1 were largely concerned with relentless natural processes without reference to humanity, and the Eiger paintings of 2003-4 were about projecting climbing and visual routes onto terrain which also had its history of dramas played out on the face of the mountain.

I wanted to reconstruct Kailas in terms of paint onto a flat canvas, bringing the mountain down to earth and into the room; perhaps equivalent to the Kailas temples which are themselves synthetic versions of the mountain, but viewed through my own western sensibility, which also included what I understood of Tibetan Buddhism. I would make a *khora*, a ritual circumambulation of the mountain, painting and recording as I went. It would be a painting *khora*.

Kailas as a subject embodies both an attitude of reverence towards the Earth and a personal, corporeal, identification with it. This might make this series close to being religious paintings themselves.

South-west face

It's 8am and dawn in Darchen, a settlement at the foot of Mt Kailas, and I'm trying to find the start of the pilgrims' path that circles the mountain. At the same time I'm trying to keep a pack of dogs at bay with my walking pole. Eventually I lose the dogs and spot a couple of people in the distance, walking in a determined way in what seems the right direction. One looks like a porter – he's carrying a heavy load – the other the client, I think. They're going faster than me, so I'm soon on my own. The way eventually ascends a pass covered with prayer flags and the first view of Kailas. I stop and look at the mountain. It does look extraordinary. Of particular interest is a gold reflection projected upwards onto an ice cliff on the shadowed side of Kailas from the sunlit snow slope beneath.

I'm joined by two shepherds and a flock of sheep, with some lambs and rams. We exchange the respective English/Tibetan names for 'sheep' and

155. Kailas south-west face (site study), 2006, oil on linen.
20 x 26ins/51 x 66cms (*Julian Cooper*)

'goats'. Then down the other side of the pass to a large flat plain dotted with boulders and covered with thin grass, leading on to a canyon further round the mountain. The sun is hot, the air cool. It all looks rather pleasant.

After a good deal of manoeuvring to get the best angle on the mountain I set everything up. It's 11am. I've got a good three-quarter view of Kailas in front of me and canvas, brushes and paints to hand. Earth colours mainly, except for the deep blue sky and white snow. The mountain looks so strange, like a space craft landed from the sky, with its pointed dome-like snow cap looming above me, ending abruptly with a monolithic black buttress like the prow of a ship, topped with a snow-cap of its own. All this is mounted on a pedestal of red sandstone conglomerate, looking like battlements.

Every now and then a large hare runs past, seemingly quite tame. It certainly feels good to be having this first session with the mountain. After a while, engrossed in the painting, I'm aware of a flock of goats and sheep surrounding me. I carry on painting, then look behind me to see the smiling face of a shepherdess leaning over the boulder forming my back-rest. I think she'd been there for some time. She could have taken my video camera if she'd wanted to; it was just there on the rock in front of her. I'd have been lost without it though, having dropped and broken my stills camera the day before on arrival at Kailas.

Whilst painting the mountain I'm very much aware of the built structures in front of me in the distance. The most prominent is a 6m pole with prayer flags radiating from it like a maypole; this is the *Tarboche*, renewed every

156. Kailas west face, 2007, oil on linen. 64 x 75ins/163 x 191cms
      (*Julian Cooper*)

June with a great festival. Further on there's the *Gagn-Ni*, or gateway *chorten*, and behind both there's a natural rock platform which forms an important sky burial site. Apart from the natural platform, I don't include these structures into the painting, although what they stand for is influencing the way I'm looking at this mountain. Four hours is about all I can usefully do on this painting, after that the light has moved too much.

It's a slog back over the pass to Darchen, the village at the foot of Kailas, because I still haven't got used to the heavy pack and the altitude. Before the end of day though I've still got to make sure of seeing the full view of the south face of Kailas in case it's impossible another day. So after a nap I climb steeply up for about 300m above Darchen to around 5000m. It's 8.30pm. The south face looks just perfect with the sun going down and a warm pink/gold colour lighting everything sideways from the west. It seems mythical even though it's in front of my eyes. I can see the great vertical gash down the side of the mountain, the terraces in horizontal rows looking like some sort of script, and great blank areas of rock like architecture. All I can do is film it, and hope to be able to return for a painting.

West face

It's 8.30am on 1 May. I'm following the same track from Darchen as yesterday but this time with 'Got', my guide and porter, who is carrying the heavier pack. He's about 50 years old, and he's done the *khora* 80 times. At the top of the first pass we pause and are caught up by two figures I'd noticed before in the distance. One large man is carrying five mattresses plus some bedding, the other smaller man is carrying a small plastic bag. He has a club foot and walks with a limp. It turns out that he is a friend of Got's and is living in a tent with his family on the north side of Kailas, where he seems to have the concession on a stone hut in which it turns out I'm to sleep, though I don't know it yet. They spend the rest of the day in continuous conversation as they walk.

Down on the plain we pass near to yesterday's painting spot and I divert to do a small *khora* round the *Tarboche* pole with its coloured streamers; the ground is covered with debris left from the year before. I'm getting used to the strangeness of being in a remote place yet with evidence of devotions everywhere; carved rock, painted rock, mani stones. We pass under a famous monastery sitting high up on the other side of the canyon. No time to visit it because the aim is to get round to the north side of the mountain before the end of day.

For a while the path follows a frozen river deep in the gorge, without sight of Kailas. Then I catch sight of it, blinding white, against the deep blue sky, half hidden behind a flat-on view of the great black buttress that forms the south pillar to its west face. This view has a savage power and significance about it, something to do with its symmetries of shape and extreme polarities of colour and tone, intensified by being seen through a gap in the red sandstone wall. All I can do is spend some time filming it, and burning it into my memory, sadly with no time for painting.

I'd read that the best views of Kailas along this stretch were from the west bank of the river and took the opportunity to cross at a small bridge. Got and his companions have continued on the main pilgrim path on the east side; I keep them in sight whilst walking on my own, which is just what I want, and there's virtually no-one else about. So quiet, but with an echo in the space.

The canyon widens a bit and suddenly there is Kailas again, totally different, this time the whole west face in view. It is an extraordinary sight, the mountain doubling back on itself, the convex south face switching into concave mode, ribbed with a complex of horizontal terraces, zipping round to a blank rock wall at the north side, ending in an abrupt ridge, the whole thing topped by an overhanging ice cliff and surrounded by demented-looking sandstone rock towers. This is what I have come for. The mountain has such a powerful presence, I should be staying here and painting it, staying the night, but it would have meant bringing a tent, which would mean an extra porter, which would mean another tent!

The next hour is taken up trying to ensure that I've got everything I might need on film to make the intended painting; stopping almost neurotically every few yards, filming again and again, from every angle, for the next mile or so. And just looking, taking it all in.

Presently I notice that the others are heading for a big tent in the valley across the river; making a rush for it across the ice, cracking as I step on it, I join them in the tent. There are two other guests there as well, a Chinese gentleman, who says he isn't going all the way around the mountain, and his Tibetan porter. The pot-noodles on offer are extremely welcome, not having had breakfast, and it was good to get indoors out of the sun. The tent has been put up in advance of the expected rush of pilgrims, due later in the month.

It is about 4pm by now, and we have yet to turn around the corner of the mountain onto the north side. This for me is a gruelling two hours, sometimes wading thigh deep in soft snow, but gaining height. At last the ground levels out, I can see some low buildings and the red *gompa* across the river and then, past a foothill, I'm looking straight at the north face and I know this is going to be worth it.

157.   Kailas north face, morning (site study), 2006, oil on linen.
         25 x 30ins/63 x 76cms (*Julian Cooper*)

North face

These Tibetans are very kind. They've shown me to an empty dry-stonewall hut I can sleep in, given me a thermos of hot water, and when I mentioned painting Kailas, brought in a cardboard box for a desk, with a candle.

A cold night, but the stone walls keep the wind out. At 8am I make coffee on my stove, then porridge . Stepping out of the hut, I am shocked at the intensity of the colour of the north face in the morning light, pink snow and golden rock with deep blue shadows. Dawn light from the east defines the forms within the mountain. Very cold; the sun hasn't reached valley level yet. It's a pity time can't be stopped when it's like this; it's perfect now, but later the light will be all wrong. I shoot 10-second bursts of video now and then to catch the change of light. Having eventually chosen a spot away from the mountain down towards the monastery and river, I set up and start painting. It's 10am.

It's fascinating sorting out the intricacies of the north face in paint. The first impact is a simple pyramid or trapezoid shape, but there are sub-shapes within this; there's a prominent terrace line running along the whole face that is about 10 degrees off the horizontal (echoing the Tibetan plateau slope), and then it breaks up into deep ridges and gullies, but the line carries on among them. Below the angled line is a blank, unbroken wall and below this a whole series of terraces one on top of another, running the whole width of the mountain, forming a base. Capping it all, against the sky, is a vast pediment, interrupted by ridges and flutings of snow. At the summit a cornice bulges over the face.

I'm using water-soluble oil paint onto pre-prepared ochre ground, which reads pretty well as basic rock colour, so I modify this and work into it with blue-grey areas for shadow, then warm white areas for sunlit snow, and pale blue-grey for shadowed snow. A deep blue Tibetan sky compresses the whole lot and keeps it unified.

Sometime during my session a man sits down right next to me. I carry on working. He stays for about 15 minutes; he's been collecting river water. I give up painting at 1pm and go back to the hut. It snows, quite a blizzard, but stops by 2.30, so I go up the hill behind the huts and tents to do another painting nearer the mountain. It's grey sky and no sunlight, windy and bleak, but I want a record of the afternoon light. I have to tether down the easel with elastic cord to stop it shaking in the wind. With this second painting it's a chance to further impress form and colour into my memory for the actual large paintings back home.

Even if these on-site paintings appear crude and sketchy, they force me to look hard at the subject and that's their main purpose. After three and a half hours the sun comes out, transforming Kailas into something epic and magical, and I make sure that I get that onto video. I also get something of it onto canvas, sunlight defining the north face from the opposite direction to this morning's session.

Packing up, I notice a lone photographer on the ridge below me; he's Japanese, I think. I wave but there's no response. He's still there when I leave. Back at the huts some people have arrived, including a Siberian who's curious to see what I've been working on. I've been given an extra duvet to go over my sleeping bag; it's going to be a cold night.

East face

I get up at 7.30am and look out of the hut. Kailas looks blindingly bright, covered in fresh snow with a semi-transparent aura of mist rising up from it. The Russians are already setting off to continue round the mountain; I pack and make breakfast, ready to set off with Got. It's a beautiful sunny day but Gott doesn't appear, and when he does, much later, suggests that it's too late now, because the snow will be too soft. I insist, and he gets ready, but it's already 10am before we're crossing the river. The ice is extremely dodgy; I have to run across, half hopping on the poles, and it breaks at every step, but not quite all the way through. Then it's a plod up to the first pass where we come across a nomad descending with his horse. The animal is bleeding and we follow spots of blood all the way from there. Next comes a snow basin; it's getting warm now and the snow is deep and soft. We have to keep moving fast before it becomes impossible to move. Splendid views looking across to the north-east side of the mountain, where it connects onto a ridge and the inner *khora* starts.

Ahead lies the Dolma La at 5630m. I ascend slowly, so it's not too bad. Got is way ahead. The top is an exhilarating and silent place, deep snow all around, the great rock covered with flags, streamers, and bits of clothing. It must be crowded with pilgrims during the season, the climax to their journey. But now it's just the two of us and we have our respective lunches. I give Got a tot of my Laphroaig; he likes it, so we share the flask during the steep descent.

It's a relief to be going downhill, but it goes on for a long time until we reach valley bottom. Resting in a sheepfold, we're surprised by a couple of yak herders who want a chat; they look a bit like Red Indians. We continue along a seemingly endless valley. I'm getting tired, but it's difficult to find any stone without sacred words carved on it, and all are therefore forbidden to sit on. The sky clouds up; it's starting to snow. I look half-heartedly up at Kailas now and then, but the east face is mostly hidden, either by cloud or foothills, and I don't care anymore.

At last the *gompa* comes into view, and a guesthouse beneath with rooms. We eat with the nice woman of the house and her young daughter; noodle soup eaten with chopsticks. I'm hopeless with chopsticks, an inability they find amusing. Before turning in the landlady needs to be paid, but won't accept either my slightly torn 100 yuan note, or the dollars I have. So the daughter takes me up the hill to the *gompa,* for change. It's dusk, and snowing gently. The girl bangs repeatedly on the great double doors of the monastery until eventually they are opened by an ancient lama in dark red robes with long grey hair. It feels like I'm in a kind of Tintin episode. The little girl skips right in, as if it's a second home, rolling the massive prayer wheel inside, and we follow the lama who unlocks an inner chamber, dimly lit, with rows of gold Buddhas and painted walls. He goes to the safe and after a lot of counting and recounting the transaction is sorted out.

Next day it is just a morning's walk to complete the *khora*, gently descending alongside a river and then onto the Barkha plain with views across to the graceful shapes of Gurla Mandhata in the distance, then onto the main Darchen track where we are overtaken by young Tibetans riding trail bikes and wearing cowboy hats. Within sight of the village, Got and I rest for the last time, sitting on uninscribed rocks, having a whisky and attending to his payment. Got shows me his shoes which were brand new at the start of the *khora* and are now completely worn through at the soles. So I give him extra for new ones.

On arrival, I'm told that my friends, with whom I journeyed to Tibet, have given up their attempt on their unclimbed 'Peak 6530' near Loinbo Kangri due to wintry conditions and are on their own *khora* of Kailas. They are due in tomorrow. I'm delighted, both at the prospect of rejoining them and because it will make it easier for us all to get back across the border to Nepal.

158. Kailas south face, morning (site study), 2006, oil on linen. 25 x 30ins/63 x 76cms (*Julian Cooper*)

South face

This is my last chance to paint the south face and I head off early. High on a ridge I stop and let a lone dog walk slowly by. I'm worried about rabies. It's cold and windy when I get to the high point looking over to the face. With sunlight and clouds moving rapidly across Kailas, it has a totally different feel from that calm evening here six days ago. I'd like to include this movement of sun and cloud shadow into the painting but that has to be left to the camera at this point. The priority is to sort out the formal complexity of the south face, which is the most iconic image of Kailas, the one that the first pilgrims would have seen on climbing up out of India.

This south face is hypnotizing me. It's a perfect symbol of *Yab-Yum,* (male/female) and I keep losing my place in what I'm looking at; there's a difficulty in getting the subtle double curve of the west skyline and I think there are nine stacks of terraces. It's a pattern of roughly equal amounts of snow and rock forming horizontal bands that move from predominately rock at the base to predominately snow at the top, with a kind of ladder of rock terraces partly showing through the snow cap leading up to the summit. It's all supposed to form a swastika but I can't see that. Then there's a great gully that rends the face from top to bottom and is said to have been formed by a *Bon-Po* priest being flung down the mountain by the Buddhist saint Milarepa.

After about three hours I've had enough. Before going, I point the video camera at myself, but forget to include Kailas in the frame, omitting the only evidence that I've been here at all. With a feeling of 'job done', I am able to appreciate the walk back down the hill to Darchen, with Nanda Devi and the Garhwal Himalaya faintly visible in the distance, Gurla Mandhata seemingly afloat beyond the Barkha plain and the half-frozen ultramarine lakes Manasarowar and Rakshas Tal in the foreground.

It's mid-afternoon when I get down to the guesthouse, and Mina, the driver insists on taking me straight to where the others have arrived. It's good to see all them again, and over beers at a teahouse we compare our respective *khoras.*

I am grateful to Julian Freeman-Attwood for his invitation in April 2006 to accompany him and fellow climbers Luke Hughes, Phil Bartlett and Mark Upton on an expedition he was leading to attempt the first ascent of 'Peak 6530', a spectacular pyramid rising from a high snowfield near to Loinbo Kangri in western Tibet. The plan was that I would paint from a high camp near the base of their mountain before heading off west to Kailas, two days away, with driver and vehicle. This part of the trip was my own eventful introduction to Tibet, involving among other things a pre-dawn exit from Kathmandu, avoiding curfew, road-blocks and riots (the slow-motion overthrow of King Gyanendra was underway), a narrow escape from a series of avalanches on the road deep in the Kyirong valley and the discovery of a 1000-year-old working monastery, apparently untouched by the Chinese 'Cultural' Revolution.

History

Rowan Huntley *Store Skagastølstind ~ Fading Light, July*
Chroma on board, 40cm x 30cm. (*Private collection*)

EVA SELIN

Carl Rubenson, Kabru
and the birth of the Norwegian AC

On 1 November 1907 Norwegian climbers received a sensational telegram:

Happily we have completed our expedition to Kabru (20th October), placing the Norwegian flag at the highest point so far reached by alpinists in the Himalaya, that is at an approximate altitude of 23,900ft. Rubenson and Monrad-Aas.

The climb to within 100ft of the summit of this outlier of Kangchenjunga by two 20-year olds on their first trip to the Himalaya was an astounding achievement and provided the inspiration for the founding of Norway's own alpine club – the Norsk Tindeklub (NTK) – which this year celebrated its centenary.

The news of the Kabru climb was also published in Oslo's biggest newspapers, *Morgenbladet* and *Aftenposten*. This prompted a somewhat sour comment by the Swedish climber Eric Ullén in the following day's *Morgenbladet*, in which he recalled WW Graham's claim to have reached 23,965ft on Kabru in 1883 before being turned back by an ice cliff. Carl Wilhelm Rubenson and Monrad-Aas seemed not to have exceeded the altitude reached by Graham, concluded Ullén, who also pointed out that the altitude record was held by the American William Hunter Workman for his ascent of 'Pyramide Peak' (23,964m) in Pakistan. Was it too hard for the Swede to put up with the Norwegian success?

Graham's claim on Kabru has since been regarded as a case of mistaken identity, and the first undisputed ascent to the 24,002ft summit was by CR Cooke in 1935. Rubenson at first hesitated about the correctness of the supposedly fast ascent by Graham but later on, when other expeditions showed it was possible to move rapidly even at higher altitudes, he was inclined to support Graham's claim. Record or not, Rubenson and Monrad-Aas's climb, without guides, was a milestone in Himalayan mountaineering.

During the latter part of the 19th century, mountaineering in Norway was dominated by foreigners, principally by Englishmen. William Cecil Slingsby, rightly known as 'the father of Norwegian mountaineering', visited the country for the first time in 1872. His ascent four years later of Store Skagastölstind in the Hurrungarne group, together with Norwegians Emanuel Mohn and Knut Lykken, was the starting point of an intensive period of ascents among the virgin peaks of the Jotunheimen. Slingsby was also the first to go by ski in Jotunheimen. Besides the Englishmen, the

Dane Carl Hall (1848-1908) was a great pioneer doing many first ascents through-out Norway.

At first the visitors were guided by people with local geographic knowledge but little mountaineering skill. However, Carl Hall was very anxious to teach the locals the basics of mountaineering and gradually they became more and more experienced. Together with Slingsby, he instructed the first professional guides: Ola Berge, Torgeir Sulheim and Mathias Soggemoen. Training took place in the early 1890s at Turtagrö, open moorland long used for summer grazing, in magnificent surroundings of sharp peaks and shining glaciers. In 1888 two hotels were built here, one belonging to Ola Berge and the other to Ola Öine. Besides the hotel keeping, both were devoted to the economically lucrative business of guiding and Turtagrö soon became a centre for mountaineering. Sadly, one of the hotels burned down in the winter of 2005 but has since been rebuilt.

At the turn of the century keen Norwegian youngsters with 'mountains in their eyes' became more common at Turtagrö. Among them were Eilert Sundt, who in 1900 joined Slingsby for a new route on Midre Skagastölstind, the legendary women mountaineer Therese Bertheau, and Alf Bryn, Carl Rubenson, Ferdinand Schjelderup and Henning Tönsberg who together would dominate the Norwegian climbing scene for 20 years, doing many notable first ascents. The ever-enthusiastic Slingsby, at this time around 50 years old, enjoyed climbing with the young tigers. In an obituary in the NTK journal of 1933, Schjelderup emphasised their friendship with Slingsby: 'With his catching enthusiasm, he inspired us to new ascents and at the same time he shared with us his exceptional topographical knowledge. But above all, he opened our eyes to interesting features and the immense beauty of the nature that we otherwise would never have been aware of. And this is the most important thing for feeling truly at home in the mountains.'

The Swede Erik Ullén and Dane Egil Rostrup were very active at this time, with several important first ascents, pushing climbing standards and safe rope management. Gradually a number of ascents were done without guides; of course it saved expenses but most important was the personal challenge. The new generation had a strong desire to find their own way and new routes in the mountains.

The 'boat' built on this intensive climbing in the Hurrungarne group and on the small crags around Oslo was then launched with the achievement on Kabru and in April 1908 the Norwegian Alpine Club (NTK) was founded. The model was the Alpine Club. Only established Norwegian male alpinists could be accepted as members – Ullén and Rostrup were thus excluded as foreigners. In 1909 Slingsby and Therese Bertheau were elected as honorary members. Today the NTK has about 500 members. In 1975 it was opened to women and in 1999 to foreigners. The Club retains the ethical heritage of Cecil Slingsby, its central objective being to promote alpinism with awareness of nature and without leaving traces.

160. *Left*
CW Rubenson
(*DNT Yearbook, 1908*)

161. *Below*
Slingsby (*left*),
Rob Baker (*centre*)
and Rubenson
in Hurrungarne, 1908.
(*NTK archives*)

The ascent of Kabru is described in the journal of the Norwegian Mountain Touring Assocation (DNT) of 1908, in the NTK journal of 1914, and in the *Alpine Journal*. In autumn 1906, Rubenson and Monrad-Aas embarked on the long journey by boat to India. Monrad-Aas was well trained, but with no alpine experience. However, according to Rubenson, he was a born alpinist.

Of Rubenson himself, who became an honorary member of the AC, I know a little more; he was my grand-mother's second cousin. Born into a prominent Jewish family in Stockholm in 1885, Carl Wilhelm's mother was Norwegian and his father Swedish. Aged one, he moved with his mother to Oslo, and there, while at college, he met Ferdinand Schjelderup with whom he started climbing.

On attaining his majority, Rubenson received a legacy that allowed him to live a more or less economically untroubled life. He began studies to become an architect but the journey to the Himalaya changed his life from an academically orientated direction to one of alpinism and business. From 1920 he worked as an advertising consultant and as a freelance journalist. He was interested in literature and wrote a splendid essay on life and nature in Kashmir and also small lyric poems as well as many articles on mountaineering.

It doesn't seem that Rubenson and Monrad-Aas had any information about Freshfield's celebrated circuit of the Kangchenjunga massif in 1898 or knowledge of other ascents in the Himalaya. Any idea about which mountain to attempt was very vague. When the pair inquired in Calcutta about possibilities, puzzled inhabitants either shrugged their shoulders or shook their heads; going to the high mountains in midwinter – impossible and stupid!

Eventually Sikkim emerged the best choice – probably their only choice as it was one of the few areas in the region where Europeans had permission to go and was also known to offer relatively safe travelling. The six-week journey to the base of Kabru gave Rubenson and Monrad-Aas a useful taste of Sikkim and of expedition life, but it was obvious that a serious attempt on the mountain would have to wait until autumn 1907. During spring and summer they undertook a long journey in the East. 'This was not the right kind of training for mountaineers as the heat encouraged us to be lazy beyond measure,' wrote Rubenson.

By the end of August preparation for the expedition was in full progress. Bags, sacks, clothing, blankets, sleeping bags, tents and other necessaries were piled in their hotel room. Rubenson laid particular stress on having the right equipment for porters.

On 16 September the two Norwegians left Darjeeling, accompanied by 100 porters and a Scot called Mason who joined as an interpreter. Base camp was established on the Rothong glacier (16,000ft) from where, on 7 October, Rubenson, Monrad-Aas and '14 of the best coolies' set off with four tents and supplies for one week. Three camps later they reached 22,000ft where they rested and acclimatised for three days. The weather was excellent, and on a calm day with a clear sky, Rubenson, Monrad-Aas and two Sherpas made what they hoped would be a final push.

'But the day was very hot; we felt very lazy and when we tapped the ridge connecting the north-eastern peak of Kabru with the Dome, we sat down, smoked our pipes, enjoyed the beautiful view and decided to have our tents brought up a bit higher the next day.'

A tent was brought up to 22,600ft; however weariness and hunger were taking their toll. Rubenson confessed to losing all taste for ox tongue and the only thing that would keep their 'pecker up' was brandy – 'even in this matter the coolies were at one with us'. On 20 October they made a last attempt, the one Sherpa who set out with them turning back with hunger pangs, leaving Rubenson and Monrad-Aas for the first time 'quite alone'. Battling strong winds, they had to choose a sheltered but steeper, icier route directly up towards the north-east peak. Great care was needed cutting steps as they had had to discard their nailed boots because freezing nails made them too cold to wear.

Rubenson reckoned he and Monrad-Aas were fifty or sixty feet below the summit when they turned back. The sun was touching the horizon, their teeth were chattering violently in the cold and the wind had hit them with such force that they dared not continue. They looked at each other and at the snow ridge slightly rising towards the long-desired white top-dome, so close and still unattainable. The descent was at times dramatic, with Rubenson being saved from a serious fall by an observant Monrad-Aas.

Rubenson and Monrad-Aas had not got their longed-for sight of Kangchenjunga from the top of Kabru, but the magic attraction lived on. In 1909 Rubenson and Ferdinand Schjelderup travelled to London to seek permission to pass through Nepal and parts of India, but without success. On 6 December a British foreign minister wrote to his Norwegian counterpart regretting to inform him 'that the objections by the Nepal government to all exploration by Europeans in Nepal render compliance with your request impossible'.

But Rubenson would not give up. In March 1911, thinking to try to get permission to visit Nepal once in India, he again left for Calcutta. A short note in *The Daily Telegraph* about his departure created alarm within the Norwegian government. Was there any possibility that the expedition would travel illegally in Nepal? The Ministry of Foreign Affairs cross-examined the chairman of the Tindeklub, Eilert Sundt, and their Norwegian representative in London, Benjamin Vogt, got in touch with Slingsby who returned a positive answer. Rubenson certainly would try to reach Kangchenjunga, but without passing through Nepal. However, Rubenson never got that far. Instead, he and his wife visited Kashmir and made first ascents of Potbury Peak (16,100 ft) and Snowy Peak (17,890 ft).

Consolation for Rubenson and Schjelderup after their unsuccessful visit to London in 1909 came with a journey north to the home of Cecil Slingsby, who, as enthusiastic as ever, opened their eyes to the possibilities of remarkable unclimbed routes in northern Norway, notably Stetind which he had attempted in 1904 with Wooley and Collie. Describing the visit in the DNT Yearbook of 1911, Schjelderup recalled asking Slingsby:

> 'Those smooth slabs, are they that hard?' The answer was immediate and short: 'There is one and only one slab on Stetind, and it runs from the base to the top'. Slingsby turned to the photograph again, pointing out some weak structures that possibly could be defeated on the impressive ridge rising steeply towards the top.

The first ascent of Stetind in July 1910 by Rubenson, Schjelderup and H Jentoft, was the breakthrough for a decade of notable first ascents in northern Norway. During the summer the party also did a couple of first ascents in the Lofoten area and in 1912 the same trio gained the inaccessible Strandåtinden on Kjerringoy island north of Bodö. (See *AJ* 2001 for an excellent article about Strandåtind by Anders Lundahl). The climb, by the exposed west ridge, is remembered by Rubenson as the hardest and most demanding he had ever done. Ten days later the same party, together with Slingsby, ascended the mountain by its north ridge. In a letter written the following December, Slingsby commented: 'I have been again in Arctic Norway climbing with Rubenson (of Kabru fame) and two other stalwart and young (comparatively with my 63 years) Norsemen.'

Further memorable first ascents for Rubenson were the long traverse of Börvasstinderne in the Beiarn area south of Bodö in 1916, with Schjelderup and W Morgenstierna, and the climb of the sharp-edged Piggtind in Lyngen, with Jensen and H Tönsberg. Five years later, with Tönsberg, Jensen and Jentoft, came firsts on Hatten in the Steigen area and Sildbottentind in the Narvik area.

162. *Left*
The first ascent of
Stetind, 1910.
(*DNT Yearbook, 1911*)

163. Stetind. (*Anders Lundahl*)

Much has changed since Rubenson's day and the founding of the Norwegian Alpine Club, but still the words of Doug Scott in *Big Wall Climbing* (1973) ring true:

> In Norway there exist not only vast areas of unclimbed rock, but also climbs in true wilderness surroundings. Very few valleys in northern Norway share the plight of Alpine valleys where commercial exploitation has brought the cities to the mountains. In Norway it is still possible to visit easily accessible valleys that have no roads running through them, not even footpaths leading to hotels and huts, and certainly no hoards of jostling climbers and trippers on conducted tours.

Hopefully it will be possible to continue to quote the same words in the future. Today it is more important than ever to conserve the possibilities of adventure in our lives.

DAVID SEDDON

The 1933 Piz Roseg Disaster
and EW Powell

This year is the 75th anniversary of the death of four Eton schoolmasters, EV Slater, EW Powell, HEE Howson and CR White-Thomson on Piz Roseg in the Engadine. On 17 August 1933 they left the Tschierva hut with the intention of climbing the Eselgrat on Piz Roseg but did not return. The following day, two guided parties climbing the same route were surprised to find three axes in a couloir above the Sella glacier. From the highest axe, a deep, narrow furrow ran down the gully and out of sight. Nothing further could be seen. The two parties continued to the summit and on their descent saw two bodies and returned to the Tshierva hut and raised the alarm. On 19 August, a search party of 19 guides found the four bodies still roped together and brought them down to Pontresina.[1] In 2006 a retired Engadine guide, Herr Kirle, could recall, as a boy of 12, witnessing this sad procession of guides and a horse-drawn cart returning to the village.

The accident could have been due to stonefall or a slip. Wet afternoon snow would have made the slide of the party, once started, impossible to control. Three days later, the men were buried in the grounds of the Santa Maria Kirche in Pontresina, each coffin carried by four guides. In 1999, as permitted by Swiss law, the headstones were taken down, although the plot where the men are buried may still be identified.

Of the four men, three, Howson, Slater and Powell, were members of the Alpine Club. This seems to have been the only occasion when three members of the Club have lost their lives as a result of a single climbing accident. The same three men were also housemasters at Eton. Claude Elliott, later President of the Alpine Club, had just assumed the headship of the school and was immediately faced with the task of replacing these men and putting the risks of mountaineering in context to the school community. Elliott gave an address in the College Chapel on 24 September 1933 and to the question: 'But, it may be asked, why should men climb mountains at all, why endanger lives that others have need of?' he responded:

It [mountaineering] *is a method of seeking, and of making touch with, something outside us and infinitely above us. They* [mountaineers] *find it above everything through a supremely intensified appreciation of all that is beautiful in their surroundings, through the vision of distant ranges, through the view from close at hand of rock tower and ice slope either gleaming in the sun or seen through rifts of cloud when every step is a struggle ...*[2]

164. EW Powell, *Wetterhorn*. Watercolour, undated. (*Private collection*)

There is a memorial to the four men in the ante-chapel at Eton and the boys of Slater's house subscribed to a memorial tablet in the Cloister.

Eric Walter Powell (1886-1933) was perhaps the most remarkable of the four men. At Trinity College, Cambridge he had been a distinguished oarsman, and a rowing Blue in 1906, 1907 and 1908. He won a Bronze medal in the 1908 Olympics. He returned to Eton in 1910 to teach French and German. At the outbreak of war in August 1914 he was an infantry officer, but by 1916 he was a squadron leader and later wing commander in the Royal Flying Corps. He returned to Eton in 1919 and spent a year (1920-1921) studying art in Paris with the intention that he should take on responsibility for the teaching of this subject.[3]

He only started climbing after the end of the war and visited Skye in 1919. He seems to have taken up Alpine mountaineering in 1922 with ascents of the Jungfrau, Wetterhorn and Schreckhorn and by 1925 he had climbed most of the Oberland peaks. He sometimes climbed with guides such as Quirin Zurbriggen and Heinrich Burgener but perhaps more often climbed guideless with Slater and Howson. He was elected to the Alpine Club in 1925 and amongst his supporters was Noel Odell.[4] He also climbed in Norway, Corsica and the Pyrenees and visited the Engadine in 1930 or earlier.

A talented amateur artist, the earliest painting I can identify is a watercolour, *Windsor Castle from the River*, dated 1908. He favoured watercolour as a medium and only rarely painted in oil. He exhibited at Walker's Galleries in New Bond Street on seven occasions between 1920 and 1933 including at least 60 pictures in 1927 and 76 pictures in 1931. Amongst these were three pictures of Piz Roseg, *Piz Roseg from Piz Morteratsch, Piz Roseg from the Ice Nose of Piz Scerscen – Sunrise, The Biancograt and Piz Roseg.*[5] Several of his pictues were exhibited at the Alpine Club in 1925 and 1930 including *Piz Roseg from the Morteratsch.*[6] A memorial exhibition of 90 of his paintings was held at Walker's Galleries in November 1933. To mark the 50th anniversary of the disaster, an exhibition of 48 of his paintings was held at Eton in 1983. Amongst these were pictures of Windsor, Paris and Venice as well as scenes from the First World War, Wales, Scotland and the Alps.[7] Eton College possesses a number of his watercolours and one oil. The Alpine Club has two watercolours; *Blumlisalphorn, Oberland* is reproduced in *The Artists of the Alpine Club.*[7]

Powell must have been very highly regarded at the Alpine Club, as well as at Eton. Irving chose to include part of the obituary notice for Powell in his anthology of mountain prose and verse.[8,9] Shortly before the accident, White-Thomson wrote in a letter to his family from the Golf-Hotel des Alpes, Samedan, '*Eric is the same, ever steady ... leading up or coming down last. In the intervals he paints.*'[10]

165. Graves of EV Slater, EW Powell, HEE Howson and CR White-Thomson in the grounds of Santa Maria Kirche at Pontresina.
(*By courtesy of Nigel Jaques*)

REFERENCES

1. *AJ* 45, 1933, 414-416.
2. Eton College Chronicle, September 1933, p1520.
3. The Drawing Schools, Eton College. EW Powell 1886-1933m November 1983.
4. Election papers of EW Powell, Alpine Club Archive.
5. National Art Library, Victoria and Albert Museum, London.
6. Exhibition Catalogues, Alpine Club Archive.
7. P Mallalieu, *The Artists of the Alpine Club.* The Alpine Club and the Ernest Press, 2007.
8. JD Hills, *AJ* 1934, 46, 185-187.
9. RLG Irving, *The Mountain Way.* Dent and Sons, London, 1938.
10. Correspondence held by Nigel Jaques.

Acknowledgements
I am grateful to Nigel Jaques, the nephew of Charles Robert White-Thomson, for the photograph of the headstones of the four men. I am also grateful to Jackie Tarrant-Barton of the Old Etonian Association and to Henrietta Ryan, Keeper of Pictures at Eton College.

C A RUSSELL

One Hundred Years Ago

(with extracts from the *Alpine Journal*)

The weather has been on the whole very fine; true, there were many laments about the meagreness of the snowfall – the winter mantle had almost reached vanishing point towards the end of January –but we have enjoyed an abundance of sunshine and the frosts have been consistently severe.

The intense cold experienced throughout the Alps during the opening weeks of 1908 did not deter the Italian climber Mario Piacenza who on 16 January, accompanied by Jean Baptiste Pélissier and Laurent Petigax, made a winter ascent of the Dent du Géant.[1] During the year the development of ski mountaineering continued apace and several notable expeditions were completed. In January, after starting from Chamonix and crossing the Col des Montets, H E Beaujard with Joseph[2] and Edouard Ravanel completed a section of the high-level route – the Haute Route – reaching Zermatt from the Chanrion hut by way of the Col de l'Evêque and the Col de Valpelline. In the same month Arnold Lunn and Cecil Wybergh, without guides, spent four days on ski at the western end of the Bernese Alps, crossing a number of passes between Montana and Villars. Peaks climbed for the first time under winter conditions with the aid of ski[3] included the Trifthorn in the Zermatt district on 21 January by C Mauler with Louis and Benoît Theytaz and in northern Europe Kebnekaise (2123m), the highest point in Sweden, on 29 March by H N Pallin.

By early summer the weather had become unsettled and the season was

... very bad from a climber's point of view. One of the oldest guides, whose exploits are well known to all mountaineers, described the season to us as 'one of the worst he had ever known.'

Although conditions were unfavourable in many regions a number of notable expeditions was completed during brief spells of fine weather. In the Maritime Alps two outstanding new ascents were completed on the Punta dell' Argentera, the highest peak in the range: the classic south ridge on 24 June by Angelo Brofferio and Vittorio Sigismondi; and, on 1 September, a fine route by Victor de Cessole with Andréa Ghigo and Jean Plent who reached the Spalla, the shoulder on the south ridge, by way of the steep west face. Following his climb on the Argentera Brofferio moved to the Mont Blanc range where on 17 July he joined forces with Ettore Santi

166. Jôf del Montasio,
Julian Alps,
from above Dogna.
(*L Pignat*)

and Ugo De Amicis to make the first ascent of the narrow east ridge of the
Aiguille de la Lex Blanche, above the Trélatête glacier. Another visitor to
this region was J J Withers who on 25 August with Adolf Andenmatten
and Andreas Anthamatten completed the first traverse of a famous pass –
the Col des Cristaux,[4] between Les Courtes and the Aiguille Ravanel.
Further along the chain in the Monte Rosa group on 28 July G B and G F
Gugliermina and Luigi Ravelli reached the summit of Punta Giordani, a
prominent shoulder of the Piramide Vincent, by way of the unclimbed north-
east ridge. In the Bernese Alps on 13 August Paul Baumgartner and Walter
Hopf forced a route up the dangerous east flank of the Lauteraarhorn to
reach the south-east ridge.

To the east in the Bernina Alps on 10 October Paul Schucan and A Pfister
made the first complete ascent of the long east-north-east ridge of Piz
Morteratsch. In the Dolomites Oliver Perry-Smith with Rudolf Fehrmann
opened two outstanding new routes: the south face of the Torre Stabeler,
one of the Vajolet Towers, on 19 August; and, on 27 August, the south-
west dièdre climb on the Campanile Basso – the Guglia di Brenta. Another
notable expedition, on 21 August, was undertaken by Frau Käthe Bröske
and Rudolf Schietzold who with Tita Piaz traversed the six principal Vajolet
Towers in a single day. In the Julian Alps on 29 August Graziadio Bolaffio
and Julius Kugy with Anton Oitzinger and Osvaldo Pesamosca established
the classic south-west pillar route on the Jôf del Montasio, or Montasch,
the second highest summit in the range.

Elsewhere in the Alps a major engineering project was severely affected by two tragic events. Construction of the Lötschberg Tunnel to provide a rail link under the Bernese Alps from Kandersteg to Goppenstein was well advanced when on the evening of 29 February a sudden wave of air pressure caused by an avalanche above Goppenstein destroyed a wooden hotel built by the contractor near the southern portal, killing 12 employees. Five months later, on 24 July, a disaster occurred when the heading of the northern, Kandersteg tunnel collapsed during blasting operations at a point some 170m below the Kander river in the Gastern valley, allowing an inflow of loose material and water. The tunnel was filled with debris over a length of 1500m and 25 workers lost their lives.[5]

In the Engadine on 1 July celebrations were held to mark the official opening of a branch railway to a famous mountain resort.

> The branch line of the Rhaetian Railway from Samedan to Pontresina will be opened for traffic tomorrow. The daily service will consist of sixteen trains each way.

On 25 May Dr William Hunter Workman and his wife Fanny Bullock Workman left Srinagar to commence the sixth of their mountain journeys. Accompanied by the guide Cyprien Savoye, three porters from Courmayeur and two surveyors, Count Cesare Calciati and Dr Mathias Koncza, the Workmans spent four months undertaking a detailed exploration of the Hispar region,[6] visiting a number of branch glaciers and descending the Biafo glacier to Askole. Many photographs were obtained during several weeks of fine weather and on 2 August Mrs Bullock Workman with Savoye and two of the porters ascended a peak[7] near the Hispar Pass to which they ascribed a height of some 6500m.

In July the American Miss Annie Smith Peck returned to the Andes, accompanied on this occasion by the Swiss guides Rudolf Taugwalder and Gabriel zum Taugwald, to make a further attempt[8] to climb Huascarán (6768m), the highest mountain in Peru. Starting on 6 August Miss Peck, zum Taugwald and a number of local men reached the saddle between the north and south peaks before being forced to retreat. At the end of the month she repeated the climb and on 2 September with the two guides made the first ascent[9] of the north, lower peak (6655m).

In the far south on 10 March a notable climb was completed by Dr A F Mackay and four other members of Sir Ernest Shackleton's *Nimrod* Antarctic Expedition who made the first ascent of Mount Erebus (3794m), a volcanic peak on Ross Island in McMurdo Sound. After leaving a base at Cape Royds the party endured very low temperatures and a severe blizzard before establishing a final camp some four hours below the summit.

In Britain, where the weather was unsettled for much of the year, many parties were active in all the principal regions. In Wales during October A W Andrews and J B Farmer made the first ascent of *Central Chimney Route*,

167. Peak near the Hispar Pass climbed by Mrs Bullock Workman's party on
2 August 1908. (*Dr WH Workman*)

a popular climb on the East Buttress of Lliwedd. In Scotland A C McLaren
and L G Shadbolt, climbing in June, scaled *Shadbolt's Chimney*, an early
route on the north face of Aonach Dubh in Glencoe.

A welcome development on 7 March was the foundation of the Alpine
Ski Club under the presidency of Sir Martin Conway,[10] the object of the
Club being

> ... to promote mountaineering on Ski and good fellowship among
> Ski-ers; to encourage mountaineering expeditions on Ski throughout
> the world; and to promote a better knowledge of the mountains in
> winter.

In the following month on 18 April the Ladies' Scottish Climbing Club
was formed with Mrs William Inglis Clark as the first President. In Norway
the Norsk Tindeklub was founded on 10 April by Carl Rubenson, Ferdinand
Schjelderup and other prominent climbers of the period.

Another event of note was the publication of *Ruwenzori*,[11] the account by
Filippo De Filippi of the expedition led by the Duke of the Abruzzi to that
range. This comprehensive work, illustrated by Vittorio Sella, was reviewed

in the *Alpine Journal* where it was considered to be 'a book which is likely to remain the classic description of one of the most interesting mountain ranges in the world.' Other books published during the year included *The Alps in Nature and History* by W A B Coolidge and *Rock-climbing in Skye* by A P Abraham.

On 1 January the death occurred of Horace Walker, a former President of the Alpine Club. A member of the famous Walker family, he took part in the first ascent of the Brenva ridge route on Mont Blanc[12] and many other notable expeditions.

This account is concluded with an extract from a paper read before the Alpine Club in the following year by Withers, who after descending from the Col des Cristaux looked up at the Grandes Jorasses.

> Scoffers indeed say, not without some reason, that the modern climber keeps only to well-worn tracks and has no initiative; but there are still some who, sitting by the winter fire, see a party of the future sturdier than they successfully breasting the last rocks of the great north face of the Grandes Jorasses. Let them so dream.

REFERENCES

1. The peak had been climbed under winter conditions by Ettore Allegra with Pierre and Jean Dayné in April 1900.
2. The famous guide Ravanel, *le Rouge*.
3. A ski ascent is defined by Sir Arnold Lunn as 'an expedition on which ski were used until the foot of the final rock or ice ridges.'
4. Named by Withers after 'a large number of fine crystals' had been found on the pass and during the ascent.
5. Construction work was delayed for seven months by the disaster.
6. The Hispar and Biafo glaciers had been explored and surveyed in July 1892 during Sir Martin Conway's expedition to the Karakoram.
7. Named Biafo Hispar Watershed Peak by the Workmans.
8. Miss Peck had made unsuccessful attempts in 1904 and 1906.
9. Although the highest point attained during Miss Peck's final attempt – when Taugwalder was severely frostbitten – has been disputed, the authenticity of her claim to have ascended the north peak has been generally accepted.
10. Later Lord Conway of Allington. He had used ski during his exploration of Spitsbergen; see *AJ102*, 233, 1997.
11. Filippo De Filippi, *Ruwenzori: an Account of the Expedition of HRH Prince Luigi Amedeo of Savoy, Duke of the Abruzzi*. London, Archibald Constable and Co Ltd, 1908.
12. With his father Frank Walker, G S Mathews, A W Moore and the guides Jakob and Melchior Anderegg on 15 July 1865.

Area Notes

Rowan Huntley *Munkan from Djupfjorden ~ Afternoon Sunshine*
Chroma on board, 50cm x 75cm. (*Alpine Club collection*)

First ascent of Nordre Munkan, July 30 1903, W C Slingsby and party
Presented to the Alpine Club art collection, 2004

The Alps 2007

This selection of significant ascents and new routes progresses, more or less, from west to east across the Alps, and all events took place during 2007 unless otherwise stated. The following are thanked for their help with this report: Jon Bracey; Nick Bullock; Andrej Grmovsek; *Montagnes* magazine; Jon de Montjoye; Tony Penning; Guy Robertson; Hillary Sharp; Luca Signorelli; Thomas Tivadar, and Miha Valic.

From 27 December '06 to 7 April '07, the Slovenian guide, Miha Valic, climbed all 82 summits that make up the UIAA's official list of Alpine 4000m peaks. Valic, who was the first to attempt all these summits in winter, had the ambitious target of completing the list in 82 days, but due to bad weather he'd 'only' managed 74 by the end of the official winter season and needed another 20 days to finish the set.

Valic's tactics were different to those of Martin Moran and Simon Jenkins, who made the first continuous traverse of what they considered to be all the 4000m peaks (the UIAA list did not exist at this time) during the summer of 1993, or Patrick Bérhault and Philippe Magnin who, in the spring of 2004, attempted a continuous traverse of the full list until stopped by the fatal accident to Bérhault. While both pairs linked the peaks under their own steam, working across the range, Valic used a van to wait out bad weather and drive to each venue, choosing peaks as weather and conditions dictated. At one point he went home to Ljubujana for almost a week.

During his odyssey the Slovenian climbed with 15 different companions and made some committing winter traverses, such as the Dent du Géant-Rochefort-Grandes Jorasses ridge, the Diable Arête and the Schreckhorn-Lauteraarhorn crossing, all serious D or D+ outings in summer. There was also a three-day traverse of the entire Mischabel Group, and another from the Aiguilles Blanche over the Grand Pilier d'Angle to the Eccles huts, then up the Brouillard Ridge of Mont Blanc and down over the Dôme de Goûter and Aiguille de Bionassay. Despite the mild winter at valley level, there was a lot of snow above 3000m and the weather in the mountains was far from mild. Strong winds made even the easier 4000m peaks a serious test and although the project was logistically and physically demanding, completing it was, according to Valic, much more of a mental and motivational challenge.

Above right
169. The south (Italian) side of Mont Blanc de Courmayeur (4765m). To the left of the summit fall-line the four Frêney Pillars rise to the crest of the Brouillard Ridge (left skyline). Dropping from the summit and marking the right edge of the Frêney Face is the upper Peuterey Ridge. (*Antonio Giani*)

Mont Blanc Massif

On the remote *Hidden Pillar of Frêney*, **Mont Blanc**, Christophe Dumarest and the evergreen Patrick Gabarrou added a second route to the right of the original line climbed in August 1963 by Tom Frost and John Harlin. Having left the Eccles bivouac huts early one morning in September, the two Frenchmen were bivouacking at the top of the pillar that same evening. Dumarest, who led the hard pitches of the new route, *Jean-Chri* (named after the late Jean-Christophe Lafaille), climbed free up to 7a+ and used aid on everything harder. He felt the route might go completely free at around 7c; no small problem when the difficulties lie at over 4400m. Next day, following Gabarrou's traditional ethics, the pair climbed up to the Brouillard Ridge and followed it to the summit of Mont Blanc through a vicious storm.

In July, Francesca Marcelli, Tullio Paravicini, Luciano Ratti and Mario Sertori put up *La Casa nella Roccia* on the west face of **Mont Noir de Peuterey** (2938m). This is a partially bolted, seven-pitch (330m) rock route with generally reasonable difficulties (mainly 5 with a crux of 6a obl). The face stands immediately above the Noire hut (aka Rifugio Borelli-Pivano: 2316m) and lies at the end of the Aiguille Noire's long east ridge. There is now a selection of single-pitch routes and a couple more longer Sertori offerings, *Mondi Sospesi* and *Bella di Giorno*, each about 250m.

On the little-visited south-east face of **Pointe 4361m** – the south-west shoulder **of Mont Maudit** (4465m), Jon Bracey and Rich Marchant made a rare repeat (and in winter) of *Nata di Pietra* (Grassi/Rossi, October 1989: 700m: IV/5), the ephemeral goulotte that cuts through the large East Buttress. Prior to this Nick Bullock and Andy Houseman made a rare winter ascent of Gian Carlo Grassi's *Overcouloir* (Grassi/Margaira/Siri, 1986: 700m: TD+: IV/5). The steep icefall through the lower rock band wasn't properly formed, so the pair created a three-pitch variation to the right, which was described as 'quite Peruvianesque'. Around on the north-east face of **Mont Maudit** above Cirque Maudit, Bullock, this time with Lake District activist Steve Ashworth, made an early repeat of *Fantasia per un Ghiacciatore* (Gabarrou/Gourdin/Passino, 1989: 400m: V/5+ and 6a), finding difficult loose pitches in the upper section. The route takes the rectilinear goulotte between the left-hand and central pillars of the Three Gendarmes (c4050m).

In August, talented Czech climbers Dusan Janak and Vasek Satava made the second free ascent of *Voie Petit* on the **Grand Capucin**. In 1997 Arnaud Petit sparsely bolted 12 pitches on the right side of the east face and eventually climbed every move free with a crux of 8a+ but wasn't able to link it all together without rests. In July 2005 Alex Huber made many attempts before finally achieving the one-day redpoint. He felt the overall grade to be 8b, making the *Voie Petit* one of the hardest 'high mountain' alpine rock routes in the world.

On the popular east face of **Mont Blanc du Tacul** above the Vallée Blanche, Nick Bullock and Kenton Cool made possibly the second complete ascent of *Slave to the Rhythm* (Parkin/Taylor, 1997: 450m: IV/6+). Although this route, left of the Piliers du Sérac, appears to have received a number of 'ascents', parties have bailed from below the last pitch – an overhanging chockstone. The crux proved to be the entry pitch, though overcoming the chockstone provided an exciting moment when Bullock, laybacking off good torques, pulled a rather large block onto his lap. Cool was belayed directly below, but the block fortunately missed him in its subsequent flight. Also during the winter and this time right of the Gervasutti Pillar, Christophe Dumarest and Patrick Wagnon made possibly only the second overall ascent and first winter of *D-Day* (Darbellay/Gabarrou, June 2004, 800m IV/5). Over the next two days the two went on to climb the *Roger Baxter Jones route* on the east face of Mont Maudit and the *Boivin-Vallencant* on the Grand Pilier d'Angle.

Just before Xmas 2006 Jon Bracey and Nick Bullock put up *Tentation* on the north-east face of **Pointe Lachenal** (3613m). The pair spotted this unclimbed line – a prominent groove round the corner right of the arête taken by the Contamine – the previous day, while making an ascent of nearby *Scotch on the Rocks*. The 260m route was completed in darkness at III/6 or Scottish VII. A couple of days later the Scottish guide, Neil Brodie, a Chamonix resident, and Jean-François Mercier made the second ascent. The pair climbed a direct finish on the last pitch, which they found to be the crux of the climb and about one Scottish technical grade harder than the rest.

With various partners Jean-Sébastien Knoertzer has been developing the mixed climbing potential on the 3541m **Gros Rognon**, a well-known rock formation in the Vallée Blanche. In the past a number of short mixed routes, which serve as excellent preparation for more remote and committing climbs elsewhere in the range, have been climbed on the south face, notably the

Pas d'Agonie trilogy by Batoux and Robert. During the winter Knoertzer added *Fanoudridou* to the south face with Jean-Luc Cuisinier to give a five-pitch II/3 M5, and *20,000 Vieux sous Méméré* (350m: 85° M5 and 4+/5a) on the north face with Jonathan Charlet, Arnaud Geldreich and Oliver Pujol. He returned about a month later to climb *Erwin et Mimie: Amour à gogo!* (III/4 M7), a more direct line just left of *20,000 Vieux*. During this period he also went to look at the **Petit Rognon** and with Benoît Chanal and Julien Duverney-Guichard came away with *Maudit Gras, une Vérité qui Dérange* on the steep NNE face (250m: M6+).

A number of interesting ascents took place on the prestigious east and north faces of the **Grandes Jorasses**. On the former, Julien Desecures and Paul Robach put up *Marine Givrée* (750m: M5+ and 5c) in mid-March. This is basically a variant to the 1981 *Boivin-Diafferia* (750m: TD, 5c and A1) and according to the authors is now the easiest line on the face. The climb avoids all the hard free and aid climbing on the lower section of the 1981 route via ground to the right and is the first winter ascent of any route on the right side of the east face, apart, of course, from the classic Hirondelles Ridge. The latter, which because of its remote situation, length and commitment actually sees few ascents, was climbed on two consecutive days over the summer with a record 11 people on the second day. One of these, the guide Matteo Giglio, has proposed a modern grade of IV 6a/A1 M for the route (replacing the old D/D+). There are now eight pegs in the crux Fissure Rey.

The only new ground climbed on the Walker Spur was an illogical variation finish to the classic *Cassin route* by Michal Burnard and Milan Maudic. Completed in August, the 260m variant, *Right Hell*, climbs the middle of three chimneys in the headwall above the upper snowfield of the *Colton-MacIntyre*. Above, it slants left through the last-named route to reach the chimney-corner system that rises to the summit ridge just right of Pointe Walker. Leaving the *Cassin* at a point just below the triangular snow patch, the two climbed 10 new pitches to the summit (between 15m and 40m), with difficulties up to UIAA VI+ and A2+. The rock was often poor, as was protection.

In the autumn, interest centred on the *Sergé Gousseault route*, which received three more ascents, most likely the ninth, 10th and 11th, but more significantly, the first all-free ascent, by the British duo of Pete Bensen and Guy Robertson. The Scottish pair made three bivouacs on the face and overcame sustained difficulties of Scottish 5-7 with a free rock pitch of British E3 high on the headwall. The new grade for an all-free ascent is now more like 1200m: ED3/4: M6 and 6b or 6c. Both this pair and Neil Brodie and Marc Challamel who climbed it next used the variation start inaugurated by Scottish climber Gordon Smith and American Tobin Sorenson in 1997 when they made the second overall and first summer ascent. This pair climbed what they felt was a more logical, and icier, line to the right of the original way and it was later incorporated into the first ascent of the

Czechoslovak route, *Rolling Stone*. One day after the Brodie-Challamel ascent, three French repeated the route, this time using the original start. Both they and Brodie felt the rock difficulties to be more like 6b than 6c.

In September Josep Maria Esquirol and Albert Salvado from Spain made the sixth overall ascent of the legendary 1964 *Bonatti-Vaucher route* on Pointe Whymper, climbing the route at ED3/4, M6, 90° and A2. It was repeated several days later by Bracey and Brodie, who made only one bivouac, climbed almost free throughout, but found thin ice, difficult mixed climbing and plenty of rotten rock. Several hard pitches were poorly protected

The *1970 Polish route* on the north face of **Pointe Hélène** got a definite second ascent in September, when it was climbed in just 10 hours by Stephané Benoist (his 10th separate route on the north face) and Patrice Glairon-Rappaz. The general impression was that protection was difficult to find, retreat would not be easy and there was virtually no in-situ gear. A new grade of TD+ 85° and M5+ was proposed. This led to a spate of ascents in October, first from Sebastien Ibanez and Christophe Moulin, followed by François Delas, Aurelie Leveque, Benoît Montfort and Patrick Pessi. It was then the turn of Julien Desecures and Paul Robach and finally by Jerome Berton and Luc Jarry-Lacombe. The later parties assessed the difficulties as TD+ V/4+ 80° M5/M5+, the crux mixed section a 20m horizontal traverse.

Tony Penning was back at work on the Italian side of the massif and his most important new route of the year was *La Fiesta de los Monsters* (11 pitches: TD+ but serious for the grade: British E3 5c obl or F6c) on the east face of the **Aiguilles de Pra Sec** (3549m), climbed with regular British partners, Gavin Cytlau, Nick Gillett and Ali Taylor. The route climbs to the left of the other three existing lines on this face (only one of which has ever been repeated) and has a very American, unprotected squeeze chimney as its crux. Access to this very rarely visited wall lies across the lower Pra Sec glacier and today the icefall at its snout makes this more or less impossible. Instead, the climbers made a monstrously circuitous traverse across ledge systems from well to the left, taking eight hours to reach the boulder-covered terrace below the start of the route. This traverse turned out to be almost as hard as the climb itself and probably scarier, traversing steep grassy slabs and several gullies.

Gillett, Penning and Taylor next headed for the untouched west face of the **Petites Aiguilles de Pra Sec** (c2960m), where they put up the six-pitch *Franci and Vale* (350m: HVS). The route follows a prominent corner system to the right of the elegant spur descending from the most northerly and highest of the three towers. It was named after the two children of local guru, Luca Signorelli, who gave the British climbers the tip about this unclimbed line.

Penning and Taylor added a sixth route to the north-east face of **Pointe 3019m**, a subsidiary summit of the Aiguille de l'Eveque above the Freboudze glacier. The 10-pitch *Checkmate* (500m: British E3 5c obligatory, F6c) takes a prominent series of chimneys left of all previous climbs (all done by

Penning). The crux was sustained and strenuous, though the rest of the route was easier.

The fourth and last route climbed in this region by the British team took place at the end of August, when Cytlau, Gillett, Penning and Taylor put up *Sexy Beast* (five pitches: British E3 5c, F6c) on what have been dubbed the **Eveque Slabs**, high on the east side of the Pra Sec basin, south of the approach to the Jachia Bivouac hut. The climb takes a big, left-facing corner splitting compact granite, and on pitch four Penning, leading the rope of four throughout, had to make an alarming hand traverse across a very steep wall to get back into the main corner system. Once there, he was confronted with six metres of almost vertical grass tufts that proved just about strong enough to climb up in order to regain clean rock and protection. A bold lead!

On the **Petites Jorasses**, many hard winter routes were in excellent condition during the season, though once word got out they became quite popular and consequently, as more and more ice was knocked off, more difficult. Notably, *Omega* (Gabarrou/Latorre, 1994: 700m: WI 6, 6a and A3: all free at Scottish VIII, 8 by Bullock and McAleese in 2005 during the third ascent) proved to have a solid ice runnel from top to bottom and saw dozens of ascents. The only new route was added by Gabarrou and Knoertzer, who climbed a narrow corner system up the buttress that lies between the Goulotte Duverney-Gabarrou (Duverney/Gabarrou, 1981: 450m: TD, II/4) and the north-west couloir of Pointe 3576m (Lambert/Perroux/Sanchez, 1981: 450m: TD II/4). Named *Goulotte Lilou* (450m: eight pitches: IV/4, M6 and A2) after Knoertzer's young daughter, it is, remarkably, Gabarrou's 10th new route on the Petites Jorasses.

On the *South Face* of the **Rognon du Plan** (3601m) Roberto Gomez (Bolivia), Andres Herrera (Ecuador) and the French guide François Pallandre opened *Los Caracoles* (280m: sustained at 5c and 6a, 5c obl), an accessible, traditionally protected climb at a reasonable grade. On the **Aiguille du Plan** there were important repeats. Several parties climbed *Bad Craziness*, first put up over three freezing days in February 1986 by Chris Dale and Phil Thornhill. The route climbs the couloir on the right flank of the classic *Ryan-Lochmatter* and the main difficulties occurred on mixed ground in the last 400m, where the granite was of good quality. Graded ED1/2 and Scottish V mixed at the time, a modern grade of V/M4 A1 has been quoted, although it is not at all certain whether the route ever had a second ascent. Several parties repeated it free and in fast times during the 2007 winter, including Neil Brodie and Kenton Cool, who graded it V/4. On the other side of the mountain, Thomas Faucheur and Didier Jourdain made a rare winter ascent of the largely forgotten *Grand West Couloir* on the west face of the Plan (3673m). First climbed in December 1975 by, inevitably, Patrick Gabarrou, with Jean-Marie Picard-Deyme, this thin chimney-gully system in the middle of the 700m face is seriously exposed to stonefall and features considerable quantities of either bare or icy rock. Current guidebooks offer a grade of ED1 or 2, V/5, 6a and A1/A2, though the route has seen very few ascents. The two French tackled the route in a modern style, using aid (A1/A2) on only two short sections and dry-tooling most of the rest up to M6. There was one section of pure rock, climbed at 5 and a small, though difficult, amount of ice (WI 5+). Above the first snowfield the chimney line was climbed in 10 pitches to reach the easier final snow ramps. They both felt the route was excellent and possibly destined to enjoy a new lease of life.

In February a French team climbed the obvious ephemeral couloir on the flanks of the **Aiguille de Grépon** separating the ESE Spur of the Bec d'Oiseau (Griffin/Sutters, 1970: 650m: TD) and the South Pillar of the Aiguille de Roc (Cordier/Remouillet, 1974: 500m: TD). The initial section of the couloir, which lies left of the start of the classic Cordier Pillar, gave a 60m near-vertical pitch on a thinly iced slab. Above, Philippe Batoux, Mathieu Cortial and Benoît Robert, with Jérémy Ponson and Jean-François Reffet, continued up the gully for nearly 500m (65° with a few steeper ice and mixed sections). Here the couloir divides: Ponson and Reffet chose the right branch, climbing it to the notch behind the Aiguille de Roc to create *Eclaires ma Nuit* (600m: III/5+ M4), while Batoux, Cortial and Robert continued on the harder, more direct line to the south-west ridge of the Grépon to create *Illumines mes Jours* (650m: III/5+ M5+).

On the nearby **Pointe Elizabeth** (c2850m) Alessandro Bonilla and Daniel Crospo added *Moonlight Shadow* (TD) to the *South Face*. The five-pitch route (220m) is fairly sustained at 5+/6a with a crux of 6a+, and is another useful addition to the many short routes at an accessible standard available from the Envers hut.

Just before the end of 2006 Pete Benson and Guy Robertson climbed the previously virgin north face of **Pointe 3650m** on the frontier ridge connecting the Pointe du Domino (3648m) and the Aiguille du Triolet (3870m). The route was named *Shining Wall* (IV/5, Scottish 6) and it is amazing that no one appears to have made serious headway on this c600m face until February 2006, when Valery Babanov and Fabian Meyer retreated after climbing nine pitches. The Scottish pair reached the summit ridge and junction with the 1905 *Fontaine-Ravanel-Tournier route* but did not continue to the highest point.

Several ice/mixed lines were established on the north-east face rock triangle of the **Aiguille Verte**, but with so many other routes on this wall, they appear to share similar if not common ground with existing climbs. Philippe Batoux and Gerald Durand climbed a 500m line at III/5+ and M7; the M7 crux a 30m dièdre with a thin sliver of ice in the back (repeated later in the year by Kenton Cool and Ian Parnell). Later, Vincent Henry Amer, Nicolas Lochu and Bruno Roche added *Camalot* with difficulties of III/6, M6 and 6b+. Both lines are close to, or in parts common with, the *1981 Gabarrou-Vogler*, a TD summer rock route with difficulties of 5/5+ in its 15 pitches to the summit of the 600m triangle.

On **Pointe Farrar** (Grands Montets ridge of the Verte), Frédérique Goujon and Thierry Renault put up the superb and varied *Y'a pas photo* (500m: II/4 M4+) on the north-east (Argentière) face. A little later Renault returned with Abigail Crofts and climbed a more direct variant he named *Hot and Cold* (II/4+ M5). These lines, immediately right of the classic and popular *Claire Chazal*, are yet more useful additions to the ice/mixed routes easily accessible from the Grands Montets station.

There were several interesting ascents of the north-west face of the **Aiguille Sans Nom** (3982m) but only one new route: *Tifeen (950m:* V/6 A1 M8+) by Christophe Dumarest and Thomas Emonet. The new line lies to the left of the *Gabarrou-Silvy Direttissima* on the steep 350m lower rock buttress and in the upper section lies just to the right, climbing ground very close to the little-known and probably unrepeated Spanish route, *Hielo Submarine* (Aguado/de Pablos/Tapia, 1981: F5+ and 90°). Climbed in July, summer temperatures allowed the use of rock boots on the lower pitches and there were excellent sections of good granite.

The *Gabarrou-Silvy* itself saw a second free ascent, when it was climbed by Slovenians Andrej Grmovsek and Marko Lukic. The first free ascent was made in 2006 by Aymeric Clouet and Christophe Dumarest at 6c and M9. The Slovenian pair found perfect climbing, good rock, good protection and a relatively modest level of difficulty in terms of sport mixed (WI 6 and M8).

Left of the Col des Drus Couloir, Vincent Henry Amar and Nicolas Lochu climbed highly technical ground on their 500m new line *Freedom* (WI 6+, M8, 6b and A1). The route follows the classic Dru Couloir, traverses left to reach the left flank of the Col des Drus Couloir, then climbs icy streaks in a corner system through steep and rather compact granite walls on the north-west flank of the **Pic Sans Nom**. On the **Petit Dru** (3733m) Martial Dumas and Jean-Yves Fredericksen became the first to climb the right side of the *West Face* since the huge rock fall of June 2005. Their line, *Les Papas*, which largely follows the crest of the pillar formerly taken by the now destroyed 1955 Bonatti route, has around 29 pitches (the first seven on snow and a little mixed ground, the last five on the original Bonatti, and the remaining all new on the grey rock scar) with technical difficulties of 6b and A3 (only half a dozen pitches near the top of the wall were climbed free). The two Frenchmen started their ascent at the end of January and made four portaledge camps on the wall.

Across the Chamonix valley on the ever-popular and seemingly stable south-facing walls of the **Aiguilles Rouges** a number of moderate new routes were created. On **Clocher, Pointe 2412m** of the **Clocher Chocheton**, Yannick Brucka, Julien Cellier and Manu Meot climbed *Label Virginie* (250m: 5c, 5b obl). On the **Aiguille de la Glière,** 10 minutes above the Index téléphérique station, Ed and Rona Grindley with Mick Johnson added *Modern Times* (six pitches: 5b on the fourth pitch, the rest easier) between Manipuliti and Nez Rouge, while on the 2511m **Central Summit** of the **Aiguille Pourrie** (2561m) Traci MacNamara and Andy Parkin climbed the south-east ridge to the top of the second gendarme to create the 180m *Baby Blue* (6a+). Further east in the neighbouring Perrons group, guidebook author Jon de Montjoye and Hillary Sharp added *A Bigger Bang* (350m: 10 pitches: 7a, 6c obl) to the sunny south-east face of the **Pain de Sucre** (2646m), left of the 1989 Ravanel route, *Squatteurs de Lune*. Apart from these summer rock routes, there was also a winter addition to the SSW face of the 2965m **Aiguille du Belvedère** when Jean Sébastien Knoertzer and Sonia Popoff Knoertzer put up the ephemeral *Emma Mousse* (TD: thin ice to 90°)

Valais

Local guide Hervé Barmasse made the first solo ascent of the *South Face Direttissima* (ED1) on the **Matterhorn**. This climb was put up in 1983 by Marco Barmasse, Hervé's father, with Valter Cazzanelli and Vittorio de Tuoni. Barmasse junior climbed the route on 16 April in just eight hours from a chalet at around 2900m. He did not use a backrope and was slowed on the low-angled section below the summit block by snow almost up to his waist. In September young Swiss guides Simon Anthamatten and Michael Lerjen set a speed record by climbing up and down the Hörnli Ridge in a total time of just two hours and 33 minutes (Hörnli hut to Hörnli hut). Their ascent time was one hour and 40 minutes, while they descended the route in just 53 minutes. Phew!

Bernese Oberland

Robert Jasper, Bernd Rathmayr and Roger Schäli climbed a new route on the north face of the 3875m **Fiescher Gabelhorn**, They started up the 700m face to the left of the *1969 Jung-Traschel route* and more directly in the summit fall line, completing their line, *Racletteconnection*, in 12 pitches after climbing unroped up the initial 200m ice slope. Difficulties were mostly M5 with cruxes of M6.

On the **Eiger** Hanspeter Hug and Roger Schali dispatched the *1938 route* in a mere eight hours on 15 October, most likely the fastest time this route has ever been climbed by a roped pair. Back in February Ueli Steck had soloed the climb in just three hours and 54 minutes, taking almost one hour off the previous fastest time (set by Christoph Hainz). Steck would not be satisfied with this and returned in 2008 to record an even faster time.

During the autumn Schali and Christoph Hainz climbed a new route *Magic Mushroom* on the right side of the north face. The route forces an exit on to the west ridge at approximately half height, just above a small but conspicuous, detached, mushroom-shaped pillar of rock. This curious formation is used by BASE Jumpers, so it will come as no surprise to find that the wall below the mushroom is extremely steep. The route lies left of *Yeti* on very compact rock and has obligatory moves of 7b and probable cruxes of 7c. However, it was not climbed without rests, making a redpoint ascent high on the agenda for Schali and Hainz in 2008. The 600m and 20 pitches of new climbing took six days to complete.

Bregaglia-Masino

From 26-31 December 2006 Fabio Valseschini made the first solo and second overall winter ascent of *Via del Fratello* on the ENE pillar of the **Piz Badile** (3308m). This seems likely to be the first time that the north-east face of this prestigious mountain has been soloed during the winter season (the claim of Dante Porta's solo of the *Cassin* in the early 1980s is now widely disputed). Valseschini made his sixth bivouac in the emergency shelter on the summit, after climbing the full spectrum of difficult rock, ice and mixed pitches (the c750m route has been climbed free at TD+ 6b). He was then lifted off by helicopter, sent by anxious friends.

Just before the end of the winter season Andrea Barbieri and Luca Maspes made the first winter, and possibly only the third overall ascent of the 1976 *Gugiatti route* on the south-east face of the **Pizzo Cengalo**. The pair climbed the route in a round trip of 15 hours from the Gianetti hut, benefitting from conditions that were reportedly quite summer-like. The original route was graded V+/VI and A1 but the two Italians completed the 450m line at VII– with a little mixed climbing, creating a three-pitch variant near the top.

During the summer Germany residents, Gabor Berecz and Thomas Tivadar, added another line to the south-east face of **Torre Darwin** (2442m) at the entrance to the Cameraccio valley. Choosing a crack system left of the existing lines, they created *Via del Invalidi* (380m: eight pitches plus some scrambling: V 5.10 A4–) in siege style, returning to a good bivouac below the face each night. The crux pitch was comparable with El Capitan's *Atlantic Ocean Wall* but a little less serious than *Zenyatta Mondatta*.

Just up the valley stands the **Torrione Moai** (aka Torre del Moai, c2700m), a curious granite tower named by its first ascensionists, Guerini and Frosi, in 1973, because of its similarity to Easter Island statues. On the 250m south-east face, Barbieri, Foglino, Ongaro, Panizza, Pavan, Sommaruga and Spennacchi became the first to breach the compelling headwall avoided by all previous routes. *Religion Rebel* (7c, 6c obl and A0) has 10 sustained pitches on compact slabs and superb, exposed cracks. The eighth pitch, high on the headwall, proved to be the technical crux but the climbers were unable to dispense with a single aid point on pitch three (6c+ and A0).

In the autumn Benigno Baletti and Valerio Corti added another route to the steep and icy 450m triangular mixed buttress left of the central sérac on the north face of **Monte Disgrazia** (3678m). This was Baletti's third new route on the buttress and reportedly his 18th on the mountain. The new line *Combi* lies between two of his own routes, *The Ghost* and *Via degli Amici*. It features a magnificent four-pitch goulotte at 75°, often no more than 40cm wide. The route, which was rated IV/4 and 5+/6a, terminates on the crest of the classic Corda Molla ridge at approximately 3450m.

Dolomites

Arguably the most significant Dolomite ascent of the year was Hansjorg Auer's free solo of the legendary *Fish* on the south face of the **Marmolada**.

The 23-year-old Austrian student climbed all 33 pitches of this 900m route without a rope at 7b+ in just two hours and 55 minutes. Auer had climbed the route roped in 2004 but at that stage was unable to do it free. The ascent prompted Messner to remark, 'This is the biggest and boldest alpine achievement in recent years.'

On the popular south face of the well-known **Piz Ciavazes** (2831m) Florian and Martin Riegler have climbed a new line up the pillar just left of the old *Demetz-Gluck-Tuntino South Chimney* (5.7) on the rarely visited upper tier above the Gamsband. *El Negrito* climbs close to the waterfall in the chimney, giving it an unusual ambience. It is 11 pitches long, the first being the crux at 7c, 7b obl.

On the 3220m **Civetta**, Alessandro Bau and Alessandro Beber made the long-awaited second ascent of *Nuvole Barocche*, an amazing line up the wall to the right of the famous *Philipp-Flamm* on the north-west face. Put up in 1999 by the prolific Dolomite activist Venturino de Bona with Piero Bez, it climbs one of the biggest and most renowned walls in the range, reaching the summit ridge of the Civetta just up and right of Punta Tissi (2992m). The 35 pitches that make up this 1250m route have maximum difficulties of 7c+ with a little A2. Bau and Beber used aid on only four pitches and think a completely free ascent might be possible at 8b.

In the Pale the great *East Face* (Andrich/Tissi, 1930: 800m: V+) of **Monte Agner** received its first ever winter ascent in mid-January by Fabio Valseschini and Ivo Ferrari.

Riccardo Scarian has become the third person to climb *Solo per Vecchi Guerreri*, a four-pitch route on the remotely situated north face of a 2000m summit dubbed **El Colaz** in the little-frequented Feltrine (aka Feltre) group. Maurizio 'Manolo' Zanolla put up the incredibly exposed route in 2006. The final pitch weighed in at an impressive 8c, 7c/7c+ obl, the grade confirmed by the second ascensionist, Mario Prinoth. Scarian commented that it is undoubtedly one of the finest routes he has ever climbed.

On the **Cima Ovest** Alex Huber, partnered on his eventual redpoint success in July by Franz Hinterbrander and Max Reichel, climbed *Pan Aroma* through the *Bauer-Rudolph route* on the north face. After climbing the first five pitches of his own 2000 route *Bellavista*, Huber broke out right. The sixth pitch is a full 60m long, protected by seven bolts and rated 8b+, while the 20m eighth pitch provides the 8c crux. Although the pitches are bolted, there are definitely long run-outs in outrageous positions and the climb is one of the hardest big-wall free routes in the world.

During the previous January David Bruder and Jonathan Trango made the first alpine-style winter ascent of the 550m *Swiss route*, which now goes free at 7b+ 6c obl. The pair opted for a light and fast ascent despite the cold, carrying no bivouac gear and wearing rock shoes. On the big roof that forms the free crux, the cold proved prohibitive and they were forced to climb it at 6c with a little A2, all on questionable rock. They reached the top at midnight and arrived back at their car after 21 hours on the go.

Russia & Central Asia 2007-2008

This report has been compiled with the assistance of the Alpinist newswire and mountain.ru. Dates refer to 2007 unless stated otherwise.

Tien Shan

During the year two new routes were climbed in the accessible **Ala-Archa** area of the Kyrgyz range. On 7 January 2007 Sergey Dashkevich and Vitaliy Akimov completed the first ascent of a new 300m 5A rock route on the left part of the west face of **Baichechekey (4515m)**. The route is immediately right of the 1977 *Kuzmenko route*. On 16 September, Ivan Pugachev and Vitaliy Chepelenko completed a new 4B route on the central buttress of the east face of **Pik Boks (4242m)**. The route is to the right of the existing 3B *Balykina route*. They climbed the route in a 15-hour push.

In the **Western Kokshaal-Too**, a strong Russian team, including Alexander Odintsov, Mikhail Mikhailov and Alexander Ruchkin, succeeded in making the first ascent of the main east or south-east face of **Kyzyl Asker (5482m)**. They reached the summit on 13 September, having started on the 5th, two days after a helicopter drop close to the face. They encountered bad weather and some difficult climbing on the face, which slowed them at one point to three pitches in 15 hours. A few valleys further east, in August, British climbers Stuart Howard and Dave Swinburne made ascents from the Malitskovo glacier of peaks 4975m and 5055m. Their plans on higher peaks were thwarted by repeated snowfall and warm temperatures.

Climbers explored several little-known ranges within Kyrgyzstan. In summer 2007, the Osh-based team of Katya Ananyeva, Dmitry Martynenko and Dmitry Shapovalov investigated the **Jamantau range** north-east of Naryn, from the road end at Jergetal village. Their main ascents were of Chontash East (4553m) at Russian 3A, Kramen (4351m) by its 500m rocky west ridge with one pitch of 5.9, and Ak-Jaman (4488m) via 60-70° ice. From this area they walked 50km south via the Arpa valley to reach the **Torugart-Too range**, close to the Chinese border. Here they reached several summits of 4800-4900m in height, on friable schist, before making an epic raft-assisted exit across the Kulun Lake.

In September 2007, Pat Littlejohn's ISM team, with Vladimir Komissarov, Barney Harford, Max Gough, Leif Iversen, Helen Griffin and Peter Mounsey, visited the higher part of the **Torugart-Too range**, not far from the Torugart Pass road into Xinjiang. From the Teke-Lutor glacier, members of the party made ascents of Piks Helen (4710m) (AD+ via W slopes to S col), Shumkar (4925m) (PD via NW flank to N col), and Bars (4800m) (PD+ via NE col). They gave the latter its name (meaning Snow Leopard) as they followed leopard tracks right to the summit. Littlejohn and Harford climbed the highest peak in the area, Mustyr ('Ice Pasture', 5108m), via a couloir on the west side to the south ridge at AD. The final peak climbed by the group was Kumay (4830m) from the north-west, following which they moved to the **At Bashi range** south of Naryn. Here they climbed Inek (4560m) and the attractive Topoztor (4600m) via the west flank to the summit dome.

Pamir Alai

Valeri Shamalo's St Petersburg team of Galina Chibitok, Dmitry Krasnov, Rustem Nagaev and Dmitry Polenov followed up their recent success on K2 with a winter ascent of the *Voronov route* on the 1200m north-west face of **Pik 4810**, above the Kara-Su valley. They reached the summit on 14 March 2008. Meanwhile, Alexander Korobkov's Ekaterinburg team of Sergey Dashkevich, Kirill Litvinov and Sergey Timofeev climbed the 6B *Kritsunka route* a little further left on the same face. They started the route on 22 February 2008 and reached the summit on 6 March.

Pamir

In July 2007, 19 inner city pupils from King Edward VII School in Sheffield undertook an expedition to the **Kinchine Kurumdy** glacier region of the north-east Pamir. The group were led by Adventureworks staff and AC member Paul Donovan plus Bill Beynon and KES staff Marc Badham, Neil Battersby, Mat Galvin and Mel Scholes. The group claimed four first British 4000m ascents, of which three were first ascents. They named the peaks Keseven (Facile, 4040m), Singing Peak (Facile, 4276m), Copper Top (4003m) and Pen Eira Fawr (Facile, 4353m). Details are available in the AC library.

On **Pik Kommunisma (Ismail Somoni, 7495m)**, in August, a six-strong Russian team from Alpclub MAI climbed the impressive south-west face. Starting on the 1968 *Myslovskiy route*, they exited onto the south ridge via the 1970 *Onishchenko route*. They were unable to continue to the summit.

In the Shakhdar range in the south-west Pamir, on **Pik Engels (6510m)**, a St Petersburg team led by Rustem Nagaev climbed a serious 6B face route as part of the high-altitude technical class of the Russian climbing championships. They reached the summit on 15 August. In the same range, in March 2008, a helicopter crashed in the Ghund valley, east of Khorog. The helicopter was transporting 11 climbers; the pilot lost his life in the crash.

170. West side of Mustyr ('Ice Pasture', 5108m), Torugart-Too range.
      (*Barney Harford*)

Crimea

On **Pik Aya**, on 6-7 May 2007 Sverdlovsk climbers Sergey Aleksandrovich
and Evgeniy Novoseltsev climbed a new route *Blik* at 6A VI A4 and 540m,
taking the overhangs on the right part of the main south-west face. The
route starts right of the route *Vorota* and finishes to its left.

DEREK FORDHAM

Greenland 2007

There were 61 expeditions in the field in Greenland in 2007 and of those 32 were planning to make a traverse of the Inland Ice, either transverse or longitudinal. However, as in previous years, enthusiasm for Greenland has not been matched by the expeditions' willingness to let the *AJ* know about their activities and this regional notes editor's enquiries met with only a 20% response rate, somewhat reducing the effectiveness of his material!

Refreshingly, in addition to the usual interest in the trade route across the Inland Ice, there were more groups than in previous years breaking away from the straightforward east-west or west-east route, including two south-north proposals and one north-south. This widening of horizons was also apparent in the expeditions to relatively new areas. Ejnar Mikkelsens Fjeld and the adjacent Sortebrae area in the Watkins Mountains have now started to rival Gunnbjörnsfjeld as popular destinations, although EMF's significantly greater difficulty than GBF, and it not being the Arctic's highest, will probably always leave it a close second to GBF. Elsewhere innovative groups visited Dronning Louise Land in north-east Greenland, Milneland in inner Scoresbysund and the far northern coast of Greenland.

Possible harbingers of climate change were responsible for significant problems with weather and snow during 2007. A number of expeditions expecting to fly in to their objectives could not be put down where they wished or, in some cases, where others had landed in previous years. The Sortebrae expedition (see below) was delayed by weather in Iceland and then spent a significant amount of their time in the field, and an extraordinary amount of effort, digging out their aircraft several times. At the time of writing, the outcome of this problem, manifested in the field by statements from the pilots that they would not in future fly into the mountains, remains unresolved.

For those parties setting off on the Inland Ice the weather was not significantly different or better than last year and most parties who did not want high winds experienced them, some to extremes. A three-member team of Linda Beilharz, Bob Rigato and Roger Chao (Australia) calling themselves the **Bendigo Bank Greenland Expedition** used a helicopter to reach Nagtvit on the east coast on 17 May and were immediately hit by a *piteraq*, the sudden katabatic wind for which this area of the coast is notorious and which has in the past proved fatal to more than one expedition. They suffered five tent-bound days and some equipment damage before getting away. The weather improved and temperatures dropped as they climbed away from the coast, first through 10 days of whiteout conditions and then into brilliant clear weather as they reached the high point of the ice. Skiing conditions were good and due to the relatively early start the party did not have big melt-water problems and reached Kangerlussuak after a rather long five weeks on the Inland Ice.

On 17 April Jan Fokke Oosterhof and Paul Kamphuis (Netherlands) commenced the second stage of their **Frozen Dreams Project**, the first stage having been the ascent of Mont Blanc in 2006. The third stage is planned to be a ski expedition to the South Pole. Intending to follow Nansen's route of the first crossing of Greenland, they were landed on the edge of the Inland Ice by helicopter and were also struck by a *piteraq* and confined to their tent for four days while having to dig the tent out every few hours. The period of whiteout which followed the storm delayed the group's progress sufficiently for them to decide to return to their starting point, which they reached safely on 11 May after covering some 340km.

Of the 10 expeditions which received permission to attempt the west-east route, only that of Frenchmen Olivier Le Piouff and Guillaume Hintzy provided details of their journey from **Ilulissat to Isortok**. Starting on 3 April in very cold winter conditions, they took 37 days to ski the 700km from Eqip Sermia on the west coast to a point on the Inland ice some few kilometres from the east coast where they were met by a helicopter. Their only problems while completing this fine trip were encountering head winds for a great part of the journey and suffering minor frostbite, probably almost inevitable at that time of year.

Of those tackling the much longer south-north longitudinal traverse, Fleming Lund and his companion Sverri formed the **Arctic Kite Tour** and left Narsaq, near to the southern tip of Greenland, on 19 April aiming for Qaanaaq. They were slowed during the first two weeks by a lack of wind for part of the day. At night on the Inland Ice in April it is too cold and dark to ski and so by 12 May, in difficult conditions, they were only just east of Pt 660, the traditional exit point for parties crossing from the east coast to Kangerlussuak, and decided to divert directly to Kangerlussuak. They plan to return to complete the job in 2009 but their experience suggests a slightly later start would be better.

This is perhaps borne out by the experience of **The Pittarakk Expedition** composed of Canadians Eric and Sarah McNair Landry and Curtis Jones who set out from Narsaq on 26 May, reaching Qaanaaq, some 2300km away, on 10 July. They had some difficulties getting all their gear to and through the marginal zone of the Inland Ice, but once through were able to use their kites and head north. In the south they encountered some head winds and wet storms but once across the Arctic Circle the winds became more constant and helpful and on 30 June, when well north and before reaching Qaanaaq, the team decided to see how far they could travel in one day and achieved 412km!

171. SMC East Greenland Expedition: view of the still unclimbed north face
of Bersaerkertinde. (*Mark Litterick*)

On the east coast, a **Spanish Army Mountain Group** expedition aiming
to climb Gunnbjörnsfjeld in the Watkins Mountains, sailed from
Isafjordur in Iceland reaching Mikis Fjord, SSE of their objective, on
2 August. This was too late as the very extensive network of surface drainage
for which the enormous Christian IV glacier is notorious, had fully
developed; the expedition was unable to cross to the mountains and returned
to Mikis Fjord.

Further north, the **East Greenland Sortebrae** expedition led by David
Jakulis, after delays in Iceland, were finally flown into their area, north
and east of Ejnar Mikkelsens Fjeld. On landing the first half of the eight-
strong group, the Twin Otter aircraft sank into the snow and required two
days of digging to get it back on to the surface again. This meant that the
pilot, when he returned with the second group, would only land at a higher
level some 30km from the first group, thus creating the need for a reunion
before the expedition could get to grips with the area. They split into two
groups and, generally avoiding the rock, made some rewarding ascents of
snow ridges and faces assessed as being of about PD standard.

With their time already limited by earlier delays, the expedition felt they should spend time making a heavily laden move to a higher level where the Twin Otter could land safely. This was not high enough and when the plane returned to take surplus gear it again buried itself, but not so deep, and this time it was on its way in a few hours, leaving the group to reach a high point on Borgetinde and make another first ascent from the Borgetinde plateau. The expedition ended with a further 30km change of position to reach a point where the pilot decreed he could safely land and take off with no chance of further burials.

Further north, on Ren Land in the inner reaches of Scoresbysund, Dick Griffiths led a 50-strong **UK Scout expedition** which efficiently carried out a comprehensive programme of climbing and exploration of this relatively little known area and an extensive science project. They also conducted a long canoe journey along the length of Scoresbysund. Many people, including the Danish Polar Centre, usually raise their eyebrows at expeditions of this size. Whatever one's view, this project was carried out in accordance with all written and unwritten rules governing expedition activities in a pristine wilderness area and seems to have been a great success.

In the Staunings Alps the **SMC East Greenland Expedition**, led by Colwyn Jones, left the UK on 29 April and then flew on to a base camp site on the Lang glacier on 30 April; the next day they made their first first ascent. The expedition subsequently achieved a total of 16 first ascents before making a ski journey to the airstrip at Mestersvig from where they were flown back to Iceland. For most of the time in the field they enjoyed excellent weather, so clear and cold that it resulted in three cases of superficial frostbite. One interesting item of concern is that the expedition experienced problems with some early model MSR XGK II stoves not working with Jet A1 fuel. Other parties planning to use this type of fuel in the Arctic, where Jet A1 is often a very available and convenient fuel, might be well advised to test the compatibility of stoves and fuel before departure.

Further north in Andrees Land, **Operation Boreal Zenith** was an eight-person Army Mountaineering Association expedition led by Sam Marshall. They established a base camp by air in Grejsdalen from where the expedition made 34 ascents of which 29 were first ascents. Peaks in the area range up to 2300m and mainly rise above snow plateaux at about 1800m leaving ascents of about 500m. Mostly the peaks are of shattered sedimentary rocks but there are a number of areas of more solid rock; among these are some large granite slabs which remain unclimbed and form a complex face on the peak named by the expedition Lizard Peak (1404m). It was noted from the aircraft that there are many interesting peaks in the surrounding unvisited areas. The expedition had generally good weather and was in the field from 3 July to 3 August.

Dronning Louise Land 2007 planned to visit the southern area of DLL which had not been visited by the two previous expeditions to the range. On 13 May, owing to perceived difficulties of landing at the chosen landing site, the three-man expedition was eventually landed some 50km north. This was closer to the planned pick-up point than intended and it was decided not to go 'back' to the initially chosen drop-off point. This entailed a revision of the plans and the expedition moved 80km northwards towards the pick-up point, climbing 19 peaks on the way, 15 of which were first ascents, before being picked up on 8 June. A small programme of geological collecting was carried out, but the meteorites the expedition had hoped to find remained as elusive as ever on the fringes of the mountains the expedition had hoped to reach, known on the maps as *Fairytale Mountains.*

Both west and east coasts were the settings for enterprising kayak journeys. On the west coast the **Paddle to the Peaks** expedition comprising Althea Rogers, Kelly Ryan and Bradford Cabot of the USA spent 65 days in the field and on the fjords, exploring the region between Manitsoq and Kangamiut. They left Manitsoq on 21 June and paddled through the coastal network of fjords, generally sleeping during the middle of the day and using the twilight hours of the midnight sun to explore the glaciers, snow fields and ridges and mountains which flanked their route. They climbed some 11 summits up to 1775m and placed great emphasis on following a 'leave no trace' ethic.

On the east coast Bill David and Beth Anne, the **East Greenland Kayak Expedition**, set out from Daneborg on 17 July, just after the fjord ice had broken up, and kayaked some 500km south to Mestersvig which they reached 28 days later using a very narrow window of ice conditions. This was emphasised when, on arrival at Mestersvig, they learnt that vessels were already having trouble with ice back at their starting point, Daneborg. During their journey through the wonderful fjord region of the 'Arctic Riviera' they made excursions inland up many of the fine valleys for which this region is noted, and experienced the prolific wildlife and wonderful weather for which the area is also famous.

In past years these Greenland notes have ended with the exploits of the ubiquitous American, **Dennis Schmitt**, and this year is no exception as he and his party discovered yet another new island. The island lies in the Bliss Bugt area of the north coast, about 60km east of Kap Morris Jessup, where Schmitt's teams have previously discovered new 'most northerly' islands, and was named 'Stray Dog Island' in American and 'Kitaa Qeqertoq' in Greenlandic. It is a small moraine-like mass rising only a little above the surrounding pack ice but it does show that new 'land' is still there to be discovered!

SIMON RICHARDSON

Scottish Winter 2007-2008

A long season stretching from November to April meant the 2007-08 winter was one of the most productive for several years. Many climbers were operating at the highest levels, and routes that in the past would have taken several attempts are now being climbed on their first try. The steady rise in standards is a combination of increased fitness, the application of leashless tools and the competitive edge provided by rival teams. Not all the key ascents can be mentioned in this brief review, but the following paragraphs indicate the breadth and variety of routes being climbed.

Ben Nevis

Ben Nevis had one of its busiest seasons for years. The first big news was in early December when Andy Turner, Steve Ashworth and Viv Scott climbed *The Secret* (VIII, 9) on 10 December. This steep crack-line slicing the right wall of Number Three Gully had been stared at by Nevis mixed climbers for a number of years, but its unremitting steepness and apparent lack of footholds meant that most looked at it in disbelief. Turner's three-hour lead of the 40-metre crux pitch was a Scottish winter climber's dream – an on-sight first ascent of a cutting edge winter-only line at the first attempt.

Situated high up in Coire na Ciste, *The Secret* is fully exposed to the blast of northerly winds and quickly becomes rimed and coated white with hoar frost and snow. In contrast to many other top Scottish winter routes which require specific conditions and several seasons' patient waiting, *The Secret* comes into condition fast and was a clear target for a quick repeat. So the next time the wall was hoared later that month, it was no surprise that it was attempted by another very strong team. The ascent by Ian Parnell, Guy Robertson and Mark Garthwaite went without a glitch, with Garthwaite quickly despatching the difficult entry pitch and Parnell taking the honours with a smooth lead of the long crux crack.

Inevitably, the relative ease of the second ascent led to some discussion about the grade. After some deliberation, based on their experience of many top-rated Scottish ascents, the first ascent party decided on X,10 for their climb; but the second ascensionists thought that the route was somewhat easier. The second ascent trio are all known to be tough graders, but they also have a vast amount of experience climbing routes at the upper spectrum of the Scottish game, and the route has now settled down at VIII,9. The team was full of praise for Andy's lead, stating that *The Secret* is one of the finest winter pitches they have ever climbed. Undoubtedly *The Secret's* quality and readiness to come into condition means that it will become established as one of Scotland's most sought-after mixed test pieces.

172. The 2008 winter was an excellent season for new mixed routes on Ben Nevis. Iain Small tackles a new Grade VIII, 8 climb, which takes the prominent rib on the left side of Creag Coire na Ciste. (*Simon Richardson*)

The second Ben Nevis route to hit the headlines was the first free ascent of *Don't Die of Ignorance* by Dave MacLeod and Joe French on the front face of The Comb on 16 March. First climbed in February 1987 by Andy Cave and Simon Yates, the route is based on the great hanging groove to the right of the crest of the buttress. A huge overhanging wall prevents direct access to the groove, so they used aid to traverse right along a wide break from the foot of Tower Face of The Comb. Their ascent was graded VI, 6 and A2 and has not been climbed since, although in 2001 Andy Nisbet and Chris Dale repeated the traverse pitch to reach a second corner-line further right. Dave MacLeod is clearly inspired by this part of the mountain. In 2005 he added the difficult summer climb *Anubis* (E8) to the crest of The Comb, and the next project on his agenda was a free ascent of the original line of *Don't Die of Ignorance.*

MacLeod had failed to free the route for the fifth time just two days earlier, so this was his sixth attempt. 'I was back once again, staring at that grim undercut crack disappearing round the prow into no man's land,' he recounted on his blog. 'I desperately struggled to seat my axe in the crux tin-opener. I screamed to Joe to expect a fall and released my left axe, cutting loose onto one arm. The axe slid and jerked a centimetre. My heart missed a beat and the jolt nearly made me fall, my hand sliding down the upside down axe to the head and rolling onto three fingers. A dynamic match and *kung fu* [move] allowed one foot to swing onto the wall to the right and up to the peg I got in on Friday. The vertical wall above was climbed in an utterly 'go for broke' style, axes ripping, dropping onto one hand and gasping with pump and shrieking for slack.'

MacLeod graded the free version of the route XI, 11, the same grade he gave to his winter ascent of *The Hurting* in Coire an Lochain in the Cairngorms, which he climbed last season.

For the vast majority of Scottish winter climbers the technical difficulty of these routes is almost beyond comprehension but demonstrate what can be achieved by talented climbers taking a modern rock-climbing 'project' approach to climbing winter routes. The majority of winter climbers, however, are happy to operate at a lower level, and climb routes on sight in the time-honoured traditional Scottish style.

In all, 12 new routes were added to the mountain, and most were in the higher grades. These included the first ascent of *Stormtrooper* (VIII, 8) on the right wall of Darth Vader by Ashcroft and Turner, and a winter version of *Subtraction* (VIII, 8) on the Minus Face by Robertson and Scott. On Number Three Gully Buttress, Ian Parnell made a bold lead of the very serious *Snuff Wall* (VIII, 8) to the right of *Babylon*, and Iain Small and Simon Richardson climbed the prominent rib on the left side of Creag Coire na Ciste between *Archangel* and *South Sea Bubble* (VIII, 8). Also of note was the second winter ascent of *Centurion* (VIII, 8) on Carn Dearg Buttress by Guy Robertson and Pete Benson.

Torridon-Skye

On 10-11 January Guy Robertson and Ian Parnell made a winter ascent of *Sundance* (VIII, 8), a summer E2 that takes a steep corner-crack in the centre of the Far East Wall of Coire Mhic Fhearchair on Beinn Eighe. '*Sundance* is a contender for best mixed route in Scotland,' Guy said afterwards. 'It's on a par with the likes of *Vertigo Wall* and *Fhidhleir's Nose*. Truly outstanding climbing – thin and delicate, then pumpy and intimidating on pitch two, then super-sustained and utterly sensational on pitch three.' The matter-of-fact nature of Robertson and Parnell's ascent was breathtaking. *Sundance* was a well-known winter objective by Beinn Eighe winter devotees but its unremitting steepness had deterred any previous attempts.

That evening, Robertson swapped partners, exchanging Ian Parnell for Mark Garthwaite, and headed off for Skye. Early next morning they abseiled from the Thearlaich-Dubh Gap to reach the Upper Cliff of Sgurr Mhic Choinnich. This is one of Skye's finest mountain rock-climbing venues and home to great classics such as *King Cobra* and *Mongoose Direct*. It has seen few winter visits, however, and the only winter route described in the guidebook is Mick Fowler's unrepeated *Exiguous Gully* (VI, 6).

Robertson and Garthwaite found the cliff covered in helpful icy hoar. After considering various options they made a winter ascent of the classic 175m-long *Dawn Grooves* but were surprised at how difficult the route turned out to be. 'We thought a summer VS would maybe give us a VI or VII,' Guy recalled afterwards, 'so we were slapped in the face a bit! It was a very sustained route, with superb climbing all the way. I was pretty chuffed with our ascent – we didn't hang about. There was a pitch of 6, three of 7 and two of 8, all of them were very sustained, so eight hours was rapid enough. That's the great thing about climbing in January – it puts a spring in your step!' *Dawn Grooves* was graded VIII, 8 and the final 10m hand-width corner crack, climbed in the dark, was the climax of a remarkable two days' climbing for Robertson.

On 18 March Steve Ashworth made a solo traverse of a very wintry Cuillin Ridge in 9 hours 7 minutes. This is almost certainly a winter record and now Steve has stated a precise time, it throws down the gauntlet for other teams to attempt the traverse and perhaps complete it in even faster times.

Cairngorm

One of the most forceful displays of mountaineering took place in the lonely Garbh Choire Mor on Braeriach. John Lyall made a lightning visit on 19 February and soloed eleven routes including the classic *Vulcan* (V, 4), a new Grade IV right of *Daddy's Gone-a-Hunting*, and second ascents of *Liaisons Dangereuses* (V, 6), *Comanche* (V, 5) and *Custer Corner* (IV, 4). Incredibly, he was back at the car, having notched up a season's worth tally of routes on one of Scotland's remotest cliffs, after a mere eight hours!

Northern Highlands

A quick thaw towards the end of the third week in January stripped many of the buttress routes in the Cairngorms and Central Highlands, but fortunately the warm air did not penetrate much further north than Inverness and the Northern Highlands escaped more or less unscathed. The forecast was cool and cloudy for the weekend, which prompted Roger Webb and Simon Richardson on 19 January to attempt a winter ascent on *Pillar Buttress* of **A'Mhaighdean** in the Fisherfield Forest, considered by many to be Scotland's remotest Munro. Tactics were all-important for this venture because the route faces south-west and strips in the sun, so a cloudy day with snow showers was ideal. The buttress is not only situated a long way from the road, but it is also tricky to get to from below, and the approach over the summit followed by an abseil down an adjacent gully took over nine hours.

The effort was worth it because the six-pitch route up the crest of the buttress was one of the finest climbs either had ever done. They topped out at 1am and it wasn't until midday that they made it back to the car after a 30-hour round trip. *The Great Game* (VII, 7) will probably only ever be repeated by the most fanatical connoisseurs of Scottish winter climbing, but they were not the only people climbing on the remote Letterewe Estate that day. Alex Runciman and partner made a rare ascent of *North Summit Buttress* (III) on the wild and lonely North Face of Beinn Lair.

PAT LITTLEJOHN

Ethiopia 2006 & 2007

Since the last report in *AJ* 2006 there has been quite a bit of development in northern Ethiopia. In the Tigray area, Pat Littlejohn and Steve Sustad returned in 2006 to attempt the impressive 'megacrack' line they had spotted on the east face of Horsetooth pinnacle (first climbed by them in 2005 – see *AJ* 2006). After two days of exhausting off-width climbing they abandoned ship at half height and sought more amenable climbing along the northern edge of the Simien mountains. Here another failure on the cigar-shaped Hawesa Tower forced a rethink and the pair retreated to Axum, probably the most interesting and pleasant town in Tigray. (Axum houses the legendary Ark of the Covenant and the unique Stele Park, a group of standing stones including the tallest in the world carved from a single block of granite). This proved to be a great decision. To the east of Axum lie the mountains of Adwa, a superb range of peaks composed mainly of solid rock – basalts, quarzites and, amazingly, marble. Many are technical summits which had never been climbed. After two further visits by the Littlejohn/Sustad team and another by Americans Mark Richey and Mark Wilford, most summits have been climbed but there is still huge scope for serious adventure/trad climbing on many untouched faces. So far this is a bolt-free area and long may it remain so!

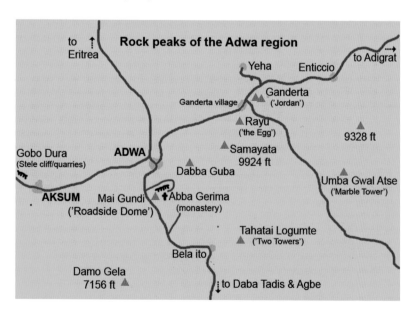

Gobo Dura
4km west of Axum is the 100m cliff where the giant stele were quarried. This gives good climbing on very hard rock and has now been visited by several climbing teams. Good for a shorter/more relaxing day.

Damo Gela
An impressive formation towering 400m above the plains, having one easy route to the summit ('climbed in the time of Haile Selassie' according to locals) and a 10-pitch E1 taking the N Buttress (PL & SS '06). Superb west face awaits ascent.

Mai Gundi
Quickly accessed from the road (20mins) with one route on the NW face (5-pitch E3, PL & SS '06) and another attempted. Easy route to the summit via NE ridge.

Abba Gerima cliff
An attractive and extensive crag overlooking the monastery (Ethiopia's equivalent of the Vatican). Two 5-pitch E4s have been climbed towards the left side (PL & SS '06).

Dabba Guba
A striking dome approached via gully bounding it on the west. 4-pitch E4 takes north ridge (PL & SS '08), easy route to the summit on the south side.

Mt Aftera
Not shown on the map as I'm not sure where it is! (ask around). 8-pitch 5.10 climbed on the west face by Richey & Wilford '07.

Ganderta
A superb and very accessible double-summited peak close to the road. Long HVS takes east ridge to east summit (easy descent); 5-pitch E2 takes south face of west summit (abseil descent). Route attempted on north face of east summit – E4 to high point. All PL & SS '07.

Tahatai Logumte
Twin towers rising 250m from the plains. 1-hour walk-in. North summit climbed by 3-pitch HVS taking north ridge, south summit by 5-pitch E5 starting from notch between towers. Abseil descents. PL & SS '08.

Samayata
At almost 10,000ft the highest of the Adwa peaks, 1.5-hour walk-in to base of south face, which is probably the highest in the area at c600m. The only route so far climbs south ridges of lower two towers near left side of face – 10-pitch E1, nice 'classic' climbing on great rock. PL & SS '08. Huge potential.

Umba Gwal Atse

Remarkable tower of marble standing in splendid isolation on the south side of the range. 2-hour walk-in. 6-pitch E2 wanders up shorter (200m) SW side (PL & SS '07), 300m east face unclimbed and very challenging.

174. Umba Gwal Atse, the 'Great Father of the Region', a 300m marble monolith on the southern edge of the Mountains of Adwa. (*Pat Littlejohn*)

Rayu

Egg-shaped formation with easy route to summit on north side and big walls to south and west. The only route so far starts up SW buttress, then veers left to line of grooves and chimneys (8-pitch XS 6a. PL & SS '08). Scope for more superb extreme adventure routes.

175. Pat Littlejohn on pitch 1 of the south buttress of Rayu ('The Egg'), an 8-pitch XS, 6a. (*Steve Sustad*)

Nebelet Tower

Rising above the town of Nebelet (1.5 hour drive north of Hawzien) is a spectacular twin-summited sandstone tower. 6-pitch 5.10 route takes steep line of cracks and chimneys on the SE side, then long traverse right to gain summit. Abseil descent. Richey & Wilford '07.

Bouldering

This can be found at Gobo Dura and a few km from the Italian Hotel in Hawzien (hundreds of round but featured boulders in pleasant setting, reputedly 'world class').

HARISH KAPADIA

India 2007

The year 2007 saw diminishing mountaineering activity in the Indian Himalaya. Among the main reasons were the stiff charges enforced by the governments of two states that contain a large number of peaks, ie Sikkim and Uttarakhand. In addition to the charges levied by the Indian Mountaineering Foundation (IMF) these two states insist on additional charges and stiff conditions which have put off many climbers. As a result, there was not a single expedition in the eastern regions, ie Sikkim and Arunachal Pradesh, and far fewer expeditions to Uttarakhand areas.

There were 113 expeditions (61 Indian and 52 foreign) and out of these about 70 expeditions were to very routine peaks which have often been climbed. Stok Kangri, a peak which can be climbed in about three days from Leh, received as many as 25 expeditions. This peak was always climbed illegally by many parties, but now the Indian Mountaineering Foundation has opened a branch office at Leh and hence these expeditions registered with them and paid the fees.

Three expeditions visited the Eastern Karakoram, which takes much organising and clearances. The Siachen area was declared open for trekkers with a fanfare, but soon Pakistan registered a strong protest. At present only one team consisting of military cadets has visited the first three stages on the Siachen, otherwise all other trekkers have been stopped. However, the rule for allowing joint expeditions to the Siachen glacier continues.

Expeditions to Kalanka and Changabang were beaten by freak storms in September and October. Many expeditions to difficult peaks like Arwa Spire and Arwa Tower were successful in the month of May. Among the other good climbs were the ascent of Kulu Makalu, Mukut Parvat East Peak, Manirang and Menthosa, all by Indian mountaineers. A trekking team was permitted, for the first time, to trek near the tri-junction where the borders of India, China and Burma meet – the easternmost point of India. Considering its sensitive nature as Indian and Chinese forces had clashed here, this was a major opening of minds.

The trekking agencies, particularly those that take students and young people to the mountains, are unregulated here. This year two deaths of young people on very routine treks have raised much controversy. Responding to a challenge by one of the parents, the High Court in Mumbai has ordered the government to frame rules for such agencies. This could be the welcome step that Indian mountaineers have been waiting for.

Many changes are evident in the Himalaya, directly due to global warming. The lower villages are receiving less snow and have complained that fields are now drier as the snowmelt used to irrigate the fields. At one village the flowers and fruits that were grown now have to be planted almost a thousand feet higher as the rising temperature has made it unsustainable at the village height. And the glaciers are certainly receding, such as the Chong Kumdan glacier.

UTTARAKHAND

The Arwa group in central Garhwal has been attracting climbers from many nationalities for a few years now. This year was no exception, despite administrative difficulties.

Arwa Spire (6193m)
Expedition: Korean
Leader: Park Heungsoo and 5 members, June 2007. Bad weather, snowfall.

Arwa Tower (6352m)
Expedition: Swiss
Leader: Thomas Senf and 4 members, May-June 2007.
Thomas Senf, Stephan Siegrist, Denis Burdet climbed the N face on 7 June.

Bhrigupanth (6772m)
Expedition: Indian; IMF Ladies Expedition
Leader: Bimla Negi Deoskar and 8 members. August-September 2007
Climbed on 19 September by Bandana Gurung, Kavita Burathoki, Chandra Bist and Kusum Chauhan with Sherpas. The climb followed the route of first ascent by Arlene Blum in 1980.

Changabang (6864m)
Changabang and Kalanka, in Central Garhwal, are major climbing challenges. Due to its steep walls, many routes have been attempted and climbed. However, storms in autumn foiled all attempts on these peaks.

Expedition: New Zealand
Leader: Brian Edward Alder and 4 members, August-October 2007.
Attempted N face, reaching 6200m on 18 September, and later tried W ridge, reaching 6000m on 1 October. Major storm in late September stopped the climb.

Expedition: French
Yannick Graziani and Christian Trommsdorff, October 2007. This two-member team reached 5800m. Two huge snowfalls stopped the attempt.

Kalanka (6931m)
Expedition: Czech Republic
Petr Masek and 3 members, September-October 2007.
Continuous bad weather; reached 5200m on N face.

Expedition: Dutch
Leader: Mike Van Berkel and 3 members, Aug-Sept 2007. Bad weather.

Changuch (6322m)
Expedition: Indian; IMF
Leader: Cdr Satyabrata Dam and members, October 2007.
While they were at camp 2, a sérac fell on the camp. Two Sherpas, Ang Nyima and Mingma Sherpa, died on the spot. One Sherpa, Pemba, was badly injured. The attempt was given up. In spite of being visible from the popular trail to the Pindari glacier, the peak has remained virgin.

Kamet (7756m)
Expedition: Indian; Howrah District Mountaineers and Trekkers Association.
Leader: NP Rao and 12 members, June-July 2007.
The team followed the normal route from Purvi Kamet glacier.

Mukut Parvat East (7130m)
Expedition: Indian; Saad Mountaineers
Leader Rajan Deshmukh and 8 members, June-July 2007. This is a satellite peak of Mukut Parvat. The summit was reached on 17 July.

Shivling (6543m)
Shivling, on the Gangotri glacier, remains as popular as ever. The most newsworthy ascent was the first successful Indian civilian climb, by Rahul Yelange and a team of young climbers from Pune, in May-June.

Nilkanth (6596m)
Expedition: Indian; The Himalayan Club, Kolkata Section.
Leader: AVM (Retd) AK Bhattacharrya and 11 members, May-June 2007.
Second ascent of the W Ridge. On 11 June, 11 members reached the summit via the W ridge route followed by Martin Moran in 2000. This was the first Indian ascent from the W ridge. The summiters were Gautam Ghosh, Debraj Datta, Subrata Chakrabarty, Gautam Saha, Bijender Sing, G Prasanna, Dinesh Rawat, Mingma Sherpa, Ang Nima, Thendup Sherpa and Pemba Sherpa.

Exploration in the Panpatia Glacier
The trail from Badrinath to Kedarnath valley, as followed by the team of Shipton and Tilman, is a fascinating piece of history. Their trail via the Gandharpongi valley was followed by a British team led by Martin Moran.

From the nearby Panpatia glacier they crossed a pass towards the southern valley, giving an easier exit to the Kedar valley. This exploration was completed this year by a team led by Tapan Pandit from West Bengal. In June they entered the Khirao valley and reached its head where the Panpatia Bamak lies. Following the northern edge they crossed Parvati Col to reach the upper plateau. Traversing SW on this plateau they crossed Panpatia Col to descend to Kachni Tal and Madhyamaheshwar. A few parties had tried to undertake this crossing from both directions in the past and failed. With this historic crossing, the routes of earlier explorations are now completed.

HIMACHAL PRADESH

Gangstang (6170m)
Expedition: British
Leader: Martin Moran and 8 members, September-October 2007.
Martin Moran, Arun Mahajan, Peter Ashworth, Gustav Fierrocarion, John Liddle, Luder Sing (LO) reached the summit on 30 September. This was a new route: W face couloir and SW ridge. They had mostly clear weather.

Expedition: Indian; Kolkata Trekkers Youth
Leader: Ashim Kr Ghosh and 10 members, August-September 2007.
After establishing three camps up to 5640m, Sanjib Kumar Dey and Mohansing Thakur climbed the peak on 31 August.

Khang Shilling (6360m)
Expedition: Indian; Snout Adventurers Association, Kolkata
Leader: Ujjal Ray and 11 members, August-September 2007.
The peak stands at the head of the Khamengar valley to the west. The N ridge of the peak forms a col with Shigri Parvat. This team approached from Khamengar valley to make the second ascent by the same route. Devdas Nandy, Surojit Bhowmick, Deepankar Ghosh, Inderjeet and Chandar summited on 3 September.

Kullu Makalu (c 6100m)
Expedition: Indian; Mountaineering Association of Krishnanagar, WB
Leader: Basanta Singha Roy and 10 members, May-June 2007.
As its name suggests, this peak stands in the Kullu Himalaya. However, its difficulties cannot be compared with those of Makalu in Nepal. The present team fixed rope to camp 2 but the final rock wall stopped them at 6200m.

Manirang (6593m)
Expedition: Indian; Himalayan association, Kolkata
Leader: Ujjwal Ganguly and 6 members, August-September 2007.

After a gap of more than a decade, this peak was climbed again. The summit was reached on 2 September via the S ridge from Manirang pass. Uttam Jana and two Sherpas, Nima Dorje and Narender, reached the summit. Earlier ascents were by J de V Graaf (first, 1952), Col Balwant Sandhu (1988) and Paul Nunn and Divyesh Muni in 1994 as part of an Indian-British expedition.

Menthosa (6443m)
Expedition: Indian; Indian Mountaineering Foundation Ladies Expedition
Leader: Chaula Jagirdar, August 2007.
This peak stands halfway up the Miyar valley above Urgus village. The team reached Tingrot by road and approached the higher slopes via Urgus nala. From Camp 2 at 5945m Bhanita Timyunpi, Tusi Das, Ms Chanda, Sange Sherpa, Lakhpa Tenzing, Lakpa Sherpa and Harsh reached the summit on 18 August.

Mulkila IV (6514m)
Expedition: Indian; Indian Mountaineering Foundation Ladies Expedition.
Leader: Deepu Sharma and 8 members, June-July 2007.
Mulkila IV is the highest and most challenging peak of the group. The team approached from the Milang glacier in Lahaul and on 14 July they reached the summit via the N ridge. They found a small box containing a paper with names of the 1939 expedition summiters who had made the first ascent. These were Parineeta Chauhan, Kusum Bharati, N Bidyapati Devi, Neeta Rani and Rinchen Sherpa.

Mulkila V (6370m)
Expedition: Indian; Bhadrakali Padatik, Hooghly, WB
Leader: Prosenjit Mukherjee and 7 members, June-July 2007.
This is a relatively easy summit of the Mulkila group. This team approached the peak from Taragiri glacier and climbed the S face. Camp 2 was set up at 5700m. All members reached the summit on 23 June.

Phawararang (6394m)
Expedition: Indian; Kamarhati Trekkers association, Kolkata
Leader: Malay Kani Halder and 7 members, August-September 2007.
The peak rises to the east of the Jorkanden massif. Approaching from the Lalanti glacier, six climbers reached the summit on 29 August.

Ramjak (6318m)
Expedition: Indian; Phoenix Kolkata
Leader: Debashish Kanji and 5 members, June-July 2007. The peak is seen from the popular trekking route from Darcha to Shingo la. It was first climbed by an Indian team in 2002. The present team attempted the peak via the SSE ridge, and reached 5350m.

Rubalkang (6187m)

Expedition: Indian-Bangladesh Joint Expedition

Leaders Basanta Kumar Singha Roy and SM Muntasir Mamun with 14 members, May-June 2007. The major achievement of this team was to be the first joint team with climbers from Bangladesh and India. They climbed this relatively easy peak in the Kullu Himalaya by its south face.

P. 6036m (Miyar glacier)

Expedition: Indian; Nilkanth Abhijatri Sangha, WB

Leader Sameer Sengupta and 7 members, July 2007.

This a small peak in the Miyar nala in Lahaul. They set up base camp near Dali got. The summit was reached by all eight members on 30 July.

P. 5617m ('Forward Peak')

Expedition: Japanese; Osaka University

Leader Daisuke Tsutsumi and 7 members, August-September 2007.

This small peak is located in the Miyar nala valley, Lahaul, near the Tarasalmu pass. The summit was reached on 8 September by the N face.

ZANSKAR AND LADAKH

P. 5200m (Kargil area)

Expedition: Italian

Leader: Mourizio Orsi and 5 members, August 2007.

A small peak in Zanskar, near Gulmotonga. The summit was reached on 20 August by all members, via the E face and the N ridge. They proposed the name 'Golden Sentinel'.

Mari (6587 m)

Expedition: Japanese

Leader: Rentaro Nishijima and 6 members, July-August 2007.

The peaks stands near the Pangong lake, village Man, Ladakh. The team attempted Mari via P.6342, hoping to traverse to Mari. But the ridge was rocky and knife-edged and they could not cross it. So P.6342 was reached by the S face by seven members on different dates.

EASTERN KARAKORAM

Chong Kumdan I (7071m)

Expedition: Indian American Joint Expedition; The Himalayan Club, Mumbai section.

Leaders: Divyesh Muni and Don Goodman with 8 members.

July-August 2007.

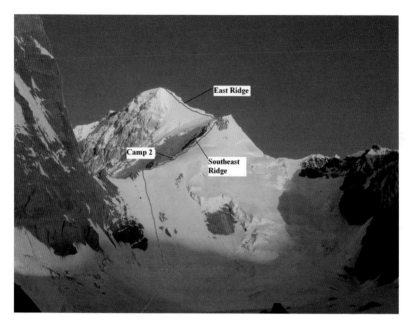

176. Chong Kumdan I (7071 m). The second ascent, a new route, was made by the east ridge. (*Divyesh Muni*)

New Route on Chong Kumdan I

On 20 August, expedition members Divyesh Muni, Donald Goodman, Marlin Geist and Chris Robertson; and Sherpas Nima Dorje, Ming Temba and Pemba Norbu climbed a new route on Chong Kumdan I. The route climbed the SE ridge to its intersection with the main E ridge, following it to the summit. This was the second ascent of this high peak, the first being by an Indian-British team led by Harish Kapadia in 1991. They had attempted this route but reached the summit via the NW ridge. The team's main ambition had been to climb the virgin peak of Chong Kumdan II (7004m). However, on approaching the glacier it proved to be too difficult and dangerous to negotiate the broken glacier.

The route on Chong Kumdan I involved 45-55° ice for 400m to the crest of the SE ridge. The team made a camp on the ridge at 6450m, spending four hours excavating tent platforms. Above camp 2 they fixed four ropes past gendarmes and corniced ridge. After this, the slopes were moderate. Due to the poor condition of the snow, it took more than five hours to negotiate the last section to the summit.

One of the Kumauni support staff, Anand Ram, passed away on 10 August due to high-altitude sickness. The Sherpa Sirdar, Ang Tashi took ill at camp 1 and was evacuated by helicopter to Hundar.

Mamostong Kangri (7516m)

Expedition: Indian French Joint Expedition
Leaders: Chewang Motup Goba and Paulo Grobel with 7 French and 9
Indian members. July-August 2007.
This high mountain ('Peak of a Thousand Devils') stands on the ancient
trade route to Saser La. The Indo-French joint expedition climbed via the
SE side, the normal route. Paulo Grobel, Gayton Michel, Sherpa and
Thinless Konchok reached the summit on 19 August.

Expedition: Indian Army
Leader: Col. Ashok Abbey and 30 members, October-November 2007.
This strong team made an ascent of the peak as autumn cold and snow was
settling in the area. They followed a new approach route. After crossing
Saser La, they turned north along the Shyok and turned further west in the
Thangman valley leading towards the Mamostong Kangri peak. Climbing
a ridge directly, they avoided the Hope Col.

Rimo I (7385m)

Expedition: Indian; Indian Mountaineering Foundation
Leader: Maj KS Dhami and team. July-August 2007.
This peak stands in the side valley to the east of the Siachen glacier. The
team experienced troubles and did not summit. Kalyansing (an instructor
at NIM) was drowned in the Terong river in the first few days. Later, the
leader Dhami suffered serious frostbite.

Unnamed Peak (6350m)

Expedition: Indian Australian Joint Expedition
Leaders Motup Chewang Goba and Geoff Bailey with 13 members.
May-June 2007. The peak is near Col Italia. The expedition had planned
to cross Saser La and follow the trail along the Shyok and Chong Kumdan
glacier dam site. However, due to unseasonal poor weather the rivers were
flooded and the expedition had to be abandoned.

ARUNACHAL PRADESH

Exploring the Lohit valley of Arunachal Pradesh

The Lohit valley, in eastern Arunachal Pradesh (formerly NEFA) is deep
and thickly wooded. It is the easternmost valley of India. At its eastern
extremity the borders of India, China and Burma meet at what is called the
'Tri-Junction'. To the north of Tri-Junction is the Jechep La (pass), leading
to China and to the south lies the Diphu La (Taluk pass) which leads to
Burma. This valley is of historical significance for several reasons. Many
early travellers approached the route from the Sadiya frontier district and

went on to Rima in the Zayul (now in China). This was the easiest route as no high pass had to be crossed. Many parties followed this trail, prominent among them being F Kingdon Ward, Col FM Bailey, TT Cooper and the Pandit explorer AK (nicknamed 'Krishna' or Rai Bahadur Kishen Singh). Both the Chinese and the British surveyed the area and built a track from their respective areas. In 1962 in a bloody war the Chinese aggressors attacked Indian posts and came down to Walong and a little beyond. The heroic battles at the Namti Plains and the (western) Tri Junction are legendary.

We aimed to reach the Diphu La at the head of the Dichu valley. Political conditions prevented us from approaching it, so as an alternative we followed the Sat Ti valley to its south. Due to local festivities, we started the trek from Dong, a village 6km north on the left bank of the Lohit. The first thing on the trail was a single log bridge 100ft above and across the Sat Ti. We had crossed many bridges on Arunachal treks in the past ('Foot Suspension Bridges') which were scary enough, but in this less trodden valley such 'single log bridges' were particularly dangerous. The trail otherwise was through thick jungle with many steep ups and downs. After several days we reached a bridge with water flowing over it. Two more such dangerous bridges were promised ahead. On the basis that discretion is the better part of the valour, we decided to return.

After many inquiries we were able to locate the Walong inscriptions on a huge rock. These were mentioned by Ronald Kaulback in the 1910 *Geographical Journal*. Kaulback was a member of F Kingdon Ward's party. On clearing the surroundings, we saw the red lettering of Chinese markings. These were partly deciphered, but this significant find will require further research.

*   *   *   *   *

During the year, two books of note were published. *Heights of Madness* by Myra MacDonald considers the war on the Siachen glacier. She was a reporter with Reuters in India and in that capacity flew over the glacier in poor weather, met army officers and talked to those involved in the war. Later, the same exercise was repeated on the Pakistan side. The other book is by leading British author Charles Allen, *Kipling Sahib* which brings out the life of Rudyard Kipling in India. It was released at JJ School of Arts in Mumbai, where Kipling was born.

Finally, the Alpine Club 150th anniversary was celebrated in the Indian Himalaya by a small expedition to the Kagbhusandi valley. The team climbed three peaks, all first ascents, despite plenty of snow on the ground. One of the peaks was named 'AC 150', fitting to the occasion. (*See 'Climbing in the Kagbhusandi Valley', page 167*)

DICK ISHERWOOD

Nepal 2007

In Nepal 2007 was marked by continuing political unrest and an uneasy truce between the Maoist group and the conventional party politicians, the future of which is still uncertain; at the time of writing the Maoists have won the April 2008 election convincingly. Trekking group numbers at last appear to be on the increase again.

The climbing pattern of recent years continued, including very large numbers of ascents of Everest, Cho Oyu and Ama Dablam, a few ascents of the other 8000m peaks, several technically hard routes on the lower Khumbu peaks, and a relatively small number of climbs in the more outlying and less frequented areas.

On **Everest** no less than 597 ascents were made, another record number, all in the spring season with almost equal numbers from Nepal and Tibet. All of these were by the standard routes. A Korean party attempted the SW face but retreated from 8000m after two members were killed in an avalanche. There were only seven deaths in total on Everest, a welcome reduction.

A Chinese party tested the Olympic torch in preparation for the 2008 ascent and confirmed that it would indeed burn up there. (Doug Scott could have told them that!) A Japanese climber set a new age record for Everest ascents of 71 years and a bit. A Dutchman in shorts reached 7400m on the Nepalese side. At least two north-south traverses were made, one by a Briton, David Tait with one Sherpa companion. Tait had planned a double traverse but after the descent on the Nepal side his knees hurt, so he decided one was enough. Conrad Anker and Leo Houlding of the Altitude Everest Expedition climbed the Second Step of the N ridge free and without oxygen, but doubted whether Mallory and Irvine would have managed it. They did not however achieve their plan of summiting in period costume of Norfolk jackets and plus fours.

Ama Dablam again saw a large number of commercial ascents in the post-monsoon season by the SW ridge, despite the large ice avalanche in late 2006 which killed six climbers and took out much of the limited tent space at Camp 3 (6300m), the usual top camp. Most people now camp a bit lower down before the summit day. All 14 parties on the standard route in the spring were unsuccessful due to bad weather and poor snow conditions; an American party of two (Aric Baldwin and James Cromie) did succeed on the more difficult NE spur, descending by the standard route.

177.   The Kammerlander/Unterkircher route on Jasamba (7351m).
(*Hans Kammerlander*)

Also in the Everest area an American party attached to the Khumbu Climbing School made an impressive winter ascent (in February) of the east ridge of **Tawoche (6495m)**. This is a 1600m route with rock-climbing up to 5.9. Their line appears to be very close to, if not the same as one climbed in 1989 by an Anglo-German pair.

There were several impressive ascents of hard routes on high mountains. Perhaps the most significant was by the Russians Valery Babanov and Sergey Kofanov, who made the first ascent of the north-west ridge of **Jannu (7710m)** in alpine style over six days in October, starting from the Jannu glacier and gaining the ridge at the col between Jannu and Sobithonge (6995m). This ridge had been attempted twice by strong French teams in 1994 and 1998. This climb was considered to be 'VI, WI+4, 80 degrees, M5'. Clearly it was quite hard, and done in the best style, unlike some other recent Russian ascents. (*See 'Nine Days on the Way that has no end', page 36.*)

In the spring, a Korean party made an ascent of the south face of **Lhotse Shar (8400m)**. The leader, Um Hong-Gil, completed the fourteen 8000m peaks in 2003 and has now added Lhotse Shar and Yalung Kang, neither usually counted as independent peaks, to his list. The route on Lhotse Shar was completed by three Korean climbers and one Sherpa in alpine style, and was reported as a first ascent but in fact appears to largely follow a line climbed by a Czech party in 1983.

Hans Kammerlander and Karl Unterkircher climbed the south-west face and south pillar of **Pasang Lhamu Chuli** (7351m, also known as Jasamba or Nangpai Gosum I) south-west of Cho Oyu in the pre-monsoon season. This was the peak on which Kammerlander lost his companion in 2006. From a bivouac at 6000m they climbed steep mixed ground to the summit in 13 hours. This line appears to be distinct from the SE face/S ridge route climbed by a Slovenian party in 2004, but may join it near the top (*see photo*).

On **Annapurna 1**, the Slovenian climber Tomas Humar soloed a line on the far east end of the south face and reached the East Summit (8026m) over three days in late October. His route was entirely on steep snow and ice above a small ice platform at 5800m and appears to have been to the right of the spur climbed by Jerzy Kukuczka and Artur Hajzer in 1988, which it joined at 7500m on the east ridge. He was unable to continue to the main summit due mainly to very strong winds. He took a companion for the very crevassed approach to the 5800m platform but climbed the rest alone. The south face of Annapurna is starting to look a bit like Stanage, with at least eight lines climbed successfully, though several, including this one, reach the east ridge a long way from the main summit.

Following page:

178. Two climbers from the Kangwon National University Expedition on the south ridge of The Fang (7647m). The peak in the background is Annapurna South. The summit of The Fang is behind the camera. (*By courtesy of Kangwon National University*)

Also in the Annapurna Sanctuary at around the same time in the autumn a Korean expedition from Kangwon National University, Gangwon, South Korea, made an ascent of **The Fang** (7647m, also known as **Varaha Shikhar**) by its east face and south ridge. This appears to be a new line and only the third ascent of The Fang. The party helicoptered into their base camp after acclimatising in the Langtang. Some fixed rope was used on the lower face leading to the 4 km-long ridge. Parts of the ridge were spectacularly corniced. One Korean climber and two Sherpas reached the summit. Two climbers took substantial falls and were evacuated by helicopter.

In the Jugal Himal the French guide Paolo Grobel, with two Sherpas, abandoned his planned attempt on Langtang Ri (7205m), owing to heavy snow cover on the very rough moraines of the long Langtang glacier, and instead made what is thought to have been the first ascent of **Gurkarpo Ri (6889m)**. They climbed it by its west ridge at a standard Difficile (using traditional Alpine grading). As with some other summits in that area, it is not impossible that it had been discreetly climbed in the past.

I would like to thank Elizabeth Hawley and Tom Nakamura for much of the information in these notes.

JOHN TOWN

China & Tibet 2006 & 2007

Qonglai Shan

The Siguniang National Park continues to be an attractive destination with easy accessibility, good infrastructure and relaxed permit requirements.

In the Bipeng valley Saburo Mizobuchi, Keiichi Nagatomo, Naoki Ohuchi and Tomohiro Sugai completed a 400m new route on **Longgesali (5420m)** on 3-4 September 2006. The group also attempted routes on **Pt 5513m** and **Jiang Jun Feng (5260m)**. In September 2007 Jon Sullivan and Liu Yong (USA) made attempts on the north face of **Dragon's Tooth/Longa Feng (5250m)**, reaching 4700m, and the nearby **Peak 5183m**, reaching 4900m.

In the Changping valley, Russians Kolesov, Shelkovnikov, and Sherstnev made a new route on the east face of **Celestial Peak (5413m)** between 17 and 19 February 2006. Later that year Ian Gibb, Felix Hoddinott, Jeremy Thornley (UK) made the first ascent of **Dorsal Peak (5050m)** on the east rim of the valley via the north-west ridge. They also made the second ascent of Jiang Jun Feng (5260m) via the south-west ridge and attempted Pk 5202m via the south flank and west ridge.

In 2007 Joe Puryear and Chad Kellog (USA) were not able to make their planned attempt on Siguniang because of news of the death of the latter's wife in the Alaska Range. Joined by Jay Janousek they did make the first ascent of **Lara Peak (c5700m)** on 18 April, which they subsequently named after Lara Kellog.

On 22 August four Italian climbers, including Elena Merino, made a new 400m route on the unnamed **Peak 4764m**.

In the Shuangqiao valley Vaughan Thomas (Australia) and Kester Brown (NZ) made the first ascent of **Daogou West (5422m)** in late September 2006 via the 600m south face.

Shaluli Shan

Genyen (6204m) received its second ascent via the north spur by the Italian team of Simon Kehrer, Gerold Moroder, Walter Nones, and Karl Unterkircher on 16 May 2006. They climbed the challenging route in two days but refrained from standing on the highest point in deference to the mountain's holy status. Kehrer and Moroder then attempted the granite east face of **Sachun (c5800m)**, but retreated on their fourth day.

In October 2007 Jay Janousek, Michelle Puryear, Peter Inglis, Julie Hodson and Joe Puryear visited the Genyen massif. On 22 October Inglis and Joe Puryear made the first ascent of **Peak 5965m**, which lies just west of Genyen.

179.   Hati (5524m) from the west. (*Dave Sykes*)

An Alpine Club team of Dave Wynne-Jones, Steve Hunt, Dick Isherwood and Peter Rowat made the first ascent of **Peak 5596m**, which lies between Dangchezhengla and Peak 5850m in October 2007.   They also made a new route from the north on **Dangchezhengla (5830m)**, joining the Japanese route on the summit ridge.   An attempt on the steep north spur of **Yangmolong (6060m)** was turned back at 5400m.

In May 2007 David Gerrard and David Sykes (UK) made the first ascent of **Hati (5524m)** which lies north-east of Xiashe in the Jarjinjabo area. The pair also attempted **Haizi Shan (5833m)** on their way back but were defeated by bad weather.

A primarily British team consisting of Theresa Booth, Charles Kilner, Simon Mills, Evelyn Mullins, Hamish Rose and Basil Thompson visited Jarjinjabo in October 2007. Booth, Kilner, Mullins and Thompson made the first ascent of **Man Chu Kangri (5434m)**. The party then attacked **Garrapunsum (5812m)**, the highest peak in the massif, and Kilner, Mills and Rose were successful in making the first ascent of the northern and highest summit via the north-east flank and east ridge.

Kangri Karpo
This beautiful range contains the longest glacier in Tibet and much of the area remains to be properly explored. The Japanese Silver Turtle Group,

consisting of Takeo Honjo, Kaneshige Ikeda, Haruhisa Kato, Isama Moriyama and Hiroshi Sagano, all over 60, continued their investigation of the Lhagu glacier in October 2006 by ski. Kato and Moriyama made the probable first ascent of **Snow Dome (5928m)**. Sadly, Honjo became ill and died at base camp at the conclusion of the expedition.

Nyenchen Tanglha East

A combination of truly spectacular mountains and some of the worst weather in Tibet make this a fearsome destination; but success is possible, as demonstrated by Mick Fowler's two recent trips to Kajaqiao and Manamcho, and Sean Water's and Jo Kippax' ascent of Birutaso in 2005. **Nenang (6870m)** is the highest unclimbed peak in the range and in October-November 2006 it was attempted for the first time by Jim Lowther (UK), Mark Richey and Mark Wilford (USA). After a very tough 13-day alpine-style push, they were stopped by a huge crevasse within 300m of the summit.

Nyenchen Tanglha West

Despite being within two hours' drive of Lhasa, boasting a rail connection and having much better weather than the eastern part of the range, this area remains a quiet and rewarding one in which to climb. Christian Haas of Austria returned to the range in 2006 with Hansjoerg Pfaundler, making the first ascent of **Sha Mo Karpo Ri (6261m)** on 5 October. They also made an impressive ascent of **Nyenchen Tanglha Central (7117m)** in a single push on 12 October.

Kun Lun

The Kun Lun remain arguably the remotest and most inaccessible mountain range in Central Asia. Russians Vasilyi Ivanov, Edmundas Jonikas, Alexander Moiseev, Tadeush Schepanyuk and Otto Chkhetiani made a 35-day circumnavigation of **Qong Mustagh (6950m)** in September 2006. Moiseev developed altitude sickness as they reached the mountain and had to be accompanied out by Jonikas. The rest of the group investigated **Peak 6946m** to the east of Qong Mustagh, via a valley to the north-west, but were stopped by a gorge at 5000m.

Aksai Chin (7167m) received its first and second ascents in 1986 and 1997 by Japanese expeditions. Bruno Paulet and Christian Trommsdorff (France) made the third ascent by a new route from the south-east, and the second ascent of the north summit, also known as **Doufeng (6957m)**, in April-May 2006.

Lungkar Shan

In August 2007 John Town, Kevin Clarke, Richard Sant and Mike Dawber (UK) made an attempt on **Tachab Kangri**, the peak at the north end of this range, shown on maps as either 6704m or 7216m. They were turned back at c6300m after snow slides swept both possible routes of ascent.

180. North-east face of Phola Kyung (6500m) from the Qulunggam glacier (c5700m). The 2006 team climbed the south-east face and upper east ridge. (*Erik Monasterio*)

181. Brian Alder on the summit of Phola Kyung (6500m). The striking light flare is natural and not a result of any filters. (*Erik Monasterio*)

182. Route taken by the British party on Yilpiz, Kuksay area, Tien Shan.
(*John Allen*)

Gangdise Shan

In 2006 a strong team consisting of Bruce Normand (UK), Brian Alder, Erik Monasterio (NZ), Monika Hrosnska, Oliver von Rotz (Switzerland) and Stephen Parker (Aus) made an impressive set of ascents in the Loinbo Kangri massif. Alder, Monasterio and Normand made the first ascents of **Chomogan (6655m)** and **Phola Kyung (6500m)** on 10 and 16 October, in both cases via the south-east face and south ridge. They also made the first ascent of **Peak 6355m** on the 18 October. Parker and von Rotz made ascents of **Peaks 6200m, 6340m, 6237m, 6240m** and **6263m**, the first of these being a first ascent with Normand and the latter with Hronska. Von Rotz also made the solo first ascent of **Peak 6044m** and the first ascent of **Peak 6202m** in the company of Hronska. Finally Normand soloed **Peak 6240m** and **Gopalho (6450m)** on 18 and 21 October, the latter being an impressive one-day first ascent via the east face.

Tien Shan

A seven-strong British party made a number of ascents in the Kuksay glacier area, approaching via Bishkek in Kyrgyzstan and entering China via the Torugart pass. John Allen and David Barker climbed **Peak 5582m**, immediately west of Kala peak, on 30 July via a 700m route on the north-west face. With Richard Taylor and Joe Howard they also climbed the north face of **Yilpiz (c5315m)**. Isobel and Kevin Mulligan and Neil Willat climbed **Tiltagh (5485m)** via its west face.

Pamir

Ivan Dusharin, Lena Lebedeva, Sasha Novik and Lev Ioffe (USA) made the first ascent of **Kokodag (7210m)** via the south spur of the north-west summit. The peak lies on the ridge extending west from Kongur, between Kongur Tiube and Aklamgam. They reached the summit on 10 August 2006 after two previous summit attempts.

A Finnish group consisting of Lauri Hamalainen, Henri Arjanne, Veli-Matti Helke, Rauno Ravantti, Teemu Saarikivi, Kalle Berg, Mikko Piironen, and Andrey Ershov visited the Kokosel glacier in August 2007. Hamalainen and Arjanne made the first ascent of **Peak 6355m** on 13 August via the 900m of the south-west face in difficult conditions. The whole team then made the first ascent of **Peak 6013m** on the next day via the 500m west face.

Himalaya

Much of the activity on the Tibetan side inevitably revolves around repeat ascents or route variations on the 8000m peaks but there was also activity elsewhere.

In April/May 2005 Stephen Chaplin (UK), Laila Ojefelt, Lars Svens (Sweden) and Damien Gildea (Aus) attempted the existing route on the west ridge of **Kula Kangri (7554m)** but were stopped by cold winds and poor weather at about 6300m. They also tried **Jiexiang (6676m)** but retreated at about the same level.

The magnificent granite of the west face of **Chomo Lonzo (7790m)** rebuffed two attempts by Valeri Babanov in April 2006 but he was successful in making a 1200m route on the south-west face of **Chomo Lonzo North (7199m)** as far as the summit ridge.

Toshiya Nakajima and Naoyuki Momose, members of a five-man Japanese expedition, climbed **Hungchi (7038m)** by a new route from the north in Autumn 2006. This peak lies on the border in the Everest region, above the West Rongbuk glacier.

Following an initial attempt in 1999, Carlos Buhler (USA) returned in May 2005 with Yuri Koshalenko and Nikolay Totmyanin to the north-west ridge of **Menlungtse (7181m)**. They retreated from 6300m, after five days' climbing, when Koshalenko became ill.

In the same year Zdenek Cervenka, Cestmir Lukes and Irene Oehninger made what are probably the first ascents of **Peak 6473m** and **Peak 6063m** at the far north-west end of the Shishapangma range.

It is possible to break new ground while operating from the base camps of 8000m peaks. Jordi Tozas of Spain soloed a new route on the south face of **Palung Ri (7100m)** from the Cho Oyu base camp on 19 September 2006 and Isomi Okanda and a porter climbed the east ridge of **Risum (7050m)** via the large glacial plateau to the north-west of Shishapangma in September 2005.

North America 2007

The Area Notes for North America would not have been possible without the help of the American Alpine Journal (AAJ) and Kelly Cordes, who provided the original background material upon which they are based. These notes cover the highlights and major ascents. For a complete report of all activity in North America, the reader is referred to the current editions of the AAJ and Canadian Alpine Journal.

ALASKA

The Denali National Park and Preserve saw some significant firsts this year with Masatoshi Kuriaki making the first solo winter ascent of **Mount Foraker** and the only successful ascent during the 2007 season. Kuriaki previously soloed Denali in the winter of 1998 and also attempted Mount Hunter three times during the 2003 to 2005 seasons. Pierre Darbellay and Raphael Slawinski climbed a new line that ends on the summit ridge of the **Kahiltna Queen**, *Le Voyage au Bout de La Nuit* (450m, WI4+ R). Their line takes an obvious gully to the right of the *West Face* (Okonek-Mannix, 1979). British climbers Jon Bracey and Andy Houseman made the second ascent of **Mount Hunter's** *French Route* (Grison-Tedeschi, 1984) climbing the route and descending in four days. On **Denali** the majority of climbers opted for the *West Buttress* route with few parties attempting other lines. Colin Haley and Mark Westman made a very fast ascent (under two days to the summit) of the *Denali Diamond* (Becker-Graage, 1983). This was only the route's fifth ascent.

As is often the case, much of the climbing in the Alaska range took place away from the main peaks. Peter Doucette, Ben Gilmore, and Freddie Wilkinson established a new line on the previously unexplored Fin Wall on a peak informally known as **The Fin**, located about four miles south-west of Mount Foraker. Their line, *Fin Wall* (3800', AK Grade 6, NEI 5+), finished on the summit ridge approximately 400' below the summit. They also made first ascents of two peaks in the left-hand fork of the Yentna glacier's north-east fork: 'Rogue Peak' (c8900') via the north-east face (3500', M5, Doucette-Wilkinson), and 'Mantok 1' (c9300') by the east-facing *All Talk Couloir* (3500', M5, Doucette-Gilmore-Wilkinson).

In the Little Switzerland area, Lucas Iten and Martin Gutmann established *Swisser than Swiss Chocolate* (10 pitches, 5.11+) on the west face of the **Throne**. The pair were then joined by Jack Sasser and made the first

183. Colin Haley on the 5th ascent of the *Denali Diamond*.
(*Mark Westman*)

ascent of the unclimbed pillar on the south side of **Royal Tower** via *Got
Lucky* (14 pitches, 5.11). Poor weather prevented the team from completing
additional new lines. Elsewhere, Ben Traxler and Mike Bromberg flew into
the Backside glacier and climbed the *West Ridge* of **Mount Grosvenor**. The
route follows the ridge (50°) to the summit pyramid where it joins the *Upper
South Face route* (Walsh-Westman, 2005). On **Mount Dan Beard** Gareth
Hughes and Vivian Scott ascended its unclimbed east face to put up *Sideburn
Rib* (4500', Scottish IV, 75°).

On **Peak 8010'**, a summit at the western end of the Buckskin glacier, Ryan Hokanson and Chris Gibisch established the mountain's second line with *A Fine Blend* (750m, IV AI6 M6+ 50°) that takes a large corner system on the east face. The only other route on the peak is the *South Route* (Allemann-Lotscher, 1968). On the south-east face of the **Bear Tooth**, Jared Vilhauer, Zach Shlosar, and Jesse (Bill) Billmeier climbed *House of the Rising Sun* (3200', AK Grade V, AI6 A2). The party rappelled the route from the ridge line rather than going to the summit.

The Ruth Gorge was also the scene for significant activity in 2007, with Fumitaka Ichimura, Yusuke Sato, and Tatsuro Yamada putting up three new routes. *Season of the Sun* (4600', V WI4R M6R) climbs **Mount Bradley's** south-east face; *Memorial Gate* (3600', V AI4+R/X) takes the central gully on the north face of **Mount Church**; and *The Ladder Tube* (3000', V 5.10R A3 WI4+R M5) on the north face and then west ridge of **Mount Johnson**.

On the **Eye Tooth**, Renan Ozturk and Cedar Wright established *Ballad of a Dead Soldier* (5.10+ R), a direct finish to *Dream in the Spirit of Mugs* (Orgler-Bonapace-Haas, 1994). They climbed a new line on the Tooth's central pillar to the summit ridge, *The Beholder* (3000', V 5.12 [5.10X]). They also put up *The Great Transformation* (5 pitches, 5.12) on the south-west-facing buttress at the end of the long ridge that extends down and WSW from the west summit of the **Moose's Tooth**. On **The Stump**, the pair also added *Brownfinger* (5.11 R/X) up the obvious corner system right of *Goldfinger* (McNamara-Puryear, 2004). They also added *StumpJumper* (5.11R) that follows the corner to the right of *Brownfinger*. Steven Lucarelli and John Parnigoni added *Choss-o-Licious* (10 pitches) to The Stump's south-east buttress.

On the **Sugar Tooth**, Peter Haeussler and Jay Rowe climbed the *South-east Buttress* (20 pitches, V 5.10, 50° snow). This was the second ascent of the mountain, the other route being the *West Face* (Bonapace-Haas-Orgler, 1994). James Mehigan and Oliver Metherell climbed *Hut Tower Couloir* (500m, ED, Scottish VII, A1), the couloir between **Werewolf Tower** and **Hut Tower**, in a single 23-hour push.

CANADA

Poor weather in the Kluane National Park and Reserve led to a reduced number of successful summits, the main summit of **Mount Logan** only seeing one ascent during 2007. Dave Hesleden and Simon Richardson managed to climb **Lowell Peak** via its *West Ridge* (45°, Scottish III), but this was one of very few successful attempts on new lines in the park in 2007.

On Baffin Island, Niels van Veen and Martin Fickweiler visited the Stewart valley and made the first recorded ascent of the **Copier Pinnacle** (N 70°44' and W 71°27'), taking eight days to ascend *A Little Less Conversation* (800m, 5.11a, A3). Ole Lied, Sigurd Felde, Audun Hetland and Lars Flatø

Nessa travelled to the Sam Ford Fjord and climbed a new line on **Kiguti**, *The Norwegian Route* (1000m, VI 5/A3+), spending fifteen days on the wall. They also attempted another aid line on the **Fin** but retreated due to strong, cold winds. Nessa and Lied also put up a line, alpine style, on the Fin, *Gud Har Ikkje Gløymt Oss, Han Gir Bare Faen* (12 pitches, 5.10, A0), which translates as 'God Hasn't Actually Forgotten Us, He Just Doesn't Give a Damn'. Also on Baffin, Sam Beaugey, Martial Dumas, Jean-Yves Fredricksen, Yann Mimet and David Ravanel travelled to Scott Island at the mouth of the Clark (also referred to as the Scott) Inlet. On **The Wall of Clouds** they climbed a line 150m right of *Aularutiksanga* (Sedeneyer-White, 1999). After seven days on the wall they completed *Nassariit* (650m, A4). The team also completed numerous BASE jumps from walls in the area.

In general, weather in coastal ranges of British Columbia and Washington was below par in 2007 but a few new lines were added. In the central Waddington Range, Graham McDowell, Ryan O'Conell and Ian Nicholson made several attempts on an unclimbed 2,000' wall on the **Blade** but O'Conell and Nicholson were forced to settle for adding a new line to the **Bicuspid Tower**, *Life in the Fast Lane* (IV 5.10c C1). McDowell injured himself on a previous attempt and had to remain at camp. Bob Hamilton, Billy Hood, Steve Kennedy, Neil McGougan, Dave Ritchie and Des Rubens visited the Frontier Group and put up numerous new lines most notably, *Caledonia* (550m, D+, 60° max, Kennedy-Rubens and McGougan-Ritchie) and *Central Buttress* (400m, TD–, 65° max, Hamilton-Kennedy-Rubens) both on the north face of **Mount Geddes**.

Significant developments also took place in the Rockies. On **Mount Yamnuska**, home of rock climbing in the Rockies, Andy Genereux added *Rejection of the Faith* (240m, 5.11c), a sport route put up with top-down bolting, while Allan Derbyshire, Kevin Embacher and Choc Quinn established *Faith* (275m, 5.11b) ground-up style with some bold climbing. These styles reflect the general trend in Rockies rock climbing: new high standard sport and trad lines being established side by side.

The most significant alpine ascent of the season was the new line on the Emperor Face of **Mount Robson** by Colin Hayley and Steve House. House and others have made many attempts on the face over the last decade, with numerous failures. In 2002 Barry Blanchard, Eric Dumerac and Philippe Pellet added *Infinite Patience* (Blanchard-Dumerac-Pellet, 2002). Hayley and House completed their line *Hayley-House* (2500m, WI5 M8) in 36 hours camp-to-camp.

On **Snow Dome** Cory Richards, Dana Ruddy and Ian Welsted climbed a new line on the north face around the corner and right of *Slipstream* (Elzinga-Lauchlan, 1979), *Polarity* (800m, V WI5+). Simon Anthamatten and Ueli Steck repeated the line a few days later adding an additional pitch through the sérac band; neither party was able to finish the route to the summit. Anthamatten and Steck climbed numerous other lines during their visit, including *Cockfight* (4 pitches, M9+ WI5+) on **Crowfoot Mountain**, one of the hardest multi-pitch mixed routes in the Rockies. On **Mount Alberta**, Raphael Slawinski and Eamonn Walsh added the obscure *West Face* (V 5.10+), a line that had seen attempts as early as 1963.

Poor snow conditions deterred many from attempting alpine routes but at the end of the winter, in March 2008, Raphael Slawinski, Eamonn Walsh, and Ian Welsted made the first winter ascent of *Northeast Buttress* (Greenwood-Jones, 1969) on **Mount Temple**. The party drytooled the entire route at M6 over a period of three days, making Mount Temple the last major north face in the Rockies to receive a winter ascent. Slawinski, along with Dana Ruddy and Walsh, also climbed *Dogleg Couloir* (V+ M7 A1) on **Mount Chephren's** north-east face right of *The Wild Thing* (Blanchard-Robinson-Arbic 1987)

Also in March, Vince Anderson and Steve House added the *Anderson-House* (1000m, WI5+ M8 R/X) to the north face of **Mount Alberta**. The route intersects with the *Glidden-Lowe* (Glidden-Lowe, 1972) at a couple of points but climbs new ground for its entirety.

CONTINENTAL UNITED STATES

As previously mentioned, the weather in the Pacific North-west wasn't conducive to climbing although that didn't stop the ubiquitous Colin Hayley and Dylan Johnson adding a new mixed line, the *Lara Kellogg Memorial Route* (IV WI6 A0), to **Mount Stuart's** north-east face. Washington Pass was the scene of several new routes over the summer, including a new line by Bryan Burdo and Scott Johnston added to the south-east face of *South Early Winter Spire*, **Hitchhiker** (IV 5.11 A0 [or 5.10 A1]). The team took three visits, spread over two months. Dan Hilden and Blake Herrington also visited the remote **Gunsight Peak** to climb the oft talked about but seldom attempted peak. Their visit yielded *Gunrunner* (1500', IV 5.10 A1), as well as some other routes.

In Yosemite, Tommy Caldwell continued to free existing lines in the valley. He and Beth Rodden completed a team-free (and second free overall) ascent of *El Corazon* (35 pitches, 5.13b), on **El Capitan.** Caldwell also freed *Golden Gate* (41 pitches, 5.13a). In the autumn he returned to El Capitan and made the second free ascent and first one-day free ascent of the *Direct North-west Face* route on **Half Dome**. Previously freed by Todd Skinner at 5.13d, Caldwell linked two of the crux slab pitches at 5.14a. Also on Half Dome, Rob Pizem and Michael Anderson freed *Arcturus* (5.13) on the north-west face.

Also on El Capitan, Rob Miller and Justen Sjong freed the *Muir Wall* via a new variation to *The Shaft* variation grading it (5.13c/d). Speed climbing continued to be popular with Alexander and Thomas Huber, who set a new record of 2:45:45 on *The Nose* route. As aid lines are being freed, more are being added. Dave Turner established *Dawn Direct* (VI 5.8 A4–) solo over a period of 16 days on El Capitan's south-east face.

The Sierra Nevada saw two new lines on the **Incredible Hulk**. Peter Croft and Conrad Anker added *Solar Flare* (V 5.12+) to the west face with the help of a few friends to take the pictures. Brent Obinger and Nils Davis added *Eye of the Storm* (12 pitches, V 5.12), also on the west face. Elsewhere in the Sierra, **Lone Pine Peak** was the scene of new routes. Miguel Carmona and Joe LeMay added the *South Corner* (V 5.9 C1) to the south face. Their line was the result of several visits over the previous year. Scott Nelson and Charles Ince made the first winter ascent of *Winter Chimney* (Carmona-LeMay, 2005). The pair completed their ascent in a single 24-hour push and graded it 5.7 M3 WI3.

A spate of new route activity took place on **Devil's Castle** in Utah's Wasatch mountains. Brian Cabe and Brian Smoot added *Shadow of the Blade* (5.10d), while Cabe and Matt Scullion added *Portable Darkness* (5.9+). The routes are 'adventurous', with loose rock, but in a fantastic alpine setting.

In the more popular Zion National Park, Bryan Bird and Dave Littman added *The Connoisseur's Variation* (VI 5.10 A3+) to **Abraham** in The Court of the Patriarchs. Their route was a creative link-up of every existing route on the wall and also added three new pitches. Local climber Michael Anderson was also active in the park. With Brian Smoot and Colby Wayment, he freed *The Locksmith Dihedral* (8 pitches, 5.12–) on the **Gatekeeper Wall**. *Hello Mary Lou* on the **Apex Wall** fell to the same team but took multiple attempts to free the line at 5.13–. Anderson also freed *Silmaril* (10 pitches, V 5.12R) on the **Watchman** with Smoot using a variation to bypass with A2 pin crack.

In the Black Canyon of the Gunnison National Park, Josh Wharton and Mike Pennings finished a long-term project on the **North Chasm View Wall**. Their line, *Black Sheep* (7 pitches, IV 5.13b), took five weeks to complete in the spring of 2007. Jared Ogden and Topher Donahue managed to complete their attempts to red point their new line, *Air Guitar* (17 pitches, V 5.12+) on the North Chasm View Wall. On the **South Chasm View Wall**, Mike Pennings and Jonathan Copp added *Dry Rubbed* (1200', 5.11+), which features serious climbing and some loose rock.

MEXICO

Notable activity occurred in the Parque Nacional Barranca del Cobre. Chris Dunbar and Ian Barrett climbed *The Main Vein* (500', 5.9 A2+) on the **Dong Tower**, one of over a hundred towers located in rough country four hours south-west of Creel. This area of towers has previously seen very little activity from visiting climbers. While in the Parque Nacional Basaseachic, Eliza Kubarska and David Kaszlikowski made a rare free ascent of *Subiendo El Arcoiris* (300m, 5.13b) and established *Arte de Malaria* (300m, 5.12c) on a wall near Guitarritas (exact location unclear).

ANTONIO GÓMEZ BOHÓRQUEZ

Cordilleras Blanca and Huayhuash 2006-2007

Translated by Erik Monasterio

This review summarises first ascents, significant attempts and other pertinent information about climbing in the Huayhuash and Blanca mountain ranges of Peru. In preparing this report I have utilised information from the archives of AndesInfo, the book of first ascents from the Casa de Guias in Huaraz and from the Casa de Zarela, *Alpinist, Desnivel, The Alpine Journal (AJ), The American Alpine Journal (AAJ)*. I have also referred to the past and present versions of Alpenvereinskarte (*Cordillera Blanca* 0/3a, 0/3b, *Huayhuash* 0/3c), maps from the Instituto Geográfico Nacional Peruano (National Geographic Institute of Peru). I have spoken with local people from Ancash and Alcides Ames, Anthony Barton, Aritza Monasterio, Brad Johnson, Carlos Buhler, Dave Turner, Evelio Echevarría, Hermann Huber, Hugo Sifuentes, Irene Beardsley, Klaus Auer, Manfred Sturm, Matt Meinzer, Oriol Baró, Pavle Kozjek, Tamotsu Nakamura, Tsunemichi Ikeda and Werner Lindauer.

Cordillera Blanca 2006

Cerro Parón (5325m)

This peak is also known as La Esfinge. In mid July 2006 USA's Dave Turner and Matt Meinzer, set off on a new route on the E face and to the right of *Papas Rellenas,* previously climbed by Cruaud, Devernay, Peyronnard and Plaze in 1999. Due to altitude problems, Meinzer pulled out after the second pitch and Turner continued on his own. Halfway up the wall, he joined the *Papas Rellenas* route and followed this to the summit. He named the route *Inferno* (650m VI 5.10b A3–). It took six days to complete. Turner enjoyed sunny days although most nights there was wind and snow.

Chaupihuanca (c 4700m)

This peak in the Rúrec valley was mistakenly named Punta Numa by the first climbers, who were unaware of its native name. Its native name is Chaupihuanca, which in the Quechua language means 'the long stone centre';

it lies just to the right of Itsoc Huanca (see *AJ* 2006, pp321-322). Chaupihuanca forms part of the SE Pumahuacanca Suroeste (5179m); please refer to Pt c4800m in *AJ* 2003 pp287-288. The NW face has three routes to the summit. On 1 July 2006 climbers Simone Pedeferri, Andrea Pavan and Fabio Palma, members of Ragni di Lecco (The Lecho Spiders, Italy), camped at c4050m in the quebrada Rúrec. They set off to the right of the 1997 *Callado-Pedrocchi route* (750m, ED 6c/A4). By the 15th, and after climbing 15 pitches and reaching c4600m, the Italians decided to turn back before the summit. They named the route *Qui io Vado Ancora* (540m, 7c, obligatory 7a, two pitches of A1). The trio free-climbed all the pitches except the 10th, which was too dirty, and the 14th (too cold). Palma estimates that the 10th pitch, once cleaned, would be F6c and the 14th F7c. In *AAJ* 2007, p216 he recommends: 'one set of Friends, from the small yellow, and doubles in sizes 1, 2, 3. The Friends are mainly useful/necessary from pitch 10 onward. Some micronuts could be used on the slab pitches. Ratings of the 15 pitches are V, V+, 6b, 7a, 7a+, 7a, 6b+, 7b, 7a+, 6b A1, 6c, V, 6c+, 7a A1, 7a. The last pitch ends, at 4600m, with a fantastic crack that needs Friends #4 and #5 (minimum #3).'

Nevado Caraz I (6025m)

On 13 July 2006, Rok Stubelj and Arcon Jernej (Slovenia) climbed the south face, to the right of the left (west) ridge, directly beneath the summit. In nine hours they reached the summit cornices, which prevented them reaching the west ridge. They took six hours to descend in 15 rappels. They named the route *Dos gringos* (800m, TD 90° 55°-65°).

Nevado Cashan (5123m)

Between 23 and 25 June 2006 a commercial expedition organised by Martin Akhurst set up camp in quebrada Rúrec, and then high camps at c4700m and c5000m. From the higher camp, Peruvian guide Damián Aurelio, Ray Tennant and David Galloway climbed the SSW ridge that climbs to the col between Nevado Cashan and Nevado Shacsha (5703m). They reached the summit on the 25th after some steep climbing and via a possible new route (AD in *AAJ* 2007 p217).

Nevado Huandoy Sur (6160m)

Almost a month alter his ascent of Cerro Parón, Dave Turner climbed the SE spur, left of the south face, in 'fast and light style'. He left Huaraz one afternoon and travelled to the Llanganuco Lakes from where he went straight to base camp. After a brief afternoon nap he climbed the SE spur (to the left of the vertical south face). He climbed steep mixed ground with unconsolidated snow. After 700m he met the 'final crux', an overhanging cornice directly beneath the SW summit ridge. He overcame this by 'using every technique possible'. He climbed the ridge at dawn, six and a half hours after crossing the bergschrund and just in time to catch sight of the final stages to the summit, before being struck by a storm. He carried on as far as he could, estimating he was 100 vertical metres from the summit. In order to avoid an exposed bivouac, he then down climbed the route of ascent. He arrived back in Huaraz 28 hours after setting off. Turner's description is insufficient to distinguish whether he climbed via the Japanese route.

Correction. The route on the NE face, climbed by Canadians A Sole and G Spohr (June 1979), repeated by Spaniards M Ábrego, J Muru, and G Plaza (May 1980), and by Slovene P Kozjek (August 1995), was climbed in 1978 by the French expedition of F Tomas, D Julien, R Mizrahi, R Müsnch, G Vionnet-Fuasset, and H Lüdi. See *AAJ* 2007, p215 or guidebook *Cordillera Blanca, Escaladas,* p218.

Nevado Huantsán Norte (6113m)

From 11-15 July, Peruvian climbers Beto Pinto Toledo, Christian Andreas Stoll Dávila, Michel Quito Bernuy and Rolando Morales Flores climbed the north summit of Huantsán. They followed the Rajucolta gorge and camped on the Huantsán glacier (c5175m). The following day they climbed the west face toward the NW (left) col of Huantsán Norte. Over the first 240m of previously unclimbed ground they encountered thin unprotectable ice on the first pitch, then two pitches of steep snow and ice to 90° and a further pitch of vertical ice and mixed climbing to the end of the face. They then made a snow cave where they sat out bad weather for one day. The following day at 2am, they left camp to climb the NW ridge. Stoll Dávila later provided the following account, entitled 'First Peruvians on Huantsan Norte' and published in *www.alpinist.com*: 'We climbed ten runout pitches, using only deadmen as anchors. The most difficult part required crossing from the W face of the ridge to the E face, over cornices and mushrooms. At 6.34am, in perfect conditions, we became the first Peruvian rope team to reach the summit of Huantsan Norte.' They descended by abseiling 14 x 60m down the NW face: '... we reached the glacier and our bivy at 5.30pm. Our supplies exhausted, we kept going, and at approximately 11.30pm, after 21 hours on the move, we feasted on the remaining food in base camp tent and drank from a nearby water-hole, having finished our almost-epic ascent of *The Wayqui Way* (850m, TD+ WI4 M4 90°; in Quechua, *wayqui* means 'brothers').' Note that the Peruvian Eliseo Vargas reached the summit of Huantsán Norte with Leigh N Ortenburger during the ascent of Huantsán (6395m) in 1958.

Nevado Huantsán Sur (5915m)

In June 2006 British climbers Matt Helliker and Nick Bullock walked from Chavin up the Alhuina river to the Huantsan gorge. They then climbed in a NE direction to the south summit. They left base camp (c4400m) on 25th and reached the moraine under the NE face at 10am. After debating the proposed route for two hours they decided to climb the NE buttress, which started at 5000m. They solo climbed over the first 200m of loose rock (V–). They then roped up, and crossed under, over and between large numbers of groaning séracs. Then, as described by Bullock in the *AAJ* 2007: 'Massive umbrellas of wind-blown, icicle-encrusted overhangs loomed atop the runnels in the afternoon sun. Speed and luck were our friends. At 5.30pm, we made a bivouac on rock to the left of a gully, near a massive umbrella at 5500m. A sérac high on the face calved in the night, debris hit us, and we cowered.' The next day they left their bivouac at 7am and after committed climbing reached the summit at 3pm. They rappelled back down to the snowfields and bivouacked (c5600m) under an ice umbrella. They then down climbed the rock section and were back in camp at 3pm. They christened their route *Death or Glory*.

Nevado Huascarán Sur (6768m)

Giuseppe Ghedina's account, published in www.planetmountain.com and dated 28 July 2006, claims a new route: 'In June, as part of a course, Davide Alberti, Marco Da Pozzo, Mario Lacedelli, Alessandro Menardi, members of Gruppo degli Scoiattoli di Cortina, together with Fabio Pavanello, Samuele Majoni, Andrea De Gasperi, Giorgio Costantini, Giuseppe Ghedina and Alpine guides Olindo De Biasio and Marco Garbin climbed a new route on the south face of Huascarán.' Towards the end of the report Ghedina states that: 'after a brief discussion the local guide confirmed that it was a new route.' However, the route indicated over the photo that accompanies the text shows the route to be a variant of the normal route, along the western slopes, on the left hand side of the Huascarán Shield. The first part of the route is the same as the original approach route taken by Broda, Merler and Segger in 1969. The final stage of the climb is the same as that taken by other climbers in previous years. The only differences are attributable to changes in the conditions of the glacier.

Nevado Shacsha (Shaqsha 5703m)

A brief note in the first ascents book of the Casa de Guias de Huaraz, p622 reveals what may be a possible new direct route on the west face. It was climbed on 14 June 2006 by a climber who did not leave his name: 'We chose a direct line towards the summit [...] the key passage is ~ 80° ice climbing for about 10 metres. Snow conditions: up to 5200m frozen, between 5200-5400m deep sugar snow [...], summit face perfect snow. Very recommendable climb, grade about AD+.'

Taulliraju (5830m)

On the 28 May 2006 Slovenian climbers Grega Lacen, Tadej Golob and Matej Flis climbed the SSW buttress by a route they christened *GMHM route* (400m, TD+ WI4+ M4). This route was climbed by Prom, Gryska and Gleizes, members of the French GMHM, ending July 4 1988 above the SSW buttress of Taulliraju. The Slovenians bivouacked on the top of the buttress. The next day they followed the *Guides' route* (800m, TD+, Balmat-Fabre-Monaci-Thivierge, 1978) to the east face, where they climbed 25m right of the route attempted by Richey and Monasterio in 2002. So far it remains unclear whether the *Guides' route* is a variation of the 1976 route by the Japanese Mizobuchi, Nagashino and Yoda. This area of Taulliraju was also climbed by Jaeger (solo, 1978), Miller and Richardson (1983), Fowler and Arnow (1988), Tamayo and Fernandez (1989), and others. Lacen wrote in *Alpinist* issue 18: 'I started up the first two pitches wearing my crampons, but after taking two falls, I changed to climbing shoes. The granite was first class, only briefly disturbed by some huge, loose flakes. On the last pitch, powder again covered the rock, and it was nearly impossible to set up belays. The sun had already set behind Alpamayo as we stood on the summit (5830m) on May 29, having completed *El Centelleo* (700m, VI 6b M6+).' They rappelled down the east face. After the first rappel line, they found an ice cave: 'After we spent an uncomfortable night, the next rappel led to an established anchor. All the following rappels were set in a similar manner to the base of the mountain. Looking over the photos back in base camp, we found we had descended directly over the Monasterio-Richey attempt.'

Cordillera Huayhuash 2006

Nevado Carnicero (5980m)
After a few rest days (see below Nevado Quesillo) USA climbers Buhler and Johnson attempted a new route on the steep 660m east face. They followed their previous steps along the glacier of the Quesillo peak. They then followed to the right and after a long approach camped next to the ridge at the foot of Jurau (5674m). With light packs and no bivouac equipment they set out at midnight, hoping for a 24-hour return trip. They crossed the glacier to the foot of the east side of the east face. They free-climbed the first 70m of the central gully before deciding to rope up. They then climbed a 70m pitch (80° AI4) to the right, then another of similar length and grade, followed by two pitches of bulletproof ice (60°-70°). On the top section of the gully system they climbed to the right, on mixed ground up to 70°-80° (AI4/4+). Thus they reached the apparently easy snow slopes on the east face, but still only halfway up (9.30am). They found rockfall and snow softened by the effect of the sun, which improved by 3.30pm. But by this stage it was too late to reach the summit, and without bivouac equipment they decided to rappel down and return to Huaraz.

Nevado Quesillo (5600m)
This peak is listed as Jurau F (5600m) in *Cordillera Huayhuash,* Alpine Mapping Guild 2004. On 9 July 2006, Carlos Buhler and Brad Johnson

reached the village of Queropalca. From there they trekked for two days to establish a base camp on the shores of the Carnicero lake. After two rest days they walked beyond Suerococha, across the glacier and camped beneath the NE face of Nevado Quesillo. The next day, 14 July, they left late, at 7am. They climbed up the glacier to reach the bottom section of the rock face and traversed to the left. They then climbed a dihedral system and followed up a 30m chimney (V– UIAA). The second pitch (70m) consisted of very loose rock and finished just below the upper snow slopes. After three further rope lengths of snow and ice (70m, 50°-75°) they reached the summit ridge, and in a further exposed pitch (70m) they reached the summit. They descended with 5 x 70m rappels on the right side of the face, including a 'treacherous' rap into the wet chimney at night. They were back in camp at 9.30am with an overall feeling that they had taken too long to climb a relatively easy route (350m, D+ V- AI3 55°-75°).

P 5740m

In the first week of August 2006 Silvano Arrigoni, Lorenzo Festorazzi, Eugenio Galbani and Franco Melesi trekked past Carhuacocha (4138m) to the Gangrahanca valley to reach Siulacocha (4290m). They climbed to the summit of a peak without any registered past ascents situated in front of the NE face of Siulá Grande (6356m). They sent the following message, published 11.8.06 on www.ragnilecco.com: 'My friends a new route has been born, 800m after 32 pitches along a previously unclimbed pillar on Siulá Grande. Overall grade up to VII (with horrendous protection due to the extremely compact nature of the granite) and AI1 and total grade ED+. The climb took place on the 3/4/5/6/7 of August 2006 with one bivouac on the face at 5200m and a nighttime descent. Our highest point was 5550m.' Lindsey Griffin provided more information in the *AAJ* 2007, pp220-221, where the peak is referred to with the name given by the Italians 'Siula Antecima'. However, Festorazzi's photo with the ascent line, printed on page 221, clearly shows that they are referring to Pt 5740m (Alpenvereinskarte *Cordillera Huayhuash* 0/3c), Jurau B (5727m) in Alpine Mapping Guild 2004 and in other previous guides.

Rondoy (5883m)

On 26 July 2006 Aritza Monasterio and Mikel S Urabain climbed the west face to a point near the col of the ridge that joins the south summit of Rondoy (5883m on the Alpenvereinskarte or 5870m in *Cordillera Huayhuash* in Alpine Mapping Guild 2004) with that of Mituraju (5684m or 5750m). The final approach to the ridge was blocked by an enormous unstable cornice. After weighing up the risks, they decided to finish the ascent there and rappel down the line, which they named *Bagabiltza* (900m, VII/5 MD+).

Cordillera Blanca 2007

Cerro Huaytapallana (c 5000m)

At the end of August 2007 British climber Anthony Barton and Jim Sykes from the USA walked up the Rajururi valley, aka Huaytapallana valley, and camped at c4500m. They then climbed 300m up the NE face to the highest summit of the Huaytapallana peaks. They believe that this may be the first ascent of these peaks.

Chacraraju (6112m)

On 21 July 2007 Felipe González Donoso, Armando Moraga and Juan Henríquez reached the Llanganuco valley and camped at Cebollapampa. On the 23rd they camped on the Chacraraju glacier and checked out their route. They left camp at 2am the following day and started climbing after 1.5 hours. They overcame difficult and committed sections of mixed climbing with soft unconsolidated snow and few security points. At 8pm they hacked out a bivouac site and three hours later they melted ice and got some rest. They set off again at 2am and after 23 pitches they reached the summit ridge (c6000m). They then attempted to climb over the ridge cornices, but retreated after three falls. After 20 rappels, to the right of their route of ascent, and 50 hours on the route, they were back at their campsite. They published together with a photo on www.alpinist.com (1-11-2007) Moraga: 'We believe our ascent line, the *Chilean route* (ED+ 95 degrees 850m), climbs new terrain between the 1977 *Bouchard-Meunier route* and the 1983 *French Direct route.*' However, the line on the photo shows they climbed part of the *Bouchard-Meunier route*.

Hatun Ulloc (Ulloc Grande c4500m)

Between 3 and 7 July 2007 Marc Wolff and Hans-Martin Tröbs climbed the east face to the height of the first prow, to the reach the summit c4500m via a new route (200m 7b 6b+ oblig. Expo. 6SL) christened *Compañía Vertical.* They rapped down the line of ascent.

Ichic Ulloc (Ulloc Chico c 4450m)

Between 3 and 6 July 2007, German climbers Alexander Schmalz-Friedberger and Michael Zettelmeyer climbed the east face via a new route *Con ojeras debajo de ojos vidriosos* (180m 5.10+ C2 6SL). This route shares the final pitch with the Mexican route *Lawak.* They called the peak they climbed Ichic Ulloc (Ulloc Chico) with an altitude of 4450m. This rock summit is the lowest peak of a mountain on the Ishinka valley, to the right of another peak called Hatun Ulloc by Crill and Gallagher; see *AJ 2006* pp320-321. The new name of Ichic Ulloc is likely to create confusion.

Nevado Alpamayo (5947m)

In www.alpinist.com (1-11-2007) Moraga describes the following: 'To acclimatize, on 19 July Felipe Gonzalez Donoso, Felipe Gonzalez Diaz and I made a Chilean variation (MD 90 degrees 400m) to the *Escruela-Tain route* – aka *Sensations of History* (ED 95 degrees Escruela-Tain, 2002) – on Alpamayo's SW face.' It is worthwhile to bear in mind that Escruela and Tain repeated the route (although with markedly different ice conditions) previously climbed by the Canadian S Parent and Peruvian P Cacha (on 9 August 1988) and before the glacier avalanche of the right side on the south-west face. I mistakenly granted the first ascent to Escruela and Tain in my book *Cordillera Blanca, Escaladas* ..., pp138-139, because at the time I was unaware of the Parent and Cacha route.

Nevado Cajavilca III (5419m)

On 14 July 2007 Anthony Barton and John Pearson, helped by four porters, climbed the trail to the Cajavilca Mine and camped at c4700m on the moraine at the edge of the eastern glacier of Nevado Cajavilca III (5419m). The porters returned to Yanama. The British climbers then easily reached the east glacier of Cajavilca II and I (5675m and 5775m and camped at c4850m. On the 18th at 4.30am they climbed the snow slopes (40°–45°) of the south-east face of Cajavilca III to reach the gully on the right of the first rock band. They climbed the gully in two pitches (55°-60°) and reached the ice ridge. After a further three long snow pitches (50°-55°) they reached the second rock band. They climbed along another gully, with a pitch that varied between 55° to 70°, and a further pitch (55°-60°) took them to the west ridge and the summit by 11am. They believe this may be a new route (550m AD+). They rappelled four times and down climbed the route of ascent.

Nevado Chinchey Central (6222m)

A Peruvian expedition made up of Quique Roel Apolinario, Elías Flores, Michel Araya, Miguel Martínez and porters David Flores, Moisés del Río and Jonathan camped in the Rurichinchay valley. They had a rest day at camp (c4950m) on the moraine of the north-east glacier. On 23 May 2007 they moved onto the glacier beneath the summits of Puntancuerno and Chinchey and established camp I (c5200m), where (due to bad weather) they remained until the 26th when they set off at 2am. After two hours they reached the NE face, which they climbed (60°-65°) as two separate teams (Araya-Martínez and Apolinario-Flores). They reached the NNE ridge of the main Chinchey peak and after two rope lengths made the summit by 1.30pm. They then rappelled back to the glacier by 8pm and descended to the camp on the edge of the moraine by midnight.

Right
184. Huascarán Sur (6768m), north-east face. *Corominas-Baró-Muñoz route.*
       (*Antonio Gómez Bohórquez 1988*)

Nevado Contrahierbas (6036m)

Between 12 and 16 August, 2007 Anthony Barton visited the eastern side of the Cordillera Blanca. He was accompanied by Xabier Arbulo from Spain. They set off during the night to climb an unclimbed crack. One and a half hours after sunrise, rockfall began in earnest and two-thirds of the way to the summit (c5650m) Arbulo was hit by rockfall as he was setting up a belay. He lost his pack and therefore they had to give up their summit attempt and abseil down.

Nevado Huascarán Sur (6768m)

After climbing Siulá Chico Jordi Corominas, Oriol Baró and Enrique Muñoz walked up the Ancosh valley and camped on the small glacier at the foot of the north-east face of Huascarán. In two days, they climbed the face via a new route *Turbera* (1200m MD+ M5/A1). This route crosses small rock steps. On the third day, they reached the summit. They bivouacked on a small ledge on the wall, then in a tent (near the north-east ridge) and finally near camp I, after descending the normal route of La Garganta.

Nevado Copa Sur (6188m)

After climbing Huascarán, Jordi Corominas, Oriol Baró and Enrique Muñoz walked up the Paccharuri valley (Ruripaccha valley in the new *Alpenvereinskarte*) to camp by a small lake before the main Paccharuri lake. In a single alpine push they climbed the south face to c5060m, where they set up their tent for the night. They didn't continue to the summit, and they christened their route *Mostro africano* (1000m ED V, 6 Scottish).

185. Puscanturpa East (5410m), seen from the Caliente valley. *Kozjek-Kresal route.* (*Antonio Gómez Bohórquez 1999*)

Taulliraju (5830m)

David Turner and Micah Retz, from the head of the Santa Cruz valley crossed the Rinrihirca-Taulliraju pass and camped (c5000m) on the Taulliraju-Pucahirca glacier, 10 minutes from the north face of Taulliraju. The next day they climbed well to the right of the *Bajan-Buch* 1979 route. The route (650m, 5.10 WI5 M6) crossed a 60m section of excellent vertical granite and a 400m perfect water-ice runnel. The runnel started halfway up the face on the right-hand side. Turner and Retz set off at 7am. They initially climbed over mixed ground before reaching the granite rock band (5.10) and then with virtually no security climbed the ice runnel (70°-85°). 'Overhanging bulges of water ice' contributed to the risk and challenge of the climb. Once they reached the summit ridge they decided against climbing this to the summit. Turner wrote in www.alpinist.com: 'At the top neither of us was willing to surf out onto the last few metres of the unstable cornice.' They abseiled down the ascent route. The climb took eight hours and the descent four hours.

Cordillera Huayhuash 2007

Puscanturpa East (5410m)

Pavle Kozjek and Grega Kresal climbed a new route on the east face of this peak. The ascent took 14 hours. The peak lies 1km ENE of the main Puscanturpa Peak (5652m). From Cajatambo they walked for two days up the valley of the Pumarinri river, to reach the head of the valley. They established base camp at (c4400m) beyond the 'Caserío de Pushca'. They set off at 4am. Within one hour they reached the start of their route. The initial 200m was over easy ice and led to the rock step on the east ridge. They then climbed two 60m pitches of slab (V, VI UIAA) to reach an obvious ledge, followed by a series of crack and dihedral systems. On the fifth pitch (VII) there were few security points and the sixth pitch (VII+) consisted of an exposed offwidth of loose rock. They then traversed to the right along a dihedral system and after a further two pitches (VI, V), on the north side reached the summit ridge. They reached the summit at 2pm on 6 July 2007. They rapped down the ascent route and named the climb *Stonehenge* (600m, 10 pitches, VII+/VI UIAA 50°-70°). The Slovenian route seems to be route 328 on the drawings 157, 159 and 160 from the magnificent Jan Kielkowski guide *Cordillera Huayhuash* vol 6, pp32-33. This description may be a mistake, as route 328 on the Puscanturpa refers to the climb of Julius Hensler and Pedro Baltazar, on Central Puscanturpa (5442m) on 20 June 1963. This guide also records that Puscanturpa East was climbed by an undescribed and unnamed British team on 12 Aug 1985. The approach to the British route appears to be identical to that followed by the Slovenian team.

Siulá Chico (6265m)

During May 2007, Catalan climbers Jordi Corominas and Oriol Baró set up a base camp on the foot of Cutatambo (c4260m) at the start of the Sarapococha valley. On the 21st they crossed the complex and crevassed west glacier and headed toward the SW face of Siula (6356m). They left equipment at (c4900m) and a tent at (c5300m) on a plateau, under the west face of Siulá Chico. They climbed this face via a new alpine route, with a portaledge and haul bag (900m, ED+ VI/A1 5+R. M/A2 Scottish grade). After six nights on the wall, they reached the summit on 27 or 28 May. They took 16 rappels to get down the route of ascent. This was probably only the second ascent of this summit, after the German ascent by Reinhold Obster, Peter Scholz and Manfred Sturm on 21 June 1966. Anze and Tine Marence attempted to reach the summit on 1 August 2004, but turned back as they found the north ridge too dangerous and difficult. The Slovenian team considered their effort a new route, which they called *A Scream of Silence*.

Interestingly, in June 1964 Lindauer, Rudl Fürst (Germany) and José Forounge (Argentina) climbed more than 900m of the NE face to within 100m of the summit, before bad weather turned them back. As they did not reach the summit, they only considered their efforts an attempt and did not claim a new route.

Yanamarey Sur (5220m)

The Chilean-North American Evelio Echevarría and the Peruvian Alberto Murguía on 8 July 2007 climbed the west ridge, which they approached from the Queracocha valley. This may be a new route and the second ascent of the summit. It was first climbed from the south by Hartmann and Reiss in 1965. The summit height is given as 5197m on page 20 of the Peru ING.

Trapecio (5653m)

On 2 August 2006 José Manuel Fernández and Miguel Ángel Pita climbed the SE face of Trapecio by following the couloir systems to the right of the July 2005 route climbed by the Slovenian team of Kozjek, Lampreht, Ivanek and the Basque climber Aritza Monasterio (refer to *AJ* 2006, pp324-325). The Spanish pair climbed nine initial pitches, with 60m ropes, even though between the fifth and sixth pitch there was a distance of 150m, and between the eighth and ninth a distance of 70m. They overcame a frozen waterfall (70°, 80°-85°) on the ninth pitch and then decided to descend after naming the route *Los viejos roqueros nunca mueren* ('old rockclimbers never die', c750m V/4+); please refer to *Desnivel*, No 51, 2007, p104. They rappelled three times: twice from rock pitons and one from a single camming device. The snow stake for the fourth rappel unfortunately pulled out of the sugary snow and Fernandez died in the fall. Pita bivouacked for 12 hours by sitting on a small ice ledge, before climbing without ropes to the summit and descending via the NW face.

MARK WATSON

New Zealand 2007-2008

Where route grades in this report use Roman numerals, these represent a commitment grade [I-VI] that is currently being adopted in New Zealand. The current Darrans guidebook lists grading criteria.

Darran Mountains
The wealth of unclimbed rock and the exposure provided by the new (2006) guidebook to the Darrans region continues to encourage new heights of activity in this primordial climbing area. Most of the activity in the Darrans region is centred on the sport climbing crags of the Cleddau valley: Chasm, Babylon and Little Babylon. These crags draw people to the Darrans like never before, and the spin-off is increased activity 'up high' on the longer multi-pitch slab and wall routes that the Darrans have traditionally been famous for.

The trio of Richard Thomson, Richard Turner and Dave Vass continue to be responsible for the most noteworthy remote climbs of the season. On a single trip in late February the team flew into Turners Bivvy, walked to the Turners Eyrie bivouac and made an excursion out to the isolated and barely known peak Ngai Tahu, where they climbed a new 10-pitch route (500m) on the previously unclimbed (and barely seen) north face. Runners and belays were reportedly scarce. *Ngai On All Night* was graded (IV, 21) (the Roman numeral representing the commitment grade). With time on their hands the trio also completed their long-term project on the south face of Makere. Previous attempts to climb the striking arête line directly have all ended at a difficult and committing stretch of climbing. This time the arête was gained via a traverse from the left, bypassing the direct start. *The Hornley Arête* is graded III, 21 (350m) – and a direct start awaits someone bold enough.

Matt Quirke and Mark Watson based themselves at Phil's Biv (Moraine Creek) for a week in January, climbing a new 13-pitch route (650m) ground-up on the north face of Marian over two days. *Electric Earth* is only the third line on this massive face and turned out to be easier climbing than the pair expected. With the second carrying a drill, the pair placed a bolt at each belay to facilitate easy descent and to open up access to the swathes of unclimbed clean rock on the face. Graded III, 19, the route features interesting, technical crux pitches interspersed with easier, scrambling sections. The whole line can be abseiled on bolts from the summit ridge.

The pair made a repeat ascent of the rarely climbed *Sarkasmos* (18) on the north-west face of Sabre Peak, finding the climbing run-out on sometimes dubious rock. Murray Ball and Nick Cradock also visited the valley in January, climbing a new beginner's slab route on the Great White slabs. *Nothing Ventured Nothing Gained* has four pitches at 14, 16, 16, 16. They also climbed a new two-pitch route nearby.

Closer to Homer Hut, Derek Thatcher and Jamie Vinton-Boot returned to an incomplete project from the previous year on the Mates Little Brother. The four-pitch line (140m), named *Revelations*, has pitches of 27, 26, 25 and 20.

On the left side of the Mates Little Brother, Nick Cradock, with Murray Ball and Glen Einham established *Where's My Epirb?* (18, 21, 21, 21) with a mixture of bolts and natural pro.

Late in the season Martin Wilson and Hugh Barnard flew into a lake-side camp on the granite ridge between the southern Llawrenny Peak and Terror Peak (1786m), climbing a six-pitch route on Terror Peak, with a crux of 21. The pair also climbed two two-pitch routes on the perfect granite slabs rising from the lake at their camping spot.

Bruce Dowrick and Martin Wilson have together opened up a new wall with significant potential for multi-pitch routes, just across the fiord from the Milford Airport – watch this space for some significant routes in the future. Dubbed the Airport Wall the pair have fixed over 500m of rope on the route.

Winter was marked with tragedy, when Te Anau climber Hamish MacDonald was killed after an abseil anchor failure while he and climbing partner Stephen Skelton were descending from an attempt on *Cul de Sac* on Mt Crosscut. Earlier in the season the pair had climbed a new winter route in Macpherson Cirque. *Midnight Cowboy* takes a spur out of the cirque, beside Talbots Ladder.

Queenstown

Winter in the Queenstown/Wakatipu region saw a few new routes climbed and a greater focus on the technical. The mixed climbing boom has taken a firmer grip in this area than anywhere else in the country, with many single-pitch and short multi-pitch mixed routes being established.

On the south-west buttress of Double Cone (Remarkables), Aaron Ford and Rupert Gardiner climbed the eight-pitch *Ikon* (M6, 350m). The route was climbed onsight, with natural pro. Reportedly the gear is good and the rock very solid, giving confidence for the dry tool moves. The pair also established *The Gambler* (M7) on the Boarder Crag at Lake Alta. In the Alta Cirque is a crag called Terminator; here Sally and Aaron Ford and Rupert Gardiner climbed a new line called *Cold November Rain* (M3, WI3, 80m). Off the beaten track Dave Bolger and Glen Aspin climbed a new line on Major Peak in the Richardson Mountains. South Taranaki (WI3, 60m) was an epic to get to in deep snow. The ice in this area can be seen from the road, and more potential exists.

At Wye Creek Aaron Ford climbed a new mixed line left of last season's *Rebirth of Cool* at around M7. Also at Wye, Kester Brown and Jono Clarke bolted a two-pitch route. They climbed the first pitch at around M7 and the second is an open project still (M9ish). There is currently a lot of activity taking place on the schist crags of the South Branch of Wye Creek with multi-pitch rock routes of up to 200 metres being established.

Wanaka

Controversy erupted in late summer as word spread that Wanaka mountain guide Marty Beare had placed approximately 20 bolts on the north-west ridge of Mt Aspiring – a classic, traditional alpine route that was first climbed nearly 100 years ago. The bolts were placed to facilitate commercial guiding on the route.

To date there has been very little in the way of retrobolting of traditional routes in New Zealand and the action was met with condemnation from most in the climbing community, although reportedly some novices said that they liked the presence of the bolts. It was not long before the bolts were hammered in (they were overdrilled in the first place as attempted removal was expected by Beare when he placed them). When interviewed by *The Climber* magazine, Beare claimed that, 'I never assumed they would last.' It's a shame that an otherwise unaltered and natural climbing resource had to be permanently scarred for the sake of an experiment where the outcome was already anticipated.

Barron Saddle – Mt Brewster

In the five years since the new edition of the Barron Saddle-Mt Brewster guide was published, more than 70 new alpine climbs have been done in the region. This is a significant number, and is indicative of the short history of mountaineering many of the peaks in this area have. The past year has been a little quieter than others, but there are a few new routes worthy of mention.

In the South Huxley valley, Tony Clarke and Hadley Slade-Jones climbed a new route on the south-west face of Peak 2090m. Mostly rock, the line goes at 16-17 overall.

In the west branch of the South Temple Valley Paul Hersey and Mat Woods completed the first ascent of *The Fend* (grade 3) on the south face of Peak 2124m. This neglected peak had been awaiting an ascent for a long time. The route follows a narrow snow-filled chute. Three months later Paul was back with Danny Baille to complete a route further right on the south face of Pakeke Peak (2237m); *Chess Geeks* (grade 3+) is a 400-500m rock route. The line follows good quality rock for eight pitches (and some simul-climbing) with a rock crux of 14. On the west face of the Dasler Pinnacles Andrew Rennie climbed a mixed winter route. It was around WI4 at the start, with a really tough last two pitches (grade 5 overall).

186. Guy McKinnon crossing a frozen lake on the approach to the
Ramsay Face of Mt Whitcombe (*centre*). July 2007. (*Guy McKinnon*)

Aoraki Mt Cook and Westland

As with the trend of the past few years, both the winter and summer seasons
at Cook have been quiet compared with the activity in the Barron Saddle-
Mt Brewster Region, The Darrans, or the Westland Névés. Still, there are
three new routes to report from the east side of the Main Divide. A 90-
metre waterfall route was climbed in Gorilla Stream (Liebig Range) by
Graham Zimmermann and Mark Kendrick. They named it the *Monk's Spunk*
(WI5). The east face of Mt Footstool was climbed by Greg Abrahams, Euan
Boyd, Steve Farrand and Florian L'Hostis. The line, named *Requiem for a
Dream*, climbs snow and ice gullies left of the main couloir. From a camp in
the Bonney glacier, Steve Dowall and Tom Wilson climbed a new rock
route on the west face of Mt Hamilton (3025m). The climb dog-legs up a
face of mostly good rock with a crux around grade 15.

West of the Divide, where there is greater scope for accessible, technical
and shorter routes, more climbing was taking place. Winter is the season
for activity and Kester Brown and Jono Clarke kicked the season off with a
free ascent of Allan Uren's mixed test piece *The Vision*. They did, however,
tackle the crux via a slight variation. Reports indicate that the climbing
was still run-out and testing at any rate. On a pre-Changabang training
trip, Craig Jefferies and Kester Brown climbed a short route on the south-
west side of The Buttress (Pt 2776m), on the Abel Janzoon glacier. The
route, *Son of a Witch*, was about five pitches long and graded WI3/4.

September saw the strong team of Matt Quirke and Mike Madden climb the most notable routes of winter with two new lines climbed on the south face of Conway Peak. *Visually Impaired* climbs a thin ice ribbon immediately right of *Moonshine Buttress*. The crux is a short, narrow chimney followed by a few metres of overhanging ice – with sparse protection. A pitch further up had little-to-no protection also, making the route a bold undertaking. The descent became a serious affair and the pair had to work hard to find anchors. The route has been graded IV, AI5, 7 pitches. The second line *Poor Visibility* (graded III, AI3, 6 pitches) offered better protection and an interesting mixed section at half-height. The route was rapped in good v-threads. In October Mike Peat and Tom Wilson climbed *Cleavage*, near earlier line *Mixed Blood*, on the south face of Matenga. The line was 200m long and has crux pitches of WI3.

Central Southern Alps

The Central Southern Alps (from Mt Cook north to Arthur's Pass) have seen some significant climbs over the past year and it's great to see a new generation of climbers returning to peaks that have been unfashionable in recent years. Guy McKinnon pulled off the climb of the year with his first winter ascent (solo) last July of the Ramsay Face of Mt Whitcombe – a face that could quite fairly be claimed as one of the last great problems in Canterbury mountaineering. Guy's was the first winter ascent of this face, and it is thought to have been climbed only twice before (in summer). Guy attempted it twice in 2006, but never got the right combination of psyche and conditions until winter 2007, when everything fell into place for an ascent of the 1300-metre route. Guy hasn't provided an overall grade for the route, named *Leviathan*, but described cruxes of WI4 in the middle of the face, during his six-hour ascent.

Teaming up with young Christchurch climber Jamie Vinton-Boot in the summer, Guy climbed a high quality rock route on the north face of Newton's West Peak (Garden of Allah) in April 2008. The face rises 400 metres above the Garden of Allah ice field, and comprises scrambling, and six roped pitches up to grade 21. Also during the 2007 summer, Rob Frost and Simon Mills made the first ascent of Mt Isabel's north-west ridge from Harper Rock bivvy. The peak was a significant, remote trans-alpine objective and featured a mix of rock climbing up to grade 14.

NICK LEWIS

Antarctica 2007-2008

As usual, the vast majority of mountaineers visiting Antarctica went to the **Vinson Massif** (now commonly referred to as Mount Vinson) and despite very mixed weather, a total of 157 climbed the mountain during the 2007-08 season. This year, Antarctic Logistics & Expeditions (ALE), the logistics operator who run the flights in and out of Vinson Base Camp and provide support on the mountain, developed a different route which climbs the shoulder immediately to the south of the old route which climbed the 'headwall' to the Goodge Col between Vinson and Mount Shinn. The headwall itself had become increasingly more sérac-ridden and subject to avalanche over the last few years and many people were becoming concerned at the increased risk. Roger Mear, Dave Hahn and others had suggested this route in the 1990s as a quick and safe way of accessing the high plateau but the route saw only infrequent ascents. ALE fixed 1200m of rope up the shoulder in November, and by December 2007 it had become the standard route for the majority of parties. In addition, several rescue caches and a radio repeater were also placed on the mountain by ALE for the benefit of all. These provided crucial support to those climbers caught in vicious storms this season.

Notable ascents of the season include Norwegians Ine-Lill Gabrielsen and Rita Glenne who climbed Vinson and then skied to the South Pole from Vinson Base Camp, unsupported, via a new route. Two groups – a Norwegian/Danish female team led by Randi Skaug and an elite Italian military Alpini team led by Ettore Taufer – skied the 200km from the ALE Patriot Hills camp in the Southern Ellsworths to Vinson before making successful ascents. Christian Stangl made a solo ascent of the mountain in December 2007, ascending and descending the new shoulder route. Contrary to popular reporting in the media, Stangl's time was slower and his route shorter than the previous solo ascents by Conrad Anker and Dave Hahn who both made very rapid round trips of the old headwall route (several other prominent guides may also have made fast times that went unrecorded). Mount Shinn, which lies immediately to the north of Vinson, receives a minute fraction of the attention given to its loftier neighbour and in the 2007-08 only two teams managed to climb Shinn during the entire season.

The arch-chronicler of Antarctic mountaineering, Damien Gildea, had another very successful season in the **Ellsworths**. Over the last seven years, Gildea, under the auspices of the Omega Foundation, has mounted annual

187. Andy Tyson (USA) at the top of the new fixed ropes on Mt Vinson.
      Knutzen Peak behind. (*A Tyson collection*)

expeditions to measure the exact heights of the Ellsworth Mountains using
GPS; in the process he has made a determined series of ascents and new
routes. For this season's foray, Gildea was joined by Antarctic veterans

Camillo Rada and Maria Paz 'Pachi' Ibarra of Chile and the talented Slovakian/Australian Jarmila Tyrril on her first visit to the continent. Kicking things off, Ibarra and Tyrril made a new 1200m route at the northern end of Vinson's west face on 20 December 2007. They continued to the summit with Rada (who had come up the normal route), reaching it on the 21st. The *Chilena-Slovak route* is the first new route climbed on Vinson by an all-female team. Following on from this, the two teams made the impressive third ascent of Mount Epperly from 27-29 December 2007 via a new route on the south face. Epperly is noteworthy for receiving both its first and second ascent by Erhard Loretan. Conrad Anker and Jim Donini then attempted the west ridge in 1997, and in 2005 Nick Lewis and Tom Nonis tried a line further to the right of the eventual Omega route before bad weather forced an eventful retreat (Lewis broke his leg and shoulder on the way down). The Omega teams encountered fresh snow on the route and this was particularly deep in the couloir which splits the upper part of the south ridge. The final three-metre-high summit pinnacle proved an insurmountable obstacle but at their highest point they were able to place the GPS, which Ibarra and Tyrril retrieved during their ascent 24 hours later. This yielded a new height of 4508m for Epperly, which is significantly higher than the old height of 4359m. This makes it the sixth highest mountain on the continent.

Gildea, Ibarra and Rada then attempted Mount Tyree in very lightweight style on 6 January (time constraints forced Tyrril to depart in early January). They reached a high camp on Mount Gardner's normal route (which they had climbed in 2005) but bad weather forced a retreat. On their descent, they managed to make the first ascent, of the recently-designated Mount Ryan, a minor peak on the northern side of Gardner's summit plateau. Another attempt a few days later ended similarly; however, they were able to make another first ascent of a rocky peak to the west of Mount Ryan. Gildea and the Omega Foundation deserve special mention for this series of expeditions and routes. In an era when too many Antarctic expeditions make false claims about scientific aims in order to obtain funding, the Omega Foundation's climbers have not only made an extraordinary number of first ascents but have also, from their GPS work, generated an excellent map of the Vinson region which will be of benefit to climbers for many years to come.

Elsewhere, Peter Clutterbuck and Simon Garrod made a very rare visit to the Mount Sporli area of the Southern Heritage Range of the Ellsworths in November and December 2007. Travelling almost 100km in two weeks, they crossed a series of cols to link the Rennell, Driscoll, Schneider, Schanz and Splettstoesser glaciers, making what are thought to be first ascents of three unnamed peaks along the way and being rebuffed by Sporli due to bad conditions. Despite its relative proximity to Patriot Hills, this was a useful exploratory trip which indicated the potential that the Southern Ellsworths hold for ski-mountaineering expeditions.

The conditions in the Ellsworths this season were varied. After a great start in November with warmer than usual temperatures and calm weather, a series of storms appeared in early December and persisted until the close of the season in late January. December produced some rather fine snowstorms, and up to 70cm of fresh powder was measured in parts of the Ellsworths in the first half of the month – remarkable given the fact that Antarctica is technically a desert. Parties on Vinson and elsewhere reported fine skiing during this period. Possibly as a result, an increased number of snow and ice avalanches were witnessed this season. Anecdotally this has been attributed to higher snowfalls and also possibly because many of the slopes in the region are thought to be getting steeper in profile owing to glacial recession. Warmer mean temperatures were recorded at both Vinson base camp and Patriot Hills this season and many continue to ask whether all these signs are just an erratic blip or further evidence of climate change.

Further north on the **Antarctic Peninsula**, the Basque team of Eneko and Iker Pou made the first ascent of *Azken Paradisua* on the highest of the three summits of the False Cape Renard Towers or The Three Pigs, a climb which marked the end of the brothers' Seven Walls – Seven Continents quest. They named the unclimbed summit Zerua Peak. The expedition sailed down the Peninsula on the yacht *Northanger* before launching their first attempt on 21 December; however, bad weather forced a retreat. A second attempt on Christmas Eve saw them climb easier ice up to a rock wall which yielded ten pitches up to E4 6b. They climbed the route in a continuous push, returning to their base camp 24 hours later. The notion of such hard free climbing in these conditions does make one shudder.

Finally to the sub-Antarctic. In October 2007, the French group of Philippe Batoux, Manu Cauchy and Lionel Daudet arrived on the island of **South Georgia** having sailed on the *Ada 2* from Ushuaia in Argentina. Their aim was to traverse the island making ascents en route. The expedition warmed up by making the sixth ascent of the island's highest peak, Mount Paget (2934m), via a direct variant on the 1995 route on the north-east face, before moving on to make the first ascent of Sheridan Peak (c 900m), a minor outlying peak. Next, the team made a quick third ascent of Surprise Peak (c 955m) by a new mixed route which was described as 'sustained'. In early December, the trio made the first ascent of Mount Worsley, but bad weather prevented subsequent ascents of Trident and Sugartop. Their 200km traverse of the island, only the third from north-west to south-east, took only three weeks from 26 November to 15 December. The expedition returned to Ushuaia on *Ada 2* in mid-January after a two-week sail home.

In an era when satellite phones and charter aircraft make rescue a possibility from even the most distant parts of Antarctica or the Himalaya, mountaineering on South Georgia – which is only accessible from the ocean – still requires the commitment it did a hundred years ago. It is reassuring to know that one of the great prizes still remains to be won on this extraordinary island.

Mount Everest Foundation
Expedition Reports

SUMMARISED BY BILL RUTHVEN

The Mount Everest Foundation was set up as a registered charity following the ascent of Everest in 1953 and was initially financed from the surplus funds and subsequent royalties of that expedition. It is a continuing initiative between the Alpine Club and the Royal Geographical Society (with the Institute of British Geographers).

Its purpose is to encourage 'exploration of the mountain regions of the earth'. This is exploration in its widest sense, not just climbing expeditions but also the application of other exploratory disciplines, such as geology, botany and zoology. It has now distributed some £900,000 to about 1,500 British and New Zealand expeditions, mostly to ambitious young climbers.

In return for supporting an expedition, all that the MEF asks is a comprehensive report. Once received, copies are lodged in the Alpine Club Library, the Royal Geographical Society, the British Mountaineering Council and the Alan Rouse Memorial Collection in Sheffield Central Library.

The following notes summarise reports from the expeditions supported during 2007, and are divided into geographical areas. Support was also given to the AC 'Summits of Learning' Seminar held at the Swiss Embassy in December as part of the club's anniversary celebrations (*see report pages 193-219*).

AMERICA – NORTH AND CENTRAL

British-Irish Ruth Gorge 2007 Oliver Metherell with James Mehigan. March-April 2007
This pair originally had designs on the east face of Mt Wake (2755m) and possibly the London/Werewolf Towers (c2250m). However, on arrival in the area, they found that their approach to Wake was barred by an open bergschrund, so were forced to seek an alternative objective on the east side of the gorge. They selected a stunning line up the couloir between the Werewolf (c2130m) and Hut Tower (c1970m), amazed that it had not been climbed already. Heavy snow falls every day set the scene for some of the most unpleasant conditions that either climber had experienced, with much of the route being up a precarious unconsolidated curtain of snow. Making the most of a brief weather window, after 24 hours on the go they were very relieved to arrive back at base camp safely having made a successful ascent of *Hut Tower Couloir* (Scottish grade VII, ED, A1). For more details see: www.super7.co.uk   MEF 07/03

Scottish Dan Beard Vivian Scott with Gareth Hughes. April 2007
Mt Dan Beard (3125m) is one of the less popular mountains to the north of
Ruth Gorge, and this pair hoped to make the first ascent of its east face.
They succeeded in reaching the summit by a route on the far right which
avoiding climbing beneath the summit séracs. Descent was made
northwards to the ridge between Dan Beard and Pt 8245 (2626m) making
a return to camp after 24 hours on the go. They have called their route
Sideburn Rib and graded it Scottish IV. They also attempted a couloir on
the mountain's SE ridge; although initially making good progress they were
halted by insufficient ice and forced to make an abseil descent. Later they
reached the summit of Mt Dickey (2909m) by its west flank. MEF 07/06

British Lowell Glacier Simon Richardson with David Hesleden. April-
May 2007
As in other areas, most expeditions to the St Elias Range of Canada's Yukon
have focused on the higher peaks, with the Lowell glacier receiving little
attention, so this team decided there would be plenty of scope for exploration
and new routes on the surrounding mountains. However, on arrival they
discovered that extremely heavy snowfall in the winter and spring had left
the whole area in a very dangerous condition, and initially wondered if
they would be able to even reach their chosen peaks. They did a
reconnaissance of Pinnacle Peak (3714m) but did not attempt it, and their
hopes of climbing the south face of Lowell Peak (3630m) were thwarted
when the entire slope slid away before their eyes. The only 'safe' line
therefore seemed to be the west ridge of Lowell, which they successfully
climbed, thus making the second overall ascent of the mountain.

MEF 07/32

AMERICA – SOUTH AND ANTARCTICA

British Graham Land 2007 Paul Josse with Steve Brown, Mark Davidson,
Mike Winters and John Venier plus Terje Lokken from Norway. January-
February 2007
This was a combined sailing and mountaineering expedition, which used
Pelagic (under Alec Hazell) to sail from Punta Williams in Chile to Graham
Land in the Antarctic Peninsula, where they aimed to explore and make
first ascents on the range of mountains inland from Darbel Bay. However,
the combination of global warming and poor weather conditions throughout
the expedition made the Erskine glacier – their intended approach –
crevassed and unstable, so the team concentrated on an unnamed glacier
between the Erskine and Cardell glaciers. From this, despite very bad
visibility, they made the first ascent of an unnamed snow peak of 1205m
via its west ridge. They graded the route as PD and have suggested *Mackenzie
Peak* as its name. They also climbed Harris Peak (1002m) on the Reclus

Peninsula via its NE ridge, probably its first ascent for many years. For more details see: www.britishgrahamlandexpedition2007.co.uk

MEF 07/04

Medical Sentinel 2007 Surg Cdr Adrian Mellor with Flt Lt Jemma Austin SSgt Jason Beckett, Flt Lt Anil Cherian, Maj Tim Hooper, Capt Stevan Jackson, Cdr Stuart Jackson, LMT Baz Lawrence, LNN Cheryl Lindup, POPTI Dave Murphy, Capt Chrissy Shorrocks, Wg Cdr Steve Swindells, LNN Jason Taylor, Capt Harry Vincent, LNN Robert Wakeford and Maj Hatty Wells. January 2007

This mixed tri-service party with widely varying mountaineering experience undertook an expedition to Argentina to carry out a programme of research into the medical effects of altitude in collaboration with University College London. (*See also Project Ref 05/15 and Expedition Ref 07/01.*) No new routes were envisaged or attempted, but to acclimatise, 15 of the team initially climbed Cerro Valecitos (5500m) before attempting the more serious Aconcagua (6959m) via the Horcones Valley route. This summit was reached by six team members – a number largely in line with expectation. The expedition was successful in all its aims, and produced data on blood pressure and oxygen saturation that should be of great value to future high altitude climbers.

MEF 07/09

British Darwin Range 2007 Simon Yates with Andy Parkin. February-March 2007

Using the yacht *Iorana* (skipper Marcel de Letter from Belgium) to access the Cordillera Darwin Range of Chilean Tierra del Fuego, this pair of climbers originally planned to explore and attempt the first ascent of the 600m south face of Monte Frances (2200m). The peak had actually been subject to at least three previous ascents over a 40-year period – the most recent being on a trip guided by Yates, who planned to use his previous route for the descent. However, adverse winds and weather made the approach difficult – first by sea and then on land, where steep broken glaciers added to their problems, and Monte Frances was almost devoid of snow and ice. They therefore turned their attention to other peaks, and were successful in making the first ascent of two non-technical (but nevertheless serious and committing) peaks at the head of Seña Pia, which they named after the yacht – Monte Iorana I (2390m) and Monte Iorana II (2075m). (NB: 'Iorana' means 'good day' in Easter Island Polynesian.)

MEF 07/10

Rio Turbo Andy Cave with James Bracken and Leo Houlding. February 2007

In 2005 (MEF Ref: 05/05), Houlding, together with Kevin Thaw and climbers from Argentina and USA planned to climb the 1000m Mariposa Wall from the Rio Turbo Valley of Argentina's Lago Puelo National Park (close to the Chilean border). Unfortunately heavy rains and swollen rivers delayed their approach so much that they had little time left to climb, so this was the inevitable return visit. However, once again they were afflicted by bad weather and delays resulting in a shortage of time plus multiple stings from a meat-eating yellow-jacket bee. As a result, they only managed to reach the lake below the route on Mariposa as their high point, and the available dinghy was not considered sufficiently robust to transfer climbers and all their equipment across such a serious obstacle. Although other objectives were reconnoitred, bad weather and a shortage of time once again meant that no climbing was achieved.   MEF 07/11A

FRCC Cordillera Carabaya 2007 Stephen Reid with Mike Cocker and Jonathan Preston. June-July 2007
The main aim of this team was to explore the little visited Cordillera Carabaya of Peru (which lies SE of the Cordillera Vilcanota, not far from the Bolivian border) and make the first ascent of the south ridge/face of Chichiccapac (5564m), the second highest peak in the area. The journey to their base camp at the western end of Laguna Chambine was something of an epic, but once there, they set to work to acclimatise, first by climbing an apparently virgin rock tower (5200m) which they named Fiesta Peak. But a reconnaissance of the South face of Chichiccapac revealed that much of it was threatened by cornices and séracs, making it too dangerous to attempt. However, they were able to make the first ascent of its north ridge (D), and also the first ascents of Mamaccapac (c5450m, PD) and the south ridge of Cornice (5660m) (D). (*See article pp55-69*)   MEF 07/14

Eastern Huayhuash 2007 Carl Reilly with Tom Bide, Lewis Fogarty, Martin Lane and Graeme Schofield. July-September 2007
The original objectives of this team – all current or former members of the University of Birmingham Mountaineering Club – were to explore the western side of the southern spur of the Cordillera Huayhuash and climb the west face of Jirishanco Chico (5467m). But on arrival in the area, the intended route was seen to be threatened by unstable snow formations, and an attempt was deemed unjustifiable. However, they did climb three new routes in the area – the east ridge of Quesillo (5600m) at TD–, and both the North ridge and NE face of Huaraca (5537m), both D. Moving to the Cordillera Blanca, they climbed a new route on the SE ridge of Point 5325m on Nevado Ulta (AD) and later abandoned an attempt on the SW face of Urus Oste (5420m) at half height when further progress would have entailed a bivouac, for which they were not equipped.   MEF 07/20

British Contrahierbas 2007 Tony Barton with John Pearson and Xabier Arbulo. June-August 2007
Although his intended climbing partner dropped out at the last minute, this leader was lucky to recruit two replacements when he arrived in Peru,

so was still able to go ahead with his 'plan A' – an attempt at first ascents of peaks in the Cordillera Blanca. On acclimatisation trips, they were successful on Nevado Raria (5576m) but were forced to abandon the first ascent of the S face of Nevado Bayoraju (5460m) when they encountered thin hollow ice guarding a gully at 5150m. They were more successful on Nevado Cajivilca III (5419m) as they made the first ascent of its 500m SE face at AD+. On Nevado Contrahierbas (6036m) they had reached 5650m when Arbulo was hit by a falling rock: although not seriously hurt, the shock caused him to drop his rucksack, thus forcing a retreat. However the leader was able to trek into Quebrada Camchas, and thus complete his exploration of the Contrahierbas massif, a task he started in 2004. Barton reported that the proposed new regulations for climbing in Peru have been abandoned for the foreseeable future. MEF 07/27

Imperial College Quimsa Cruz 2007 Hal Watts with Bernard Lam and Ben Withers from UK, Virgil Scott from Canada and Markus Roggen from Germany. June-July 2007
For their first trip to the greater ranges these five young students selected an area to the east and north-east of Laguna Blanca of the Cordillera Quimsa Cruz of Bolivia as offering plenty of scope for exploration and new routes. Although prior to the trip they had named two specific objectives, once in the field they decided that neither looked particularly attractive, so turned their attention to others. In total, they climbed 11 routes, 10 of which were thought to be new. Eight were purely rock routes, two long scrambling 'alpine' routes and one was a mixed route. They felt that the area was an excellent destination for future rock-climbing expeditions. For more details see: www.quimsacruz2007.co.uk MEF 07/33

GREENLAND

Dronning Louise Land 2007 Russ Hore with Gerwyn Lloyd and Tim Radford. May-June 2007
Although a very detailed survey was carried out of the northern part of Dronning Louise Land as long ago as 1953, the southern part remained largely unexplored, being marked on the map as 'Eventyrfjelde' (Fairy Tale Land). Due to badly crevassed blue ice, it was not possible for this team's aircraft to land at the intended drop-off site, so a point on the edge of the ice cap 40km to the north-west was selected instead. Plans had therefore to be modified, and over the next three weeks they skied north setting up camps and climbing 19 peaks en route (to many of which they gave Welsh names): 15 of them, between 2000m and 2600m, were believed to be first ascents. Although they collected small geological specimens from each peak, there was little evidence of the meteorites they had hoped to find. For more details see: russ-hore.co.uk/expeditions/d11_2007 MEF 07/07

Exercise Boreal Zenith WO1 (ASM) Sam Marshall, with Capt Sally Brown, Maj Cath Davies, Maj Kev Edwards, Capt Beth Hall-Thompson, Cfn Ollie Noakes, Lt Dave Stanley and Ocdt Joe Williams. July-August 2007
This expedition, in celebration of the 50th anniversary of the Army Mountaineering Association, visited Andrees Land in north-east Greenland – an area possibly not visited by climbers since the fifties – to explore and climb new routes. With fairly good conditions throughout and only three days lost due to bad weather, they made 34 ascents, ranging from simple snow plods to steep north faces (Alpine PD to D, and up to HVS on rock). Of these, 29 were first ascents.   MEF 07/13

West Lancs Scouts East Greenland 2007 Dick Griffiths with 24 Mountaineering/ Support leaders, 7 Explorer Scouts and 19 other members of the Scout Network (July-August 2007)
This positive 'invasion' of Ren Land in NE Greenland celebrated the centenary of the Scout movement. Although it was understood that several SMC members had been there recently, this is one of the lesser visited areas of Greenland. Existing maps are based on aerial photography. Expedition members were able to explore some 2,500 sqkm of glaciated mountainous terrain in the centre of the area that will improve knowledge and detail on the 1:50,000 maps: in an area they described as a 'milieu of spires and minarets' they climbed 32 separate mountains, all of which are thought to be first ascents. They are still waiting for approval of the names which they proposed for them.   MEF 07/19

SMC East Greenland 2007 Colwyn Jones, with Laubus Laubscher, Mark Litterick, Ken Moore, Brian Shackleton and Brian Whitworth from UK plus Heike Puchan-Whitworth from Germany and Stephen O'Sullivan from Ireland. April-May 2007
Despite long-term popularity with climbers - particularly members of the Scottish Mountaineering Club – the Staunings Alps in NE Greenland still harbour unclimbed peaks for those who search for them, as was proved by this team. They hoped to make first ascents of four peaks c2500m around the Lang glacier (aka Stor Gletscher), plus new routes on other peaks such as Dansketinde (2795m) and Bersaerkertinde. In fact, neither of the latter peaks was attempted as they were not in condition, but the team far exceeded their aim, ticking off more than a dozen peaks up to 2600m. MEF 07/25

East Greenland (Sortebrae) 2007 David Jakulis with Andy Garman, Alasdair Garnett, Rob Green, Clare O'Sullivan, Jonathan Philips, Tracey Quine and Malcolm Sloan. June 2007
There have been very few previous visits to Sortebrae by climbers, so this team felt that it would be a good area for an exploratory expedition with the opportunity to make some first ascents. However, unusually warm

temperatures had an immediate effect on their trip when the aircraft flying in the first members became stuck on the glacier, taking two days to extract. The second group was therefore landed some 30km away. A number of glaciers received their first visits, and eight peaks up to 2800m were climbed by routes up to PD+, of which four were first ascents.　　　MEF 07/30

HIMALAYA – INDIA

New Zealand Himalaya Alpine Style Brian Alder with Marty Beare, Kester Brown, and Craig Jefferies from New Zealand plus Adam Darragh from Australia (August-October 2007)
These climbers attempted two new routes on Changabang (6864m) in the Kumaon Himalaya. Brown and Jefferies attempted the north face and Alder, Beare and Darragh the west ridge, both groups operating independently above ABC. Unfortunately, both were curtailed at c6200m by a massive storm that dumped 50cm of snow at BC. This also prevented them attempting their secondary objective, a new route on Purbi Dunagiri (6489m).
　　　MEF 07/12

Kalanka North Face 2007 Nick Bullock with Kenton Cool.
August-September 2007
Although several teams have tried to climb the north face of Kalanka (6931m), so far only one, from Czechoslovakia, has been successful, and that was with the aid of fixed ropes. As the face is considered to be 'one of the great prizes of the Garhwal', this strong duo was determined to climb a new route in more modern – ie Alpine – style. After acclimatisation sorties to 5800m on a nearby peak, they set off up the massive fluted snowfield at the far left of the Kalanka's north face. Although hampered by regular snowfalls, they continued for four days to a shoulder at 6200m which led to the stunning NE ridge. With food running out and the probability of several more days' technical (and 'not very appealing') climbing to the summit, they decided to curtail their ascent at this point (*see article 'Bittersweet Desire', pp14-21*). (This expedition received the Nick Estcourt Award for 2007.)
　　　MEF 07/15

2007 Kharchakund Pat Deavoll (NZ) with Bruce Normand (UK) and Paul and Shelley Hersey (NZ). September-October 2007
Although Deavoll and Normand originally planned to make another attempt on Jankuth (6805m) at the head of the Gangotri glacier, the Uttaranchal state government refused a permit. However, they were able to obtain one to attempt the unclimbed east ridge of Kharchakund (6612m) in the Garhwal, and were joined by the Herseys, who had designs on other unclimbed aspects of the same peak. After scouting out two routes,

the Herseys decided that the sérac danger was too great and turned their attention to Yeonbuk (5953m). After climbing several 'bullet-proof' pitches of 60 degree ice Deavoll and Normand established themselves on the east ridge of Kharchakund, but overnight a snow storm struck and they decided to withdraw. When the weather improved six days later, they discovered that the east ridge was now out of condition, so they decided to have a look at the SW ridge, but soon realised that it would be too dangerous. However, Deavoll remembered seeing an unnamed 6465m peak further up the glacier in 2004. In a two-day push with deteriorating weather they reached its summit – probably the first people to do so – and returned to base camp where they met up with the other team members who had decided that the avalanche risk on Yeonbuk was too great to continue.   MEF 07/40A

British Sikkim 2007 Roger Payne with Julie-Ann Clyma. October-November 2007
Persistence eventually paid off for this pair when they at last received permission to climb in north Sikkim, although not on Gurodongmar, at 6715m the highest peak in the area and their hoped-for objective. They were able to explore two glaciers, climb Brumkhangshe South (c5635m) and Brumkhangshe North (c5450m), make the first ascent of Eagle Peak (c5540m), make the second ascent of Pheling (c5500m) and two other sub-6000m peaks, and check out a number of routes on Chombu (6362m).
MEF 07/41

HIMALAYA – NEPAL

Caudwell Xtreme Everest Dr Mike Grocott with Summit Climbing Team: Dr Sundeep Dhillon, Patrick Doyle, Paul Gunning, Nigel Hart, Chris Imray, Daniel Martin, Dr Roger McMorrow, Mick O'Dwyer and Dr Jeremy Windsor plus Support Climbing Team: Vijay Ahuja, Maryam Koshravi, Dr Denny Levett, Paul Richards and Andre Vercueil plus Climbing Filming Team: Michael (Charlie) Brown, Graham Hoyland, David Rasmussen and Jack Tankard plus Camp 2 Support: Simon Lowe and Araceli Seagara plus 200 'volunteers'. March-June 2007
This was a complex medical research expedition studying the effects of altitude on the human body, in particular on the level of oxygen in arterial blood. More than 200 subjects were studied at a range of altitudes from sea level (in the UK) via Kathmandu, Namche Bazar, Pheriche, Base Camp to (just below) the summit of Mount Everest (8850m) which was reached by 8 doctors, 2 cameramen and 15 Sherpas. The results will take many months to analyse, but, combined with the Study carried out in 05/15 (*see below*) will provide valuable data for future individuals suffering the effects of low oxygen levels, be it due to illness or ascent to high altitude. (*See article 'Caudwell Xtreme Everest', pp220-226*)   MEF 07/01

Kanti Himal Julian Freeman-Attwood with Nick Colton, Luke Hughes and Phil Wickens. September-October 2007
When permission for his intended 'McMahon Line 2007 Expedition' (MEF Ref 07/02) was withdrawn due to internal political problems less than a week before departure, with no alternative Tibetan peak offered, this leader was fortunate to obtain a permit to attempt Rongla Kangri (6647m) in Kanti Himal, an unexplored area of west Nepal. So remote is the area that with very severe post monsoon weather all over Nepal, they never even reached the mountain. However, they were able to make the first ascents of two peaks at the head of an unnamed glacier west of the Rong La – Pk 5984m by its north ridge and Pk 5930m by its west ridge. During their debriefing back in Kathmandu, the team learned that Nepal has some 2200 peaks over 6000m, less than half of which have names and even less have been climbed. Some 250 of these lie in west Nepal, so this area alone offers plenty of scope for future exploratory trips. MEF 07/02A

CHINA AND TIBET

British Manamcho 2007 Mick Fowler with Steve Burns, Ian Cartwright and Paul Ramsden. April-May 2007
During his expedition to Kajaqiao in 2005 (MEF Ref 05/17) Fowler discovered that the name had originally been attributed to a very shapely peak to its south whose true name was Manamcho (6264m): Tom Nakamura described is as 'the Matterhorn of the Nyenchen Tanghla'. Amos and Thomas had attempted its NW ridge while Fowler and Watts were on Kajaqiao, but only reached 5880m. However, Fowler had been so impressed with its appearance that this return visit was inevitable. In a round trip of eight days from base camp (including one spent exploring the 'most beautiful area ever visited') Fowler and Ramsden completed the ascent of the NW ridge (at TD) and thus the first ascent of the peak. Unfortunately, photographs from the summit, rather than the hoped for panoramic extravaganza, 'could have been taken on any cold, snowy, misty and windswept place anywhere in the world'. Meanwhile in a four-day round trip, Burns and Cartwright made the first ascent of Peak 5935m which rises to the north-west of the large glacier plateau north and west of Manamcho and Kajaqiao. This climb involved superb mixed climbing of AD standard, and the excellent views from the summit helped to clarify the layout of the mountains in the area. MEF 07/05

British Yangmolong 2007 Dave Wynne-Jones with Steve Hunt, Dick Isherwood and Peter Rowat. October 2007
Yangmolong (6066m) is one of the few remaining unclimbed 6000m peaks in Sichuan, and only appears to have had one previous 'official' attempt.

To acclimatise, this team made the first ascent of an unnamed peak of 5596m (GPS reading) between Dangchezhengla (5847m) and Peak 5850, and then a new route from the north on Dangchezhengla, joining the Japanese route at the summit ridge. Then, in deteriorating weather, they made an attempt on the north face of Yangmolong, but found that it was steep and difficult with sérac barriers. They reached 5400m before retreating. MEF 07/22A

British Zhopu 2007 David Gerrard with Dave Sykes. April-May 2007
These climbers – aided by Zheng Lin ('Lenny') Chen, a well known local 'travel consultant' who proved to be an excellent companion – visited the Zhopu Pasture area in Tibet's Shaluli-Shan range with the intention of exploring and attempting a number of first ascents. They were successful on Hati (*aka* Hadi or Nazdenka, 5584m) via a gully line on its west face (AD, Scottish III, pitch of rock UIAA III). They also carried out a reconnaissance of the 5812m highest peak in the area which Chen insisted was called Garapinsung and not Jarinjabo as marked on Nakamura's map. A period of bad weather in the area then encouraged them to relocate to Tagong, from where they made an attempt on the south face of Haizi Shan (*aka* Ja Ra or Yala, 5820m), but after establishing a camp at 4800m they retreated due to a storm with high temperatures which caused a high risk of avalanche. MEF 07/31

British North Lungkar John Town with Kevin Clarke, Mike Dawber and Richard Sant. July-August 2007
Maps of remote areas can be most unreliable, with different heights – and names – being allocated to the same peaks. From several maps, this team spotted an unclimbed peak about 100km south-west of Gertse (*aka* Lumaringpo) in northern Tibet, variously marked as Peak 6704 and Peak 7200, and planned to make a reconnaissance and hopefully its first ascent. Satellite and Google Earth pictures proved helpful on their approach to the area from the north, and they were able to drive to a base camp at c5000m. From here they progressed via easy slopes to a camp at 6017m in the centre of a glacier. Although they did not expect to encounter monsoon conditions in this area, heavy snowfall suggested otherwise, and they triggered a number of massive snow slides which warned them of the danger in progressing any further. Although they did not have an opportunity to confirm the true height of the peak – known to locals as Tachab Kangri – they were convinced that the greater height was most unrealistic. (*See article 'The Sliding Snow of Tachab Kangri', pp84-92*) MEF 07/35

Zhongdian Caves Gavin Lowe with Sam Allshorn, Pip Crosby, Pete Hartley, Chris Rogers and Paul Swire. July-August 2007
Continuing the Hong Meigui series of expeditions (MEF 02/48, 03/49, 04/54, 05/51, 06/01 & 06/35) this team set out to prospect for caves in a compact block of mountains rising to 4706m above the Jinsha Jiang (Yangtse

river) in Sanba County, Yunnan Province, some 50km south-east of Zhongdian. With solid beds of limestone and no surface streams, the area seemed to have a lot going for it and a depth potential of more than 3000m. Despite poor weather with frequent fog and heavy rain, the area was fully explored, and nearly 30 caves found. All turned out to be very disappointing, as none were more than 60m deep. The consensus was that although the mountains are almost entirely limestone they had been raised too quickly – in geological terms – for decent caves to develop. MEF 07/42

PAKISTAN

NZ Womens Beka Brakkai Chhok   Pat Deavoll with Lydia Bradey. June-July 2007
Beka Brakkai Chhok (6940m) lies in the Batura range of Pakistan. Although some years ago an unauthorised attempt was made from the north via the Batura glacier, this was the first official expedition to the peak. Weather conditions throughout this trip were generally excellent, but poor snow conditions and a rock band that required fixed ropes (which they did not have) led to an attempt on the south face being abandoned at 6200m – with possibly three days more required to reach the summit. They did however make the first ascent (up steep snow and ice) of another peak, which they named Wahine (5835m). For success on Beka Brakkai Choka the climbers recommend acclimatising on another peak and also having an additional team member to help with load carrying (including rope for fixing) and leading, although it would sometimes be difficult to find anywhere big enough for a three-person tent. MEF 07/16

Hispar   Peter Thompson. August-September 2007
This trip was originally planned for a three-man team, but when both his companions withdrew prior to departure, the leader decided to attempt first ascents of peaks close to the Hispar glacier on his own. Despite breaking the pick on one of his tools on very hard ice low down, on Haigutum Middle (6031m) he was within 50m of the summit via an Alpine AD route on its north face/east ridge when he was avalanched, falling more than 150m down the Kero Lungma side of the mountain. The lack of a second tool (and any companions), plus the onset of bad weather prevented him from attempting other peaks, but he was able to carry out a reconnaissance of the unclimbed west side of Tahu Rutum (6651m). MEF 07/28

Shingu Charpa 07   John Arran and Anne Arran. July-August 2007
Although only two days' march from Kande and thus a fairly popular area, the Nangma valley still offers opportunities for exploration plus some *very* serious rock climbing. The unclimbed east face of Shingu Charpa (aka The

Great Tower, 5600m) is one such, and was initially the main objective of what was to be a 3-person team. However, when one member withdrew, the remaining pair felt it better to concentrate on other routes. On these they were very successful, firstly in freeing the Czech aid route *Bloody Mary* on Denbor Braak (4800m) and establishing a new climb *Welcome to Crackistan* on the granite spire of Zang Braak (also 4800m). Using a portaledge on both, the routes – each with pitches of 5.12d – took seven and nine days respectively, completion of the latter being accelerated when they ran out of food. With a wealth of experience for comparison, they considered it to be one of the most continuous hard jamming routes on *any* big wall.

MEF 07/37

Ikhatta Karna Luisa Giles (UK) with Sarah Hart (USA) and Jacqueline Hudson (Canada). July-August 2007
These three Canada-based rock climbers hoped to make the first ascent of the NE ridge of Peak 5700, (south of the Choktoi glacier) which they had dubbed 'Hidden Tower'. However, an early reconnaissance proved that the rock quality on the mountain was generally poor with exfoliating loose granite, so they turned their attention to a rock peak down-valley and slightly east of their original objective. They made three attempts on this, reaching a northern sub-summit (c5200m), on the multi-pinnacled summit ridge but stopping short of the highest point when they were hit by bad weather. Nevertheless, their third excursion was a fine achievement involving a 19-hour round trip.

MEF 07/39

CENTRAL ASIA AND THE FAR EAST

Kuksay 2007 John Allen with David Barker, Joe Howard, Isobel Mulligan, Kevin Mulligan, Richard Taylor and Neil Willatt. July-August 2007
Although close to the ever popular Mustagh Ata, the Kuksay glacier of West Kunlun still had several significant unclimbed peaks, and this team (all making their first visit to the greater ranges) hoped to make some first ascents. From a base camp at 4500m, they climbed several peaks with grades varying from PD to TD, giving each a local (Kyrgyz) name, viz: Pt 4976m = *Kichinekey Tagh* (Small Mountain), Pt 5582m = *Chiatuk*, Pt 5315m = *Yilpiz* (Snow Leopard), and Pt 5485m = *Tiltagh* (Tongue Mountain). They also put up a couple of traditional rock routes, no doubt the first in this area. For more details and photographs see: www.alienmountain.com

MEF 07/08A

Alpine Club Ak-Shirak on Ski Dave Wynne-Jones with Stuart Gallagher, Gethin Howells, Adele Long and Gordon Nuttall. April 2007
Based on his experience of Kazakhstan in 2003 (MEF 03/30) and 2006 (MEF 06/09), this leader selected April as the most suitable month for a

circuit on ski of the unexplored glacier systems of the north-eastern Ak Shirak area. Unfortunately the ubiquitous 'climate change' had caused an unusually warm winter with less snow than usual, making glacier travel more hazardous than anticipated. Despite this, the team managed to establish the feasibility of the trip, and succeeded in making the first ascents of five summits between 4720m and 4901m, the highest being Pik Snow Leopard. (*See article 'Ski Tracks in the Kyrgyz Tien Shan', pp163-166*)

MEF 07/17

Malitskovo Glacier Stuart Howard with Dave Swinburne. July-August 2007
The Malitskovo glacier lies in the central section of the Western Kokshaal-Too region of Kyrgyzstan, close to the border with China; in fact, according to recent border realignment, it now lies within China. Until 1999 visits were restricted to climbers from the USSR, but in 2006 the main glacier was visited and partly explored by an expedition from the ISM. The American Alpine Club produced a 1:150,000 map of the area in 2005 from which this year's pair identified a number of peaks c5000m which appeared to offer reasonable objectives as first ascents. They were successful on two, marked as Pik 5055m and Pik 4975m, although their own GPS, which they believe to be more accurate, recorded 5061m and 5100m respectively. They also made an attempt on Pik 4995m on which the ISM failed, but proposed the name 'Pik Kanashay'. Unfortunately a heavy dump of snow made the final slopes unstable, so they did not reach the summit.   MEF 07/21

MISCELLANEOUS

Xtreme Everest Genotype Study Dr Hugh Montgomery with Dr Mike Grocott and Dr Julian Thompson. 2005 onwards
This ongoing study, being carried out at the Centre for Aviation Space and Extreme Environmental Medicine (CASE), is integrally linked to the Caudwell Xtreme Everest Expedition, 07/01 (*see above*). It is intended to expand knowledge of the physiology of normal adaptation to hypoxia, and involves studies of the DNA and high altitude performance data from several cohorts of mountaineers. In addition to the 300+ trekkers and mountaineers on the linked expedition, data have been collected from over 350 Everest summiters plus a further 140 subjects attempting to ascend above 8000m. Future studies will include 250 subjects attempting Kilimanjaro (5894m), 150 attempting Aconcagua (6960m) and 100 attempting Shishapangma (8046m). The information obtained should not only aid understanding of the variability of performance at altitude, but also identify strategies for improving the care of critically ill hospital patients suffering from low oxygen levels. One paper has already been accepted for publication, but full analysis of the results is likely to continue for several years.   MEF 05/15

ALISON CHADWICK MEMORIAL GRANT

In 1978 the British climber Alison Chadwick died close to the summit of Annapurna I whilst a member of the successful American women's expedition. Three years earlier, together with Janucz Onyszkiewicz (her Polish husband) and Wanda Rutkiewicz, she had reached the summit of Gasherbrum III, at the time the world's highest unclimbed summit, and probably for ever the highest virgin summit climbed by a woman.

Following her death, a Memorial Fund was instituted in her name 'to provide grants to further British and Polish women's mountaineering in the world's greater ranges, ie: further afield than the Alps'. At the end of 1990, the entire assets of the fund were very generously passed to the Mount Everest Foundation which has continued to award grants broadly in line with the original guidelines.

However, rather than administer the Award as a separate fund, the MEF decided that it would award the grant to an applicant for MEF support – either an all-female expedition or an individual female team member – which also meets the above criteria. Hence, there are no separate application forms, and there is no need for an applicant to indicate that she wishes to be considered for the Award: eligibility is considered automatically during the normal MEF screening process. In view of the rather stringent criteria, it is perhaps inevitable that some of the country's leading female climbers have received the Award more than once.

Requests for MEF Application for Grant forms can be downloaded from the website or obtained direct from the Hon Secretary. In either case, *they must be completed and returned to him by 31 August or 31 December of the year preceding the expedition*. Early applications will be interviewed in November and the later ones in March. It is advisable to submit applications as early as possible.

MEF Hon Secretary:
WH Ruthven,
1 Sarabeth Drive
Tunley
Bath BA2 0EA
Website: **www.mef.org.uk**

The Alison Chadwick Memorial Grant for 2008 has been awarded to **Anne Arran,** who is leader of the **Chimanta 2008 Expedition** to Venezuela, on which she and her husband (plus one of the most accomplished local climbers) plan to explore the Grand Sabana Chimanta Massif of Venezuela and attempt to make the first recorded ascent of the steep rock walls of Chimanta (2700m). Previous exploration of the peak by cavers and ecologists has been very limited, as it has the most overhanging wall in the world (100m + overhang).

Reviews

Chris Smith

BOARDMAN TASKER AWARD 2007

Chairman of the judges for the Boardman Tasker Award for Mountain Literature in 2007 was AC honorary member Lord (Chris) Smith of Finsbury. Announcing the winner at a packed event at the Kendal Mountain Festival last November, Chris gave such a comprehensive and thoughtful summary of the best of 2007's books, that it seemed appropriate and a pleasure for the journal to reproduce his speech in full:

Judging the Boardman Tasker Award this year has been a real delight. This has partly arisen because of the sheer quality of much of the writing that we had to consider, but it has also resulted from the commitment, insight and assiduousness of my two fellow judges, Alison Fell and Tim Noble. Alison is a Scottish poet and novelist, whose novel *Mer de Glace* was a joint winner of the Award in 1991; Tim is a life-long climber, writer and teacher of English, author of *Great VS Climbs in the Lake District*, and has just completed 10 distinguished years as editor of the *Climbers' Club Journal*. I want to pay tribute to both of them. I couldn't have wished for better colleagues. The fact that we were unanimous not only in our choice of winner, but in our selection for second and third places too, speaks volumes.

As usual we have been ably served by Maggie Body, the Administrator of the Award, whose hounding of publishers, treks to the Post Office, production of information and wisdom when needed, and cheerfulness throughout, have been exemplary. It is a fitting tribute that Maggie plays a near-starring role in one of our short-listed books, Stephen Venables' *Higher than the Eagle Soars*.

Before I turn to the six short-listed books, I want to mention with honour three that didn't quite make it to the list. Owen Sheers' *Resistance* (Faber) is a first novel that anyone would be proud to have written. As befits a poet of huge talent and integrity, Owen has brought to his novel set in an imaginary period of German occupation in the Welsh hills – full of the stresses, tensions, turmoils and attractions that throws up – an intimate sense of the strength of the living landscape. The land of the Black Mountains becomes almost an actor itself in the story, a brooding and powerful presence. It is a wonderful book, but we felt we couldn't really put it on the Boardman Tasker list because it didn't quite fall into our remit of 'mountain literature'. Go and read it, though.

A F Whyte's *A Cairngorm Chronicle* (review, p382) was in fact written some 60 years ago, but Fred Whyte had buried it in a drawer and his daughter only discovered the manuscript after his death, and then again long after that it has been published by her in a very handsome small volume. Because of the posthumous nature of the publication, we didn't feel we could include it on our short-list, but we found it full of flowing and enthusiastic, if slightly dated, writing. Rich phrases such as 'a coign of vantage' emerge that take us back to a bygone and better time. And the sheer rollicking fun of the 24-hour walk over the four four-thousanders comes shining through.

And Mike Cawthorne's *Wilderness Dreams* (Neil Wilson Publishing £14.99) takes us romping through some of Scotland's wildest places: a canoe trip down the River Dee, a blizzard in the Monadhliath, the dangers facing the Flow Country in Sutherland. The heart of the book, though, is the story of an expedition across the Munros in 1986, accomplished on no money and with falling-apart boots, and despite an occasional over-excitement in the landscape description, this is exciting stuff, and it's written with humanity, passion and a touch of anger. For anyone who loves the Scottish hills, this is a book to read.

So, to our short-list of six books. I will, if I may, keep the three best to last. I say 'best', but that belies the value of the others. All six were worthy contenders. I'd recommend all of them to you. It's invidious to have to choose.

Judith Brown's *Happy Climbing Tells No Tales* (Troubadour Publishing Ltd, £5.95) is a compendium of well-told short stories, capturing the fun, the excitement, and occasionally the terror of climbing. Some of the stories here are gloriously surreal. *Troll Climb*, for example, speeds along for six pages with a brilliant description of a difficult climb on a big wall, and then for the final two suddenly turns into a nightmare where the cliff engulfs the climber and turns him into stone. This is no stuff for the faint-hearted. But some of these tales are subversive and funny, and told with real verve.

Bernadette McDonald's *The Brotherhood of the Rope* (reviewed *AJ* 2007, p344-346) is an excellent biography of the great American climber, explorer and scientist Charles Houston. It's well written, but it's the subject of the book that glows through its pages. It charts Houston's early expeditions with his father, with Bradford Washburn, and with Bill Tilman. It tells the 1938 story of the attempt on K2, and then again in 1953, when eight climbers had to retreat and miraculously seven survived. And it describes how Houston went on to become a leading expert in high-altitude science and to lead President Kennedy's Peace Corps in India. And throughout it all shines the honesty, the courage, and the commitment to his climbing companions – the true 'brotherhood of the rope' – that is deep at the core of Houston's being. He is a real hero, and this book shows why.

I first came to Hamish Brown's writing as a youngster, exploring Scotland's hills, and regarding *Hamish's Mountain Walk* as something of a bible. What's more, it was written with a mixture of wisdom, humour, informative fact, and total irreverence that captured the spirit of waywardness and exploration that brought us out into the hills and glens we loved. Hamish has recaptured all of that same spirit in writing now about the Atlas Mountains in Morocco, in *The Mountains Look on Marrakech* (Whittles Publishing, £25). Few Europeans know the Atlas Mountains as intimately as does Hamish, and there's no-one else could have written this book. It describes a 96-day, 900-mile traverse of the Atlas in 1996, by Hamish, Charles Knowles, and two Berber muleteers. The description of the mountains is threaded through the narrative of the trek; it is both a story and an inspirational guidebook; it is packed with anecdotes and stories and history and moments of pathos and of humour. There are moments of poetry, too. It is imbued with an affection and respect for the Berber people. It makes you want to go there.

And now to our three finalists. All three are experienced and published writers with honed and polished styles; and they have provided us here with three distinctly different genres of mountain writing, about critically important issues and climbs. The quality and range of their writing is formidable.

In third position we placed Stephen Venables' *Higher than the Eagle Soars* (review, p375). This autobiography of an extraordinary climbing and exploring life is surely appropriately high up on our list, in this important year of the 150th anniversary of the founding of the Alpine Club. This book is a classic of mountain autobiography. It fleshes out the life left unrecorded in three successful expedition books including the Boardman Tasker winner *The Painted Mountains*. Stephen delights the reader with the depth of his – sometimes painful – self-awareness. A classical music buff but poor team player at public school and university, and self-confessed emotional hesitant all his life, he nonetheless finds in and from climbing – particularly solo climbing – the inner resolve and strength to devote his life to high-standard mountaineering: culminating in the outstanding and highly dangerous ascent of Everest's Kangshung Face, when he summited without oxygen and alone, and was lucky to return alive.

We found ourselves wishing for a fuller analysis of the thoughts and feelings and inner struggles about selfishness and companionship when serious decisions are taken at extreme moments like this. And there is perhaps too much hesitation in the book about his placing his life and achievements in the full context of changing social and mountaineering *mores*. Stephen's life, after all, is contemporaneous with many readers' experiences: one of the judges was in Chamonix at exactly the same time as, and emotionally caught up with, a climbing tragedy that Stephen records with real feeling. But the writing about the ascents sparkles with iridescence and immediacy. You are there with him, battling with the external elements and sharing the internal anxiety. And you follow this remarkably told journey through suffering and adversity to a modest acceptance of world-wide acclaim, always rooted in a passion for the mountains and the almost superhuman effort they call forth from those who venture to them.

(This is the moment where I give everything away, but please bear with me nonetheless!)

Our second place goes to James Tabor's *Forever on the Mountain* (review, p372). This book re-examines the worst disaster in American climbing history, when in 1967 seven young, idealistic, fit and experienced climbers died in a freak storm somewhere under the summit of Denali. This is a forensic and densely-researched book, but is startlingly fresh in both style and narrative drive. It engrosses from start to finish. It has impact and immediacy, being written largely in the present tense. James Tabor examines the evidence rigorously, he looks at contemporaneous accounts, extant writing, and considers the participants dispassionately. He turns over all stones, theories, received opinions and reputations. That one of the most revered figures of international mountaineering, map-making and scientific research, Bradford Washburn, comes out with a dented reputation, but with the writer's integrity intact, is a measure of the stature of this book. And it is very hard to avoid ending the book in a state of huge rage at the bureaucratic incompetence of the then National Park Service.

This is a book with a very American flavour, but for British mountaineers – used perhaps to the more intimate post-Hunt approaches to expedition selection and execution – it is nevertheless an essential and compelling read. It lays bare some of the crucial issues facing serious mountain expeditions, then and now: exuberance, incompatibility or mutual support, blame, error, or accident, and the relentless nature of the mountain, its weather and its wilderness. James Tabor's resolve and sustained engagement, his determination to uncover the truth, and his lucid and consistent style of writing whilst exploring and including a wide range of source material, make this book, we believe, a touchstone for the future.

Which brings me to our winner. Robert Macfarlane's *The Wild Places* (review, p371) is neither a book of forensic investigation, nor autobiography, but it would be impossible to say that elements of both styles are not vibrantly present in this moving, challenging, luminously written book. A few years ago Robert's *Mountains of the Mind* was shortlisted for the Boardman Tasker Award, and narrowly missed winning. *The Wild Places* is even better. He wants to search for, and find 'wildness' – noticeably, he never uses the term 'wilderness' – but not only to find it: to sense it, feel it, understand it, capture something of its soul. This is a magical book, written in the finest evocative prose, in which hedgerow, summit, crag, tree, storm, shingle beach, bivouac and solo exploration are discovered and described anew.

Robert writes with a poet's eye and mind, but without ego. His evocations of the ordinary are extraordinary. A spurt of birds driven down the wind; a tall bright sky; a flash of the sea grass; a shrapnel-blast of shingle. And alongside the arresting words, there are the quiet and moving meetings with extraordinary people, first among whom is the late, great Roger Deakin. Indeed, part of the true delight and revelation of this book is the integration he achieves, melding disparate sources, observations, facts and first-hand experience; he leads us to see and think the way he does. He seeks to find and to feel the nature of Nature itself, and it is after all our only true context. He shows us how wildness exists just round the corner, as well as in the remote mountain peaks and vistas. That we can be moved to visit our own little pieces of wildness and come to terms with our real responsibility to preserve them for others to discover anew, is gloriously celebrated in this book. As TS Eliot wrote in *Little Gidding*,

> We shall not cease from exploration
> And the end of all our exploring
> Will be to arrive where we started
> And know the place for the first time.

Robert Macfarlane's *The Wild Places* is an outstanding winner of the Boardman Tasker Award for 2007.

Classic Rock
Compiled by Ken Wilson
Second Edition 2007 Bâton Wicks 300pp £32

A long time ago in a distant part of the Galaxy (East Finchley actually), a long-haired climbing youth laboured long in a garden shed. No ordinary garden shed this, but a darkroom. No ordinary darkroom either, but the hallowed home to the enlarger of one Ken Wilson who, back then in the autumn of 1973, stood astride the climbing world as the colossus editor of *Mountain* magazine. I, the long haired youth, was working out my notice as Assistant Editor (don't ask), having let slip that I could print – at which point Ken marched me out into the garden, locked me in the shed with a arm-load of negatives and commanded me to print. Two weeks later I emerged blinking into the daylight, reeking of hypo, but having printed up a vast selection of images that would become very familiar to the climbing world over the next decades. What I didn't know was that Ken was planning a series of climbing books and it turned out that these pictures would grace the pages, not only of subsequent issues of *Mountain*, but *Hard Rock*, *Classic Rock*, *Cold Climbs* and *South West Climbs*.

I had been working closely with Ken over the previous months, following a learning curve of Ceüsean steepness. His energy was, and is, legendary and limitless, so once a plan was laid nothing: the weather, people, God, fellow road users, would or could interfere. For example, in that fine September of '73, Ken decided he needed to fill in some photographic gaps in the 'Rock' books, so we'd go to Scotland, via the Lakes, to get crag and action shots for *North Crag Eliminate*, *Shibboleth*, *Raven's Gully*, Craig a' Banchair, *Clachaig Gully*, and *Centurion*. In four days, mid-week, he got the lot: good light, dry rock, people. (My subsequent efforts to emulate this feat during the assembly of *Extreme Rock* met with dismal and repeated failure, but that's another story.)

So the various books were produced and became part of the furniture of British climbing literature. A whole generation of climbers grew up with the images and words of *Hard Rock* and *Classic Rock* hard-wired into their climbing psyche. At the time they were published, trad' climbing in Britain had reached its high water mark: the ethos was set in stone and subsequent advances during the Eighties and Nineties were only of degree, doomed to share the limelight with the *bête noire* of bolted sport climbing.

Of all the books, *Classic Rock* was perhaps the most inspirational and accessible, for it encompassed not only climbs that were do-able by the majority, but also the wealth of history and anecdote that came with them. Accessible also because most, if not all, of the routes included were done prior to 'modern protection' the application of which could render them a safe-ish introduction to leading.

Fast forward the decades: of bolting, sport climbing, bouldering and indoor walls and all the while this collection of ageing black and white photos and fine essays waited in the wings, selling steadily, it must be said, enough to justify a couple of slightly tweaked reprints. However the routes didn't fall into obscurity – far from it. These classics remained popular with grassroots climbers from beginners to seasoned veterans. Contrary to popular belief amongst climbing feature writers, 95 per cent of us only climb to VS, a point which I have tried to ram home to contributors throughout my stewardship of various magazines.

So, at a time of glitz and glamour and the pursuit of big numbers it was time to redress the balance. Arise the once and future king in our time of need: Ken decides to produce a second edition of *Classic Rock*. Three years of trawling photos and a series of his by now legendary photographic *enchaînements* later, the deed is done.

Now this hardly qualifies as a second edition, more like a completely new book: larger format, nearly all new photos, mostly colour (I struggle to find examples of my lovingly crafted shed period black & whites), all augmented with new historical perspectives and profiles woven around archive photos. This last feature was the real winner for me: having read most of the essays several times over the years (Alan Austin's *Clachaig Gully* is still the best), I savoured the new extended captions and historical box-outs. The front and back of the book are crammed with new lists and tables and charts and time lines which can easily convert a quick dip into a lost hour.

There are of course a few technical problems with the book; he was at times not best served by either Kodachrome 200 or his colour scanners (tell me about it ...) but this doesn't detract from the wealth of brilliant new pictures. Which brings me at last to a rather unsettling conclusion. All the images in this book are from slides and black & white prints with insignificant input from digital cameras. I have a horrible suspicion that here we see the end of the photographic history of climbing. Digital photography is so vulnerable and ephemeral that in a few years time there will be no accessible record of climbing from the point where people abandoned their film cameras.

Previously, lackadaisical climbing photographers (is there any other kind?) would consign prints and slides to a shoebox to languish in attic or drawer. Twenty years down the line they'd be re-discovered with joy and amazement (or embarrassment) as part of climbing history. No problem, I'm often berated, you just update your storage media. Sorry, this is just not going to happen and whole climbing lives will be consigned to landfill along with their obsolete PCs. But hey, digital is so quick and convenient and you can spray them to the news web sites! And when their servers go down? No old magazines to trawl or journals to thumb through ...

And what of Ken? What if he ever decides to retire (though he might not get the chance if he continues to solo about on crags with his Leica trying to get action shots like some suicidal paparazzi)? Will anyone come along with anything approaching his obsessive, almost brutal attention to publishing rigour and detail? I doubt it.

This latest edition of *Classic Rock* is a great book: absorbing, informative, inspirational – you stand back from it and think 'blimey!' and this is only *part* of climbing.

Bernard Newman

Albert Steiner: The Photographic Work
Edited by Peter Pfrunder and Beat Stutzer
Steidl, 2006, pp239, 136 colour illustrations, £45

Albert Steiner, born in 1877, managed his parents' bakery in Thun for some years before setting out to make a living as a self-employed photographer. In 1904 he opened his own photography studio in Geneva and later lived and worked in St Moritz. Steiner was one of the outstanding Swiss photographers of the 20th century. Like Ansel Adams, he translated his artistic vision of mountains into black and white to reveal all its majesty. Steiner's photographic work spans the period before World War I, with its pictorially inspired images that look like oil paintings, to the straightforward and elegantly modern photography of the 1930s. Unlike other Swiss photographers of his generation, Steiner considered himself to be an artist. He saw photography as a completely appropriate means of creating works of art.

This is a very fine coffee table book that captures the atmosphere of the times in Switzerland. As a member of the SAC, Steiner ventured into the high mountains and produced beautiful images of the Alps in their pristine state at the turn of the 20th century. Interestingly enough I was able to buy his other book *Engadiner Landschaften*, published in 1929, on the internet. Remarkably, the printing in this 80-year old book is on a par with this contemporary offering.

The narrative explores his contribution to Swiss and European photography and compares him to the British and American masters of the time
like Frank Smythe and Ansel Adams. It places Steiner in context with
modern masters like Balthasar Burkhard and with his Italian predecessor
Vittorio Sella.

I recommend this book to all connoisseurs of fine mountain photography
and for its history. For me, it is all the more fascinating as Steiner was my
uncle's uncle.

Alex Milne

The Wild Places
Robert Macfarlane
Granta, 2007, pp340, £18.99

Presumably, one of the reasons we go to the mountains is to reconnect
with wild places, leaving behind domesticated lowlands, agricultural and
urban spaces in hopes of reviving that wild spark in ourselves by negotiating
our journeys in the unpeopled, uplifting, wild places. So, in Robert
Macfarlane's Boardman Tasker-winning account of his tour of the wild
places of Britain and Ireland (after first climbing a beech tree close to a
road and the hospital, airport and housing estates of Cambridge where
he lives), he heads to the far north and the far west of the archipelago for
more satisfying encounters with wildness. Bivvying out is one of his modes
of reconnection in these places, each rendered generic by his chapter titles:
'Island', 'Valley', 'Moor', 'Forest', 'Cape', 'Ridge', etc. But on the summit
of Ben Hope Macfarlane makes a strange discovery for the author of
Mountains of the Mind (2003). He cannot connect. During his winter night
on the single summit of these journeys, he experiences, not the hostility,
but the indifference of this wild place: 'Here, there was no question of
relation. This place refused any imputation of meaning.'

Much could be written about these two sentences, and perhaps already
has been, for example, by Menlove Edwards in his poem 'You rock, you
heaviness'. Jim Perrin's deft discussion of this poem in his biography
Menlove (1985: 156-7) concludes that the alienating 'feelinglessness' of rock
is either desirable or annihilating according to the inner mind of the climber
at the moment of contact. 'Relationship', or even more demanding 'meaning', might seem 'refused' by a mind trying too hard. To some readers this
will be a shortcoming of the book, resulting in too earnest a temptation to
significance, like folding the wings over the body of a dead seagull, or taking
back a symbolic item from each journey that really needs poetry such as
Seamus Heaney's 'Shelf Life' sequence to explore its significance. I regard
it as a strength of Macfarlane's book – the mind trying hard to understand
experience, to read around it and to reflect upon it, in the richest resources
that language can muster.

The key to this book's success is its honest self-criticism, its capacity to learn from its earnest endeavours and its clear, imaginative, at times stunning language that impressed the Boardman Tasker judges in what has been another bold judges' decision. Bold because the result of Macfarlane's enquiry is that little places, often in the lowlands, often close to habitation, offer insights into the nature of wildness: 'It seemed to me that these nameless places might in fact be more important than the grander wild lands that for so many years had gripped my imagination'. In the chapter following the summit experience, the epiphany comes when looking down into a gryke in the Burren at the jungle of miniature, complex, wild life. Thus the following chapters of journeys engaging with a holloway (sunken track), storm-beach, saltmarsh and tor, connect with wildness through new eyes and mindset, leading back to a new experience of wildness in the almost urban beechwood with which the book began.

Early for my meeting with Robert Macfarlane yesterday, I wandered about Lime Kiln Hill, above his Cambridge suburb. I struggled on our weekly winter school cross-country runs up here 50 years ago. Brambles, mud and a slippery slope beside the old chalk quarry are what I remember. I was shocked to find that it now carries the designation 'Nature Reserve' – still brambles, mud and a slippery slope, but apparently one of Macfarlane's designated local wild places. As we talked about his recent skinning up Ben Alder from Culra bothy we noticed a crow disturbing the display encirclement of two sparrowhawks above us. Suddenly a heron flew low over the hedge. His small children went on playing wildly with soil, grass, beans and the bubbles I'd brought. 'Aren't children natural tree-climbers?' he said. We were in town, at his home, in the wild, as this book leads the reader to appreciate.

Terry Gifford

Forever on the Mountain
James M Tabor
W W Norton and Company, New York, 2007, pp374, US$26.95

When seven climbers died on Mt McKinley in July 1967, engulfed by the mountain, their bodies never recovered, the tragedy ranked as the worst disaster in North American mountaineering history. Two books by survivors of the doomed Joseph F Wilcox expedition and reports of the inquiries left many questions unanswered over the conduct of the climb and the subsequent search and rescue operation. Forty years on we now have a third book, *Forever on the Mountain* by James M Tabor, which cuts through the acrimony, blame shifting and contradictions to weigh the hard evidence and set a distorted record straight. Grand tragedies, he points out, require a singular confluence of time, fate, circumstances, will and mishap. What he identifies in a painstakingly thorough evaluation of the facts is a trail of wrong decisions, financial pressures, bruised egos, personality clashes and bureaucratic delay compounded by the worst weather that this crucible of storms can generate.

Mt McKinley (6194m) was first climbed in 1913 by Hudson Stuck, Episcopal Archdeacon of the Yukon, who was a hardy, Scottish-trained mountaineer. Measured from base to summit the mountain ranks as the highest climb on earth, exceeding Everest's bottom to top elevation by more than a vertical mile. Its status as the highest summit in North America, its Arctic isolation and thin air has created an iconic challenge for aspiring mountaineers. Among them in 1967 was Joseph F Wilcox, whose nine-man eponymous expedition began planning at the same time as a group of three 'alpha male' mountaineers from Colorado had McKinley as their goal. National Park rules did not allow attempts by fewer than four climbers, the Wilcox expedition was struggling to raise funds, and so joining forces offered an obvious but uneasy all-round solution.

Seeking funds to attempt a mountain first climbed half a century ago was a problem for Joe Wilcox. His innocent proposal to attract publicity and media interest by climbing and camping out on the north and south summits of McKinley simultaneously brought a caustic response from Bradford Washburn, doyen of McKinley pioneers and fountain head of the mountain's history, when he was approached by Wilcox for guidance. 'For your information, according to our records,' Washburn replied, 'McKinley has not yet been climbed blindfold or backwards, nor has any party of nine persons yet fallen simultaneously into the same crevasse. We hope that you may wish to rise to one of these compelling challenges. Sincerely, Bradford Washburn.'

His letter ignited a searing response from Wilcox who accused Washburn, his 'childhood idol', of hypocrisy considering the amount of publicity Washburn's own climbs on McKinley had received.

Thus began 30 years of smouldering dislike between the two men with Washburn actively attempting to frustrate the expedition, advising the head of the National Park Authority: 'Don't let those stupid asses on the mountain,' before the climbers had even set foot on McKinley.

When they did, it was quickly apparent that the two groups were ill-matched with the Coloradoans proving faster and able to acclimatise more easily than some members of the Wilcox team. The climb began on 18 June and after weeks of gruelling load carrying seven camps were established on the Muldrow glacier and the icefalls above, culminating on 15 July when Wilcox with Coloradoans, Paul Schlichter and Jerry Lewis, reached the summit. Behind them, a second group was gathering at the high camp ready for their own attempt the following day.

But even as the successful climbers were descending from the summit, following a route marked by wands planted earlier, the weather began to deteriorate. Poor visibility and increasing wind delayed the second team for two days. Leaving one man ill in the high camp, six others set out into cream-thick whiteout, following a sparse line of wands towards the summit ridge some 650m above. Progress was slow and the climbers chose to dig snow caves to bivouac the night below the summit. The following day they called the park headquarters by radio to say they were healthy, uninjured and had linked arms on McKinley's summit. The wind was 15 miles an hour but there was no view and they were about to descend. Shortly after this call, ominous lenticular clouds gathered around the summit signalling a storm of violent wind and heavy snow that was to last 10 days, stranding seven men high on the mountain.

Overflights by light aircraft or an air force C-130 to check on the climbers or to drop emergency food and equipment were impossible in the storm which dumped unprecedented amounts of rain that washed away roads and bridges and winds that disrupted radio and telephone services. Meanwhile, at camp 6 on the mountain, Wilcox and the Coloradoans had spent 11 days at 5000m, storm-bound and in no condition to climb through deep fresh snow to reach the climbers higher on the mountain.

Tabor graphically describes the frustrated attempts to coordinate a rescue, the heroic efforts of the climbers who survived and the search team who did eventually climb beyond the high camp and discover the bodies of three of the climbers. No trace was found of the other four.

The tragedy has already been described in *White Winds* by Joe Wilcox and *The Hall of the Mountain King* by Howard Snyder, both with their individual slant on the expedition and the succeeding furore. What Tabor does in the final one-third of *Forever on the Mountain* is give close scrutiny to the reports, statements, excuses and press coverage that emerged as the mountaineering world sought for reasons for the disaster and as blame circled looking for somewhere to land. A conference in Anchorage some six weeks after the event had a Who's Who of Alaskan mountaineering, among them Washburn acting as a National Park Service consultant. The Wilcox tragedy's five survivors were conspicuous 'not for their illuminating testimony but for their absence'. The conference's leitmotif was 'tactical errors' with the spotlight on Wilcox, allowing the National Park Service bureaucrats to slip quietly from the stage.

The next report, an anonymous account in the annual compendium of accidents by the AAC and Canadian Alpine Club, equally contained false statements and assumptions according to Tabor who attempted unsuccessfully to discover the author. He concluded: 'after all the wild geese had been chased…it appeared likely that Brad Washburn had written the report himself or, if not, had strongly influenced the person who did.' Tabor then tracked down the precise meteorological records for July 1967 around McKinley. They showed all the ingredients for winds of extreme strength and turbulence with jet streaks deflecting the energy and velocity of the jet stream down to McKinley's summit area. He also interviewed the remaining survivors of the tragedy and recorded their recollections and recalled how, in 1997, Wilcox had presented a slide show about the 1967 tragedy to a conference of McKinley personalities, among them Bradford Washburn. The show ended in absolute silence with pictures of seven dead young men and Wilcox saying: 'These were my friends.' At this point Washburn rose from the front row, shook Wilcox by the hand and said softly: 'You did everything as well as it could be done.' Much has since changed in the organisation and the emergency services guarding Mt McKinley, and Tabor's forensic examination of how the tragedy happened may have at last brought closure.

Ronald Faux

Higher Than The Eagle Soars: A Path to Everest
Stephen Venables
Hutchinson, 2007, pp370, £18.99

In this his latest book, Stephen Venables presents the reader with a standard format autobiography covering his early years, climbing initiation and a huge variety of mountaineering experiences around the world leading up to his historic mask-less ascent of Everest in 1988.

Stephen is an accomplished writer (as one would expect from an Oxford English graduate) whose work I always look forward to reading. Although some of the expeditions have been covered in previous books (*Painted Mountains* and *Everest: Alone At The Summit*) I did not find that this detracted unduly from the story he has chosen to tell – a personal, physical and spiritual journey from childhood to reaching the summit of the world's highest mountain, alone by a new route.

I could have left the childhood memories, but they are there for those who find these things compelling. As a reader your attention has already been grabbed by the summit day prologue on the South Col of Everest, and Stephen soon returns to the meat of the book – climbing. On this theme he writes as well as anyone. On numerous occasions I found his eye for detail of the intricate beauty of the mountain environment struck particular chords, transporting me back through time and space to some of the places we have both been fortunate enough to visit. Stephen's love of these places and his chosen sport is very evident.

This book does not carry the same narrative drive of *A Slender Thread* or *Ollie*, the previous two titles of Stephen's that I sampled, but as a climber I was pleased to find it a more comfortable read that allowed my delusions to remain intact.

Ultimately, *Higher than the Eagle Soars* is a joyful celebration of our unique and special pastime, the strange bunch of misfits who pursue it and the truly magical places it takes them to. In summary: a piece of timeless mountaineering literature that will sit very comfortably on any AC member's bookshelf.

Simon Yates

On My Own Two Feet
Norman Hardie
University of Canterbury Press, 2006, pp324, Aus$37.95

New Zealander, honorary member of the Alpine Club and one of the four summiteers on the first ascent of Kangchenjunga in 1955, Norman Hardie has written an absorbing and at times inspiring account of his life. The book is written in an unpretentious style that carries one along on an increasing wave of respect for a man who, as he puts it, would like to put the record straight.

His accounts of boyhood and early manhood are fascinating; an unhealthy child who was excused from sports at school, he grew up in a strict rural family and, with regular chores on the farm from an early age, he learnt that life can be hard. By 16 he was deer-culling in the New Zealand bush and packing out vast loads of skins on his back and had made a 260km cycle trip on a bike with no gears, on dirt roads – and in one day. Those experiences stood him in good stead for the privations of the war for which he was just too young to be actively involved in but which saw his brother shot down on a raid over Germany.

A largely unmapped South Island was on his doorstep and, learning technique from experience and friends, he explored vast areas of unpenetrated country. His accounts of journeys in the Landsborough area south-west of Mt Cook are typically understated and one needs first-hand experience of New Zealand bush to understand what was involved. It's hard to imagine a climbing expedition these days in which you carry a rifle and live off deer! But here lies a minor criticism: for non-Kiwi readers, Maori names are a bit like characters in a Russian novel – they may be pronounceable but they all sound the same. A large-scale map early on would be a great asset. I didn't find the two less than adequate maps of New Zealand until I stumbled upon them attached to the block of plates in the centre of the book.

It was during those early explorations amidst the mountains of the South Island (and the good fortune of being influenced by the big names of New Zealand mountaineering at the time) that he acquired his formidable skill on ice. And it was here, on a rescue on Mt Perousse that he first met Ed Hillary. The rescue took seven days and underlines the toughness of New Zealand mountaineers. The carry first went upwards almost to the summit and then down the valley of the Cook River – untravelled by man for the previous 10 years. At the end the professionals drove home by car while Hardie tuned round and marched non-stop across the divide to Pukaki where he was working on an hydro-electric project, had a quick breakfast and went to work.

Hardie qualified as a civil engineer, and engineers will enjoy the glimpses of his professional career; all will appreciate his skill in surveying in the

Himalaya in previously uncharted country and his insights into dam construction.

1951 saw Hardie arrive in England. Typically, he worked his passage as a tourist-class steward on a cargo liner and his picture of Britain in those bleak post war years is a sharp reminder of a world almost forgotten. Three months after his arrival, Norman married Enid Hurst, a girl he had met through the tramping club while at university in Christchurch. It seems to have been a happy and successful union and it is clear that she brought to his considerable intellect a broader appreciation of music, literature and the arts. To me she is the unsung heroine of the piece – the perfect wife who accompanies her husband on some expeditions (she was the first woman to reach Everest base camp) or, apparently uncomplaining, guards home and hearth while he is away on others: three seasons in the Antarctic including one as base commander of New Zealand's Scott Base when he managed to get to the South Pole and, famously, to Kangchenjunga.

Hardie must have been a strong contender for a place on the 1953 Everest expedition but the powers that be thought two Kiwis were enough, although he acted as one of the secretaries at the RGS for the expedition. He was in the Himalaya in 1954 (his book *In Highest Nepal: Our Life Among the Sherpas*, 1957, provides a record of a way of life now almost disappeared under mass tourism) and he was a natural for selection for the 1955 expedition to Kangchenjunga – which it is worth remembering was intended to be a reconnaissance rather than a full-scale assault. Hardie's account of that successful attempt indicates a deep friendship with Charles Evans and paints a portrait of a very happy group and a strong feeling that success had been a team effort.

It is clear that Evans was concerned that upon their return to civilisation they might experience the 'who was first?' problem experienced by the 1953 returning Everest party and one suspects that Hardie, evidently not keen on celebrity, may have had this in mind when he decided to stay in the Himalaya and explore with three Sherpa friends rather than return to Britain immediately. That the expedition's return was greeted with something of a yawn by a population sated on Everest, the coronation and the 'New Elizabethan Age' must have been anticlimactic and that none of the successful party has been honoured seems, to say the least, churlish.

Between the lines one gains the impression of a polymath who, never having sought the limelight, deserves greater recognition than he has received. He reminds us, in the days when people queue at the Hillary Step and the Chinese take the Olympic Flame to the summit of Everest, of a time when exploration was exploration and when a Himalayan attempt meant a commitment of six months without pay. This book provides a valuable record of a pioneering age in mountain history and the story of a life lived to the full.

Nigel Peacock

Beyond Seven Years in Tibet
My life before, during and after
Heinrich Harrer
Translated by Tim Carruthers
Labyrinth Press, 2007, pp512, £25

John Lennon put it pithily in an interview for *Rolling Stone* magazine. 'You have to be a bastard to make it,' he said, then added, 'and the Beatles were the biggest bastards on Earth.' Doubtless there have been exceptions to the Lennon rule of bastards, but Heinrich Harrer was probably not one of them. He was certainly a tough bastard. The Austrian mountaineer-explorer weathered avalanches on the Eiger, imprisonment in India, a bone-shattering fall into rapids in New Guinea, a near-fatal bout of malaria and a whole lot more. I was going to say a lucky 'b' too. But Harrer made his own luck. He was a ruthless opportunist, and that, together with his iron constitution, carried him through a lifetime of adventure.

Tim Carruthers warned me, as he was engrossed in the translation, not to expect any surprises or confessions. This, we should remember, is the work of a man in his late eighties and unless there are hidden letters or diaries it represents his last testimony. It is Harrer's life as he wants to be remembered, told in his direct style. He is centre stage and the seismic changes he witnessed in pre-war Austria and in Tibet are merely backdrops.

One photograph in this marathon of a book epitomizes Harrer's life post-Tibet. He is seated, shirt off, in a dug-out canoe on a river in French Guyana, peering at the jungly bank, cradling a cine-camera, sun hat and camera cases to hand, while an Indian paddles the craft. Filming and writing, he had embarked on another half century of globetrotting. He also chalked up some notable first ascents, including Ausangate (6384m) in Peru, Mounts Hunter (4442m) and Deborah (3822m) in Alaska with the prolific Fred Beckey, and Carstensz Pyramid (4833m) in New Guinea.

Harrer – an AC honorary member – died in January 2006, aged 93. This autobiography first appeared in German in 2002 under title *Mein Leben – My Life*. Publishers Labyrinth Press clearly thought English language readers might be less familiar with Herr Harrer (remember, this book is not primarily aimed at mountaineers) and went for a more portmanteau title: *Beyond Seven Years in Tibet: My life before, during and after.*

Carruthers, a climber himself, has deftly caught Harrer's voice. One can easily imagine the old man seated at his desk at home in the Carinthia hills, the journals and clutter of his travels spread about him, recalling with evident satisfaction his glory days on the Eiger and escape from the Raj, then a wounded tone as he excuses his 'mistakes' in the Nazi era, and a touch of melancholy pervading the later journeys as he sees the modern world encroaching on tribes who had lived in harmony with nature. Not only was Harrer one of the last westerners to witness the old lamaist Tibet, he was also one of the few to experience life as it was in the Palaeolithic and Neolithic eras – the former in New Guinea and the latter among the Xingu Indians. In one poignant passage, he illustrates the corrosive effect of outside contact on the Indians of the Xingu River in Brazil – despite the area being designated a reservation and national park. Along with new diseases had come an erosion of traditional skills:

'For example, in order to collect the splendid coloured feathers of the toucan, the Indians used to entice the birds closer by imitating their calls, whereupon they would shoot them from the tree branches with arrows dipped in a mild poison, pluck a few of the bright red and yellow feathers and set the birds free again. Now the Indians were proud possessors of rifles, with which the birds could be killed outright from a great distance, and their bows and arrows had become redundant, but they had lost the ability to imitate birdsong and other animal sounds.'

This is Harrer the ethnologist. But frustratingly such observations come as isolated vignettes between the jungle bashing and the endless name-dropping as he meets and basks in the reflected celebrity of an oddly varied cast from his hero Sven Hedin, pioneer explorer of central Asia, to golfer Jack Nicklaus, Bing Crosby, the Duke of Windsor and the artist Balthus.

Harrer was born in July 1912 and paints a warm picture of his upbringing in a former miner's cottage in the hills of Carinthia, southern Austria. (The first of three fine sections of photographs capture this long gone period in a backwater of the collapsed Austro-Hungarian Empire.) His father worked for the Post Office on mail trains and was a member of the Socialist Party. As such, Dad was angered when 'Heini' left the Children's Friends Association, who would hike in the hills behind a red banner, and switched to the German Gymnastics Club.

In 1927, when the family moved to Graz, provincial capital of Styria, Harrer joined the junior section of the Austrian Alpine Club (ÖAV) and soon began climbing and skiing. He was chosen for the Austrian national ski squad for the 1936 Winter Olympic Games in Bavaria, but never got to race as the Austrian government withdrew the team in protest at the politics of Hitler's National Socialists.

This is the shadow time for Harrer and an area for further potential disclosure. The ÖAV was a hotbed of anti-Semitism and Graz, where Harrer studied geography and athletics at university, was the scene of Nazi demonstrations with the right-wing students to the fore. Harrer does not touch on this but gallops on through climbs in the Dolomites to his limelight moment as a mountaineer – the first ascent of the north face of the Eiger in July 1938 with his fellow Austrian Kasparek and the Germans Heckmair and Vörg.

We know Heinrich Harrer from two best-sellers – *The White Spider*, recounting that ascent of the Eiger *Nordwand* with a verve that made the book an inspiration to post-war climbers, and *Seven Years in Tibet*. Confident of his place in history, Harrer was cruising along comfortably into old age, when in 1997, as his Tibetan adventure was being turned into a film starring

Brad Pitt, his dalliance with National Socialism came to public attention. There are documents stating he joined the thuggish *Sturmabteilung* (SA) in 1933, but Harrer says he had been advised to make this 'false' claim in order to speed up his marriage to Lotte Wegener, from a family well-connected to the Nazi elite, and that he only applied for membership of the Nazi party in 1938 in order to take up a teaching post. At this time he was also working as a sports and ski instructor for the Syrian SS, though we're told he only wore the SS uniform once, on the day of his marriage to Lotte.

It was a difficult time for a proud old man, seeing the golden sunset he believed was his due clouded by a 'smear campaign' by journalists and others who, he complained, had not been born at the time. Harrer says he has thought 'long and hard' about his behaviour in 1938. 'Maybe it was youthful opportunism or maybe it was blind determination to subordinate everything in order to achieve my sporting objectives. Whatever it was, it was a mistake.'

At the close of the book, Harrer engages in a rambling valediction, taking another swipe at the duplicity of the journalists who beat it to his door following the disclosures of the late 1990s, engaging in a Desert Island books diversion – he would take the Bible, *Don Quixote*, Ovid's *Metamorphosis* and *Kim* – and declaring his abhorrence of violence.

Of the hack pack, Harrer says that by the summer of 1998 he and Carina, his third wife, had got to know the correspondents of all the newspapers and magazines in the world, or so it seemed. 'The journalists' expressions of gratitude and respect filled 22 pages of our guest book, but unfortunately their kind words only rarely matched those that subsequently appeared in print.' Knowing the tactics of my trade, I have to say that this rings painfully true. I guess we all have our place on that Lennon scale.

Stephen Goodwin

When a Woman Becomes a Religious Dynasty: The Samding Dorje Phagmo of Tibet
Hildegard Diemberger
Columbia University Press, 2007, pp. xx+394, £32

Samding monastery stands on a hillside within a vast plain south-west of Lhasa, overlooking a lake known as 'demoness lake'. The monastery's name means 'Soaring Meditation' and it is the seat of the Samding Dorje Phagmo, the most famous female incarnation lineage in Tibet. According to popular legend it is only through Dorje Phagmo's power that the lake's waters are restrained from bursting out to flood the whole of Tibet. Stories of the austere and beautiful Tibetan landscape are one with its religion and the history of its people, as Hildegard Diemberger's book demonstrates in exploring the lives of the remarkable women who together form a dynasty of female leaders in religion and politics.

Diemberger provides extraordinary insight into the life of the very first woman in this lineage, Chokyi Dronma, through a recently discovered 15th century biography. We learn that Chokyi Dronma was born a Tibetan princess in 1422 and, although early in her life she felt the desire to renounce worldly status and become a nun, political obligations compelled her to marry into a neighbouring royal family. Following the death of her baby daughter, however, she resolved to leave her marriage and take religious vows. Her husband, family and the local people opposed her decision but she was determined to dedicate herself to a spiritual life, and ultimately achieved ordination, an extremely unusual attainment within Tibetan Buddhism for a woman. Chokyi Dronma's spiritual masters recognised her as the emanation of the tantric deity Dorje Phagmo.

The book opens with introduction to the life of Chokyi Dronma and her historical and cultural contexts, followed by Diemberger's translation of the biography. Armed with the information from the previous chapters, this text is fascinating reading, delivered in a fluid, engaging style, mixing drama with pursuit of spiritual ideals. In one memorable scene Chokyi Dronma learns that her religious master, the great scholar Bodong Chogle Namgyal is approaching death and she races to him across high mountain passes, 'riding fast with snowflakes hitting her eyes, hurting like thorns'. These passes appear throughout the story as places of meeting and departure.

The biography is followed by chapters on the later incarnations of the Samding Dorje Phagmo and detailed explorations of the meaning of reincarnation and the role of women in Buddhism. The last chapters explore the life of the current twelfth incarnation, a woman who has lived through a period of extreme change. Born in 1938, she saw the Chinese annexation of Tibet in 1951 and fled to India during the uprising seven years later. She chose to return, was fêted by Mao and appointed to various government positions, used for her symbolic value against Tibetans who chose exile. Even so, Samding monastery was destroyed in the Cultural Revolution. Since then Samding has been rebuilt and is now physically impressive, if spiritually malnourished. The Dorje Phagmo remains a high government cadre in the Tibet Autonomous Region. Diemberger delivers a nuanced account of these events and it is typical of her careful presentation of Tibetan voices that this section is largely made up of and structured around the recollections of the Dorje Phagmo's sister.

The book combines scholarly analysis with occasional anecdotes of personal encounters. In the last of these, Diemberger meets a cheerful young nun on a dirt lane wearing monastic robes but with her hair long and a mobile phone in her hand, who gives her name as Dorje Phagmo. Diemberger learns that the woman is thought by some to be an emanation of the deity, said to be 'just one of the many new incarnations and oracles that are emerging these days'. The resilient Tibetan women portrayed in this book evidently inspire this tentative but hopeful conclusion.

Kathleen Palti

The Cairngorms
Andy Nisbet *et al*
Scottish Mountaineering Trust, 2007, pp492, £23.00

The SMC's latest compilation of mountain routes lying east of the A9 continues their modern tradition of fabulous looking, highly articulate climbers' guides. After a brief experimentation with a two-volume approach covering the climbs of this area, the SMC have, despite the significant increase in recorded routes, reverted to a single-seater design for the latest model. Strictly speaking, its title tells only a fraction of the story, for this data-stoked tome covers not just the Cairngorms/Am Monadh Ruadh proper, but also everything recorded in the Mounth. As a consequence, the guide is quite chunky but still manageable – think of it as a slightly overweight but fit and happy labrador, rather than a run-yourself-ragged border collie. The guide 'modernises' the presentation of Cairngorm data with many of the old crag line drawings done away with and replaced by the now-familiar and attractively clear panoramic colour photo-topos. However, given the fact that the prevailing weather conditions in these parts 'occasionally' renders these beautiful depictions largely irrelevant (as a character-building maelstrom of cloud, rain or snow engulfs the land), a useful innovation might have been the judicious mention of grid co-ordinates to aid navigation to and from climbs (especially given the fact that these days most people with a healthy survival instinct carry a GPS in the 'Gorms, especially in winter).

This is a minor gripe however. The crag and route information, as expected from a publication with Andy Nisbet leading the writing team behind it, is authoritative and enthusiastic – while the numerous photographs of often remote and exciting climbs sharpen the exploratory urge in the reader. It's a combination that both informs and inspires. Who needs the Alps when we've got one of the best wilderness climbing areas in Europe within our own borders? *The Cairngorms* provides a compelling argument to support this view.

Colin Wells

A Cairngorm Chronicle
A F Whyte, illustrated by Rose Shaw-Taylor
Millrace, 2007, pp158 £14.95 list / £13.50 website

To the polymath A F Whyte, politician, journalist and lecturer, the Cairngorms were 'the home of the spirit, the shrine to which the wanderer returns to recapture that which he dare not lose'. In his long career, travelling widely in India and the Far East, he often turned to his journal as a means of revisiting his beloved mountains. It is this journal, written for his own pleasure and discovered by his daughter after his death, which appears in a beautifully compact offering from the excellent Millrace list.

The centrepiece of the book is a remarkable day's foray in 1904 when Whyte and two companions set out from the Shelter Stone before dawn and completed a circuit of 38 miles, climbing 9300ft including nine Munros. Although the physical exertion is remarkable, it is the innocent pleasure of companionship and the historical and linguistic digressions which most entertain the reader. Whyte's discussion of the subtleties of interpretation of the Gaelic names of the mountains and the natural features around them form a scholarly yet absorbing strand of the narrative.

However, this gently anachronistic book does much more than record, though it charts more than 50 years of outings in Whyte's beloved mountains. It contains a wealth of curious detail, such as instructions for the preparation of the Herring Bap and on the necessity of soaping one's socks to ensure comfort on a long walk, a wry sense of self-mockery when an anonymous stream is named Allt Eggie after an eggshell race down its course. As Whyte puts it, with eloquent cheerfulness, 'matters of great moment have sometimes turned on trifles.'

At its best, it gives us writing which lights up the landscape – 'Loch Avon has ... a flavour of claret, too indeterminate to be called purple, too cloudy to be called violet, yet somewhere in the spectrum near indigo, with an olive-green shadow shot through it' – and a clear and sturdy sense of place, reinforced by Whyte's wide-ranging and apposite literary allusions.

Perhaps most seductively of all, it affords us a glimpse into a world long-gone and innocent pleasures now too rarely appreciated – a world which is not a literary or historical construct but the very centre of one man's lifelong passion.

Val Randall

Darkening Peaks
Glacier Retreat, Science and Society
Edited by Ben Orlove, Ellen Wiegandt and Brian H Luckman
University of California Press, 2008, pp296, £26.95

It is as if heralds had been sent with a warning. First there was 'Ötzi – the Ice Man' – discovered by two hikers in the Ötztaler Alps in 1991. The Bronze Age fellow had emerged from the melting Similaun glacier after 5000 years. But perhaps we were all too focused on what he had in his pockets and whether he was Austrian or Italian property and so we missed his most important message. Anyway, global warming was not an issue we were receptive to back then.

So another herald was despatched. Kwaday Dan Ts'inchi emerged from the edge of a retreating glacier in Canada in 1999. The name was bestowed on this second ice man by the indigenous people of the region and translates as 'long ago person found'. By this time we were waking up to the message. These chaps were turning up because glaciers around the world were melting, and maybe human activity was a part of the cause.

I suppose I have lit upon these two particular exemplifiers of glacier retreat because I am a scientific illiterate and symbolism is easier to absorb than the mass of data presented in this authoritative study. However even I can see where the figures are leading; many of the glaciers that have seemed permanent features for millennia will be gone in decades.

Academic, yet accessible, *Darkening Peaks* provides an integrated, multi-disciplinary, global exploration of the scientific, social, and economic dimensions of the phenomenon of glacier retreat. It brings together contributors from five continents to discuss the ways that scientists have observed and modelled glaciers, tells how climate change is altering their size and distribution, and looks closely at their effect on human life.

Of thought-provoking interest is the attention given to the cultural significance of mountain glaciers. For many there is a spiritual connection, and for particular communities – such as the people of Seattle looking up to Mt Rainier or those of Yerevan in sight of Mt Ararat – the glaciated peak is part of their idea of home. Even among the majority of us, without a specific connection, there is a deep response to glittering white peaks as one of great treasures of the world. The idea that this purity should dissolve to leave dark, crumbling rock is somehow shocking.

Orlove, Wiegandt and Luckman suggest that hope may lie as much with this cultural attachment to glaciers as much as our reckoning of the downstream hazards and economic consequences of their retreat. They posit two scenarios: waves lapping the lower stories of skyscrapers of former coastal cities due to the shrinkage of polar ice caps, first signalled by the reduction of mountain glaciers to small fragments; or new technologies and new patterns of consumption (surely that can be summarized as 'a lot less'?) averting such catastrophic change.

'If the world does address the great challenge of global warming, it will be in part because of the way that glaciers serve as icons to make this change visible,' the authors conclude. But how big is that 'If'?

Stephen Goodwin

Thin White Line
Andy Cave
Hutchinson, 2008, pp.186, £18.99

Andy Cave is truly a Renaissance Man. In one month he climbed Fitzroy, saw Marc Almond perform live at the Buxton Opera House and watched his beloved Barnsley FC beat Liverpool in the FA Cup. And, somehow, in between, he finished writing his latest collection of mountaineering reminiscences, *Thin White Line*. It's a book that reflects Cave's eclectic interests and his voracious curiosity about the world by describing expeditions and first ascents in Patagonia, Norway, Scotland and Alaska, touching along the way on history, geology, triumph and tragedy, as well as providing plenty of dry, understated humour.

A sequel to his award-gobbling first volume of autobiography *Learning to Breathe* (lauded by non-climbing and climbing critics alike for mixing vivid depictions of elite mountaineering and life underground as one of the last generation of British coal miners), *Thin White Line* continues the story of Cave's adventures in the aftermath of his bitter-sweet triumph on the north face of Changabang when, after successfully making the first ascent, his good friend Brendan Murphy was swept to his death in an avalanche. It is an account of how Cave gradually came to terms with the emotional scars left by the tragedy, and how he learnt to fall back in love with the big mountains and expeditionary alpinism after a period of wariness.

Although relatively short, *Thin White Line* packs the punch of a far weightier tome thanks to the condensed quality of Cave's writing. His voice is a welcome and much-needed addition to mountain literature in a decade in which the genre has been eclipsed by spectacular climbing films. Cave has been one of the few writers to make an impact and advance mountain writing; indeed there are few interpreters of the climbing experience who are both as eloquent and as active in cutting-edge and multi-faceted aspects of the sport. As Cave himself concedes: 'Being a mountain guide doesn't help; just because you're quite good with an ice-axe, it doesn't necessarily follow you'll be as good with a pen'. Luckily for the rest of us, Cave is pretty handy with both, deploying a deft prose style that is as efficiently spare and carefully considered as a climber negotiating an overhang of chandelier ice, each stroke of the pen, like an axe blow, having been weighed first and used for a specific purpose. In the same way that his first book, *Learning to Breathe*, was characterised by being as much about non-climbing subjects as climbing, so *Thin White Line* is elevated above mere mountaineering narrative – although there's certainly plenty of action. This comprises gripping first-person accounts of battling anorexic ice lines in Patagonia (the eponymous 'Thin White Line' of the title), a vivid account of the pursuit of a hard first ascent in the depths of a Scottish winter (*Genesis* on Beinn Bhan), the excitement of hard, big wall climbing in remote Norwegian fjords and the huge adventure of climbing a new alpine-style route on Mount Kennedy in remotest Alaska. Linking and threading the climbing action are insightful observations on the landscapes Cave has travelled through, their history, parallels between the bush pilots of Alaska and South America and mountaineers, and pithy character portraits of many of his travelling companions, especially the contrasting personalities of a young Leo Houlding and Mick Fowler.

It is clear from the latter vignettes that climbing partnerships are important to Cave, perhaps even more than the climbing itself. 'It is firstly about choosing the companions – and then the place, the adventure,' he has said. 'Fun' is always the main motivation, although Cave's idea of fun – which often seems to involve terrible suffering in inhospitable weather – is perhaps not one that might be recognised universally. After reading *Thin White Line* however, even the most cautious and wary mountaineer cannot fail to appreciate the motivations that drive the best climbers to such extremes, and to gain an insight into the thin line separating their perceptions of fun and fear.

Colin Wells

Tomaz Humar
Bernadette McDonald
Hutchinson, 2008, pp258, £18.99

For her third book in as many years, the industrious Bernadette MacDonald, former director of the Banff festival, has skipped a couple of generations after her biographies of Himalayan record keeper Elizabeth Hawley and K2 veteran Charles Houston to tell the story of Tomaz Humar. While Humar may lack the hinterland that comes with age and gives any biography an added dimension, the Slovenian *uber*-alpinist rather makes up for this with the emotions he excites in his contemporaries and among commentators. Humar's media-event rescue by helicopter from the Rupal Face of Nanga Parbat in 2005 seemed to confirm his reputation in the eyes of critics as an arrant self-publicist, yet two years later he made a stunning solo ascent of the south face of Annapurna – no rope, no harness, no helmet, *and no cameras*. It had been done without fanfare, though, consciously or otherwise, success would only heighten interest in the enigma. Humar's quotes here often seem to come from the Eric Cantona school of cod philosophy, but the deeds speak louder.   *SG*

Los 6000s de Chile. Ascent routes for the summits over 6000m
Edited by Rodrigo Jordán
Banco de Chile, Santiago, 2006, pp284, npq

Planeta Antártica. Antarctica Planet
Rodrigo Jordán
Vertical S.A., Santiago, 2004, pp126, npq

Bilingual and even trilingual mountaineering books are becoming common in South America. One Andean author who, in his several books and videos, has consistently been putting bilingualism to good use is Rodrigo Jordán, a Chilean member of the AC, an Oxford graduate and at present a mountaineer who ranks as one of the foremost in South America. His forte includes expeditionary leadership as well as writing about his expeditions. He has climbed on four continents; in 1992 he led the Chilean expedition that made the second ascent of the Kangshung face of Everest.

Edited by Jordán, *Los 6000s de Chile* is a massive picture book describing the ascents of 38 major peaks on the Chilean northern and central Andes that were the goals of national climbers enlisted for the project. It took two years to complete. For each mountain peak the accompanying text covers a number of related topics: access, routes, local or regional characteristics, registered waypoints, acclimatization and the use of vehicles in the desert of Atacama. There are no maps but readers are referred to the 1:250 000 and 1:50 000 charts of the Instituto Geográfico Militar of Chile. Photographs of the peaks and their surroundings are good and numerous.

Jordán's book *Planeta Antartica* relates the story of a 403km crossing along the east side of the Ellsworth mountains that took place during the last eight weeks of 2003 (see *AJ* 109, p123-131, 2004). Jordán and his three companions explored 9 mountain passes and 17 glaciers and made the first ascent of Mount Segers (2460m) plus an attempt on Mount Giovinetto (4089m).

Considering how scarce the literature is pertaining to purely Antarctic mountaineering, this work deserves close study. Travellers and climbers planning to operate in polar conditions stand to benefit from several appendix-like chapters, found between pages 92 and 109, on health, diet, photography, communications, gear, possible scientific research and flights. Along with the text and excellent illustrations, the characteristics of Antarctic mountaineering are clearly revealed.

Evelio Echevarría

Wielka Encyklopedia gor i Alpinizmu
Jan and Malgorzata Kielkowski
Vol I Wprowadzenie, Stapis, Katowice, 2003, pp535, npq
Vol II Gory Azji, Stapis, Katowice, 2005, pp808, npq
Vol III, Gory Europy, Stapis, Katowice, 2007, pp848, npq

I hasten to confess that I know no Polish, but I can unhesitantly declare that the publication of the projected seven volumes of this 'Great Encyclopaedia of Mountains and Mountaineering' will rank as a major event in the history of our sport. For the first time we will have within our reach a comprehensive encyclopaedia with international scope.

The first volume, published in 2003, covered the subjects of mountains and mountaineering in all their diverse aspects, including paintings, postcards and stamps. The second, issued in 2005, surveyed the immense mountain world of all of Asia, reviewing not only the major peaks but also the lesser ones. The statistics of Soviet and Russian ascents in Asia alone would justify the purchase of this great volume. The third volume deals with the mountains of Europe. Western Europeans will find this particularly attractive because of its massive amount of data and illustrations, a large number of the latter belonging to traveller-geologist Jan Kielkowski himself. Included are numerous reproductions of 19th century mountain paintings, those of Edward T Compton clearly being particular favourites of the author.

All three volumes so far published are rich in both text and illustrations. There are sketch or ridge maps and bibliography for every area treated. There are photographs in both colour and black & white, and line-drawings and logos are so numerous that it is safe to say that there is at least one on every page – and these three volumes contain a total of almost 2,200 pages! Volumes IV to VII will cover mountaineering in other continents and will include biographies, supplements and indices.

The great appeal of this massive collection, currently being published in Poland, is the overwhelming amount of information it contains. But in addition to quantity there is accuracy. One has to ask: how did authors Jan and Malgorzata Kielkowski accumulate so much data and thousands of illustrations and how long did it take them to prepare a single volume for publication? The answers to these questions alone would be a story well worth recording. Within the realm of world mountaineering literature, I know of no similar enterprise. Editions in other languages are needed.

Evelio Echevarría

Gable & Pillar – FRCC Guide
Phil Rigby and Stephen Reid
FRCC, 2007, pp402, £16 (AC members £12)

The FRCC have begun their latest series of definitive climbing guides to rock climbing in the Lake District appropriately enough with the two mountain crags that form the cradle of the sport in Britain – Great Gable, at the head of Wasdale, and Pillar, the 'grand stone' of Ennerdale.

There is a wonderful hark back to those early days in a frontispiece photo of the first ascent of North West Climb (MVS) in 1906. Both LJ Oppenheimer and Dr JH Taylor carried cameras on the climb. Indeed from the historical photos interspersed in the guide, it is clear the pioneers were as keen on self-advertisement as their modern counterparts. And cameras cannot have been too diminutive a century ago. What with manhandling the camera, a hemp rope, and the essential pipe and tobacco, it perhaps as well they weren't further encumbered by cams, nuts or anything else in the way of protective hardware.

Part of the pleasure of the new guides, under the direction of series editor (and AC member) Stephen Reid, is the combination of clear direction to every known route in the area together with endlessly browse-able history, including snippets inserted into the first ascents list. For example, 1980 brought the first 'new wave' route on Pillar – Tapestry E4 – with 6a crux negotiated by Tony Stephenson, watched ashen faced by his three companions. Stephenson recalls the moves, then adds: 'We join on the ledge – four friends, all aware of just how close this one has been, and summed up by Chris (Sice) in typical fashion – "That should send the price of diarrhoea crashing!"'

The great innovation for the FRCC is the introduction of colour photo-diagrams, beautifully clear, a boon to first time visitors, particularly to the remoter corners of Ennerdale, or for picking out routes that somehow one had overlooked. There are routes from moderate to E9, with more than 150 new ones added since the last guide to the area 16 years ago, many of them by Reid and friends in Ennerdale.

Gable & Pillar sets a high standard and generates a sense of anticipation for the rest of the series to come. Taken together, the new routes, photo-diagrams, history and a mass of associated info and ephemera, skilfully compressed into 400-pages, amounts to a resounding re-affirmation by Reid and his team of the case for good, well-produced, definitive guidebooks.

Stephen Goodwin

Buttermere & St Bees
FRCC Guide
Colin Read and Paul Jennings
FRCC, 2008, pp356, £16 (AC members £12)

'If you have not savoured the delights of *Eagle Front* or *Oxford and Cambridge Direct* in Buttermere then in climbing terms you have not lived,' says Stephen Reid in his introduction, as series editor. I'd guess that a respectable percentage of AC members have ticked at least the second of those two climbs, and for most of the remainder of you, well, surely there's still time. And here's the inspiration.

This is the second in the series of new definitive guides from the FRCC and embodies much the same features – photo-diagrams etc – that distinguished the *Gable & Pillar* offering. Amazingly for such a relatively quiet corner of Lakeland – certainly on its crags – the 15 years since the last Buttermere guide have seen the greatest number of new climbs recorded in any edition of the guidebook for the two valleys of Buttermere and Newlands. And they kept coming right up to copy deadline, with one of the final routes added being *Bathsheba* (E1***) on Miners' Crag, reckoned by co-author Colin Read to be one the best climbs in Newlands – but then Read was also one of its first ascensionists, partnered by Philip Fleming.

This bonnie guide also marks the end of the forced marriage of Buttermere with the 'Eastern Crags', a curious coupling by the FRCC that persisted through three series from 1970. Buttermere lies in the north-west corner of the Lakes, and so the two areas were not contiguous at all. Next year should see publication of *Eastern Crags and Outcrops*, which will also include the Eden Valley and South Lakes Limestone.

Buttermere, now, is linked much more logically with the sandstone sea cliffs of St Bees – for sunny afternoons of boulders, bolts, sea birds, and multi-pitch routes the seriousness of which carry red ink warnings from Paul Jennings.

Stephen Goodwin

The Kaçkar
Trekking in Turkey's Black Sea Mountains
Kate Clow with Terry Richardson
Upcountry (Turkey) Ltd, 2008, pp176 +map, £13.99

Kate Clow is the redoubtable mother of trekking in Turkey, ebullient on the trail, as I can testify, and enthusiastic in her detail-packed guidebooks, of which this is the third – a lover of Turkey's mountains, its yaylas and sheperding families, wildlife and wild flowers. An Antalya resident, with this book she and Terry Richardson have left the scorched limestone of Taurus range (guidebooks *The Lycian Way* and *St Paul Trail*) for the cooler granite massif of the Kaçkar, close to the Black Sea.

Contained here are 32 trekking routes ranging from half-day walks to multi-day treks, plus the first map to the old, often-paved trails of the range. Unlike Kate's previous routes in the south, which she waymarked herself, sometimes in defiance of official ire, the Kaçkar walks are not signposted. Instead, both as a downloadable file on www.trekkingturkey.com and in the book, there are GPS points for the routes.

Kate and Terry hope the guide will encourage the expansion of environmentally-responsible tourism in an area which in terms of population and cultural diversity is dying. Many of the stone and timber summer sheilings have been abandoned as villagers have given up trying to wring a living from the mountain pastures and moved to the cities in search of employment. The EU and UNDP, among others, have projects to protect the old-growth forests with their rich bio-diversity and Kate hopes the guide will play a complementary role, helping locals earn a living by providing accommodation, services and food to visitors and thus stemming the flight from these beautiful mountains.

Stephen Goodwin

In Memoriam

The Alpine Club Obituary   **Year of Election**

Sir Edmund Hillary	1953
	Hon 1983
Lt Col Charles Geoffrey Wylie	1947
	Hon 2004
Brigadier John Richard Gerard Finch OBE	1953
Wing Commander Henry David (Harry) Archer DFC	1973
Phyllida Marianne Methuen Roberts	LAC 1948
Paula Biner	
Michael Wilhelm Jolles	1963
Ken S Vickers	1967
Rick B Eastwood	2004
Denise Escande	1992
Ruedi Schmid	1947
Robert Milne	1993
F David Smith	1961

As usual, the Editor will be pleased to receive tributes for any of those not included in the following pages.

Sir Edmund Hillary 1919-2008

I first met Ed in 1953, on disembarking in Bombay en route for Everest. With him was George Lowe. The two New Zealanders already had a considerable reputation and had been strongly recommended to John Hunt by Eric Shipton. Those of us who hadn't met them were curious to see what sort of people they were, and a bit shy. Ed said little, which didn't help, but the ice was broken by George Lowe, who took out his false teeth, grimaced and started to play the fool. We relaxed. Then Ed flew to Kathmandu to join John Hunt, while most of us started on the long journey overland.

We then all walked from Kathmandu to Khumbu. The trouble with walking with Ed was keeping up, so conversation on my side was difficult. Much the same was true later, when a small advance party was tackling the Everest icefall. But I cherish the memory of a few days with Ed alone, cutting steps and fixing ropes on the upper section while the bulk of the expedition arrived and started the build-up of stores below us. In the tent, relaxing after the day's work, he was good company – also prepared to cook, and to go out into the cold and tighten the guy ropes.

But my most vivid cameo, reinforced I suppose by having seen it so often on film, is of Ed, with Tenzing and George Lowe on the rope behind him, walking stiff-legged into camp IV, on 30 May, as George signalled that they had made the summit the day before. We dashed out to meet them, and John Hunt, tired and strained as he was, embraced them both.

One more personal memory - of Ed's reaction when he heard during the walk back to Kathmandu that he had been knighted. We were all very scruffy, mostly unshaven, in shorts and gym shoes, trudging through the mud of the incipient monsoon, badly needing a bath. He was amazed, somewhat shocked. 'How can a bee-keeper like me, in patched jeans, be a knight?' He did get used to it, but he remained an unassuming man, in spite of being lionised and asked to pose for photographs wherever he went.

Edmund Percival Hillary was born in Auckland, and lived in New Zealand's North Island all his life. From boyhood he was restless and independent, devouring books of adventure stories, and incurring the wrath of his father, a stern disciplinarian. He went to Auckland Grammar, and to the University, where he lasted two years, not passing any exams but acquiring a taste for strenuous 'tramping'. So he returned to help in his father's bee-keeping business; arduous work, helping to manhandle 90lb boxes of comb honey. During the Second World War, he applied to join the Air Force, but bee-keeping was a reserved occupation, so it was not until 1944 that he joined the NZAF. He did very well in his exams after training and became a navigator on Catalina flying boats, seeing service in the Solomon Islands. Back home, he returned to the bee-keeping business, where at last he was paid a modest salary.

His first introduction to snow and mountains had been as a schoolboy in 1935, on a trip to Ruapehu. He also climbed Mt Oliver, in the South Island,

and during his air force training there began to spend all his spare time and money climbing; notable was a solo ascent of Tapuaenuku one weekend, including an 80-mile journey hitchhiking and on foot. After the war, holidays were devoted to climbing. In 1946 he made the acquaintance of Harry Ayres, the doyen of New Zealand guides, and with him went up Mt Cook, first by the normal route and two years later together making the first ascent of the difficult south ridge. Accompanying his parents to Europe in 1950, he did some modest climbing in the Alps.

It was not until 1951, at the suggestion of George Lowe, that he went to the Himalaya, on a four-man, low-budget trip attempting Mukut Parbat (7550m) in Garhwal. Neither he nor George got to the top, which was reached by Earle Riddiford, Ed Cotter and Sherpa Passang, who got ahead on the final ridge. But then came the opportunity that was to lead to Everest. Eric Shipton, who had been impressed with the ability of New Zealand climbers to reach and tackle remote peaks, invited two of the party to join his reconnaissance of the Nepal side of Everest. Hillary and Riddiford set off to meet the party at Dingla. Ed records that he expected to meet 'pukka sahibs', who might even dress for dinner, and how relieved he was to meet Eric and his scruffy companions, Mike Ward, Bill Murray and Tom Bourdillon.

The 1951 reconnaissance was the first serious attempt to find out if there was a route up the mountain from Nepal, the political situation making it possible at last to approach from that side, whereas Tibet was now closed. The party found a way through the icefall to about 6500m before retreating. On returning to Europe, they were horrified to hear that the Swiss had earlier applied for permission to go to Everest in 1952. The British had permission for 1953, and meanwhile decided on a training climb on Cho Oyu in '52. This was led again by Shipton, but the easiest route to the top seemed to be from the Tibetan side, which for political reasons could not be attempted. However, Hillary and Lowe crossed illegally into Tibet to explore the north side of the range. They were stopped by a party of Tibetan irregulars, but their Sherpas managed to negotiate their release and 'no questions asked' for a trifling sum.

Returning to Khumbu, they learned that the Swiss had narrowly failed, Raymond Lambert and Tenzing Norgay having got within 3500m of the top. There was further suspense later in the year, when a second Swiss party got only to the South Col, in very bad conditions.

British preparations for an attempt had already begun - with Shishapangma as an objective if the Swiss had made it in the autumn. Shipton was at first automatically invited to be leader, but there were those who thought he might not be the man to organise a single-minded drive up Everest. In the upshot, John Hunt was appointed overall leader, and invited Shipton to be climbing leader. Shipton thought this unworkable, and refused. He was deeply disappointed, however generously persuaded Hillary and others, whose first reaction to Hunt's appointment had been very negative, that they should go with him.

188. Everest 1953: Ed Hillary and Tenzing Norgay en route to establish a final camp at 28,000ft. (*Alf Gregory*)

Each member of the 1953 expedition would have been glad of a chance to go for the top, but all cooperated in doing the essential jobs lower down. Ed was even more determined than most. He deliberately sought out Tenzing as a partner, reckoning that John Hunt would not nominate two New Zealanders as the lead pair. None the less he had no hesitation in doing his share of load carrying. He went twice to the South Col with Tenzing, on the first occasion persuading two parties of Sherpas, reluctant to leave camp VII, to get their loads there. Five days later, he was there again, tired, yet ready to help an exhausted Hunt who had dumped a load higher up, and to receive Evans and Bourdillon as they staggered down from their climb to the south summit. Next day, 27 May, the weather was poor, and they rested on the Col as best they could. On the 28th, with Lowe and Ang Nyima ahead of them, they started up the couloir leading to the south-east ridge. There is a well-known photo of Ed standing, with Tenzing in front of him, at the start of the ridge proper – he looks fit for anything. The four of them continued, picked up the loads left by Hunt and Ang Nyima, and went on about another 150m to a sloping shelf, which was all they could find for the final camp.

They had limited oxygen for their sleeping sets, which enabled them to doze fitfully. Early next morning, Ed had to thaw his boots over the primus before leaving at about 6.30. They followed the tracks left by Evans and Bourdillon to the south summit and then made their way along the ridge towards the unseen top. They came to a very steep 15m section, now known as the Hillary Step, with rock on the left and overhanging snow on the right. Ed insinuated himself into the crack between the two and fought his way up it. That was the crux of the climb, but they had to keep on and on, traversing snow to the left of the crest, wondering all the time whether the summit was just beyond the next rise. At last it was there and they stepped on top. It was 11.30am. Ed and Tenzing embraced, and Ed briefly removed his oxygen set and took photographs of Tenzing on top holding his ice-axe with flags attached, of the ridge down to Tibet, and all other directions.

After 15 minutes, they started down. Their oxygen supply was none too plentiful but Ed had calculated that if they restricted themselves to 3 litres a minute for the ascent they would just have enough. They made the South Col, moving slowly, at about 5pm, to be greeted by George Lowe with hot soup and more oxygen. Then came the immortal words, 'Well, we've knocked the bastard off.'

So much for Everest. None of us then anticipated the extent of public interest, to say nothing of the Bengali communist attempt to sow conflict in Kathmandu between Asians and Europeans by asserting that Ed had been dragged to the top (if indeed he got there). Tenzing was threatened with a beating if he said that Ed stepped on the summit a few paces ahead of him, so we agreed to say only that they got there 'almost together'. Once we reached New Delhi, Tenzing publicly came out with the truth. But we are still being asked the question! The coincidence of the Coronation, the day the news was available in London, has also led to accusations that the whole business was stage-managed. After a generous and colourful reception by Pandit Nehru and the Indian government, we flew to London, to be greeted with enthusiasm. Clad in unaccustomed morning dress, Ed was tapped on both shoulders by Her Majesty to signify his knighthood. He and George then flew to New Zealand where he married Louise Rose (the daughter of the president of the NZAC), to whom he had been quietly engaged. The three of them then embarked on a lecture tour in the USA, the first of many, before coming back to England.

Ed records his reluctance to leave home yet again, but he had agreed to lead an NZ expedition in1954, with Baruntse as the main objective - and Louise, as always, encouraged him to go. In the event, it was a disaster. Two members of the party broke through the lid of a great crevasse. One climbed out and Ed went down on a rope to extricate the other. In the process he broke three ribs. Any normal man would have called it a day, but Ed joined the rest of the party in an attempt on Makalu, to which their ambitions had switched. It was too soon. In his own words years afterwards, 'I made the unbelievably stupid decision to push on.' At about 6700m, still aiming to go higher, he collapsed and had to be evacuated. It was a three-day ordeal and only the expert attention of Charles Evans saved his life. Ed later reckoned that he never fully recovered from the effects of the collapse and that he should not have gone high after the accident.

Opportunity for another adventure soon turned up. In 1953 he had met Bunny Fuchs, who tried to interest him in Antarctic travel – partly, no doubt, because of Ed's ability to attract sponsorship. He did not react at first, but after Makalu welcomed a government invitation to lead an NZ expedition from the Ross Sea to support and partly provision Fuchs' trans-Antarctic journey, as well as carrying out research. This occupied him until 1958, visits to Antarctica being slotted in with spells at home and lecture tours abroad. From the start, he planned, if all went well and he had laid down the supplies needed by Fuchs to complete the crossing, to reach the Pole from the Ross Sea side with his party. He said as much but was not taken seriously.

In December 1955, he went with Fuchs on the *Theron* to the Weddell Sea, to land a small wintering party to establish Shackleton Base. He was not impressed with either the organisation of the expedition or with Fuchs as a leader, being particularly riled at Fuchs' refusal to invite anyone not in his crossing party to attend meetings. On the *Theron*'s return to the UK, Ed took the trouble to visit in Norway the developers of the Ferguson tractor system for use on snow and ice, and was presented with five vehicles. He describes the next eight months, before sailing south on 21 December, as probably the busiest he had ever spent. But he found time to send a brief message to Fuchs and the Ross Sea Committee saying that he planned to have enough in the way of resources to reach the Pole if that was practicable. This message also was ignored, and he was too wise to repeat it.

The plan recommended by Fuchs was to start from the Ross Sea and journey inland via the Ferrar glacier. However this was soon found to be impracticable. Instead, with the advice and help of US Admiral Dufek, he established Scott Base on Ross Island. From the ship, he flew inland to reconnoitre the unknown Skelton glacier. In the next few days, large quantities of supplies were flown in to the Skelton and Plateau dumps, at the foot and head of the glacier. The dogs and their drivers were landed and traversed the route between Plateau and the Base. The ship then left for New Zealand, taking with it the construction party that had built a comfortable camp.

The one major project for the winter was to try out the Ferguson tractors. Ed chose to visit Cape Crozier and look for the remains of the improvised hut in which Wilson and his companions had spent a miserable winter in 1911. They took three days, found the hut with some difficulty and returned rapidly to base, in the process learning a lot about managing the tractors in the rigorous conditions. The rest of the winter was spent in meticulous preparations, as well as scientific work. At one point, the 'scientists' claimed their work was so important they should be excused their share of cooking and other chores. Ed would have none of this. He and Harry Ayres took over for the first week, after which there was no difficulty.

The crossing started on 14 October. At first they were desperately slow and had to unload some drums of fuel to achieve a reasonable mileage.

They had to stop at the Skelton dump for two days. The dogs had been flown in there, and were to go some way further towards the Pole. On the 22nd they were off again, with the crevassed glacier to overcome, and did well to reach Plateau Depot by the 31st. Here they were held up for 12 days, by minor injuries to two of the party and by difficult flying weather. Starting again, they were slowed by deep snow and then by a very badly crevassed area in which they were lucky not to lose a tractor. The struggle with crevasses continued, almost to Mile 700 depot.

They were there five days and Ed was much engaged in furthering his plan to make for the Pole. Fuchs was against it, but asked for a further dump of stores beyond Mile 700. This done, Ed would have gone on himself, with only Peter Mulgrew to drive the second tractor, but in the event the others decided to join them. By Christmas Day they were 270 miles from the Pole. They waited a day, but there was no message from Fuchs, so Ed issued a press release saying they were 'hell-bent for the Pole', and pressed on. There was then a message from Fuchs, asking for yet another fuel-dump to be established, and that they should wait there for him. This was clearly not on; in the event it would have meant a four-week wait. So they carried on, reaching the Pole on 4 January to a very warm welcome

The rest of the expedition story is quickly told. Fuchs, too, received a warm welcome. After about three weeks, he left to continue the crossing while Ed flew to Scott Base. Profiting from Ed's tracks, in 15 days Fuchs reached D 700, where Ed flew to meet him and accompany him to Scott. He again records his irritation with Fuchs, who would not have him in the lead tractor unless he needed his help with the route. After reaching Scott Base, Fuchs and his party left for London, where they were suitably fêted. But Ed preferred to go home to New Zealand.

In mid-1959, Ed was approached by Field Enterprises Corporation with a view to organising an expedition for them. He suggested scientific research into acclimatisation to altitude, and also a search for the yeti, though he was sceptical about its existence. In September he was in Nepal again, and in Khumjung negotiated for the loan of a 'yeti scalp', which turned out on examination to have been pieced together from the fur of a brown bear. Norman Hardie and others had meanwhile brought material to Khumbu for the construction of a hut, in which the altitude researchers could spend a reasonable winter. The 'Silver Hut' was erected at 6000m, after which Ed flew out, returning to Khumbu later with Louise and with June Mulgrew.

On his return, he found that Mike Ward and others had climbed Ama Dablam without official permission. There was a big fuss, and Ed went to Kathmandu to deal with the situation. Nine days in government offices were followed by an acrimonious meeting with the minister, after which Ed was fined $60. He flew again to Khumbu and, going up to 7000m far too soon, was struck by what was called 'a cerebral vascular accident'. Again he had to be evacuated, but appeared to make a rapid recovery. He took part in the construction of a school at Khumjung, and then returned home, unusually remaining there a year, before going to the USA with the family for most of 1962.

It was back to Nepal again next year. The Khumjung school had prompted requests from other locations, and Field Enterprises and others put up the money for further construction. To facilitate supply by air, Ed organised, and physically took part in, the construction of an airfield at Thamserku, later commissioning Paphlu Hospital. Meanwhile, he went to the Antarctic again, taking part in the first ascent of Mt Herschel, but not attempting to go to the top himself.

Tragedy struck in 1975. Louise and their younger daughter Belinda died when their aircraft crashed taking off from Kathmandu. Ed was distraught. Being the man he was, he took refuge in ever-harder work for the Sherpas, but it was some time before he was able to share his grief with others.

Adventuring was not yet over however, and his 1977 project was to go up the Ganges in a jet boat to Garhwal, then walk to Badrinath and climb Akash Parbat. At 5800m, he yet again collapsed with altitude sickness, and had to be sledged down, unconscious. Nevertheless he was persuaded, four years later, to go with an American party to the Tibetan side of Everest, which involved repeated visits to 5000m, and finally a climb to nearly 6000m. Again, he paid the penalty of headaches and sickness, though he did get down on his own two feet.

This time, it took him some months to recover. He was helped in this by his growing friendship with June Mulgrew, Peter's widow. He threw himself into his work for the Sherpas, and June went with him to Nepal and also on further fund-raising trips to the US. Then in 1984 he had a surprising call from Prime Minister David Lange. Would Ed be prepared to take on the job of NZ High Commissioner in Delhi? The answer, after some hesitation, was 'Yes'. He was reluctant to lose June's company yet dared not ask her to go with him in case she refused. June solved the problem by suggesting that she become his 'official companion'. They had four happy and successful years in India, interspersed with visits elsewhere. He managed to see Tenzing occasionally, and was shocked by his unhappiness and physical deterioration. When Tenzing died in 1986 Ed was the only European to attend his funeral.

On return home, Ed and June were married, partly at the suggestion of their sons and daughters. Not long before, Ed had gone to Thyangboche at the urgent invitation of the Sherpas, as the monastery, not able to cope with the new-fangled electricity, had burned to the ground. Ed flew round the world to raise money for the rebuilding and in 1993 he and June went to Khumbu in for the monastery's reopening. They were there again in 1995 and had a surprising phone call. Ed had been proposed as a Knight of the Garter, to be appointed by the Queen (the AC's third KG, with Quintin Hogg and John Hunt). Lady Thatcher turned out to be his companion at the ceremony.

Annual visits to Nepal continued while he was physically capable of going there; he had at last realised that he had to be very careful of going to any altitude. He flew rather than walked to Khumbu to see his many Sherpa friends. His last illness, at home before he died, looked after by June, was mercifully short. Essentially a modest man, he might have been somewhat appalled by the elaborate arrangements for his funeral.

Mike Westmacott

More than a decade ago, the obituaries department of The Independent *newspaper, planning ahead as they must, asked John Hunt for his reflections on Edmund Hillary. Hunt's response was published in* The Independent *on 12 January 2008 as a postscript to the main obituary, written by the AJ editor, and is reproduced here by the newspaper's kind permission. (John Hunt died 7 November 1998)*

Edmund Hillary's name will be associated for all time with Everest. I met him and his compatriot George Lowe at the British Embassy in Kathmandu, in March 1953, before we set forth for the mountain. The two New Zealanders were the only members of the climbing party whom I had invited to join simply on repute; they had greatly impressed Eric Shipton during his preparatory expeditions in 1951 and 1952.

I think that we had both entertained doubts about one another before the first encounter; but for my part, I need not have worried. Ed Hillary was not one to nurse a grievance over the decision of the Himalayan committee to appoint me as leader in place of Shipton and I sensed, in his wide smile and forthcoming manner, the qualities I needed in my team, apart from his reputation as an exceptionally strong climber. Those impressions deepened into a growing respect and ripened into an abiding friendship.

Hillary's contribution to our success was not limited to the fact that he was the first to reach the summit with Tenzing Norgay. I often think of the crucial role he played, with Tenzing, in resolving a crisis which arose only seven days beforehand, when two of our carrying parties, with loads to establish camps on the South Col and above, had come to an exhausted halt at Camp VI, halfway up the 1200m Lhotse Face.

Aware as I was of the implications for their own chances of reaching the summit as the second assault party, and for the whole plan which had been so carefully worked out, I asked Hillary and Tenzing to go up at once and get things moving. They set forth immediately, inspired the climbers and Sherpas at Camp VI to fresh efforts, and led them all the way to the South Col.

On my way up the Lhotse Face with the first assault party on 21 May, I met them on their way down, very tired and with barely enough time to recover their strength before returning three days later. It was an example of the selfless spirit which underlay the whole great adventure.

189. John Hunt and Ed Hillary in the Royal Geographical Society garden on the 40th anniversary of the 1953 Everest climb, 24th May 1993. (*John Cleare*)

We met again five days later, when Da Namgyal and I returned to the South Col after carrying loads up the south-east ridge to 8335m. Hillary and Tenzing, with the second assault team, had just reached the Col, very tired after their second climb up the Lhotse Face. I will never forget how they helped Da Namgyal and myself in our own state of exhaustion.

Evans and Bourdillon had that same day reached the South Summit at 8760m, but there remained the uncertainty about the final stretch of narrow ridge; in particular, a vertical section of 10-15m. In his lead up that pitch, Hillary showed exceptional strength and courage, lumbered as he was with his heavy oxygen equipment.

When they returned triumphant to the South Col that evening, Hillary broke the news to George Lowe with typical nonchalance: "Well," he announced, "we've knocked the bastard off."

After Everest, Hillary had the world at his feet. He was presented with difficult decisions about his future career. The sudden translation from work on his father's bee farm to worldwide journeys as an international hero was, to say the least, a bewildering experience. On receiving news of his knighthood he was, in his own words, 'appalled'.

Yet, he came to enjoy fame and exploited it to good purpose. At one point his thoughts turned to the diplomatic service; at the time I assured him that this would not suit his spontaneous and outspoken character.

I was to be proved wrong many years later when, in 1984, he was appointed as New Zealand's High Commissioner in India and Ambassador to Nepal, posts which he filled with great success.

Continuing contacts with the Sherpa communities in Solu and Khumbu provided an opening for other facets of Hillary's nature: his warm-heartedness and social conscience. He learned about their life-style and its problems: in regard to health, education and travel in that remote land. The Himalayan Trust is a permanent memorial to his labours in promoting a social revolution in east Nepal. That work gave rise to some soul-searching on Hillary's part. But, as he said:

'The traditional Sherpa way of life was doomed in any case. If contact with the West has made them lose their traditional hospitality, their religious motivation and their community spirit . . . foreign money, they tell me, is a powerful panacea for such ailments.'

There is a touch of unaccustomed cynicism in those words.

Success, with all its attendant euphoria, counted for nothing when his wife Louise and his daughter Belinda were killed; this was a terrible blow, from which, I suspect, Hillary never fully recovered. In Louise he had found the partner he so greatly needed to restore a sense of proportion amid so much adulation, high expectations and media exploitation. She described their life of high jinks and 'razzmatazz' in a delightful book, *Keep Calm If You Can* (1964). She was his soulmate, who provided him with some of his most precious moments: 'For what can surpass a tear on your departure, joy on your return and a trusting hand in yours?' wrote Hillary before her death.

His marriage to June Mulgrew ensured a happy ending to the life of a remarkable man, great in his achievements and possessing other attributes of greatness, too: his honesty, his generous and warm-hearted nature and his readiness to acknowledge his errors. Ed Hillary, 'Action Man' in the eyes of millions, was very human.

John Hunt

Lieutenant-Colonel Charles Geoffrey Wylie OBE
1919 - 2007

Charles Wylie performed with calm efficiency the seemingly mind-boggling task of marshalling the hundreds of porters and two-score Sherpas without whom Edmund Hillary and Tenzing Norgay would not have reached the summit of Mount Everest.

A fluent Urdu and Nepali speaker, Charles, as transport officer, was almost literally responsible for keeping the show on the road, ensuring the movement of men and supplies up the mountain, soothing porters' grievances and keeping their spirits up through bad weather and hard toil. In this he worked closely with Tenzing whom he had helped persuade to join the expedition as *sirdar*, just as he was looking forward to a rest after two exhausting expeditions with the Swiss in 1952. The two had previously met in Kashmir in 1948. The partnership formed between Tenzing and Charles as they handled the Everest bundobust was probably as central to the expedition's success as the pairing of Tenzing and Hillary for the summit bid.

John Hunt, in his book *The Ascent of Everest*, introduced the members of his team with short biographical notes. Of Wylie he wrote as follows: 'Charles' services had already been obtained from the War Office early in September. He was working as organizing secretary during the interim period before my arrival and he was to continue in that capacity, as my invaluable assistant, throughout the preparatory period. Charles is a serving officer of the Brigade of Gurkhas; he had spent most of the war in a Japanese prison camp. That he had weathered this so well was doubtless due to his selflessness and sympathy for others, his faith and his cheerful disposition. We have to be grateful to him that the expedition's equipment was so meticulously prepared and documented, that every minor detail was thought of and provided for.'

At this stage there was, of course, no mention of the further immense contribution he was yet to make.

The success of our 1953 expedition was, as Hunt was always at pains to point out, the result of unstinting teamwork. Yet inevitably the names that are remembered are those of the New Zealander and the Sherpa who stood on top. Charles, however, was modesty personified, to the extent that his vital role in the enterprise is all-but unknown except to those familiar with mountaineering history. Imperturbable and unfailingly polite, he really did fit the image of the quintessential English gentleman.

Yet perhaps it wasn't his Englishness that made him such an ideal manager of 350 porters – 'coolies' in the imperial parlance – along with Sherpas, cooks, and mail runners, but three generations of association with Nepal and its Gurkhas. Indeed Charles's very gentleness might be said to be more of a Nepali than an English quality. His grandfather was the British Resident in Kathmandu in the 1890s and his father, commissioned into the 4th

Charles Wylie 1919-2007

Gurkha Rifles, became Chief Recruiting Officer for all the Gurkhas. Charles was born on Christmas Eve 1919 at Bakloh, regimental home of the 4th Gurkhas in the Punjab hills, and was fluent in the language of his garrison playmates by the age of six when he was 'sent home' to school – promptly forgetting Gurkhali, though it proved easy to relearn.

I had always been rather vague about Charles' mountaineering record; John Hunt had merely mentioned that he had good Alpine and home experience and had climbed in Garhwal shortly after the war. So I looked up his application for the Alpine Club, approved in December 1947, and was astonished to read that he had been proposed by no less than Geoffrey Winthrop Young and had already made four visits to the Alps, climbing over 25 respectable peaks while still a teenager. His course for Everest was probably as good as set at Marlborough College where his housemaster was Edwin Kempson who had been on expeditions to the mountain in 1935 and 1936. Kempson also influenced two other alumni on the 1953 expedition, John Hunt and Michael Ward who, with Charles, later held an impromptu Old Marlburian Dinner at over 20,000ft in Everest's Western Cwm!

Passing out fifth of 180 cadets from the Royal Military Academy, Sandhurst, in 1939 (the same year he was also the British Pentathlon Champion) Wylie was commissioned into the 1st Gurkha Rifles and returned to India one month before war was declared. There was time for just one more climb, in the Dhaula Dhar range of the Punjab lesser Himalaya.

The regiment was sent to Malaya where it was driven back by the invading Japanese. Charles was taken prisoner and made to work on the infamous Burma-Siam railway, enduring three-and-a-half years of cruelty, deprivation and disease. He spoke little of this experience, though in an interview recorded by The Gurkha Museum three years ago described in detail his capture, ensnared in a bungalow on a rubber estate, after days on the run through jungle without food. Arriving at the bungalow, Charles and the other soldiers flopped on the floor exhausted and slept, but were woken by being fired upon. They had virtually nothing for any fight-back, just Charles's pistol and ammunition that 'would have gone in about two seconds'. Rather than waste lives, they surrendered and a Japanese soldier entered the bungalow.

> 'He was astonished to see all of us there with our hands up. Anyhow he thought he had better kill somebody, I suppose, and he came straight for me (I was the little one). But he was a bit hesitant. I detected it. He was just about to shove a bayonet into my stomach and I very quietly put my hands down and pushed his long bayonet to one side and then I handed my pistol to him. And that was it. They were funny little chaps.'

Charles drew back from revealing his feelings about subsequent brutalities and when asked what kept him going through his years of captivity replied simply: 'Hope. Hope kept us going.'

In 1947 Charles rejoined his regiment in Peshawar, on the North West Frontier. When, on Independence, the 1st Gurkhas remained with the new Indian army he transferred to the 10th Gurkha Rifles (later Princess Mary's Own) going on to see more action during the Malayan Emergency and eventually retiring, in the 1970s, as a lieutenant-colonel.

At the Memorial Service for Charles, General Garry Johnson described a counter-terrorist action in Malaya carried out by a small group of Gurkha soldiers, the success of which, he said, was due to 'a mixture of careful planning, focused activity and the leadership by example of the company Commander, Charles Wylie. Charles had only just returned from leave in England. His reputation as a soldier and mountaineer had preceded him. As a very raw subaltern in the battalion, I had expected a whirlwind, but this man of action turned out to be the most courteous and modest person one could hope to meet. I was fascinated by the paradox which Charles presented, a mixture of action and modesty. But I soon realised that these two aspects of his character existed together in complete harmony, and were his constant hallmarks.'

Charles returned to mountaineering in 1947 with an attempt on the much-coveted Nilkanta (6596m) in the Garhwal Himalaya, with five camps above the snowline. That same year he climbed in the Bernina Alps and the Valais with Jimmy Roberts, a fellow Gurkha officer and one of the founders of trekking in Nepal. With a guide, he also traversed the Matterhorn by the fine combination of ascent by the Zmutt ridge – the true classic of the mountain – and descent via the Italian ridge. In a rare venture into print, Charles wrote an article for the *AJ* entitled 'A Long Day on Piz Palü', describing one of the climbs with Roberts and wondering if their zeal for big traverses that year stemmed from 'a sense of seasons wasted in war'.

When in September 1952, the Himalayan Committee appointed Charles organising secretary for the 1953 Everest expedition, it was assumed Eric Shipton would be the leader. But the committee being desperate for success conspired to replace the veteran mountaineer-explorer with a soldier of known drive. Both Wylie and Roberts were briefly in the frame; however, the leadership passed to John Hunt. As another Everester, the schoolmaster Wilfrid Noyce, observed: 'It would have been difficult to find two more gentle, gentlemanly military men to rule over us than Charles and John.'

On leaving the UK, Charles ceased to be organising secretary and took on the mantle of transport officer. He was also in demand as a translator, notably for the expedition's audience at the Thyangboche monastery, and was also, of course, a member of the climbing team. During the build up, Charles received news of the birth of a son, the telegram being forwarded over the Indian wireless link to Namche Bazar and on up the Khumbu valley by runner. The head of the wireless station had added a flourish of his own to these glad tidings: 'I am transported with great exultation to announce the birth of your son. I hope that you have cause for similar rejoicing at least once a year. Please pay the bearer one rupee baksheesh.'

Charles's great contribution high on the mountain was on the South Col 'carry', a crucial breakthrough after the expedition came close to being beaten by fresh snow, cold and fatigue on the Lhotse Face – the1220m barrier that has to be climbed to reach the col from the Western Cwm. Some 500lbs of equipment and stores were needed on the col if the team was to make any bids for the summit, but for 12 days the expedition was stalled on the face.

The golden moment for Hunt and those of us at advanced base camp down in the cwm came on 22 May when we saw 17 figures strung out on the traverse between camp VII at 7300m and the Geneva Spur at 7900m, just before the col. Hunt had rushed up Hillary and Tenzing to give fresh impetus, and in their footsteps on the face came Charles and his 14 Sherpas, each with a 30lb (14kg) load. One Sherpa faltered, but Charles took over his load, completing the ascent to the col without the assistance of bottled oxygen which had run out. They had carried a greater quantity of stores than ever before to a height the equivalent of Annapurna, then the highest summit yet climbed. As Charles and his men dumped their loads at the col the expedition's progress was back on course. It was the Sherpas' finest hour.

Three years after Everest, Charles was a member of an expedition led by his friend Jimmy Roberts to climb Machapuchare, the 6992m 'Fish Tail Peak' above the Nepali lake resort of Pokhara. Wilfrid Noyce and David Cox were halted by columns of blue ice 45m below the summit. At Roberts's suggestion, no permits have since been issued for Machapuchare and it has remained officially unclimbed.

Charles became British Military Attaché in Kathmandu from 1961 to 1964, a posting that enabled him to take up the offer of a present Tenzing had wanted to give him since their days on Everest – a Lhasa Apso puppy. Tenzing bred the dogs at his home in Darjeeling. After retirement Charles worked on behalf of charities as Secretary of the Gurkha Welfare Trust and the Britain-Nepal Medical Trust and was Chairman of the Britain-Nepal Society for five years. He was awarded the OBE in 1995.

In 1948 Charles married Diana Lucas and they had three sons and a daughter; she died in 1974. The 25th Anniversary of the Everest success was in 1978, and several members of the team celebrated by trekking with their wives from Darjeeling to the Everest area. Charles had just married Sheila Green so for him it was a second honeymoon. I took the accompanying photograph in the village of Godal, East Nepal, where we had a rest day, 2 November, which turned out to be the fifth day of the Dewali festival. The schoolmaster invited us to a *tikka* ceremony for his Governing Board. We were each garlanded with marigolds and marked with tikkas. As Charles' expression rather suggests, we all consumed rather more *rakshi* than was probably good for us.

Charles died in Guildford on 18 July 2007. In his final years he was working on his memoirs *Peaks and Troughs* which have yet to find a publisher. On Everest's 50th anniversary, he retold the story of the 'Great Carry' at a Royal Gala Celebration in London, entitled 'Endeavour on Everest', in the presence of the Queen. Answering questions put by Sir David Attenborough, the normally reticent Charles gave one of the most emotionally charged performances of the occasion, reliving an endeavour he had shared with the Sherpas, for whom he had a lifetime's respect and affection.

George Band
With assistance from Stephen Goodwin

Brigadier John Richard Gerard Finch OBE, 1911-2007

'Gerry' Finch, who died a venerable 96, led an adventurous, distinguished and varied life both as a soldier and mountaineer. Born in Southport on 26 February 1911 he was educated at Rugby but broke with the family's legal tradition by reading engineering rather than law at Caius College, Cambridge before entering the Royal Military Academy, Woolwich, from where he was commissioned into the Royal Engineers in 1929. Arriving in India in 1934, aged 23, to join the Bombay Sappers and Miners, he was first posted to 17 Field Company Royal Engineers at Quetta. This ancient, mountain-girt frontier fortress was then the capital of British Baluchistan and the main garrison town guarding the southern passes into Afghanistan. Although Quetta had been the Indian Army's Staff College since 1907, Finch's Sapper Company had neither wireless nor telephone so messages were still sent by runner. Their most effective form of transport was by mules imported from Argentina.

For the remainder of his peacetime service in India, Finch took every advantage of local leaves to explore little-known mountain areas in Tibet, Sikkim, Chitral and Kulu. In 1935 he visited Gyantse fort in Tibet where the British Trade Agent's Indian Army escort was mounted on shaggy Tibetan ponies. On returning to Quetta via Northern Sikkim, he found the place devastated by the disastrous earthquake that claimed more than 20,000 lives. In 1937 he was posted to Chitral, the most spectacular and romantic of all North West Frontier provinces, renowned for its polo-playing tribesmen, its hundred peaks exceeding 6000m and Tirich Mir, at 7688m the monarch of the Hindu Kush. Then, as now, Chitral was the buffer zone that guarded the northern passes through the Hindu Kush and Pamirs into the Indian sub-continent.

In 1938 with war looming, Finch returned to England for two years' training before being posted back to Bombay in September 1940 to command the Depot Battalion of the 45 Army Troops Company. In 1941 he took over the newly raised 91 Field Company RE and in March 1942 joined the 23 Indian Division at Ranchi in Bihar Province to prepare for Burma operations. Initially, there were no weapons available for his company and no transport save one air-compressor truck. Three months later they moved on to Assam after taking 48 hours to cross the flood-swollen Brahmaputra, passing en route streams of refugees, only to find Imphal in chaos with the pathetic remnants of a demoralised Burmese and Chinese Army.

For the next 14 months Finch served under Lt Col J H Williams, the famous 'Elephant Bill', whose Sappers and elephants, under persistent Japanese harassment, built the infrastructure, roads and bridges that provided a launch pad for Slim's Burma campaign. In July 1943 he was recalled to the Quetta Staff College and in March 1944 transferred to the Italian theatre, taking command of 21 Field Company during the final stages of 4th Indian Division's engagement at Monte Cassino. Zigzagging across Italy in pursuit of the retreating Wehrmacht, he met John Hunt in the Maiella mountains and thus began a lasting friendship that was cemented later that year in Greece when Finch was appointed Chief Royal Engineer 4th British Division in Athens. In Cyprus he was largely responsible for rebuilding Limassol in the face of EOKA terrorism. Returning to England after the war, his appointments alternated between the War Office, Nigeria, Egypt, Cyprus and the USA. He commanded 35 Field Engineer Regiment both in the Canal Zone and in Cyprus where he had the dual responsibility of rebuilding the RAF base, combating ENOSIS and dealing with civil unrest.

Tall and powerfully built, Gerry Finch's mountaineering enthusiasms were fostered at Cambridge. He was already a powerful and competent rock climber by the time he reached Quetta and was soon co-opted to lead senior officers on climbs on the nearby Takatu mountain (c3350m). While on local leave in Sikkim in 1935, he investigated an approach to Lacksi (c6400m) from the north-east. The following year he returned for a serious attempt which he had to abort just short of the summit due, in his own modest words, to 'inexperience'. On this same expedition he narrowly failed to climb another Sikkimese peak, Lama Anden, owing to foul weather.

Three years later, emboldened by experience in the Alps during home leaves, he conceived the altogether more ambitious aim of reconnoitring a route up Tirich Mir (7,688m) which had first been investigated by Charles Bruce when establishing Chitral as a forward military base with Francis Younghusband in 1893. Finch's modest recce party, consisting of himself and two Chitrali porters, made lodgement on the mountain's south ridge before going on to explore the South and North Barun glaciers. They then crossed the Pharsan An to make a bold attempt on Buni Zom (6551m) only to be frustrated by illness. Their subsequent recce of Pushari (c5800m) was cut short by an accident. Finch's last Himalayan venture was to Kulu in 1941 with his wife Tricia whom he had married in 1939.

During his post-war tour in Cyprus, Gerry teamed up with his Regimental Chaplain Fred Jenkins (subsequently the AC's unofficial lifelong chaplain) to share many mountain adventures together. Finch was already an active member of the Climbers Club and climbed frequently in North Wales with his AC seconder Lt Col Gavin. Gerry's election to the Alpine Club in 1953 was warmly supported by John Hunt and it was their friendship that led to Finch's close involvement with the establishment of the Duke of Edinburgh's Award scheme and the Army Mountaineering Association. In the immediate post-war years, Gerry regularly attended AC meets – as often as not with his family giving moral support from base camp – until his knees and hips lost their youthful pliancy and he turned to sailing.

Gerry's lifelong enthusiasm for skiing was sparked in India. At Quetta he had met a fellow skiing and mountaineering spirit in Eric Gueterbock, a subsequent President of the Alpine Ski Club and first Chairman of the National Ski Federation of Great Britain, who became his AC proposer.

During home leaves in 1937 and 1939, Gerry made ski ascents of the Mönch, Fiescherhorn, Grünhorn, Mont Blanc de Seilon, Pigne d'Arolla and Monte Rosa and in 1938 undertook a pioneer ski ascent to the head of the Pushkari glacier in Chitral. He also played a supporting role to Alan Blackshaw's first British Alpine Ski Traverse in 1971 and became the ASC President in 1982.

Finch was a modest, perceptive man of outstanding courage, initiative and determination. Writing about his time in the Canal Zone, a comrade in arms Maj Gen Fursdon, subsequently the *Daily Telegraph's* military correspondent, described Finch as a 'towering figure' whose commanding presence and massive clasped hands placed firmly on an otherwise empty desk at his Commanding Officer's Orders left miscreant soldiers in no doubt about the firmness but fairness of his judgements. He conducted ASC committee meetings with that same quiet authority and a wry humour. Having served his country with distinction and outlived almost all contemporaries, Gerry's memory will be cherished by all those who knew him and particularly by his children and numerous grandchildren. In compiling this obituary I am indebted to his son Sir Robert Finch, latterly Lord Mayor of London.

J G R Harding

Wing Commander Henry David (Harry) Archer DFC
1922-2007

Harry Archer was an enthusiastic member of the Alpine Club to which he was elected in 1973 and was Honorary Secretary 1978-1982. He was also a member of the ABMSAC (1967) and was its Vice President in 1984, President from 1985 to 1987, and at his death an Honorary Member. In addition he was a member of the SAC (Diablarets 1952).

The son of Canon George Archer, who served as a Military Chaplain throughout the First World War, Harry had an early introduction to the Alps when his parents took the family on skiing and climbing holidays, mostly to Zermatt. This instilled in Harry a great love of the mountains that remained with him for the rest of his life.

Educated at Winton House Preparatory School and St Edwards, Oxford, he was too young to enlist at the outbreak of the Second World War so he went to work as a clerk at the Bank of England. He was living in a flat in Dolphin Square when the property was severely damaged by a bomb but Harry, in bed at the time, managed to escape uninjured together with most of his possessions. In June 1941 he volunteered as a pilot in the RAF, was accepted and sent to the USA for his training. On completion of his Advanced Training he was retained as a Flying Instructor – an early indication of his exceptional flying skills. After accumulating some 1000 instructional flying hours he returned to UK in the summer of 1943 and was posted to a Lancaster squadron.

Over the next 14 months Harry flew virtually non-stop on day and night bombing raids, surviving many near-misses but always managing to get his damaged aircraft safely back to base. During this period 450 of his Squadron's aircrew were killed. On completion of this tour Harry was awarded the Distinguished Flying Cross. He was then posted to the Far East with a new crew to fly Liberators out of India and the Cocos Islands and more drama was to come. In August 1945, when Harry was briefed to attack and destroy Japanese aircraft on an airfield on the west coast of Sumatra, his aircraft was hit by cannon fire, setting the starboard outer engine on fire, damaging the pilot's instruments and severely wounding the Navigator. Doubting the Liberator's ability to survive a ditching (it had a bad reputation in this respect), Harry decided to try to fly back to the Cocos Islands some 600 miles away. Now at only 300ft and in the dark, all moveable equipment was jettisoned and with a reducing fuel load the aircraft was able to climb to 2000ft. Four hours later Harry made a safe landing on the Cocos runway. Happily the Navigator subsequently made a full recovery.

After the war, Harry was posted to Transport Command where he took part in the Berlin Airlift and in 1956 greatly enjoyed flying Fitzroy Maclean (*Eastern Approaches*), then a junior minister at the War Office, to Kathmandu where he enjoyed his first views of the Himalaya. Prior to retirement from the RAF in 1977 Harry filled a number of staff appointments at Command Headquarters and the Ministry of Defence. He then went into the engineering manufacturing industry until finally retiring in 1997 at the age of 75.

In 1957 Harry married Valda Mildred Smart a former WRAF Officer and they were blessed with four children, two boy and two girls. Tragically, Valda was taken seriously ill around the time Harry retired from the RAF and she died in 1978. This left Harry in sole charge of four teenage children in addition to a full-time job; however, all difficulties were overcome by the family pulling together as a team.

I first climbed with Harry in 1961 when we were both stationed at RAF Eastleigh in Kenya. Together we climbed numerous routes on Mount Kenya, Kilimanjaro and Mawenzi and he accompanied me, providing wise advice, on the recce that led to Tommy Thompson and I achieving the first ascent of the east face of Mawenzi in 1964 (see *AJ 2007*). We also enjoyed two wonderful expeditions to the Ruwenzori, a range that fascinated Harry, and were able to climb all the peaks and manage a couple of first ascents. On return from overseas we climbed together in the UK, the Alps and the Himalaya. He was an adventurous mountaineer but always prudent and safe and I shall forever remember his favourite dictum which probably saved my skin on more than one occasion when I had wanted to press on in adverse conditions: 'John, the mountain will still be here in the morning – let's make sure we are!'

Harry Archer 1922-2007

Harry's climbing activities were severely curtailed as a result of an horrific accident in 1998 when he was hit by a speeding car while crossing the road on his way to church one Sunday morning. He underwent a series of operations during a lengthy stay in hospital. However, Harry still enjoyed a number of excursions with his old friend George Watkins. They had made a trip to New Zealand prior to the accident and undertook a series of treks in the Mount Cook and Mount Aspiring range and climbed Mount French. During this visit they went to the New Zealand Pilots' Association Museum where Harry met an ex-Wing Commander who had also flown out of the Cocos Islands, thus providing an excellent opportunity for exchanging a few reminiscences and more than a few beers. After the accident Harry and George confined their trips closer to home visiting the Orkney Islands, the Hebrides and a mad quad-biking holiday at Aviemore.

Having touched and enriched the lives of so many, Harry died peacefully on 11 April 2007 after a long illness borne with characteristic fortitude. He is survived by his children John, Margaret, Charlotte and Matthew and seven grandchildren.

John Edwards

Phyllida Marianne Methuen Roberts 1922-2007

Phyllida Thornton was born in 1922, in Nairobi; she started her travels early, the family moving to the South of France. The development of juvenile rheumatoid arthritis led to more travels, as her determined mother took Phyllida around Europe and Egypt looking for a cure. One outcome of this was that she became trilingual, including German with a Viennese accent, and she learnt to ski.

Finally settling in England, Phyllida went to Bedales School and then studied medicine at University College, London, qualifying MB BS in 1946. Her subsequent hospital appointments included working in Berne for Professor Tobler, who had treated her for arthritis as a child.

In 1948 Phyllida saw a need for doctors in China and she went to Nanjing with the Friends' Ambulance Service. Fortunately the expected bloodshed with the establishment of the Communist Republic did not happen and Phyllida enjoyed treating the locals, particularly the children, about which she had many delightful stories. Phyllida interrupted her return from China in 1950 with a visit to New Zealand, including a spell in general practice in Wellington and a visit to the New Zealand Alps.

Back in Europe she went to a climbing school in the Dauphiné and there met her husband-to-be, Paul; climbing and skiing together established them as a good team and they married in 1952.

Developing a career in laboratory medicine at University College Hospital and then at the Royal Free Hospital, Phyllida's final move was her appointment as Consultant Haematologist at St. Albans City Hospital at an exciting time when haematologists were taking over the clinical care of patients with blood diseases. Never one to waste time, early on in her career Phyllida gained an MD and took the D. Path and DTM & H, somehow managing to produce a daughter and two sons over the same period.

Phyllida loved music, particularly Beethoven and Sibelius, and was a frequent visitor to the Royal Festival Hall. She was a faithful attender at the Crown Court Church of Scotland in Covent Garden. Moving out of London she joined the Society of Friends and was for many years a member of Jordan's meeting.

Phyllida was a very early, probably a founder member of the London Graduate Mountaineering Club; she was an active member of the Ladies Alpine Club until its amalgamation with the Alpine Club in 1975 and was probably not entirely happy to see the Ladies lose their independence.

Until she retired in 1983, mountain holidays had to be squeezed into a busy life, but most years included both climbing and skiing in the Alps, with hectic sorties to the British hills, particularly north Wales. Climbing on the Dorset cliffs was particularly popular with the Ladies Alpine Club, referred to by a member as 'heavenly rock dear'. Phyllida loved long walks over the hills, scrambling and climbing. Joints damaged by juvenile rheumatoid arthritis made rock climbing a particular challenge and she frequently had to invent her own ways of getting up a move, but she liked challenges. One of the original 'hippies', Phyllida skied for many years on two artificial hips, although she noticed that her balance was 'not quite so good' and she gave up rock climbing.

A fearless skier, Phyllida enjoyed both downhill skiing and touring; tours included the classics, Ötztal, Ortler, Stubai and Silvretta, with one tour with a dog-sledge in Norway. A notable feat in May 1953 was to climb in one week five 4000m peaks: the Alphubel, Strahlhorn, Rimpfischhorn, Allalinhorn and Breithorn, mostly on skis, with crampons to the summits.

In addition to ski tours, Phyllida climbed many of the Valais mountains in the summer, including the Weisshorn, Matterhorn, Monte Rosa, Mont Collon, Douves Blanches, Aiguille Rouge and many others. She had a particular association with the Zinal Rothorn, traversing it from Zinal on her honeymoon, climbing it from Zermatt 10 years later and being robbed of a third ascent from Zermatt 20 years later by bad weather. One of her sons claims, probably correctly, to have climbed the Matterhorn in-utero.

Phyllida climbed in many other areas. In 1951 she did many climbs based on Pralognan, including a traverse of the Grande Casse. She was in Chamonix in 1967 and 1968, climbs including the Aiguille du Géant and Rochefort Arête, Requin, Grépon and the Moine. She loved the sunshine and warm rock of the Dolomites, making four visits in the 1970s, doing many climbs unguided and some substantial routes with a guide. A novelty of these trips was the family rope, including the three children, along the *via ferrata*.

Phyllida Roberts on Cima Grande.

In the early 1970s Phyllida had a particularly successful visit to the southern alps, routes including the Punta Razica, the east ridge of Casnile and the north ridge of the Badile.

Phyllida just loved to be in the mountains and did not have to be doing something difficult. In 1963 and 1965 she was camping in the Encantados region of the Pyrenees; in 1964 and 1966 she was walking and scrambling in the Corsican mountains, and in 1979 she did the GR20 traverse in Corsica, repeating this in 1985. In 1974 Phyllida trekked in Nepal with Bill Murray, when they met one other trekking party in three weeks. In 1977 she was in the Kulu Himalaya. A holiday in Peru in 1980 included the Inca Trail, with the party carrying their own gear and having the route to themselves, and an exploration of the Cordillera Carabaya. Then followed a trek in Lahoul, in 1982, to the Myar Nula and Gumba Nula. In 1984, aged 62 and with a replaced hip, Phyllida climbed Lenana in the Mount Kenya group, and then Kilimanjaro. Back in Nepal in 1985 she went to the Everest base camp and in 1987 she followed the GR route in the Alpes Maritime. In 1988 Phyllida did many treks in New Zealand, including a crossing of the Copeland Pass. In California in 1989 she was trekking in the Sierra Nevada, ending up on Mount Whitney.

Sadly Phyllida's last years were blighted by illness. An emergency heart valve replacement was life-saving, but after this she never regained her old self. Phyllida died peacefully on New Years Eve 2007. She had lived life abundantly.

Paul Roberts

Paula Biner 1916-2007

Paula Biner was a friend and hostess in Zermatt to generations of British climbers. She ran the Hotel Bahnhof, a home-from-home for so many of us, while Bernard, her much older brother, supervised and sat outside, welcoming and freely giving advice. Bernard, who had been chief guide for a number of years (obituary *AJ* 1965) had a soft spot for the British, which Paula certainly seemed to share. On returning from a climb, one could always rely on having a bed, at least in a *dortoir*, even if it meant that some of the guests who had been hanging around in Zermatt without actually climbing anything were relegated to what was called 'the chicken house'. And some of us were at times privileged to occupy a bed in her office or even accommodated in her chalet.

The Bahnhof, which she and her brother opened in 1951, was very suitable for the post-war British, short of foreign currency – and indeed often short of any currency. There was a large communal kitchen/dining room in the basement, with cookers, on which a variety of concoctions were produced from whatever the climbers had brought from home or could afford to buy in Zermatt. At night, the question was whether any of one's fellow guests were late partiers or snorers, similar peril as in the SAC huts which in those days did not have rooms for singles or doubles. Over the years, the facilities were greatly improved, and there were proper bedrooms, but there is still a *dortoir* and the communal kitchen.

After Bernard's death, Paula carried on the welcoming tradition, continuing to run the Bahnhof until eventually handing over to her niece, Kathy Lauber. She was well informed about climbs from Zermatt, somehow kept in touch with what her guests were doing, but did not presume to give advice, which she properly thought was for the guides to provide. I remember her concern when Sally and I and Chuck Loucks returned from the Younggrat on the Breithorn having been caught in a storm when we were halfway up. 'Of course you didn't climb it,' she said, and was horrified to hear that we had finished it in the storm.

She was Zermatt born and bred. Her father was the mountain guide of the Seiler hotels and the family held firmly to traditional Swiss values. She was, for example, reluctant to allow an unmarried couple to share a room. She was for 70 years a member of the church choir. She looked after her ageing parents for a number of years. Her nephew said, in a brief obituary at her funeral, that she continued to organise a family Christmas party every Christmas Eve, 'with everybody celebrating and singing'. In her youth, she skied and took part in ski races, long before there were such things as chair lifts and cable cars. Her brother Bernard took her up the Matterhorn and other peaks. She said she really enjoyed the Matterhorn: 'It was one of those beautiful September days.' They had the mountain to themselves and could move at their own pace.

Paula Biner
1916-2007

It was great to see Paula at the AC 150th birthday celebrations last year, carrying a stick and limping a bit after a bad fall while out walking above Zermatt, but looking far younger than her 91 years. She came to the service in the English church and to the celebrations organised by the commune of Zermatt. Many of her AC friends enjoyed visiting her in the care home where she had been since her accident. Zermatt will not be the same without her.

Mike Westmacott
(*with assistance from Mike Esten*)

Michael Wilhelm Jolles 1910-2005

Micha Jolles died in November 2005 at the age of 95. He read law at the University of Amsterdam. At the end of his professional career he was a director at the Amsterdam-based Dutch Reinsurance Group. Micha had a keen interest in history, was very well read and published frequently on historical topics. In addition he was interested in music and played the flute.

For 30 years Micha was editor of the journal of the Dutch Alpine Club. It is fascinating to read those old issues, in which he published many articles striking for their style and language. In the quiet of his study I found 20 heavy notebooks in which he had described all his climbs over a period of more than 50 years. Many were serious undertakings, sometimes guided, very often not. Too many to mention, but let me make one exception: in his notebook for 1936 he describes his climb of the Peuterey ridge with his brother and guided by a Rey and a Grivel. In a letter in February 1991,

Micha Jolles 1910-2005

written in response to an article I wrote about a stupid bivouac in a wet forest in the Kaisergebirge, Micha wrote me that something similar had almost happened to him during a descent from the Col Torino. He describes that descent in the dark and ends with: 'Shortly before midnight we knocked on the door of a hotel in Entrèves, slept well and after a day's rest we returned to Chamonix over Peuterey.' In those modest words, as if describing a casual stroll, is hidden what has been called one of the major achievements of Dutch climbing between the wars.

Let me mention also that Easter weekend in Belgium back in 1934 when he visited Freyr and thus became the first of so many, many Dutchmen who have spent their weekends climbing there. In 1994 we celebrated its 60th anniversary; all Presidents past and present of the Dutch Alpine Club with Micha and his wife Lotte on a boat trip on the Meuse along the Freyr crags, a sunny and warm picnic on the grounds of the Château de Freyr and a dinner in Falmignoul.

A few days later Micha wrote me a note: 'No long stories after our weekend in Falmignoul. Except for: how warm it was in both meanings of the word.' Although much younger, we regarded him as one of us. That was easy enough, because Micha always kept his sparkle and flair even in old age. With his passing Dutch climbing lost one of its grand old men.

Robbert Leopold

Ken Vickers 1941 - 2007

To us Leicester climbers, Ken was a Leicester man through and through, an encyclopædia of climbing and mountains, the creator of an epic out of any event, the anarchic innovator and storyteller, the master of memorable moments – and always known as 'the trespasser'. Ken's wider reputation rests on his immense influence on the availability and quality of British climbing guides.

Born 17 August 1941 as a twin to Sandra and younger brother of John, Ken Vickers established his rebellious style early on by setting fire to Braunstone Hall Primary School when the head of a match broke off and fell between the floorboards. In his early teens, he became a member of the Leicester Museum Club and developed an interest in fossils. This led to prospecting caves at Matlock and elsewhere in the Peak District and then on to rock climbing.

With a group of friends, mainly from the British United Shoe Company, who later became the Leicester Association of Mountaineers, Ken explored the Leicestershire outcrops and quarries, creating many classic routes such as *The Sorceress* (A3) on Forest Rock, *Sailaway* in the Brand and *Virago* at Craig Buddon. He wrote the first two Leicestershire guidebooks – the 'Red Guide' in 1966 and the 'Yellow Guide' in May 1973, as well as venturing further afield.

Ken left Ellesmere Secondary School at 15 to join Cundy's of Leicester, painters and decorators. On completion of his apprenticeship, his talent for design and style led to a job with Leicester City Architects whilst he studied for a diploma in interior design.

In 1967 Ken was a member of the Midlands Hindu Kush Expedition with Doug Scott but otherwise he restricted his climbing to the British Isles and the Alps. He became an AC member that same year. His immense knowledge of the western Alps was stimulated by three seasons instructing for the Mountaineering Association, based in Arolla.

Ken met his wife June in 1970 at the housewarming of their mutual friends Dave and Di Draper at Whitehall in Derbyshire and they married the following year. He started his first business – a design consultancy EXPO-TGV – with four friends. In his spare time Ken was elected to the publications committees of both the BMC and the Climbers Club. When he was asked to represent climbers on the Sports Council he used his influence to get the council to support publication of the BMC guidebooks, the first one of which, the Staffordshire Gritstone guide, was designed by EXPO-TGV in 1973.

When EXPO-TGV folded in 1973, Ken and June started a company, from the front room of their house in Knighton Church Road, dedicated to distributing and publishing guidebooks. He named his business Cordee – which had been the name of the journal of the Leicester Association of Mountaineers.

Ken was the last LAM member to defect to the Bowline Climbing Club where he exerted a strong influence over its independent spirit. He will be remembered by many fell runners as the creator of the Charnwood Hills Race, for more than 20 years a highlight of the Fell Running Association calendar. With the Bowline his reputation as the arch trespasser, whether climbing, running or swimming in forbidden waters, lives on.

Very occasionally the trespasser was caught: driving June's VW on a visit to the Cairngorms, Ken and a few friends found the gates at the end of the Linn of Dee locked. On inspection of the gatepost they found it could be lifted out and replaced once the VW had driven through. After climbing on Ben a Bhuird for the weekend, they returned to the car to find a note on it from Mar Lodge Estates. Not daring to risk the wrath of June, Ken meekly turned up at the Braemar police station and asked if there was anything he could do to make amends. The policeman, realising he was on to a winner, said £5 should sort it out. Imagine the policeman's astonishment as Ken handed over £5 – and asked for a receipt. This receipt resides in the Bowline Bullshit Book.

Ken was a key influence in the development of British climbing. He provided the volunteer authors with the means by which their research became a first point of reference for the burgeoning ranks of British climbers. From the late 1960s it was commonplace to search out routes from the guidebook either at home, in the café or in the car on the way to the crag.

Ken's great contribution came with his involvement from the mid 1970s with the publication and distribution of Climbers Club guidebooks. Working closely with Robert Moulton and others he formed a dynamic and wise central figure that ensured the CC's guidebooks were published smoothly and efficiently. This combined marketing, design and editing expertise, for club guidebooks was soon emulated (in various bespoke forms) for the BMC, FRCC, the SMC and the YMC. In addition, Cordee assisted other groups to publish more localized guidebooks during this time. It provided a reliability that enabled the information of the climbing world to be efficiently circulated from that time right up to his death where previously it had been erratic and unpredictable. Ken can take the lion's share of the credit for this. 'The Trespasser' may have exhibited strong anti-authoritarian tendencies but he himself became an authority, through the guides, on which British climbing could depend.

Two Kens, Vickers and Wilson, both trained in architecture, linked up in 1978 to establish Diadem Books Ltd. Following the groundbreaking new format established by *Hard Rock* and *Classic Rock*, edited by Ken Wilson and published by Granada, Diadem published a stream of books including *Classic Walks*, *Big Walks* and *Cold Climbs*, plus anthologies and biographies by British climbers. Go into the house of any climber in the country and you will see several of these masterpieces on the bookshelf. The pair sold the business to Hodder and Stoughton. Ken sold Cordee in 2002 and fully retired three years later. He died in May 2007.

Ken Vickers on *Fionn Buttress* (VS),
Carnmore in 2001. (*Miles Hillmann*)

Ken Vickers had a massive impact upon the lives of so many British climbers, many of whom he did not personally meet, and provided much wisdom, warmth and entertainment to us Leicester friends.

Miles Hillmann

Richard Eastwood 1951-2007

Richard (Rick) was a man of many talents, accomplished yet supremely modest about his achievements. Essentially a very private person, his precise and thoughtful contributions will be missed by many. Never one to share his personal feelings, Rick was an agreeable companion quietly ploughing his own furrow. One sensed inner tensions but these rarely surfaced.

Born to a family with a strong Peak-based hill-walking tradition, Rick grew up in North London prior to reading architecture at Manchester where for seven years he was an active member of the university climbing club. With a strong aptitude for languages, he became an unofficial translator of technical documents for the fledgling BMC. Fluent in French, in later life he added German, Spanish, Italian, Arabic and Mandarin to his repertoire.

1977 saw Rick lead a university expedition to the Zebak region of the Hindu Kush. The team, with the exception of Rick who was delayed by his professional examinations, travelled overland by truck via Turkey and the Salang Pass, establishing an advanced base camp in the Galat valley south of Eshkashem and the Oxus. This was an era when an expedition's essential skill set always included motor mechanics, given equal prominence to climbing experience in grant applications. By any standards the expedition was successful, with a range of new routes on peaks from base camp and an advanced base north of the Qualat head wall. Rick wrote with astonishment of their encounter with a ridge of penitentes high on Kalisa Sangi that delayed progress on their ascent. We now know that these strange ice spikes are rarely found outside the Andes. The team climbed seven peaks between 5200m and 5900m including Harame Safed and Sare Kalan. The expedition report to their sponsors and patrons, edited by Rick, was a model of content and balance. Rick later recalled a chance meeting with Stephen Venables in Afghanistan, an acquaintanceship renewed 30 years later in the Clubhouse.

Rick's architectural talents were in demand and he acquired successive placements with Hugh Casson and Basil Spence prior to a nine-year appointment with the Architects Partnership that included projects in the Middle and Far East. He enrolled in the Insead MBA programme before accepting an architectural appointment with a European-wide brief, basing himself near Cannes.

Balancing the spiritual with the secular was a consistent life theme and Rick became an active Baptist, closely involving himself with the English Church in Cannes. The Church was also an important outlet for his musical talents. Rick was an accomplished pianist and keyboard player ranging across classical and modern ecclesiastical swing styles, often playing keyboard for Church bands. I recall a campsite discussion with an evidently less musically talented climber on the finger positions for a complex series of harmonious chord transitions through various major and minor keys.

Rick Eastwood on *Leviathan* (VS 4c ***)
at the Dewerstone, Devon, 2006. (*Jason Parker*)

Not daunted by the absence of a keyboard, Rick drew one on a camp table to demonstrate the optimum finger sequence. He recounted with amusement arriving at a BBC concert only to find that the soloist's Clavinova had developed a fault. Realising that the offending instrument was identical to his own, less than two miles distant, he led a team of BBC technicians to his flat. After rapid dismantling, transport and reassembly the concert started on time.

While based in France, Rick continued his climbing, mainly concentrating on rock climbs; however, his location also gave reasonable access to ski slopes in winter. He was a natural skier with grace and flair. It was only after his death that I discovered Rick had also been an expert dinghy sailor. Returning to London in 1997, Rick joined a consultancy where he led a succession of large and complex property projects. Deciding to rekindle his climbing, he became an active member of SaKMC and latterly the Alpine Club, attending Alpine and UK meets. Setting ambitious goals on standards, in the space of a year and with regular training, Rick's climbing standard rose, his forte being steep, fingery walls. Naturally cautious, he was the reluctant star in a gritstone spectacular when his leader, many kilograms heavier, fell from a high position. In the absence of a ground anchor and with an intermediate runner acting as a pulley, Rick's vertical takeoff and the inevitable mid-air head to toe collision was the stuff of legend.

Always in demand from friends for advice, Rick's common sense, business and property expertise were quickly recognised and he was elected to the Alpine Club committee. His final contribution was to organise the Zermatt church service for the Club's 150th anniversary, a perfectly structured event that gave him and the congregation great pleasure. It was just weeks later, on an Alpine Club Meet, that he tragically died when in-situ belays failed while descending the Grand Capucin after an ascent of the Swiss Route. He is survived by his father, Bernard.

Bill Thurston

Denise Escande 1914-2007

Denise Escande... However impressive her list of routes it is as nothing compared to the warmth of her friendship and the kindness of her welcome. How many, French and foreigners alike, have not benefited from her little chalet 'La Tirelire' on the edge of the forest at Les Moussoux in Chamonix? True, it was not big, but all those in need were welcomed, even if only to pitch a tent when indoors was full. And she looked after all alike, concerned by everyone's needs and problems. None of those whom she received will ever forget her. No need for her to be there. Everyone knew if she was away in the mountains that the key was left on the beam above the door for them

Denise nearly always climbed as a second, but that was as she wanted it; she was 37 when she first started climbing. Once, when I hardly knew her, I asked a strong mountaineer: 'Why do you climb with Denise? She is old enough to be your mother and never leads?' 'First of all,' he replied, 'she is an excellent second, but in addition she has excellent qualities, she is good humoured and looks after everything …'

So which from her long list of routes should be singled out? The south face of the Fou, the Swiss and Bonatti routes on the Capucin, the west face and the American on the Dru, the Gervasutti Pillar, the south face of the Guglierminia, the north face of the Badile, the Old Brenva, many Dolomite routes including a remarkable visit in 1977 which included the Brandler Hasse and Cassin routes on the Lavaredo and the Constantini on the Pilastro di Rozes in a four-day push, followed by the Philip Flamm; and her string of routes in the Verdon and particularly in the Vercors where she did many of the hardest is simply too long to even try and make a selection. Denise was an Alpine encyclopædia in her own right, without even starting to consider what she also did in Morocco, Mali, Nepal or the fact that she took part in a new four-month north to south crossing of the Sahara.

Yes, an exceptional list of routes, but when you have known Denise Escande, what sticks in the memory above all is her hospitality, her vitality and her smile.

Anne Sauvy

Alpine Club Notes

CELEBRATING SIR EDMUND

On 29 February this year, the ashes of Sir Edmund Hillary were scattered by his widow Lady (June) Hillary and children Peter and Sarah from aboard the sailing vessel *Spirit of New Zealand* in the Hauraki Gulf, near Auckland, Hillary's home for much of his life.

Sir Edmund died in Auckland on 11 January, aged 88 (*obituary, p392*). He was accorded a state funeral – an unprecedented honour for a private citizen – on 22 January and on 2 April the Queen hosted a special memorial service for him at St George's Chapel, Windsor Castle.

In his book *View From the Summit,* Sir Edmund wrote that he did not want his final resting place to be in some crevasse on a mountain, observing that he had 'been down too many of them for that to have much appeal'. Instead he wanted his ashes to be 'spread on the beautiful waters of Auckland's Hauraki Gulf to be washed gently ashore maybe on the many pleasant beaches near the place where I was born. Then the full circle of my life will be complete.'

The New Zealand government generously invited the surviving Everest 1953 climbers and their wives as official guests for the state funeral; the AC thereby being well represented by George Band and Alf Gregory, George Lowe and Mike Westmacott. Also invited was Jan Morris, who as James Morris, correspondent for *The Times*, made the scoop of a lifetime on cue for the Coronation of Queen Elizabeth II.

A wave of emotion swept over the people of New Zealand. Led by their Prime Minister, Helen Clark, they mourned their greatest Kiwi as he lay in state in Holy Trinity Cathedral, Auckland, Everest ice-axe and Maori ceremonial staff on top of the casket, and a selection of his medals and decorations on velvet cushions at his feet. The service was followed by a special reception hosted by the Governor General, Anand Satyanand, who represented the Queen, not only officially but also personally at the funeral. This was followed by a more informal 'Mountaineers' Farewell' organised by the New Zealand Alpine Club at which a dozen of his friends recalled facets of Sir Edmund's varied life.

The Service of Thanksgiving at St George's Chapel, attended by the Queen and Princess Royal and led by the Dean of Windsor, saw the laying up of Sir Edmund's banner as a Knight of the Garter. As Helen Clark, who had flown especially to Britain, reminded the congregation, when Sir Edmund was appointed to the Order in 1995 it was the first time the honour had been conferred on a person resident outside the UK.

On appointment, every knight is required to display a banner of his arms in the Chapel, together with a helmet, crest and sword and an enamelled stallplate. These 'achievements' are taken down on the knight's death and the insignia are returned to the Sovereign, with the stallplates remaining as a memorial.

Projected against the refined bulwark of St George's, Sir Edmund's more down-to-earth style shone out via music and rituals drawn from his native land. Sarah, his daughter, read Allen Curnow's elegiac poem *You Will Know When You Get There*. The young baritone Jonathan Lemalu sang Mendelssohn's aria *Lord God of Abraham*.

As the great and the good, sprinkled with the faces of friends from the high Himalaya, belted out *Praise My Soul the King of Heaven*, Sir Edmund's banner was paraded through the chapel. Featuring Tibetan prayer wheels against a blue background and a Kiwi bird brandishing an ice-axe, the knights escorting it paused at the back of the chapel while Mereana Hond, a human rights lawyer and TV journalist, performed the karanga welcome call, a ceremony traditionally performed by Maori women in part to acknowledge ancestral spirits. It is an invitation to reflect on the lives of those who have passed on. Hond's voice cracked with emotion as the Queen looked on.

Again the surviving 1953 Everesters were in attendance, including Sir Edmund's fellow New Zealander, George Lowe, who shared in his charitable work in Nepal. Peter Hillary said his father was most proud, over his long life, of the work he had done with the Sherpas of Nepal, building schools and hospitals, and earning the respect of the people who had worked alongside him in the Himalaya. Sir Edmund, his son said, was revered among the people he loved best. 'And it doesn't get any better than that.'

Norbu Tenzing Norgay, the eldest son of Hillary's Everest partner, Tenzing, flew in from California for the service; Alexandra Shackleton, granddaughter of Ernest Shackleton, Hillary's great hero, joined survivors of the 1958 Trans-Antarctic Expedition, along with Sir Vivian Fuchs's son, Peter. Non-mountaineering celebrities included Sir David Attenborough, and the actor Sir Ian McKellen, who arrived wearing what looked like, appropriately enough, glacier glasses. The New Zealand rugby star Sean Fitzpatrick was also there, along with Lord Falconer, who represented the British government at the state funeral in New Zealand.

In a neat reminder of Sir Edmund's no-nonsense approach, Peter Hillary recalled the moment in 1990 when he himself reached the summit of Everest for the first time and used a new-fangled satellite phone to call his father. As pleased as the old man must have been to hear his son's voice from the roof of the world, his advice was typically to the point: 'You're not done until you're down.'

Ed Douglas, George Band and Stephen Goodwin

Hillary Lying in State 21.1.08, viewed by family members.
Peter Hillary on the right. (*George Band*)

ALPINE CLUB LIBRARY ANNUAL REPORT 2007

As we come to the end of our 150th year, this report must open with our
major achievements. It must also give a testament to the effort and hard
work provided by the members of the Alpine Club Library team that made
these happen.

Firstly, the Club published two books to coincide with the 150th year
celebrations. These are *Summit: 150 years of the Alpine Club* by George Band
and *Artists of the Alpine Club* by Peter Mallalieu; George's book was published
late in 2006 and many copies were sold in this year. Peter's book was
launched early this year and has done very well. Both books highlighted
the collections of the Club and both needed the expertise and equipment of
the Photo Library to help provide many of the illustrations.

Our considerable thanks are due to Rachael Swann and then Anna
Lawford (supported by David Baldock and others of the Library team)
who put in long hours of work to ensure the timely arrival of both of
these books. We continue to receive compliments on these every week;
both are great achievements. George's book has already made money
for the Club and the Library, and Peter's book should contribute profits
to the Club.

The celebrations in Zermatt included a lecture by Peter Berg, our retiring
Hon Archivist, which was a re-creation of *My scrambles amongst the Alps* by
Edward Whymper, probably first given in Davos in 1896; it used the original

glass lantern slides now in the Photo Library. Also, the Club press release and other PR activity for Zermatt were enhanced by a good supply of historic photographs arranged by Anna Lawford.

The second key achievement was the mounting of the *Treasures of the Alpine Club* exhibition to tell the story of the pioneering of mountaineering in the Alps and the greater ranges using around 100 historic 'treasures' from the Club's collections. Books and photographs cared for by the Library were shown along with paintings and artefacts. This was a splendid opportunity for many members to see Club 'treasures' that only come out of storage from time to time.

The exhibition was held in Christie's Ryder Gallery in St James's, London, in September. We are extremely grateful to Christie's for the free loan of the gallery and to our sponsors and benefactors, First Ascent, PAYE Stonework and Nick Clinch, who ensured that this event did not require a subvention from the Library's funds. I must also thank the many people who helped make this happen, particularly Jerry Lovatt and Barbara Grigor-Taylor who really drove the project forward. We estimate that nearly 25 per cent of Club members visited this show and the supporting events; again, we received much appreciation.

Within the Library, Glyn Hughes took on the Hon Archivist position and Mike Hewson took over from Bob Lawford the work with books donated by members; both have made very professional approaches to the work. I should explain that all books donated are carefully vetted; some are retained to become part of the Club's collections and some are sold to members via the second-hand book sales lists – this is very helpful to both Club members and Library coffers.

So, what are the next challenges? We will be examining budgets to ensure that we only spend within our income; this will mean a re-appraisal of our opening hours and possibly an increase in our charges (which will remain free or very modest to members). Generally, the Library will move towards a smarter operation, partly electronic, which will include better access to books, archives and a selected collection of historic photographs.

New guidebooks will begin to appear on the shelves in March 2008; initially, these are for the Alps; we will move on to cover wider areas. Also now on the shelves is a specialist full set of large-scale maps of the Himalaya, donated by our member, Harish Kapadia, in memory of his son, Lt Nawang Kapadia. I should mention that we have no intention to compete with the extensive map library of the Royal Geographical Society – where AC members are welcome – but we do see the need to have some specialist maps in the AC Library, readily available to help members referring to books and journals to plan expeditions.

Yvonne Sibbald, who has been our Librarian since November 2003, has decided to retire. I am sure that many Club members and other Library visitors will support me in thanking her for her contribution to the work of the Library over her years with us: we all wish her well.

Finally, it is right and proper that all members of the Library team take pride in all the achievements this year and we must congratulate those who did the heaviest work. My personal thanks go to the Trustees and Officers of the Alpine Club Library who have worked – entirely voluntarily – to ensure the success of the Library; I am confident that it will go forward and hold a proper place in the Club's activity for another 150 years.

Hywel Lloyd
Chairman of the Council of Trustees of the Alpine Club Library

THE RISE AND FALL
OF THE NATIONAL MOUNTAINEERING EXHIBITION

Now that the National Mountaineering Exhibition has closed at Rheged, Cumbria, we should record the nine-year history of its success and termination. It is the story of a huge amount of voluntary effort, of a heroic commercial bailing out of the BMC and its ultimate failure as a commercial museum.

It was in the spring of 1999 that I received the first call from George Band, then president of the British Mountaineering Council (BMC), who had been charged with identifying a location to establish a repository for the archive associated with mountaineering history worldwide. This had come as a response to a call at the BMC AGM from Barbara James to ensure that this heritage was preserved.

With an initial budget of £3,000 we visited buildings that were available in Windermere, Kendal and Keswick; none of them proved to be ideal.

In Penrith much publicity surrounded the prospect of a new underground building to be called Rheged which was being marketed as a 'discovery centre'. In the spring of 1999 it was a very large hole in the ground and George Band and I met the owner of the project, John Dunning, on site to discuss the possibility of a tenancy. John Dunning was immediately enthusiastic and in due course offered us 5000 square feet of exhibition space.

Rheged opened in 2000 – an £18m development in a former limestone quarry housing beneath the largest turf-covered roof in Europe, an IMAX cinema, visitor centre, exhibition space, restaurant, shops and motorway-style service station. The same year, the BMC formed Mountain Exhibitions Limited (MEL) to run the proposed exhibition on a commercial basis and simultaneously the Mountain Heritage Trust (MHT) was formed as a charity with Sir Chris Bonington as founder Chair.

On behalf of MHT, John Porter, a founder trustee, negotiated substantial funding from European Regional Development Fund which enabled the employment of John Sunderland (of Jorvik fame) to design and build the first national mountaineering exhibition. This he did on time, finishing on 15 July 2001, ten days before the exhibition was opened by Prime Minister

Tony Blair to a background of crisis in the Lake District caused by Foot and Mouth disease. Mountains and paths surrounding the exhibition building were closed indefinitely. The total cost of the project was reported at £750,000.

MHT commissioned Colin Wells to write *A Short History of Mountaineering* which formed the theme of the first exhibition and also commissioned Julian Cooper to create a painting of the Scafell range with help from the Northern Arts Foundation. Tony Blair's words on leaving the opening were 'this is a fantastic project, not just an exhibition of mountaineering but an important slice of our history as well'.

George Band was the host that day and in his speech welcoming the Prime Minister, he said 'on the morning of your birth Prime Minister, I see from my diary I was in Camp VI on Everest with Tenzing Norgay', to which Tony Blair remarked enigmatically that he was in greater danger at that moment than George.

Several days prior to the opening, in my position as Curator, I had received a packing crate from the USA containing all the artefacts removed from George Mallory's body in 1999. And here I faced my first real test; the Prime Minster asked to try on George Mallory's watch … and I had to refuse. The loan of these precious artefacts led to the establishment of the Mallory Replica Clothing Project, financed by the Heritage Lottery Fund and managed by Prof Mary Rose and Mike Parsons of Lancaster University on behalf of MHT. This resulted in the production of meticulously replicated garments that were tested before being exhibited at the NME. The remarkable discoveries made during this project are published in *Mallory Myths and Mysteries*, available from MHT (www.mountain-heritage.org).

The first exhibition covered the Greater Ranges, but most importantly the early days of mountaineering in the UK with archive footage of Joe Brown, Tom Patey and a young Chris Bonington. The majority of the artefacts were sourced thanks to the generosity of the FRCC, together with personal items from the collections of Chris Bonington and Doug Scott.

By now MHT trustees included Roger Chorley, Paul Braithwaite, Audrey Salkeld, Jerry Lovatt and Ron Kenyon. All came together to help in the creation of a new exhibition to mark the 50th anniversary of the first ascent of Everest. On 10 June 2003 an exhibition devoted entirely to the 1953 expedition was opened by the Duke of York and I was privileged to act as host together with George Lowe and Michael Westmacott. The exhibition was enthusiastically received and coincided with celebrations in London hosted by the Queen.

In the intervening period the BMC decided that the exhibition hitherto owned by MEL should be sold and the owners of Rheged, the Westmorland Group, stepped in to purchase the NME. Westmorland appointed as exhibition manager Robin Ashcroft whose influence and vision contributed, through NME, much to the public understanding of our sport as he organised film, lecture and literary events at Rheged.

In September 2004 MHT appointed its first professional archivist, Maxine Willett, who is employed to preserve and catalogue MHT's collection of archives and artefacts and ensure displayed items are secure and are not exposed to any potentially damaging conditions. The archivist also helps BMC clubs preserve their unique heritage and maintains a database of collections in the UK.

The new owners were keen to support a small exhibition celebrating the 50th anniversary of first ascent of Kangchenjunga, duly opened on Saturday 9 April 2005 by George Band and Joe Brown. In 2007 this exhibition was replaced by the final exhibition of the NME, one marking the centenary of the Fell & Rock Climbing Club. With hindsight it seems appropriate that the NME should mount its last exhibition covering the history of climbing and exploration in the Lake District.

It became clear that the NME was in need of completely new exhibitions for which funding would need to be sought, as it had been in the initial creation of the exhibition. But it was also clear that such funding was more easily available for regional rather than national exhibitions. In December 2007 the Westmorland Group decided that the NME was no longer commercially viable and that it would close on Christmas Eve.

The NME fulfilled many objectives, among which was the need for MHT to connect its work and collections with the public and for the public generally to discover the history of mountaineering adventure worldwide which many would argue had its birth in the British Isles.

Times have changed in the last nine years and the activities of MHT must balance the urgent needs of preservation with the wider need for education about our mountaineering heritage. The Mountain Heritage Trust now offers public outreach through its website and is seeking to display its archive through a series of smaller exhibitions. But at a time when the American Alpine Club has joined other European countries in establishing a museum of national mountaineering, the treasures of our own heritage lack a permanent exhibition space in Britain.

John Innerdale
Curator and former Chair of the Mountain Heritage Trust

OFFICERS AND COMMITTEE FOR 2008

PRESIDENT	P Braithwaite
VICE PRESIDENTS	C Watts
	M Scott
HONORARY SECRETARY	F Call
HONORARY TREASURER	R N K Baron
HONORARY LIBRARIAN	D J Lovatt
HONORARY EDITOR	
OF THE *Alpine Journal*	S J Goodwin

Contributors

VALERY BABANOV is one of the foremost exponents of pure alpine-style at high altitude. Born in Omsk, Russia, in 1964, he is resident in Canada and works as a guide out of Chamonix. He has twice been awarded the Piolet d'Or – 2001 Meru solo, 2003 Nuptse East via SE pillar – and this year was awarded the first Grolla d'Oro of the newly instituted Saint Vincent Award, for his ascent, with Sergey Kofanov, of west pillar of Jannu.

GEORGE BAND was the youngest member of the 1953 Everest team. In 1955 he made the first ascent – with Joe Brown – of Kangchenjunga, and subsequently climbed in Peru and the Caucasus. More recently he has climbed in Bhutan, and escorted treks for 'Far Frontiers' in Nepal, Sikkim and Central Asia. AC President from 1987 to 1989 and President of the BMC from 1996 to 1999. His books *Everest: 50 years on Top of the World* and *Summit: 150 years of the Alpine Club* were written to coincide with their 50th and 150th year celebrations in 2003 and 2007 respectively.

ANTONIO GÓMEZ BOHÓRQUEZ lives in Murcia, Spain. A librarian and documentalist (information scientist), he specialises in ascents in the north Peruvian ranges. He has written two books: *La Cordillera Blanca de los Andes, selección de ascensiones, excursiones* and *Cordillera Blanca, Escaladas, Parte Norte*. He has climbed since 1967, with first ascents including *Spanish Direct* on the north face of Cima Grande di Lavaredo, Italia (1977), Pilar del Cantábrico del Naranjo de Bulnes, Spain (1980), east face of Cerro Parón (La Esfinge, 5325m), Peru (1985) and the south-east face (1988).

NEIL BRODIE lives near Chamonix in the French Alps. He has fully embraced the local mountaineering ethos and always tries to be back in the bistro by nightfall. He enjoys short approaches and easy descents, and regularly delves into the black arts of skiing and sport climbing. Occasionally he has a relapse and does a climb that involves a bit of discomfort.

NICK BULLOCK was a PE instructor for the Prison Service until he became a nomadic full-time climber and writer in 2003. He discovered climbing in 1991 on a work-related course at Plas y Brenin since when he has established himself as one of Britain's leading alpinists. He has put up new routes in Wales, Scotland, the Alps, Peru and Nepal. He also rock climbs a bit.

ALTON BYERS is a mountain geographer and climber specialising in integrated conservation and development programmes, high altitude ecosystems, and field research methods. He has more than 30 years of experience working and living in remote mountainous regions of Africa, South America, Asia, and North America. He has worked for the Mountain Institute since 1990, and lives in Elkins, West Virginia.

NICHOLAS CLINCH is a past president of the American Alpine Club and an honorary member of the Alpine Club. He has led or co-led a number of expeditions including the first ascents of Hidden Peak and Masherbrum in the Karakoram, Vinson Massif in Antarctica and Ulugh Muztagh in the Kun Lun of northern Tibet. He is the author of *A Walk in the Sky*.

MICHAEL COCKER has climbed extensively throughout Britain and the European Alps as well as in East Africa, the Andes, Himalaya, North America and Arctic Norway. He works as a physiotherapy clinical specialist and is interested in mountaineering history and literature. He wrote and edited the *Wasdale Climbing Book* (Ernest Press, 2006).

ROB COLLISTER lives in North Wales and earns his living as a mountain guide. He continues to derive enormous pleasure as well as profit from all aspects of mountains and mountaineering.

JULIAN COOPER is a painter living in the Lake District specialising in mountains and rock faces. He has also worked in the Alps, Andes, Himalaya, and Tibet. Mountains as a subject provide him with a means of touching upon wider themes. His current project is set in the marble quarries of Carrara, Italy, and the slate quarries in Cumbria.

HENRY DAY has been driving Land Rovers to the Greater Ranges for more than 40 years, starting with the Elburz (Alam Kuh) in 1963, pushing on the following year to Swat (Mankial) in Pakistan. Since retirement from the Army the 'Maschina' has seen Kilimanjaro, the Karakoram Highway, Khiva and the Kun Lun; and now the Caucasus – via the Rockies and the Andes. Some mountains were climbed too, though Annapurna, Indrasan, Shishapangma and Everest were, sadly, Land Rover free ascents.

ED DOUGLAS is a former honorary editor of the *Alpine Journal*. His books include *Tenzing*, published by National Geographic, and *Chomolungma Sings the Blues*, published by Constable, both prize winners at the Banff Mountain Book Festival. When not flogging his soul as a freelance journalist, he can be found on the gritstone edges near his home in Sheffield.

RONALD FAUX worked as a journalist on *The Times* for 30 years and covered three expeditions to Everest, respectively in 1976, in 1978 when Messner and Habeler made the first 'unmasked' ascent, and in 1986 with the British team attempting the pinnacles of the north-east ridge. He is the author of *Soldiers on Everest*, jointly with Jon Fleming, *High Ambition*, the authorised biography of Reinhold Messner, *Everest Goddess of the Wind* and *The West*, a sailing companion to the west coast of Scotland. He claims many unspectacular visits to climb and ski in the Alps and the hills of Scotland and the Lake District where he now lives.

DEREK FORDHAM, when not dreaming of the Arctic, practises as an architect and runs an Arctic photographic library. He is secretary of the Arctic Club and has led 21 expeditions to the Canadian Arctic, Greenland and Svalbard to ski, climb or share the life of the Inuit.

LINDSAY GRIFFIN, after a lengthy and enforced break from activity, has returned to rock climbing, re-discovering all the anticipation and excitement of teenage years. He is still keeping up to speed on international affairs through his work with Mountain INFO and as Chairman of the MEF Screening and BMC International Committees.

MICK FOWLER works for Her Majesty's Revenue and Customs and, by way of contrast, likes to inject as much memorable adventure and excitement into his climbing ventures. He has climbed extensively in the UK and has regularly led expeditions to the greater ranges for more than 25 years. He has written two books, *Vertical Pleasure* (1995) and *On Thin Ice* (2005).

CLAUDE GARDIEN works as an editor for *Vertical*. He discovered climbing when he was 15 on the crags of Burgundy, and started a mountaineering career a few weeks later in the Mont Blanc range. He later climbed in the Alps, Morocco, Algeria, Jordan, Nepal, Pakistan, and worked as a mountain guide as well as a writer and photographer.

STEPHEN GOODWIN renounced daily newspaper journalism on *The Independent* for a freelance existence in Cumbria, mixing writing and climbing. A precarious balance was maintained until 2003 when he was persuaded to take on the editorship of the *Alpine Journal* and 'getting out' became elusive again.

MIKE GROCOTT is a consultant in Intensive Care Medicine at Southampton University Hopsitals Trust and Senior Lecturer at University College London. He is director of the UCL Centre for Altitude Space and Extreme Environment Medicine and was expedition leader of the Caudwell Xtreme Everest medical research expedition in the spring of 2007. He has 15 years experience of high altitude mountaineering and summited Cho Oyu in 2006 and Everest in 2007.

GEOFF HORNBY is a consulting engineer now resident in the Italian Dolomites. He has made almost 325 first ascents in mountains outside of the UK and is looking forward to 175 more, inshallah.

ROWAN HUNTLEY, artist and AC Associate, is never happier than when painting rock, snow, ice and sky, and she explores away from her base in Cardiff whenever she can. With Norway, Switzerland, France and the Italian Bregaglia under her palette, Greenland is firmly on her agenda for 2009.

DICK ISHERWOOD has been a member of the Alpine Club since 1970. His climbing record includes various buildings in Cambridge, lots of old fashioned routes on Cloggy, a number of obscure Himalayan peaks, and a new route on the Piz Badile (in 1968). He now follows Tilman's dictum about old men on high mountains and limits his efforts to summits just a little under 20,000 feet.

HARISH KAPADIA has climbed in the Himalaya since 1960, with ascents up to 6800m. He is Hon Editor of both the *Himalayan Journal* and the *HC Newsletter*. In 1993 he was awarded the IMF's Gold Medal and in 1996 was made an Hon Member of the Alpine Club. He has written several books including *High Himalaya Unknown Valleys*, *Spiti: Adventures in the Trans-Himalaya* and, with Soli Mehta, *Exploring the Hidden Himalaya*. In 2003 he was awarded the Patron's Gold Medal by the Royal Geographical Society.

PAUL KNOTT is a lecturer in business strategy at the University of Canterbury, New Zealand. He previously lived in the UK. He enjoys exploratory climbing in remote mountains, and since 1990 has undertaken eleven expeditions to Russia, Central Asia, Alaska and the Yukon. He has also climbed new routes in the Southern Alps and on desert rock in Oman and Morocco.

NICK LEWIS has worked in polar matters since 1991 when he first started at British Antarctic Survey's Rothera Base. He has a penchant for cold mountains with favourites being the Tatra, Alaska, the Yukon, Patagonia and, of course, Antarctica. He is an environmental consultant and lives in New England where he enjoys the most frigid winters of all.

PAT LITTLEJOHN is known for a 'clean climbing' ethic and adherence to the lightweight, alpine-style approach. His worldwide portfolio of first ascents include the NE Pillar of Taweche (Nepal), Raven's Pyramid (Karakoram), Poi N Face (Kenya) and Kjerag N Buttress (Norway). He succeeded Pete Boardman as director of the International School of Mountaineering in 1983. Pat enjoys passing on the skills acquired over nearly four decades of alpine climbing, and is keen to ensure that climbing's unique 'spirit of adventure' is kept alive, both on the rock and in the mountains.

NICK MASON is a doctor, photographer and mountaineer based in Cardiff. A Consultant in Intensive Care Medicine at the Royal Gwent Hospital, Newport, he has been fortunate for over a decade to combine his love of mountaineering with research into high altitude physiology in the mountains of Nepal, Central Asia, North America and the French Alps. Nick is a member of faculty of the UK Diploma in Mountain Medicine.

Along with his wife, Emma, he is a representative for the International Porter Protection Group and worked at the IPPG rescue post at Machermo in Nepal's Gokyo valley during the autumn seasons of 2005 and 2007.

JOHANNA MERZ joined the Alpine Club in 1988 and has devoted most of her energies to the *Alpine Journal*, first as assistant editor, then as honorary editor from 1992 to 1998, and currently as production editor.

ADE MILLER lives and occasionally works in Redmond, Washington. This allows him to spend his weekends climbing in the mountains of the Pacific Northwest, specializing in winter ascents. He has also visited and climbed in numerous mountain ranges but has spent the last few years climbing in British Columbia, the Yukon Territories and Alaska.

TAMOTSU NAKAMURA was born in Tokyo in 1934 and has been climbing new routes in the greater ranges since his first successes on technical peaks in the Cordillera Blanca of Peru in 1961. He has lived in Pakistan, Mexico, New Zealand and Hong Kong and in the last 18 years has made 30 trips to 'Alps of Tibet in East of the Himalaya' – the least-known mountains in East Tibet and the Hengduan mountains of Yunnan, Sichuan, East Tibet and Qinghai. He is currently editor of the Japanese Alpine News and has received the RGS Busk Medal 2008.

ANDY PARKIN is still pushing at frontiers as both an artist and mountaineer. Active on the UK rock-climbing scene in the 1970s, he settled in the Chamonix valley, gaining a reputation for his painting and sculpting, along with hard routes such as *Beyond Good and Evil* on the Aiguilles des Pèlerins. Andy is committed to exploratory mountaineering: Patagonia and Tierra del Fuego have become favourite locations.

DAVID PICKFORD is a freelance photographer and writer, and the editor of planetfear.com (a climbing and adventure sports website). He has established many new rock climbs around Britain and across the world. David is currently pioneering a more direct route from his desk to the front door.

SIMON RICHARDSON is a petroleum engineer based in Aberdeen. Experience gained in the Alps, Andes, Patagonia, Canada, the Himalaya, Alaska and the Yukon is put to good use most winter weekends whilst exploring and climbing in the Scottish Highlands.

C A RUSSELL, who formerly worked with a City bank, devotes much of his time to mountaineering and related activities. He has climbed in many regions of the Alps, in the Pyrenees, East Africa, North America and the Himalaya.

BILL RUTHVEN was appointed Hon Secretary of the Mount Everest Foundation in 1985 so is now something of an institution in his own right. He is always happy to discuss the plans of people planning expeditions to high and/or remote areas and advise on their eligibility for MEF support.

VICTOR SAUNDERS was born in Lossiemouth and grew up in Peninsular Malaysia. He started climbing in the Alps in 1978 and has climbed in the Andes, Antarctica, Papua, Rockies, Caucasus, India, Pakistan, Nepal and Bhutan. Formerly a London-based architect, he is now a UIAGM guide based in Chamonix. When not working he likes to relax on steep bits of rock and ice. His first book, *Elusive Summits*, won the Boardman Tasker prize. In 2007 he received an honorary MA from the University of Stirling for services to Scottish mountaineering and between 2004 and 2008 has successfully guided Everest four times.

GRAEME SCHOFIELD is a teacher of Geography in a secondary school in Derbyshire. Walking up to his classroom, on the top floor of the school building, is how he keeps in shape for alpine adventures. Over the past five years he has been steadily building his experience of alpine mountaineering through climbing trips to the European Alps and as a member of two successful expeditions to the Bolivian and Peruvian Andes.

DAVID SEDDON is a physician in Nottingham. He has walked, climbed and skied in a number of unusual places, often in the company of John Harding or Derek Fordham. He continues to be interested in the painting of TH Somervell.

EVA SELIN is president of the Swedish Alpine Club, elected in 2001 and the first woman to hold this office. She is also a member of the Norwegian Alpine Club. Eva's climbing career began in 1978 with an ascent of the Troll ridge in Romsdalen together with her husband Anders Lundahl and blossomed during autumn of the same year at a BMC meeting where she climbed at Stanage with, amongst others, Dennis Gray. She is a professional botanist at the Museum of Gotland.

JOHN SHIPTON is the younger son of the explorer Eric Shipton. In recent years he has taken a passionate interest in his father's career and has been retracing some of his expeditions in the Himalaya and Patagonia. John has worked, travelled and sailed in many parts of the world, sailing in 1975 to Greenland with Eric's great climbing partner Bill Tilman. He now runs a plant and bulb nursery in west Wales and leads botanical treks in the Himalaya.

JOHN TOWN is a retired university administrator. He has climbed in the Alps, Caucasus, Altai, Andes, Turkey and Kamchatka, and explored little-known mountain areas of Mongolia, Yunnan and Tibet. He is old enough to remember the days without satellite photos and GPS.

STEPHEN VENABLES has just completed a busy term as president of the Alpine Club. He made many Himalayan ascents between 1977 and 1992, including a new route on the east face of Everest and more recently has climbed in South Georgia and Tierra del Fuego. He is a freelance writer and lecturer and has published a string of mountain travel books including the BT award-winning *Painted Mountains* (1986).

MARK WATSON works for the New Zealand Alpine Club as editor of both *The Climber* magazine and the *New Zealand Alpine Journal*. Mostly found hanging out at various crags, he can also be seen in the mountains from time to time. Mark's favourite New Zealand area is the Darran Mountains. He has also rock-climbed extensively in the USA, UK, western Europe and Australia.

DAVE WYNNE-JONES used to teach before he learnt his lesson. He has spent over 30 years exploring the hills and crags of Britain and climbed all the Alpine 4000m peaks. By the 1990s annual alpine seasons had given way to explorative climbing further afield, including Jordan, Morocco, Russia and Ecuador, though ski-mountaineering took him back to the Alps in winter. Expedition destinations have included Pakistan, Peru, Alaska, the Yukon, Kyrgyzstan, Nepal, India and China with a respectable tally of first ascents.

Index 2008

NOTES FOR CONTRIBUTORS

The *Alpine Journal* records all aspects of mountains and mountaineering, including expeditions, adventure, art, literature, geography, history, geology, medicine, ethics and the mountain environment.

Articles Contributions in English are invited. They should be sent to the Hon Editor, Stephen Goodwin, 1 Ivy Cottages, Edenhall, Penrith, Cumbria CA11 8SN (e-mail: sg@stephengoodwin.demon.co.uk). Articles should preferably be sent on a disk with accompanying hard copy or as an e-mail attachment (in Word) with hard copy sent separately by post. Their length should not exceed 3000 words without prior approval of the Editor **and may be edited or shortened at his discretion.** It is regretted that the *Alpine Journal* is unable to offer a fee for articles published, but authors receive a complimentary copy of the issue of the *Alpine Journal* in which their article appears.

Articles and book reviews should not have been published in substantially the same form by any other publication.

Maps These should be well researched, accurate, and finished ready for printing. They should show the most important place-names mentioned in the text. It is the authors' responsibility to get their maps redrawn if necessary. This can be arranged through the Production Editor if required.

Photographs All images must be pin sharp with good colour saturation. Digital images must be of high resolution, minimum 300dpi, and submitted on CD, not by email. Each image must be individually captioned. Please be selective and do not send large collections. Colour transparencies are still desirable. These should be originals in 35mm format or larger. Prints (any size) should be numbered in pencil on the back and accompanied by captions on a separate sheet/document (see below).

Captions Please list these **on a separate sheet/document** and give title and author of the article to which they refer.

Copyright It is the author's responsibility to obtain copyright clearance for text, photographs and maps, to pay any fees involved and to ensure that acknowledgements are in the form required by the copyright owner.

Summaries A brief summary, helpful to researchers, may be included with 'expedition' articles.

Biographies Authors are asked to provide a short biography, in about 60 words, listing the most noteworthy items in their climbing career and anything else they wish to mention.

Deadline: copy and photographs should reach the Editor by 1 January of the year of publication.

Rathbones welcomes private investors

Discretionary portfolio management

How often do you receive a truly personal service today?

At Rathbones we offer a bespoke service with a dedicated investment manager from £100,000, including SIPPS.

We also welcome directly invested portfolios when some other investment managers may insist on a restricted list of unit trusts.

We listen to your needs and plan your strategy together.

Rathbones manages the investment funds for **The Alpine Club, The Alpine Club Library and the Mount Everest Foundation.**

Drake Davis
Investment Director

Tel: 020 7399 0000
drake.davis@rathbones.com
www.rathbones.com

RATHBONES
Established 1742

MOUNTAIN
EQUIPMENT

above & beyond since 1961

23,000 square kilometres of Alaskan wilderness, 4,441 metre peak of Mount Hunter, 4 days, one stunning route: Moonflower Buttress. Jon Bracey. Andy Houseman. Mountain Equipment.

Be inspired to go **above and beyond** by this and other stories at **www.mountain-equipment.co.uk**

The Mark Clifford Grant

Jon Bracey and Andy Houseman were assisted on their Alaskan expedition by the Mark Clifford Grant. The grant's purpose is to support and encourage ambitious young mountaineers by providing financial assistance to enable new routes, exploration and education. Find out more at **www.markclifford.co.uk**

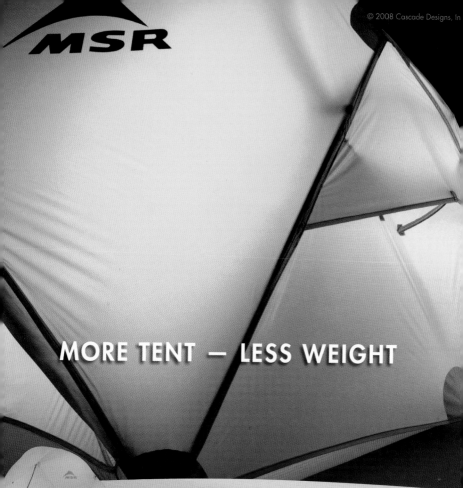

© 2008 Cascade Designs, In

MSR

MORE TENT — LESS WEIGHT

JBBA HUBBA™ HP
Person,
69 kg

BBA HUBBA™
Person,
1 kg

The new Hubba Hubba™ HP brings increased foul-weather protection to the best-selling Hubba Hubba tent. Utilizing the latest ultralight fabrics, we've delivered that added performance while actually saving you weight. Our proven hub design offers fast and easy set-up, superior ventilation and interior space, along with two vestibules and StayDry™ entrances. It's what we call livability, and you'll find it in every tent we make.

Go to www.firstascent.co.uk
or call 01629-580484 for
more information.

MSR®

MOUNTAIN SAFETY RESEARCH®

www.msrgear.com

PROVEN IN REMOTE PLACES
REDESIGNED FOR TIGHT SPACES.

For over 30 years, MSR's XGK™ has been the world's most reliable extreme-condition stove, trusted by mountaineers everywhere. Our new XGK EX™ builds on that legacy. Like its predecessor the EX boasts unrivaled performance, dependably burning a greater variety of liquid fuels than any stove on the market. It also features a new flexible fuel line that allows it to pack smaller than ever, as well as attached retractable legs and pot supports for superior stability — no matter where your next expedition takes you.

Go to www.firstascent.co.uk
or call 01629-580484 for more information.

MSR

MOUNTAIN SAFETY RESEARC

www.msrgear.co